S0-AZS-414

Mirror, Mirror
on the Page

Mirror, Mirror on the Page

Identity and Subjectivity
in Spanish Women's Poetry
(1975–2000)

W. Michael Mudrovic

Lehigh
University
Press

Bethlehem: Lehigh University Press

Associated University Presses
2010 Eastpark Boulevard
Cranbury, NJ 08512

The paper used in this publication meets the requirements of the American National Standard for Permanence of Paper for Printed Library Materials Z39.48-1984.

Library of Congress Cataloging-in-Publication Data

Mudrovic, W. Michael.
　　Mirror, mirror on the page : identity and subjectivity in Spanish women's poetry (1975–2000) / W. Michael Mudrovic.
　　　　p.　cm.
　　Includes bibliographical references and index.
　　ISBN 978-0-934223-84-3 (alk. paper)
　　1. Spanish poetry—20th century—History and criticism.　2. Spanish poetry—Women authors—History and criticism.　3. Identity (Philosophical concept) in literature.　4. Women in literature.　I. Title.
PQ6055.M83　2008
861′.64099287—dc22

2007036043

For the four generations of women in our family

my mother, Lucille
my sister, Denise
my niece, Laura
and my great niece, Brianna

with love always

Contents

7

Acknowledgments

WITHOUT ENCOURAGEMENT AND SUPPORT FROM MANY DIFFERENT sources, I would not have been able to complete this book. First, I would like to express my gratitude to Skidmore College for the generosity shown in the granting of a Faculty Development Grant, a Major Project Completion Grant, and a sabbatical leave to work on this project. In addition, the support of my colleagues in the Department of Foreign Languages and Literatures has been indispensable. I am particularly grateful to my late colleague, Juan Carlos Lértora, with whom I shared many meaningful discussions about poetry and who was a valued and discriminating reader of my work. The other members of the Spanish section, Patricia Rubio, Grace Burton, and Viviana Rangil, have also been stimulating colleagues and valued friends. Several other professors of Spanish at other universities have also read and commented on distinct chapters of this book, and I am grateful for their insights. With the risk of omitting someone, I most sincerely thank Martha LaFollette Miller, Margaret Persin, Cecile West-Settle, Sylvia Sherno, David Thompson, and John Wilcox. I am also heavily indebted to my editor at Lehigh University Press, Judith Mayer, whose patient and wise counsel have contributed significantly to the final product. It would be remiss of me not to mention two other colleagues who contributed directly and indirectly to the completion of this study and who have passed away: Andrew P. Debicki and Lori Pattison. Hence, the publication of this book is bittersweet, as nearly all our endeavors must be. *Ave atque vale.*

Another group of individuals has contributed to what I hope is the success of this study: the poets themselves. In particular, I am grateful to María Victoria Atencia and her husband Rafael León for their hospitality and friendship, to Ana Rossetti for her stimulating, provocative, and humorous insights into literature and life, to the sensitive and passionate Margarita Merino de Lindsay, and to a new friend I recently met in Pamplona, Maite Pérez Larumbe, a consummate poet and warm human being whom I am so happy to have met. Although I do not personally know Blanca Andreu, Luisa Castro, Almudena Guzmán, and Amalia Bautista, I thank all these poets profoundly for allowing me to cite their works in this study.

9

I am also indebted to a number of student assistants who participated in various and sundry tasks in the completion of this project. Many thanks to Brian Cugell, Morgan Caldwell, Whitney Nuchereno, and Emily Maskin.

Several other people have provided moral support and inspiration on a personal level. It would be futile to try to list all of them, but some merit special mention: my good friend Joan Headley, one of the most courageous women I know; my long-standing friends Skip and Darlene Gatermann, and Mike and Mary O'Brien; a good friend and spiritual guide, Rosalyn Schultz; and the current mainstays of my life, Chris Livingston, the dark-chocolate-imbibing Aztec avatar, who constantly urges me to view the world from radical perspectives and encourages me to reach beyond self-imposed limitations, and my dog Rusty, the best golden retriever mutt that ever came out of an animal shelter.

Let me also mention an intelligent, humorous, and insightful friend who has always been generous with his time, his knowledge of poetry and art, and his deep appreciation of the Spanish language: the Segovian poet, Luis Javier Moreno. Luis and I met nearly thirty years ago at Washington University in St. Louis, and our friendship, along with the warmth of his entire family and the embrace of his friends and *contertulianos* in Segovia, has enriched my life on many levels.

℘

Finally, I wish to acknowledge permission to include material from these articles published prior to this book:

"Un ménage-à-trois inesperado: Lou Andreas Salomé, Nietzsche y Ana Rossetti," *Explicación de Textos Literarios* 32 (2003): 143–54.

"Espejito, espejito: La recuperación de la voz poética reprimida en los poemas de 'Blancanieves' de *Marta & María* de María Victoria Atencia," *La poesía de María Victoria Atencia: Un acercamiento crítico,* (pp. 171–82).

"Re-visiting Mary and Martha: Passing the Torch from One Generation to the Next," *Journal of Hispanic Higher Education* 1 (2002): 195–210.

Mirror, Mirror on the Page

Introduction: The Page as Mirror

MANY REMARKABLE CHANGES—SOCIAL, ECONOMIC, CULTURAL, PO-litical, aesthetic, technological—have occurred in Spain since the death of the dictator Francisco Franco in November 1975 and the institution of a democratic constitutional monarchy in 1978.[1] Among the most noteworthy phenomena of the post-Franco era has been the burgeoning of women's poetry—poetry written by, about, and/or for women. A restructuring of the paradigmatic image of "woman," a shift from the conservative, traditional, submissive spouse and mother (as defined by the Franco regime and the Sección Feminina) to a more contemporary image based on feminist principles, has resulted in more advantageous conditions for women to express themselves lyrically.[2] As major editorial venues became available and presses like Torremozas were established to foment women's writing, women of all ages perceived and took advantage of a more open and receptive climate for their literary aspirations.

Spanish women poets have also realized that the opportunities they now enjoy entail certain obligations—to women of the past, of the present, and of the future. The poets of the post-Franco era (particularly of the late 1970s to the early 1990s) found themselves at a pivotal historical moment. As their voices began to emerge, many poets understood that they were entrusted with solidifying—not establishing, but consolidating—a women's poetic tradition. This task required them to define themselves not only as poets with their own voices and their relationship to their medium (the largely male poetic tradition as well as language in and of itself), but also as women, a viable, powerful new force emerging in Spanish society and culture in the public sphere. Consequently, a paramount vein of poetry has emerged in which women poets use the "page as mirror."

Catoptric imagery—images that deal with the reflection of light from mirrors or mirrorlike surfaces—provides an apt metaphor for the type of poetry defined here. Sabine Melchior-Bonnet agrees that "the mirror, 'matrix of the symbolic,' accompanies the human quest for identity. . . . To see oneself in the mirror, to identify oneself,

13

requires a mental operation by which the subject is capable of objectivizing himself, of separating what is outside from what is inside. This operation can be successful if the subject recognizes the reflection as his own likeness and can say, 'I am the other of that other.' The relationship of self to self and the familiarity of the self cannot be directly established and remains trapped in the reciprocity of seeing and being seen."[3]

Along with this emphasis on the process of self-identification, Melchior-Bonnet makes a further comparison between painting and the mirror: "The notions of subjectivity and identity were first established within religious and social realms, where self-portraiture and autobiography, the habitual practices of reflection and of introspection, are first played out. Against this backdrop, one who gazes at himself in the mirror strives to regain the resemblance that unites man with his creator and the solidarity that links him to his peers. . . . The mirror thus underscores the hazy, inverted, and intentionally distorted nature of any self-portrait."[4] It is therefore not coincidental that portraiture, three-dimensional perspective, and the individual identity and style of the artist (painter, sculptor, poet) is coetaneous with the technological advances that produced and refined the first truly planar mirrors.[5]

Finally, Jean Delumeau, prefacing Melchior-Bonnet's book, maintains that "the mirror was and is particularly ambiguous for women. It is true that woman 'awakens to life when she has access to her image' and the mirror will always be 'the privileged province of femininity.'"[6] It should not be surprising then that the mirror appears with amazing frequency in women's writing, particularly in Spanish literature of the post–civil war era, as Spanish women writers avail themselves of the page as a "reflective surface."[7]

The basic premise for this study derives from Jenijoy La Belle's *Herself Beheld: The Literature of the Looking Glass*.[8] Although her study specifically examines works of literature by both men and women in which the physical object of the mirror appears, toward the end of her panoramic discussion La Belle postulates a related idea that has provoked my reading of post-Franco women's poetry in Spain. In La Belle's chapter on the semiotic surface, a poem by Louise Bogan allows her to see "a connection between reading and mirroring that hints at a shared semiotic ground" (155). It is only a short logical step, then, to the following ideas: "Both looking into mirrors and reading/writing are attempts to create the self without another person literally present. In the reflection or in the book, there is another presence. Once you objectify yourself into a mirror or onto a page, then that image has a separate reality. The poem [Bogan's 'Man Alone' as well as the literary genre in general] suggests that there is a difficulty in finding one's identity in writing or in a mirror because the objectified self has an independence that is disturbing and is subject to multiple distortions" (155). This link leads La Belle to the conclusion that "for a woman, to write, to create a persona, can be a substitution for looking in the mirror" and that "although some women see writing as an escape from mirroring, others see it as an extension—a supplement rather than a substitution" (159).

When Spanish women poets of the post-Franco era represent a female figure in their poems, that figure serves as a "mirror image" or reflection (in both senses of the word) of the implied author. The image represented on the page as mirror generates a dialogue of sameness and difference between the image and the woman who is speaking/writing the poem. This dialogue opens a textual space that can function in a variety of ways in accord with La Belle's understanding of the mirror. There obtains "an intimate and significant relationship between the mirror and a woman's conception of what she is, what she has been, and what she will become" (2). Using the image of the self as other (and/or the other as self), a woman poet can invent, revise, discover, analyze, evaluate, describe, emphasize, reject, deny, celebrate, enhance, affirm, and/or interrogate who she is. The page as mirror thus can be considered a "useful tool for the reaffirmation of [a woman's] identity" (19). La Belle continues: "The mirror is used merely as a tool to see the exterior evidence of an immaterial being we call 'character' or 'personality.' There is no implication that the reflection (or even the face) *is* the character or the personality or the self. The external presence registered by the glass can never be more than a sign of a reality which is within, but different in kind from, that sign. What is remarkable, then, about so many women in front of mirrors is that the image in the glass *is* the character, the personality, the soul" (22).

Many Spanish women poets of the post-Franco era avail themselves of the page as mirror, allowing them to delve into issues of identity and subjectivity at the historical moment when the Spanish nation itself is undergoing a radical transformation and redefinition of its identity in the transition from dictatorship to democracy. This assertion is replete with pitfalls of both practical and theoretical dimensions. The following salient issues have arisen that merit further comment: first, a consideration of the mirror as trope, its symbology and some of the psychoanalytic considerations it raises; then, some basic definitions and discussion of the terms *identity* and *subjectivity*, with specific reference to Kelly Oliver's concept of witnessing; and finally, a brief overview of the gynocentric tradition in late nineteenth and twentieth-century Spain, especially the role of Gloria Fuertes in establishing the type of poetry described here.

The Mirror as Trope

To understand the concept of the page as mirror, we first need to delve into the symbology of the mirror and some of its psychoanalytical facets with regard to female identity and subjectivity. In addition to the information gleaned from Melchior-Bonnet, several other authors have explored the implications of the mirror as trope.

Although most people tend to associate it with the single theme of narcissistic vanity, the mirror is a symbol with multiple resonances. Juan Eduardo Cirlot affirms that "from the earliest of times, the mirror has been thought of as ambivalent," and Michael Ferber asserts that "the symbolism of mirrors depends not only on what things cause the reflection . . . but also on what one sees in them—oneself, the truth, the ideal, illusion."[9] Most authors also agree with Cirlot that "the mirror is both solar and lunar as the sun disk, sky and light, and as the reflected light of the moon. It is also regarded as having magical properties and is the gateway to the realm of inversion." For these reasons La Belle maintains that the mirror entails a paradoxical or, as she puts it, "oxymoronical" structure in that "mirroring is, quite literally, a mode of figuration or figuring-forth an image which, like metaphor, is inscribed with both identity and difference" (42). She notes that "in European literature through the eighteenth century, a woman looking in a mirror only rarely escapes its traditional emblematic meaning—vanity" (14). However, she asserts that a major shift in the paradigm begins to occur in the novels of the nineteenth century, so that a new relationship obtains between a woman and her reflection: The mirror becomes a medium for interrogating and defining the self. Moreover, she emphasizes the mirror's semiotic nature that involves both aspects of the sign: the signifier (the visual, two-dimensional image of the reflection) and the signified (what one reads into that image, its meaning, the third dimension of interiority that accompanies and arises from the exterior properties of the signifier, however arbitrary their connection may be).[10]

We are then confronted with what seems to be a major difference between a man and a woman's use of the mirror.[11] In general, men have a different relationship with and use for the mirror than women. In accord with the more radical separation from the mother, men tend to view only the surface of the reflection in the mirror. "Men," La Belle notes, "look at their faces and their bodies, but what they *are* is another matter entirely—ultimately, a transcendental concept of self" (9). Because a male must make a definitive separation from the mother and identify with the father, he continues to gauge his masculinity in the mirror's reflection. That reflection is, in effect, the ego ideal that the father represents. When a man looks in the mirror—beyond purely pragmatic purposes—he looks for confirmation of and delights in his approximation to the ideal of masculinity. In semiotic terms men perceive a one-to-one relationship between signifier and signified: surface equals depth. In terms of repetition theory we could say that it represents the Platonic concept in which every repetition (reflection, image) is a reproduction of the ideal and equivalent to it.[12]

Women, on the other hand, have a more nuanced way of reading the signifier/reflection. In the Oedipal process a female must separate from the mother but also identify with her. The individuation and separation is subtler, not as radical (and violent) as the male's. As a result, a woman's reading of the sign in/of the reflection encompasses a wider scope of signification and encourages a more indeterminate interpretation, one that goes beyond the surface and a one-to-one correspondence of signifier to signified. It also consists of more fluidity (less rigidity) over time, prompting La Belle to challenge Lacan's concept of the "stade du miroir": "The mirror phase . . . is for Lacan a single, originary event. I have found that, for women, mirroring is not a stage but a continual, ever shifting process of self-realization" (10). Again, in terms of repetition theory this position constitutes the Nietzschean concept in which each repetition is slightly different from the previous model.[13] In sum, men and women (as subject positions that do not depend on anatomical configuration or sexual orientation) use the mirror for different purposes, depending on how they have learned to read what they see in the reflection.

IDENTITY AND SUBJECTIVITY

A second and related issue concerns the very definition of *identity* and *subjectivity*. These terms and their various explanations have been debated from many points of view without definitive resolution or consensus. In fact, one could assert that they are often synonymous and used indiscriminately. Throughout this study I have employed a wide variety of approaches to these concepts. It has not been my purpose or my politics to settle on one definitive or consistent approach to these issues. I have, in contrast, taken advantage of different theories and concepts depending on the applicability of those ideas to the poetry under consideration. After all, if the poets have diverse opinions and ways of representing themselves, the critic must take advantage of all available resources. No one approach is sufficient and may even be unjust and/or distorting if applied stringently in all cases. My analyses of Spanish women's poetry intend to illuminate the various ways in which individual women writers come to an understanding of themselves as women and writers (what Paul Smith in *Discerning the Subject* calls "unified loci"), and how they attempt through their writing to effect changes in the sociopolitical status quo in contemporary democratic Spain.[14]

Whereas Paul Ricoeur has stated that the word *identity* encompasses both sameness (*idem*) and difference (*ipse*), Paul Smith points out that etymologically the word *individual* suggests the wholeness or unity of the subject, a concept that, according to Lacan and others, is a misconception.[15] In addition to the indivisibility implied in *individual* (*not* divisible), which would point to a coherence or coagulation of complex parts (traits and characteristics) that *internally* define the person (pace metaphor), we can also posit the external perspective of a society "divided *into*" discrete entities, the combination of which conglomerate to form society (pace metonymy). Thus identity and subjectivity are imbricated mirror images of one another: Identity entails the aggregation of multiple, often incompatible personalities that cohere to a greater or lesser extent to form a unique individual (a unified locus). On the other hand, society consists of the same type of aggregation, but of many individuals who can be grouped arbitrarily along lines of gender, race, class, and any number of other attributes, depending on their subject position(s).

In general terms, then, I understand *identity* as a process that occurs and recurs within a human being that, consciously or not, provides that person with an understanding of who s/he is (however equivocal and evolving that conception may be). This process involves contact with the external world from the beginning of life and never reaches definitive resolution. It is, however, fundamentally an internal phenomenon in which the person comes to know her/himself. Identity is the comprehension and affirmation—however tentative, transitory, and partial (some refer to it as only a "glimpse")—of who one is at a given time and in a given place. Certainly, this definition of self can change and does change in its very articulation. *Subjectivity*, in contrast, places the emphasis on the relationship and definition of the individual with society and from society's point of view. I associate subjectivity with the concept of *subject position*, which the individual identity can accept or reject in part, in whole, or variously. An individual can occupy one or more subject positions at any given time. But those positions are not determined a priori by the individual but by the society of which s/he is a part, ranging from familial and local to national, continental, and hemispheric. Subjectivity, then, refers to the projection of the individuation in the agentic assertion of identity.

This distinction is moot in that the internal understanding of one's identity and the external perception of it are in constant reciprocity and always contingent on historical, cultural, social, and personal contexts. Just as the Spanish nation as an entity has had to (re)define itself in the context of Franco's death and of the "new Europe" along with advances in the technological world, so Spanish women/poets have (re)defined themselves vis-à-vis society, language, and the poetic tradition. Hence, identity refers to the largely internal process in which a Spanish woman (in these instances, a poet) defines herself for herself in the act of writing and in her representation of a female figure; subjectivity defines that individual's relationship to and position in her society at large (and the poetic tradition), an external process albeit still addressed through the same act of writing. Both processes are simultaneous, and neither holds teleological sway over the other, even though individual writers may approach the question from different directions.

While I still rely on traditional psychoanalytical concepts (such as Freud's discussion of mourning and melancholia), I find the discussions of more recent thinkers provocative and useful. Many of Julia Kristeva's concepts are quite applicable to many of the texts examined. Solidly grounded in Kristeva's philosophy, Kelly Oliver's work, especially *Subjectivity without Subjects: From Abject Fathers to Desiring Mothers* and *Witnessing: Beyond Recognition,* has profoundly affected my thinking.[16] Oliver's concept of witnessing stems from the Lacanian definition of the mirror stage and the *méconnaissance* (misrecognition) and alienation produced when an infant recognizes itself in the mirror. But where Lacan (following Hegel's lead) interprets this encounter with the "other" (the reflected self) as antagonistic, Kristeva argues for an alternative or complementary relationship. Rather than antagonistically rejecting—in effect, violently "killing the other"—Kristeva advocates an embrace of otherness. The underlying justification for this stance is that "Without this splitting, the child would not have the recognition of itself as a unified self. This is the paradox of self-consciousness: to become one, you must become two." Oliver then adds a comment that goes to the heart of a consideration of the page as mirror: "Only through representation does self-recognition take place. . . . [But b]ecause we can never adequately or completely represent ourselves, we keep trying, we keep talking"—and, I would add, we keep writing.[17] Hence the integral part the other plays in the determination of subjectivity and the need to embrace the other rather than repel otherness. Oliver provides a summary of this situation in a passage that warrants quoting in full:

> Subjectivity is not the result of a dialectic jerking back and forth from self to other. Rather, if anything, self and other are the illusory by-products of subjectivity, perhaps even the refuse of the continual process of inter-subjective exchanges that nourish and sometimes threaten. Identity is not necessarily bought through the abjection, exclusion, or domination of others.
>
> Hegel and his willing (and unwilling) followers are right in thinking that the subject is desire (which is to say that it is no subject at all). But desire is not as they describe it. Desire is not the urge to overcome the otherness in the self and to recuperate oneself from the other. Subjectivity does not attempt to close in on itself and fortify itself against the other. Rather, subjectivity opens itself onto the other, multiplies itself but not in the sense of reproducing itself. Desire is the urge to move out into otherness. I do not define myself in relation to a hostile external world against which I am me by virtue of denying everything that I am not. The self and the other, the I and the I am not, are never fixed; and they are certainly never polar opposites.[18]

Therefore the mirror image—and by extension any representation —generates multiple exchanges. The distance created by vision also transfers to that obtained in the act of writing and opens up a space between self and other (the "space of the text" in both its narrow and broad definitions). Again, Oliver astutely summarizes the importance of this space:

> Because of the interconnection between the senses and the elements that make vision possible, the distance necessary for vision is not alienating but enabling. Vision does not necessarily put the world or others or our own image at an unreachable distance. If vision is part of a sensory system that includes what we take to be more proximal senses like touch, taste, or smell, vision becomes a sort of touching, a palpitation with the eyes. If the eyes are porous membranes and not solid mirrors or windows, then vision like the other senses necessitates a type of interpolation of elements that challenges any neat distinctions between inside and outside, or self and other.[19]

The page as mirror, then, allows the poet to "recognize" herself in the representation of an other, a female figure, in the poem and establish a dialogue, an exchange, a dialectic between self and other.

But Oliver discovers that this Hegelian recognition is only the first step in the process and that it is necessary to move "beyond recognition" to witnessing.[20] Recognition is unidirectional or uni-intentional in spite of its dialogic nature because of the antagonism involved. Witnessing, on the other hand, is reciprocal because it entails "address-ability and response-ability" (7). Oliver bases this duality or reciprocity on the two contradictory definitions of the word *witnessing:* "*eyewitness* testimony based on first-hand knowledge, on the one hand, and *bearing witness* to something beyond recognition that can't be seen, on the other"—which she asserts is "the heart of subjectivity" (16). The tension between eyewitness testimony and bearing witness both positions the subject in finite history and necessitates the infinite response-ability of subjectivity. The tension between eyewitness testimony and bearing witness, between historical facts and psychoanalytic truth, between subject position and subjectivity, between the performative and the constative, is the dynamic operator that moves us beyond the melancholic choice between either dead historical facts or traumatic repetition of violence (16).

This combination of and tension between eyewitness testimony and bearing witness leads not only to self-awareness and the possibility of personal change brought about by the opening of space between self and other, but also to a resituation of the self with regard to others. Mirroring, using the page as mirror as I am defining the process, "depends on constantly renegotiating self and other to expose the connections between them" (219). Thus Kristeva and Oliver see no conflict between identity and difference. The "loving eye" that Oliver describes in the following passage epitomizes the relationship between the implied author and the representation of a female figure on the page as mirror.

> Self-reflection is not a turn inward but a turn toward otherness. . . . If the self is by virtue of a witnessing relation to another, then self-reflection is the reflection of what makes reflection possible, the process of reflecting that makes mirrors send back images. The loving eye is a critical eye in that it demands to see what cannot be seen; it vigilantly looks for signs of the invisible process that gives rise to vision, reflection, and recognition. The loving eye is a critical eye in that it insists on going beyond recognition toward otherness. The loving eye is a critical eye in the sense that it is necessary, crucial for establishing and nourishing relationships across difference. (219)

In other words, subjectivity obtains in a reciprocal process, a "response-loop," as psychologist J. J. Gibson has called it.[21] And this reciprocity depends on both *address-ability* and *response-ability,* terms which Oliver appropriates from Lévinas and which correspond to the two definitions of witnessing in that witnessing allows for the other's response, the other's ability to respond. When a woman poet recognizes herself in the representation of a female figure in the mirror, the intermediate space allows for the mirror image to respond. This moment of realization materializes because of the tension between self and other, similarity and difference, reflection and self-reflection. The implied poet recognizes herself in the other but then opens herself to the response of/to the other. This circularity functions as a Moebius strip because of its fluidity from inside to outside and from self to other, epitomizing the interaction between the implied author and the image on the page as mirror, a process that also then inscribes the reader in a "chain of reflections."[22]

The focus of this book privileges a phenomenological representation over language per se, although the distinction is purely arbitrary and abstract. It is impossible to talk about poetry without talking about language, and I certainly concentrate my focus on words and other linguistic sememes. Yet I concentrate here on the image of woman as represented in the text. The vision is Gestalt in that I attempt to envision—on the basis of the language of the poem—an image of the woman described and of the woman doing the describing so as to draw comparisons and contrasts and thus to arrive at the poet's perception of feminine identity—or what it is not.

PRECEDENTS: THE GYNOCENTRIC POETIC TRADITION IN SPAIN

The issues with which post-Franco women poets deal have their precedents in poets and novelists writing during the Franco era and earlier. Indeed, Rosalía de Castro (1839–85) is a seminal model for late twentieth-century women poets for the depth of her emotion and her linguistic restraint. Like her male counterpart Gustavo Adolfo Bécquer (1836–70), Rosalía de Castro appropriated romantic imagery and thematics, but without falling into cliché, melodramatics, or saccharine sentimentality when dealing with the profound issues that defined her life, such that at times the overt expression of her religious doubts shocked her audience and caused the emendation of some of her texts following her death.[23] For that reason and for the affective intensity of her poems, *linguistic restraint* may seem an inappropriate term; but much of her power resides in the language of her poetry and her difference from the trite, sentimental effusion of other poets (male and female) of the same era. A quick glimpse at a poem from *En las orillas del Sar* will illustrate my point.

Cerrado capullo de pálidas tintas,
modesta hermosura de frente graciosa,
¿por quién has perdido la paz de tu alma?,
¿a quién regalaste la miel de tu boca?

A quien te detesta quizás, y le causan
enojo tus labios de cándido aroma,
porque busca la rosa encendida
que abre al sol de la tarde sus hojas.[24]

Despite the traditional floral imagery of the rose as symbol of female sexuality, other characteristics prevent this poem from deteriorating into excessive sentimentality or vituperation. In spite of the poem's compression (similar to Bécquer's *rimas* and forerunner of María Victoria Atencia's and Clara Janés's signature brevity), a contrast between the rosebud (*capullo*) of the first stanza and the full-blown rose of the second stanza posits a duality of innocence versus experience. This duality points to the consolatory speaker who addresses a young woman disillusioned in love. These dualities, underscored by the division of the poem into two stanzas, suggest that the speaker is an older and wiser woman who has experienced a similar disillusionment with men. The emphasis thus shifts subtly to balance the anger and pain the young woman feels and transfers it to an echo, redefining and amplifying the emotions without erasing them. The force of these emotions can be perceived in the third line of the second stanza in the alteration of the established rhythmic pattern. The dynamic tension between self and other that plays out on different levels deepens the affective thrust of the poem rather than converting it into diatribe. Empathy wins out over greeting-card sympathy, as the older woman and the younger one mirror each other.

For whatever reasons—political, social, economic, religious—it is not until after the Spanish civil war that the inroads made by Rosalía de Castro again come to the fore. As the recent book by Catherine Bellver attests, the tendencies in post-Franco poetry are not manifest in the women poets of the 1920s and 30s.[25] We might adduce arguments put forth by Susan Bordo who explains this hiatus as "the dilemma of twentieth-century feminism," "post-feminism":

Then as now, there was a strong backlash, particularly among professional women, against feminist talk about gender difference. . . . Professional women in particular shunned and scorned the earlier generation of activist women, who had made themselves a "foreign, irritating body" to prevailing institutions and who attempted to speak for an alternative set of emphatic, rational "female" values. Instead, women were urged to adopt the rationalist, objectivist standards they found in place in the professions they entered. . . . Professional women saw in the "neutral" standards of objectivity and excellence the means of being accepted as humans, not women. In any case, . . . to have mounted a strategy *against* those standards (to expose them as myths, to offer other visions) would have surely "marked them as outsiders."[26]

Bordo's arguments evoke undeniable parallels when we consider the Spanish women poets of the 1920s and 30s and the hegemony exercised by their male counterparts. Bellver also presents cogent arguments for the eclipse of women's poetry during this period.

Because many of the authors of this era went into exile during or following the civil war, a new generation of women poets emerged during the Franco years. In spite of key figures such as Carmen Conde and Angela Figuera Aymerich, Gloria Fuertes stands out as the most significant if controversial poet of her time. Other poets contemporary with Fuertes—Francisca Aguirre, María Victoria Atencia, and Clara Janés, most notably—either began later or interrupted their poetic careers to follow more traditional feminine roles in the Franco era, while Fuertes demonstrates the greatest degree of exploration and oppositional politics of the era. Although many poets of the post-Franco era disavow Fuertes's importance and influence on their poetics, and others—mostly males—emphatically deny that Fuertes is a poet at all, her contribution to Spanish poetry cannot be underestimated.[27] Even if today's women do not uniformly acknowledge her contributions, Fuertes pushed the envelope to such an extent that contemporary women may seem mild in comparison and therefore have realized greater possibilities of expression. Fuertes, then, exemplifies a woman "who [made herself] a 'foreign, irritating body' to prevailing institutions," an "outsider," in Bordo's words.

American scholars have focused primarily on Fuertes's humorous and highly irreverent appropriation of diverse discourses (for example, slang, advertising slogans, references to trivial events) to create what has been called her antipoetry.[28] Andrew Debicki summarizes this characteristic, saying that Fuertes's "inappropriate language . . . explicitly (when two easily identifiable modes of expression clash . . .) or implicitly (when the language merely suggests a conflicting convention or form of expression) . . . deliberately disorients its implied reader."[29] This disorientation generally results in either humor or social criticism (and at times a combination of both).[30] John Wilcox approximates the concept I am investigating with his gynocentric focus on Fuertes's poetry. Noting that Fuertes's poetry often "textually foregrounds imagery of women's bodies which it develops into metaphors of female thoughts and feelings," his discussion of Fuertes's portrayal of herself as poet comes closest to mentioning the definition of self and subjectivity that constitutes my approach.[31]

In my view Fuertes's experimentation with different discourses and the presentation of her persona to emphasize "a very strong sense of self-sufficiency and self-dependency" opens the possibilities for using the page as mirror.[32] In effect, she avails herself of a variety of images to meditate on her identity as woman and as poet through an interplay of sameness and difference. These images take the form of other women in everyday situations, of animals, of cultural and popular icons, and of autobiographical characterization. Through a variety of costumes, gestures, and stances, the poet attempts to define her identity—both poetic and personal—while interacting with an image of herself in the poem. In this game of dress-up she often uses artifacts that establish distance between herself and her image, emphasizing the sense of the other so crucial to the definition of self. Fuertes's ludic posturing in the poem as mirror has ambivalent and paradoxical consequences, however. While it affords her opportunities to assert her individuality and define her identity, it also problematizes the concept of self. The interaction between self and image displaces the location of meaning and blurs the distinction between self and other.

In addition, the concept of the poem as mirror enables Fuertes to inscribe a place for herself within the patriarchal poetic canon as she simultaneously affirms her marginality and difference. "The problematics of what constitutes self, where it resides, and how it comes to be through objectification" form the basis of one of Fuertes's signature poems, "Puesto del Rastro."[33] At first glance, this poem appears to be little more than a catalog of second-hand objects found in one of the stalls of Madrid's flea market. But since "El poema es una especie de auténtico pregón" (as a footnote informs us, "the poem is a type of authentic sales pitch"), we soon recognize the rhythm, internal rhymes, and caesura characteristic of poetry.

> —Hornillos eléctricos brocados bombillas
> discos de Beethoven sifones de selt
> tengo lamparitas de todos los precios,
> ropa usada vendo en buen uso ropa
> trajes de torero objetos de nácar,
> miniaturas pieles libros y abanicos.

(vv. 1–6)[34]

From the midst of this collection of odds and ends a distinct voice emerges, a voice that addresses an audience. After the reader has succumbed to the rhythmic and phonic mesmerism of this list, the word *joyas* resonates in the silence of the poem's conclusion.

> Y vean la sección de libros y novelas,
> la revista francesa con tomos de Verlaine,
> con figuras posturas y paisajes humanos.
> Cervantes Calderón el Oscar y Papini
> son muy buenos autores a duro nada más.
> Estatuas de Cupido en todos los tamaños
> y este velazqueño tapiz de salón,
> vea qué espejito, mantas casi nuevas,
> sellos importantes, joyas . . .
>
> (vv. 26–34)[35]

Are there really jewels amid the junk, moments of intense emotion, true poems, beneath the apparent meaninglessness of the words? By placing herself in the role of the vendor surrounded by others' cast-off junk, Fuertes is able to appropriate various voices or discourses to construct a poem from which her own voice emerges. The poem as mirror defines her view of her poetry as a crazy quilt and of herself as a crazy textual quilt maker. This interplay between anecdotal reality, poet, and text calls into question the locus of meaning. Like a cubist portrait, this poem defines recognizable characteristics of the subject, but it does so from different perspectives simultaneously, scattering identity and emphasizing its instability and continuous evolution. "Puesto del Rastro" questions the unity of self at the same time that it defines essential characteristics of Fuertes and her poetry.

In another poem exemplifying the page as mirror, the speaker of "Disco de gramófono en una tarde de gramófono" (Gramophone Record on a Gramophone Afternoon) adopts the persona of a blues singer. In addition to merging the poetic voice with that of the singer, Fuertes creates a metonymic chain by availing herself of another object, the gramophone (note the metapoetic etymology). First, the voice emerges from the bell, in effect broadcasting the speaker's protest against an oppresive order. In yet another metonymic move, the RCA logo of a dog sitting before a gramophone and recognizing "His Master's Voice" provides an ekphrastic image.[36] Multiple interpretations of this image are feasible, including the ironic relationship between the poet and "el Gran Marionetista" (the Great Puppeteer, mentioned earlier in the poem and referring to God, male poetic inspiration, or the patriarchal order) or between the reader and the poetic voice. These possibilities disperse the speaker's identity by calling into question hierarchical (patriarchal) relationships by means of metonymic displacement.

As we can see, Fuertes avails herself of objects and the ekphrastic principle, concepts evident in other poets studied here. She employs yet another object that appears frequently in women's poetry: the doll.[37] If in "Puesto del Rastro" the poet hawks her poetic identity in the guise of a vendor and in "Disco de gramófono" she confronts the patriarchal dominance of poetic convention by singing the blues, in "Muñeca disecada" (Dissected Doll) she exposes a more tender and intimate side of her character. While still using the poem as mirror with ambivalent consequences, Fuertes explores its temporal possibilities.[38]

As though based on an article in the *National Geographic* about the archeological find of a rag doll in a child's tomb, this poem begins with seemingly objective information. But by dint of the interaction between herself and the doll, the poet confronts her own past and the emotions attached to it. When the poet then echoes an earlier phrase with "mucho trapo en la tripa" (a lot of rags in its guts), it acquires additional significance as an image of reproductive organs that have not borne a child. The profundity of these reflections is heightened by images of death ("un gusano en el gozne" [a worm in the hinge] and "telaraña en la ceja" [spiderwebs on the eyebrow]) or of feelings that have been stored away and out of sight for a long while ("mucho olor a alcanfor" [a strong odor of camphor]). The discovery of the doll has brought these feelings to the surface and revivified them, demonstrating the temporal dimension of the mirror. The final three verses complicate the interaction between poet and doll, past and present, self and other.

> La muñeca sin vida la muñeca que vive,
> la muñeca sin pelo la muñeca que llora,
> la muñeca que ríe, la muñeca que espanta.
>
> (vv. 17–19)[39]

As these verses describe the doll, they also define the poet. Fuertes sees the doll as a representation of a former self, a part of herself that has died and is now alien to her, causing her to reject it and distance herself from it. At the same time, she identifies with and is attracted to it because of the love and hope it recalls. In this poem the mirror has an inverse function. The deep chords of emotion the poet strikes through her honesty with herself confirm that what appears to be frightening and repulsive on the outside may conceal an inner beauty and tenderness. La Belle describes this potential characteristic of the mirror when speaking of a passage in one of Virginia Woolf's novels: "The physiognomic mirror tells the woman, 'you are what you look like.' Woolf says in effect, 'you are the exact opposite of what you look like.' This is not an utter rejection of the mirror, for the glass is used as an instrument to reveal an inverse proportion relating outer beauty and inner being" (147).

As noted above, Fuertes frequently evokes recognized cultural or religious icons to posit her "reflections." One of her favorite figures is the Virgin Mary, as the poem "Virgen de plástico" (Plastic Virgin) exemplifies. Since at first she does not seem to recognize herself in the image of Mary, the poetic voice satirically jibes at this tacky object (similar in configuration to a doll). The figurine's halo is lighted by an electric bulb instead of true saintliness, and there are batteries where her heart should be; she wears both a synthetic cloak and an oxymoronic "sonrisa triste."[40] Moreover, traditional representations of Mary are undercut by banality: The accumulation of trivial and mundane details, including those of size and color, creates humor, further distances the speaker from the image, and emphasizes her rejection of it.

> Es un cruce de Virgen entre Fátima y Lourdes,
> un leve vaciado con troquel "made in USA,"
> tiene melena larga y las manos abiertas
> es lavable y si cae no se descascarilla.
> Las hay de tres colores,
> blancas, azules, rosas
> —las hay de tres tamaños—
> —aún la grande es pequeña—.
>
> (vv. 11–18)[41]

A subtle shift in the final verses understates the duality of the poem as mirror and allows us to glimpse a change in the poet's attitude. She no longer snickers, digging her elbow into our ribs, but engages in direct discourse with the Virgin. This change in address may indicate a realization that she is looking into the mirror and that she shares something with this representation of the Virgin, causing her sorrow ("me diste pena"). She may recognize that in criticizing this tacky item she has done what many men do to women. Just as men expect women to be ideal, whether virgin or sex partner, Fuertes has imposed her religious and artistic criteria on this female figure. By refusing to ask the Virgin for a miracle, she rejects those unrealistic patriarchal expectations imposed on her (and her poetry) and so frees herself from them. She rejects not the image itself but the ideals imposed from without, which tend to make all women the same (in spite of differences in size and color). Through her empathy with that image she affirms her individuality and valuation of herself and the need to express that self in her own voice. Seeing herself in the poem as mirror causes Fuertes to modify her initial reaction and to affirm her own identity.

The artifacts that Fuertes uses to mediate the space between herself and the image in the mirror have a dual and ambivalent effect: They disguise the image of the self, creating a sharper sense of alterity, an essential part of the process of self-definition, and they fill the gap between self and other, blurring the distinction between them and confirming that the self is "a double or complex self, one that is both subject and object."[42] In still other poems the mediation is more tenuous. It may be linguistic, as in the autobiographical poems in which she names herself, uses second- or third-person pronouns and verbs, and supplies a personal history. Or it may be the more explicit image of a woman, such as the cleaning woman in "No dejan escribir" (They Don't Allow One to Write). Then again, the figure of an animal, as in "Cabra sola" (Lonely Goat) or "A un raccoon muerto" (To a Dead Raccoon), disguises the poet to a greater extent. In the adoption of different guises and stances in the poem as mirror, Fuertes shows that "the mirror's [the poem's] power resides in its ability to reveal alternative selves out of which [she] can mold the self. Before she can have any control over what she is, she has to be able to conceive what she can be. The mirror [the poem] allows her to do that."[43] Fuertes's emphasis on and acceptance of the unattractive and unconventional in herself and in her poetry contribute to the development of her personal and poetic identity by using the poem as her mirror. Gloria Fuertes is the founding mother of the page as mirror because of the numerous ways in which she explores her personality as both woman and writer.

Whereas Fuertes demonstrates the most diversity in using the page as mirror, she is not the only poet of her generation or her era to use a female representation to reflect on sameness and difference in the understanding of identity and subjectivity. Other poets are more revisionist in their appropriation of cultural icons.[44] Angela Figuera Aymerich titles her first book *Mujer de barro* (1948), and Carmen Conde rewrites the creation myth in *Mujer sin Edén* (1947). Francisca Aguirre rereads the Odyssey from Penelope's point of view and thus interacts with this epic figure to speak of her own life and that of contemporary women in *Itaca* (1966). Later on, Concha Zardoya similarly chooses the figure of the woman philosopher Diotima from

Plato's *Symposium* to define herself as a poet, a scholar, and a woman versed in the theme of love.[45] All of these works and others prefigure the much more extensive use of the page as mirror in the post-Franco era, but Fuertes is the most daring, diverse, and iconoclastic in her exploration of female identity and subjectivity during the Franco era.

THE PAGE AS MIRROR

In approaching the poetry analyzed in this book, a primary concern has been—as always—to discover the various ways in which these poets make language signify. Conceiving of the page as mirror provides an insightful means of access into the poems, some of which—particularly Andreu's *De una niña de provincias* and Castro's *Los versos del eunuco*—are challenging poetic texts. Again, La Belle's study has provided a fundamental template to which I have added other aesthetic, psychoanalytic, and feminist lenses. In her chapter on "Introductory Reflections" in *Herself Beheld*, La Belle provides a lengthy enumeration of different types of mirrors: wavy-surfaced mirrors, swinging mirrors, triple mirrors, windows as dark mirrors, convex pier glasses, shattered mirrors, magnifying mirrors. Moreover, she asserts, "If a mirror cannot be found, one can be created" (7).

A few telling criteria have governed my choices of the authors considered here: First, a wide range of authors from different age groups, regions of Spain, and historical moments in which their poetry appears; second, selecting works from different decades (the seventies, eighties, and nineties) shows not only that the phenomenon of the page as mirror is pervasive but also that it has undergone changes over this time period; and finally, this concept knows no aesthetic boundaries: poets with quite different aesthetic approaches and ideologies can employ the page as mirror, although their poetic praxis will have an effect on the process and the outcome.

This study begins with two women who have achieved canonical status in Spanish poetry: María Victoria Atencia and Ana Rossetti. Because they are from two different generations and begin their aesthetic project with different purposes in mind, their poetry is quite distinct, but both manifest a rejection of the predominant image of woman as defined by the Franco era. In *Marta & María*, Atencia manifests a conflicted attitude with regard to her self-image. In accord with the Franco ideal and a traditional role for women, she temporarily abandoned her poetic career for a domestic one. However, with the end of Francoism on the horizon and her own duties as wife and mother—her Martha personality—reaching satisfaction, the aesthetic side—her María personality—reasserted its desire and need for recognition. The tension between these two impulses, reinforced by the social pressure of the epoch in which she matured as a woman, provokes her to reflect on her identity. Many of her works in the early period of her return to writing show her questioning and defining her identity through a process of comparison and contrast with female figures represented in her poems. In addition to *Marta & María,* Atencia wrote *El mundo de M. V.* (which contains the unforgettable and paradigmatic "Godiva en blue jean"), *Paulina o el libro de las aguas,* and the first poems that will eventually—and continuously—expand into *Los trances de Nuestra Señora,* a meditation on various aspects of the Virgin Mary.[46] As La Belle has suggested, mirroring is not a single event in Atencia's poetry. In her book *La intrusa,* which appeared much later in her career (in 1992), Atencia returns to this device to consider the process of aging and her changing identity.[47] At the same time, however, another of the poet's interests provides the theoretical balance for the page as mirror: painting. Margaret Persin's inveterate interest in ekphrasis along with Atencia's recounting of her training as an artist and her desire to be a painter leads to viewing this poetry as an ekphrastic mirror.[48]

Rossetti, in contrast, has always been involved in theater, which led me to investigate the role of play and masquerade in her first book, *Los devaneos de Erato.* Whereas Atencia chronologically belongs to the Generation of the Fifties (the Second Generation of the Post-War or the poets of discovery), Rossetti is a *novísima* who begins her career during the famous *movida madrileña,* a sociocultural period of liberation following the adoption of the Constitution of 1978. Whereas Rossetti's ingenuity and ludic experimentation rival those of Gloria Fuertes, her choice of figures is more culturalist, more learned and intellectual vis-à-vis Fuertes's more popularist, socially engaged approach. Rossetti playfully dresses up in various guises or costumes depicting different characters and then observes herself as if she were standing in front of funhouse mirrors. Her costuming and her baroque poetic language deform the original image to highlight misperceptions or distortions of women in an attempt to subvert those images and bring about changes in society's thinking. In that sense these poems are revisionist.

Blanca Andreu's *De una niña de provincias* provides a smooth though painful segue into the eighties. Her surrealistic imagery and eclectic intertextual references evince the *novísimo* influence like Rossetti, but her image as *poète maudite* prefigures the emergence of attitudes of protest in the mid-eighties in the work of Luisa Castro and Almudena Guzmán.[49] As *Bildungspoesie, De una niña de provincias* portrays the concept of the shattered mirror and the reconstruction of identity after traumatic loss, providing many parallels with Sylvia Plath's poetry and prose. In conjunction with this concept, this work reads as an elegiac text in which repetition leads to a degree of consolation and a reconstruction of identity from the broken fragments of the mirror and of language. This process also entails Kristeva's concept of the abject and the *sujet-en-procès* as a way of redefining the image of a woman poet in post-Franco Spain.

Following the transition from dictatorship to democracy, the mid-1980s is a critical period, especially with regard to women. A new generation of children born just before the end of the Franco era begins to come of age but confronts the residual framework of Franco ideology and conservative, phallocentric attitudes in the poetic establishment. Because the children of this generation come of age in the democracy, their expectations conflict with the regnant structures of social and cultural power, producing angry rebellion in Luisa Castro's *Los versos del eunuco* and Almudena Guzmán's *Usted.* As both these titles indicate, these young poets meet condescending patriarchal attitudes head-on in a bitter coming of age. We might adduce Ramón Buenaventura's irritatingly patronizing tone in the introduction and presentations of *Las diosas blancas,* the first anthology of women's poetry in the post-Franco era, as typical of the prevailing attitudes.[50] In some ways it would be illustrative to present specific passages from this text to appall the reader with Buenaventura's insensitivity and condescension, but such citation would only perpetuate those attitudes in a work that proposes to extol women poets' aesthetic achievements.[51] Even the choice of the title *Las diosas blancas* (taken from Robert Graves's mythological studies) is sarcastic. Suffice it to say that Buenaventura and Castro did not get along well![52]

In *Los versos del eunuco* Castro challenges the Freudian concept of woman as castrated male (*homme manqué*) and the subsequent attitudes it spawns: that women are lacking; that women envy the male his penis; that women are therefore incomplete and inferior to men. That Castro is an intelligent woman who also comes from Galicia and from a working-class background only exacerbates her anger. To protest these intimations of her inferiority, the poet feigns complicity in adopting the image of woman as eunuch. Her purpose is to debunk these outdated attitudes and assert her self-esteem and self-valorization in the new democratic atmosphere.[53] The irony and sarcasm of Castro's book is echoed in Almudena Guzman's *Usted,* although in a radically different way. By sequentially ordering short lyric pieces, Guzmán creates a narrative of the deleterious effects of hegemonic aesthetic attitudes on young women writers. Even though the protagonist of her work is named Almudena, the poet steadfastly denies that the work is autobiographical. It does, however, comment on the paternalistic reception of her poetry and that of other young women. The mirror as male gaze thus determines the dispiriting sense of inferiority and inadequacy that society can create in young women. Insofar as this atmosphere can eviscerate and disempower young women of their aspirations and potential, *Usted* attests to the psychological violence done to young women. Patriarchal attitudes are equivalent to rape, clitorectomy, and the infantilization of women.

Young poets are not the only ones to raise their voices in protest. Born in 1952, the same year as Ana Rossetti, Margarita Merino unleashes her rage against provincial conservatism and a masculinist double standard in *Baladas del abismo*. Like Fuertes and Rossetti, Merino demonstrates an amazing range of personalities that function as the mirror image on the page, but all have one common paradigm: the abandoned woman. Having been abandoned by her lover, Merino abandons herself to criticizing male privilege and a society that endorses women's silence and suffering. The paragon figure here is Emma Bovary, but Merino adopts various avatars such as her housekeeper, a medieval lady whose lord does not return from war, a prisoner of courtly love, and even her own father to reflect on her identity and to define the plight of the abandoned woman. Lawrence Lipking's well known study, *Abandoned Women and Poetic Tradition*, provides the basis for this discussion.

The final two poets could both be called revisionist, thus pointing to an adjustment in the purpose of the page as mirror. In general, critics have miscategorized Amalia Bautista's *Cárcel de amor* as poetry of experience, the predominant though controversial poetic aesthetic of the 1980s and '90s in Spain.[54] In very general terms, the poetry of experience posits a familiar voice in a commonplace situation on the basis of which that voice discovers deeper meaning. A throwback to the poetry of discovery of the 1950s and a reaction against the *novísimo* aesthetic of distancing and cultural reference, this trend has been hailed by many self-promoting poets as the ideal of poetry.[55] But more recently readers have become tired of this style (equivalent to official verse culture in the United States), and criticism of the exclusivity of this approach has arisen.[56] Just as countertendencies have appeared in the United States, Bautista's *Cárcel de amor* (and her subsequent book, *Cuéntamelo otra vez*) are better characterized as expansive poetry because of their proselike versification and their narrative style.[57] In any event, the poems of *Cárcel de amor* present a woman's point of view on love relationships in such a way that they call for changes in men's attitudes. Highly ironic and subtly ludic, *Cárcel de amor* culminates with a section devoted to the modern revision of traditional female figures: Judith, Columbine, Galatea, and others.

In the same vein, the poems of Maite Pérez Larumbe's *Mi nombre verdadero* entail the revision of biblical women, quite similar to Alicia Suskin Ostriker's project delineated in *Feminist Revision and the Bible*.[58] Larumbe's poems function as two-way mirrors in that the speaker of the poem portrays herself as a biblical figure and then turns the mirror so that it reflects a certain type of contemporary woman or issues that many women are encountering in contemporary society. The image in the mirror thus reflects traditional situations and ways of defining women, but also offers possibilities for revising and altering those possibilities from a feminist perspective.

Hence, the page as mirror proffers a useful tool to women poets of the post-Franco era. It enables them to define their identities not only as women in a new democratic society but also as poets in a more open literary environment. The page as mirror is not the only tendency in women's writing during this period, nor is it an obligatory practice. Nor does the momentary image presented in the poem straitjacket the poet or define her essence. It is a (transient) moment of recognition of self that empowers a woman by giving her the ability to define who she is and/or to demolish rigid masculinist or patriarchal conceptions of woman.

1
The Ekphrastic Mirror: María Victoria Atencia's *Marta & María*

In spite of a fifteen-year hiatus in her poetic career, María Victoria Atencia has become a canonical figure, one of the more prolific and renowned poets of post-Franco Spain. Although we can attribute this hiatus to many different causes, one of the principal reasons was that the author was raising her family and fulfilling her obligations as wife and mother.[1] Her first work published after that silence, *Marta & María* (Martha and Mary) (1976), reflects the tension between two opposing but inextricably commingled aspects of her identity. Hence the title *Marta & María* and its biblical allusion to two sisters: the practical Martha who is anxious and harried with the preparations for a meal and the innocent Mary who quietly sits at the feet of Jesus and listens to his words. Others have described it as a contrast between *la vida activa* (an active life) and *la vida contemplativa* (a contemplative life).[2] Martha and Mary are also sisters of Lazarus, which posits a subtext of death and resurrection, a prominent motif in *Marta & María*.

Each of the three sections of *Marta & María* represents a step in the process of reconciling these two spheres—the domestic and the aesthetic—and recuperating the repressed poetic voice.[3] This progression is particularly evident in the three poems—one in each section—dedicated to a young woman named Blancanieves (Snow White) who was a friend of the poet and who died prematurely. Here the poems delineate the resurrection and revitalization of the repressed poetic voice through descriptive settings and female figures that mirror the poet's creative self.[4] This process entails a coming to terms with the assimilated and engrained image of woman during the Franco era and the conflicts generated by the proposed reemergence of the aesthetic self.

In light of her later work that increasingly evokes, describes, and interacts with specific works of visual art, the poems of *Marta & María* draw their aesthetic effect from the ekphrastic principle. As Murray

35

Krieger has noted, Horace's injunction *ut pictura poesis* has only recently encompassed verbal representation of a visual work of art.[5] But Krieger, investigating the history of this trope, expands its definition, affirming that "the early meaning given 'Ekphrasis' in Hellenistic rhetoric . . . referred, most broadly, to a verbal description of something, almost anything, in life or art. . . . It was, then, a device intended to interrupt the temporality of discourse, to freeze it during its indulgence in spatial exploration." In truth, the trope that best describes Atencia's poetics is *enargeia:* "[t]he capacity of words to describe with a vividness that, in effect, reproduces an object before our very eyes (i.e., before the eyes of the mind)."[6]

This understanding of the ekphrastic principle makes it clear that in her poetry Atencia paints pictures with words. She describes reality *as if* it were a work of art, *as if* she were painting. Hence her poetry exemplifies the injunction *ut pictura poesis.* By extension, then, the ekphrastic scenes depicted in her poems serve to mirror the woman presenting that scene to the reader, with all the implications of the mirror as a means of exploring and discovering the self. At times, the scene becomes an objective correlative as a physical or geographical setting reflects the mental state of the poet. But as this process continues to develop in the poems of *Marta & María,* the depiction of female figures becomes prominent. In effect, the poet's identity emerges from her surroundings and then becomes sharper in the interaction of similarity and difference with these other female figures. Blanca, the poet's recently deceased friend, is one of the most important of these female figures and enables the reader to discern the different stages in the poet's rediscovery and the reemergence of her aesthetic self. This process culminates in the eponymous final poem of the collection, "Marta y María."

The initial section of *Marta & María* contains a predominance of poems in which the speaker's surroundings function as an objective correlative of her state of mind, as some of the titles suggest: "1 de diciembre" (First of December), "Entre los que se fueron" (Among Those Who Have Gone, describing a visit to a cemetery), "Puerto llovido" (Rainy Port), "Cuanto escondió el olvido" (What Forgetfulness Hid), and "Mar" (Sea), for example. Out of these surroundings there emerges a renascent passion for the poetic act, an urge that had lain dormant for fifteen years. Toward the end of this section, the figure of Blanca appears in "Ahora que amanece" (Now That It Is Dawning). An examination of some of these poems shows how this figure materializes and emerges from the dullness and grayness of a life devoid of the aesthetic act.

The opening poem, "1 de diciembre," is typical of this section, for it is not until the very end of the poem that we perceive the small point of light and warmth, the ember of poetic stimulation and inspiration in the midst of gloom. In December the days grow shorter, darker, and colder, heading for the winter solstice. As the poet herself mentions, it is also the beginning of Advent, the start of the liturgical year, in anticipation of the birth (death and resurrection) of Christ. The evocation of the single lit candle on the Advent wreath is consonant with this moment in the speaker's reawakening to/of her poetic talent. The description of the scene in the first stanza, however, stresses repetition and dullness.

> Marchaba por su curso el Adviento y se estaban
> quedando los jardines a merced del poniente.
> Algunos animales prosiguieron en celo.
> Escurrían los peces su plata en las orillas.
> Derramaban serrín las muñecas de trapo
> y sintieron las tejas verdecer sus aleros.
>
> (vv. 1–6)[7]

One aspect common to all these metonymically juxtaposed images is the use of past-tense verbs. Although there are two preterits, the others are imperfect, connoting routine and constancy. Yet even the preterit verbs express a continuing state: *prosiguieron* is literally continuous, while the personification of the roof tiles allows these inanimate objects to feel the growth of moss on the eaves, a traditional symbol of aging and decay.

If we look closely at these mimetic images, other archetypal signs of repetition and return emerge. The phrases *Marchaba por su curso* and *a merced del poniente* obliquely allude to circadian and seasonal cycles. The garden and the sunset point to the end of a process, the loss of productivity, and the brevity of light/life. Given that Atencia was born in 1931 and *Marta & María* was published in 1976, these images might reflect her entry into menopause and the conclusion of the reproductive cycle, provoking a return to the production of poetry. Certainly, the "animales . . . en celo" introduce this theme, reinforced by the rag dolls losing their sawdust filling, echoing Gloria Fuertes's "Muñeca disecada" discussed in the introduction. The value suggested in the fish's silver scales is elusive, evading capture, and even the green color of the moss on the roof tiles—which could have positive connotations of growth and life—is negatively marked by dampness and the parasitical nature of moss. In short, the predominant tone of this stanza is one of loss, gloom, chill, and emptiness.

But these images also point to hope in their differential opposite:

Every cyclical process suggests a beginning in its ending, as does Advent in December and Christ in the human world of sin and death. This countermovement manifests itself in the second stanza.

> La tristeza en los barcos no aumentó con la lluvia
> ni lloraron los sauces más de lo conveniente.
> Encontró el recental las ubres deseadas.
> Ajenos, los amantes continuaron su sueño.
> Y aunque un frío finísimo paralizó mi sangre,
> estuvo a punto el té, como todos los días.
>
> (vv. 7–12)[8]

Unexpectedly, the sadness does not increase when it starts to rain. This could mean that the speaker's emotions have reached a nadir and cannot go any lower, but also that she sees some hope in the gloom as crying alleviates her sadness. Her assimilation of the traditional romantic symbol of the weeping willows is gently self-mocking. And she finds new life in the continuation of cycles: the calf suckling at the cow's udder and the dreamy lovers—perhaps her children— who will continue procreating and creating life.

The final two verses neatly juxtapose the contrast, and it is here that the speaker enters in the first person. Her emergence at this moment is significant insofar as her presence pulls together the disparate images of this "1 de diciembre." Certainly, she participates in the chill and gloom of this sense of loss, emphasized in the phrase "un frío finísimo paralizó mi sangre." But the adjective *finísimo* could mean "very sharp and painful" or "very delicate and just barely perceptible, but wonderful." The custom of taking tea on this chilly afternoon may seem trivial and unimportant, but the opposite is true. If the "frío finísimo" refers to the slight twinge of poetic inspiration that prompts the poet to write, the tea's warmth and (honeyed) savor represents a small spark of life and hope in an otherwise gloomy existence. By having the speaker enter in the very last lines, the poet shows that the scene is a reflection, an objective correlative, of the subject in front of the mirror.

The interface between interior and exterior, surface and depth, the conscious and the subconscious takes many forms in Atencia's ekphrastic mirror and lends significance to what would otherwise seem to be concrete, trivial details. Many of the poems in this first section of *Marta & María* are set in the tangible imagery of her hometown, Málaga, and other sites in this maritime setting. In addition, Atencia is fond of using regional and colloquial expressions, further strengthening the poems' grounding in a mimetic, concrete context, as several commentators have already noted. Yet many poems also take place at night or involve hidden interior spaces, suggestive of the poet's exploration of her subconscious. Similar to Fuertes's use of objects, Atencia's concrete imagery adopts symbolic proportions, giving fuller depth to the image the poem reflects/projects as a mirror.[9] Such an effect is created in the poem "Mar," where a dim, still imprecise image of the poet's self moves among the shadows of night. The seascape under the speaker's bed represents one of those hidden, subconscious spaces that disturbs the speaker's sleep and compels her to explore her self in spite of herself.

> Bajo mi cama estáis, conchas, algas, arenas:
> comienza vuestro frío donde acaban mis sábanas.
> Rozaría una jábega con descolgar los brazos
> y su red tendería al palo de mesana
> de este lecho flotante entre ataúd y tina.
> Cuando cierro los ojos se me cubren de escamas.
>
> (vv. 1–6)[10]

Metaphorically transforming the floor of her bedroom into the sea and her bed into a boat, the poet determines a contrast between the bed's warm security—her present life—and the cold awakening and insecurity of the sea—her subconscious and the source of her poetic inspiration. The sea is both nutritive and dangerous, as the shells, the algae, and the sand suggest. We might also question whether she is on the beach (the very edge of the sea before taking the plunge) or in the depths of the sea itself (dreaming).

The conditional tense of the verb *rozaría* and the pending act *con descolgar los brazos* show the speaker's reluctance to let herself explore, to relax enough so that she can cast her net over her subconscious to see what she can catch. Her bed is both coffin and bathtub: It can be cold or warm, it can lead to death (unconsciousness, unawareness) or to a relaxing purification (heightened awareness). Do the scales that cover her closed eyes form a protective barrier that induces her to sleep calmly? Or do they give her the means to dive into the sea of the subconscious and maneuver her way through that watery world? The image is both grotesque and beautiful, indicative of the attraction and reluctance the speaker feels toward the risk she is taking. Repetition of the phrase *Cuando cierro los ojos* makes a smooth transition from one world to the other at the same time that the stanzaic break imposes a barrier, gulf, abyss, or threshold that still poses an obstacle.

> Cuando cierro los ojos, el viento del Estrecho
> pone olor de Guinea en la ropa mojada,
> pone sal en un cesto de flores y racimos
> de uvas verdes y negras encima de mi almohada,
> pone henchido el insomnio, y en un larguero entonces
> me siento con mi sueño a ver pasar el agua.
>
> (vv. 7–12)[11]

On a literal level, we understand the "Estrecho" as the Strait of Gibraltar. But this interface between two continents, the passageway between two bodies of water, forms another threshold that both bars and facilitates passage. The wind, a traditional symbol of inspiration, brings an aroma that invests clothes hung out to dry—perhaps the very sheets that cover the speaker's bed at that moment, that is, her quotidian surroundings—with wildness, tropical lushness, and exoticism (Guinea). She also mentions the pillowslips on which her head lies, decorated with traditional embroideries of baskets of flowers and bunches of grapes. The wind puts the salt of the ocean on these traditional motifs providing both an acrid, pungent covering, and a seasoning adding zest and enhancing flavor. As embroideries, they allude to textuality, already latent in the images of sheets and pillows. What Krieger would call "natural signs" thus acquire symbolic proportions belying the mimetic relationship between sign and referent.[12] The speaker then states that this wind—poetic inspiration on the threshold between sleep and wakefulness—"pone henchido el insomnio." But it is unclear whether her insomnia is fruitful, laden with images (*henchido* even suggests pregnancy) that delight and sate her, or if it becomes swollen and painful, wakes her, and interrupts her comfortable status quo.

In the final verses of the poem the speaker again situates herself on a threshold (*larguero*) between inside and outside, entry and exit. Her *sueño* could be either her sleepiness or the images culled from her dream, so that the final phrase is enigmatic. The grammatical construction *a ver* could indicate that the water is passing before her and that the speaker sits down to watch it: to lull herself to sleep with the monotonous passage of time? Or to contemplate the process of that passage and to try to find meaning in that which slips away? We might also interpret *a ver* as indicative of some future occurrence: that the water is not yet flowing, but that the speaker will see if it will flow. This flowing could be her sitting down with paper in front of her to see if, by meditating on her dreams or her insomnia, she can write. The speaker's uncertainty, however, is patent. Even though she feels the urge to write, even though these images are presenting themselves to her, she is not sure that she *can* write a poem. If at the end of the first stanza she recognizes her resistance to creativity and imagination, at the end of the second she fears taking that risk because of failure, perhaps, or because of what she might discover—even that she might realize she has no poetic talent and should abandon her dreams of writing. The thresholds, gaps, and liminal spaces of the poem point to the speaker's wavering, uncertainty, and the hesitant emergence of her renascent impulse after fifteen years of poetic inactivity.

As stated above, each of the three sections of *Marta & María* contains a poem dedicated to Blancanieves, a young woman who has died prematurely. This figure enables the poet to reestablish contact with her creativity and imagination, the fanciful side of her personality that she wishes to recuperate and revitalize, that part of herself that will not be denied or taken from her, that part of herself that hears inspired words. The rediscovery of the imaginative inner self takes place in "Ahora que amanece," the first of these three poems, where dawn represents an awakening and a new beginning after a long hiatus in creative activity. Ambivalence in the addressee of the opening verse causes us to question whether the poetic voice speaks to the dead woman in apostrophe or if she sees herself as a younger woman returning in her dream.

> A veces por la noche vuelvo, niña, a tu lado
> y hacia las cuatro cruzo por un camino tuyo.
> ¿Mi amistad precisaba más tiempo compartido
> o tuvimos las dos algo en común más serio
> que mi vida y tu muerte: un sueño de muñecas
> de trapo y volaeras color arropía?
>
> (vv. 1–6)[13]

The image of the girl allows her to reencounter herself in the guise of the other at this liminal moment between waking and sleep, so that the *tú* addressed could be either the girl or the speaker's alter ego. This ambiguity continues in the question culminating the first stanza, for what could be more serious than the speaker's life and the young woman's premature death? The colloquial language and allusion to childhood in the images "un sueño de muñecas /de trapo y volaeras de color arropía" at once reinforce the dreamlike vision and suggest a world of fantasy, imagination, and vivid color. Given that *arropía* is a colloquial expression for toffee, this synaesthetic image enhances the swirling visual effect of the pinwheel with another layer of sensorial childhood delight: sweetness. This capacity for fanciful musings and unexpected metaphor couched in everyday language unites the speaker with the child and signals the poet's rediscovery of her creative self. To name the other is to resuscitate her; but the poet deliberately refrains from specifically naming the other.

> Nombrarte es poseerte, y yo digo tu nombre
> de un candor repetido, y esta noche a las cuatro
> el nombre contradice tu morenez resuelta.
> Como la última vez que en la playa estuvimos,
> nos sentaremos contra la barca repintada
> para ver el mar juntas, ahora que amanece.
>
> (vv. 7–12)[14]

Not specifying the name calls attention to the redundancy and double voicing of this negative affirmative. The name *Blancanieves* redoubles the whiteness of snow and the innocence of the young woman who has died. Moreover, it recalls the fairy tale of Snow White and posits the topos of dormant youth and resurrected beauty. But the name *María Victoria* could also fall under the rubric of a name "de un candor repetido" as it too hagiographically implies a saintly purity and innocence and a triumph over sin and death. A repetition of the hour (*las cuatro*) and the young woman's *morenez resuelta* (suggesting shadows, sadness, and death) contrasts with the connotations of the name. The chiaroscuro iterates the reemergence and resuscitation of what had been hidden, suppressed, and dormant (both the image of the young woman and the light of dawn).

As the speaker recalls a past event ("la última vez que en la playa estuvimos"), the play of verb tenses allows her to project that scene into the future at the transitional moment of dawn; and when she states, "nos sentaremos contra la barca repintada / para ver el mar juntas," imagination takes over. The poet paints a colorful, intimate picture in which two female figures—one an adult, the other a younger woman (similar to the poem by Rosalía de Castro discussed in the introduction)—share the unique moment of sunrise on the beach that is both transient and transcendent. Whereas the boat may seem to be a trivial detail, the archetypal symbolism of a journey, here refreshed by a new coat of paint, a bright splash of color, points to a renewal of life through the resuscitation of a former perspective. The reference to paint also links this scene with the (ekphrastic) representation of reality in the artistry of the poem.

Dawn embodies the magical turning point at which the poet recuperates a dormant part of her self and begins to experience a reawakening of her imaginative and creative abilities. The ambivalence of address, the topos of sleep and waking, the play of light and darkness, and the image of dawn all express a transitional moment as the poet attempts to revive the inspiration of the past. This uncertain transition characterizes the first section of *Marta & María*. The next two sections and the poems dealing with Blancanieves reveal the poet's growing confidence as she gains control of her abilities and becomes more determined to reassert her poetic talent.

Atencia devotes the second section of *Marta & María* to an exploration of the past, especially to the recuperation of female figures who can supply the inspiration and stimulation to continue her poetic career. Many of these delvings are tinged with sadness because the poet recognizes that she has lost something. But her return to these figures stimulates her to pursue her poetic activity precisely so that she can rescue, preserve, and prolong the traditions and values she finds in them. The first poem of this section typifies this stance toward women of the past, as it not only describes "a room of one's own"— Atencia's own study—but also is addressed to Rosalía de Castro.

> La ventana da a un mar gris plata, con su jábega,
> y hay en el cuarto música de Haendel y Corelli.
> Repaso tu tristeza, amiga Rosalía.
> Si pudieras cederme tu correlato justo
> de saudade, alcanzara a dejar este peso
> y a subir poco a poco por tus altas ternuras.
>
> (vv. 1–6)[15]

The title of this poem, "Saudade," is a Galician word referring to the profound nostalgia and love that the Galician people feel for their "patria chica" (regional homeland), the most northwestern province in Spain, the geographical and climatic opposite of Atencia's sunny Málaga. In spite of the usual sunny weather, the speaker opens the poem with reference to "un mar gris plata." Because of the frame of the window through which she observes this scene and a fishing boat, the windowscape ekphrastically reflects the speaker's life and emotions at this time. Life in general seems gloomy and gray, and her life in particular seems to be adrift, as was the case in the poems in the first section (although the silver does indicate value).

The speaker then draws us into the interior of her room, where she is listening to Handel and Corelli. At first, these references may appear gratuitous. These two composers and their music, one German, the other Italian, reflect the gloomy, gray, dour Northern character in contrast with the sunny, lively Southern art, evident in painting as well as music since at least the fifteenth century. These two musicians are also among the founders of Western music, revealing the motif of roots of art in the past. The musicians' explorations of the possibilities of music are similar to Atencia's experimentation with her own voice in these poems. Therefore, even though the world on the exterior looks gloomy, routine, colloquial, the interior is celebratory and sunny, filled with music.

When the speaker engages directly with her predecessor, a poet whose world was sad and full of disappointment, she establishes a relationship of similarity and difference with the other in the mirror. This mirror could quite literally be the page, as we imagine Atencia reading Rosalía's poems. The verb *repaso* is appropriately equivocal: In going over the other poet's words/poems, the present poet (re)experiences "her" sadness—both the other's and her own. Using the words *correlato justo* invokes a sense of logic, of mathematical equation and balance, of measure. Because this is a "correlato . . . / de saudade" (the enjambment is very effective), the writing of the poem seeks a balance between emotion and art, inspiration and skill, similar to that which she finds in Rosalía's poetry. Moreover, the imperfect subjunctive verbs *pudieras* and *alcanzara*—especially the second, which is the main verb of the sentence—capture perfectly the poet's "saudade." The contrast between the phrases *dejar este peso* and *subir . . . por tus altas ternuras* underscores the tension. And the rhythm, the alliteration, and the placement of *altas* before the noun *ternuras* build expectation and tension while at the same time gently relaxing it. Having reread her predecessor, the poet-speaker now emulates her in her own words/poems. This play of sameness and difference stands out in the emblem of the mirror in the next stanza.

> ¡Qué reseco este sur y qué húmeda tu tierra!
> En Padrón me dirás el nombre de las flores.
> Confrontaremos épocas, repasaremos cartas,
> tu bargueño abriré más que exhaustivamente.
> Déjame que me vea reflejada en tu espejo
> y no falte a mi canto la palabra precisa.
>
> (vv. 7–12)[16]

Echoing the contrast of Handel and Corelli, the opening exclamation differentiates the two women, separated geographically and temporally. The speaker feels uninspired, infertile, in comparison with her counterpart; but this contrast merely goads her more insistently to emulate the other. Curiously, the speaker now switches to the future tense, expressing her optimism and enthusiasm (cf. "Ahora que amanece"). By meeting the other on her own terrain (not only in the town of Padrón where Rosalía lived, but also in her poems), the speaker will learn from the other how to name her feelings. She will compare the problems and issues of her time with those she perceives in Rosalía's poetry. They will exchange and reread letters with one another in mind to illuminate what they find there. The image of the "bargueño" shows to what extent the speaker is prepared to delve into the world of the other. This antique piece of furniture normally functioned as a desk and writing table and contained innumerable drawers, slots, cubbyholes, and even secret compartments. The speaker will enter these nooks and crannies "más que exhaustivamente" to savor the subtle nuances and the most hidden emotions in the words of her predecessor.

Atencia's plea/request/hope, "Déjame que me vea reflejada en tu espejo," is a strong affirmation of the thesis of this book. The overemphasis and mirroring placement and usage of the pronoun *me,* the word *reflejada,* and the emblem of the mirror underscore the interaction of sameness and difference, self and other. The virtual act of observing oneself in someone's mirror and imagining that person's same gesture, and the symbolic reading/writing of poetry to reveal one's identity are synonymous yet different. The signs are simultaneously transparent (*natural*) and an illusion, arbitrarily symbolic. The return to the present subjunctive in the final verses provides a fitting balance between doubt in the imperfect subjunctive and the enthusiasm of the future tense. "Saudade" thus functions as an invocation of the past whereby the speaker will learn to know herself better so that she can continue her career and continue to improve as a poet. The sadness of the *saudade* is counterbalanced by the hope of converting loss into discovery.

The middle section of *Marta & María* entails the poet's return to the traditions and memories of the past in order to recapture that other part of her self. This invocation of the past to enliven and enrich the present in spite of the passage of time and loss is evident in the next poem, the second of the three dedicated to the poet's deceased friend, Blanca. By adopting the voice of the deceased and speaking as if from the grave in "Blanca niña, muerta, habla con su padre" (The Young Blanca, Dead, Speaks with Her Father), the poet turns the perspective inside out and sets up parallels between the dead woman speaking to her grieving father and the inner creative voice which speaks to her adult self. On the one hand, the poetic voice empathizes with the father—a masculine other who allows her to recognize her own grief and regret for time lost, time not dedicated to poetry but to other (domestic) activities. On the other hand, that voice attempts to console the adult and provides a solution for grief: the cultivation of beauty.

Aparta el ave umbría que se posó en tus ojos
para quebrar por siempre su vuelo en tu mirada.
¿Era razón de vida que yo me anticipase?
Tanto amor tengo tuyo que no te estoy ausente
pues mi sangre retorna nuevamente a la tuya
y aguardo desde el polvo, floralmente, tu mano.

(vv. 1–6)[17]

Although the title announces that Blanca will be the speaker of this poem, the use of the third-person voice to make this announcement creates an ambivalent play of perspectives that continues in the opening verses. First the speaker admonishes the grieving adult to remove the sadness that has settled over his/her gaze. The imperative (spoken in the present but deferring the action into the future) contrasts with the preterit of the verb *se posó,* while the image of the shadowy bird suggests a sadness naturally associated with death. The phrase *para quebrar por siempre su vuelo en tu mirada* may mean that the bird will never take flight again (the sadness will never lift) or perhaps that this sadness softens and filters the gaze of the aggrieved, forever altering his/her view of the world.

We might imagine the poet gazing at herself in the mirror as she reflects upon the father's grief and relates it to the loss of her own parents shortly before she wrote these poems, a connection she has mentioned elsewhere.[18] The poet is able to identify with the perspective of both the child and the adult, so that the young woman's voice speaks simultaneously to both the grieving father and the adult poet looking at herself in the lyric mirror. A return to writing becomes a means for the poet to come to grips with her own grief for/as a lost child at the same time that she sympathizes with and consoles the adult whose child has been lost.

A similar play in perspectives is perceptible in the question of verse 3, especially in the phrase *que yo me anticipase.* The verb could indicate the young woman's premature death, which has preceded that of the adult; but it could also describe the young woman's precocious ability to fathom life's mysteries. Paradoxically, this anticipation is expressed in a past tense. Inasmuch as grief can only be felt in proportion to the amount of love that exists, the reciprocal relationship between child and adult makes each immediately present to the other. The child returns the adult's grief with love and awaits only the adult's delving into memory to reemerge. Once again the child anticipates the adult's act of recalling the past to the present, and thus of undoing the seemingly irreversible. The second stanza continues the development of the horticultural imagery, echoing the opening image both to explain and to expand it.

> Me fue puesta esta casa más allá del estiércol:
> no podrá contra ella el terral que propaga
> a la dama de noche, ni el viento de poniente.
> Mi jardinero y padre, siempre aquí es primavera:
> tu majestad prosigue sobre las rosas rojas;
> sonríe, pues que vives sólo para lo bello.
>
> (vv. 7–12)[19]

The young woman's dwelling is beyond decay ("más allá del estiércol") and beyond the ravages of time and death: "No podrá contra ella el terral que propaga / a la dama de noche, ni el viento del poniente." In spite of or even because of her premature death the child lives in a perpetual springtime: Having died young, she remains young in perpetuity. Her father is a gardener, one who has the power to keep her alive in his memory, just as he fertilizes and mulches the roses. While the adult grieves for the lost child, the child sympathizes with the adult. By remembering the beauty each brought to the other, grief flowers into beauty.

The image of the adult's "majestad" in the context of a garden and perpetual spring transforms the father figure into the sun (warmth and light, love and poetic inspiration). This warmth results in the flowering of red roses, traditional symbols of the transience of life, its intensity and passion, and perfect, everlasting beauty (which apply as well to the poem). The imperative of the final verse parallels that of the first, creating a frame that both closes and opens the poem. To smile is to remove the shadowy bird from one's gaze, i.e., to part the clouds so that the sun can shine and stimulate the majesty of the roses. On one level, then, grief for a lost past becomes a source of inspiration and beauty, while on another the poet recognizes that her former self has not been lost but continues to exist within her and can be recuperated through memory. To give voice to that inner self, the poet must adopt its perspective and immerse herself in the fertile loam of memory (and by extension in the poetic tradition).

At the end of "Dejadme" (Leave/Let Me), another poem in this section, the speaker avers her desire to take in the messages of the past as if they were her mother's milk: "Dejad que sin zapatos siga andando y regrese / de muy lejos al pecho caliente de mi madre" (Let me, without shoes, continue walking and return / from afar to the warm breast of my mother). The qualification of the adjective *caliente* not only makes reference to the physical warmth of the mother's body, but also calls attention to another layer of meaning. The word *pecho* metonymically stands for the heart as well as the breast, so that the speaker will gain both physical and emotional sustenance from drawing upon the sources of her poetic identity.

This couplet—a variation on Atencia's sextets—leads directly into two important poetic statements: "Muñecas" (Dolls) and "Mujeres de casa" (Women of the House).[20] In both of these poems, the speaker returns to her childhood in search of female models on which to nourish her renascent poetic identity. And in both cases the multiplicity indicated by the plural nouns in the titles attests to the variety of the models upon which she now draws. The dolls of the first of these poems represent female figures that comfort the speaker in her fever—physical and emotional.

> Tenéis un renovado oficio cada noche,
> muñecas que pasasteis un día por mis manos.
> Como un vaso de fresca naranjada reciente
> llegáis hasta el embozo de mi fiebre con vuestros
> tirabuzones lacios de estropajo teñido
> y ojos de aguas azules.
>
> (vv. 1–6)[21]

A contrast between past and present obtains in the opening pair of verses, but the temporal order is reversed, as is the relationship between the grown speaker and her dolls. In addition to addressing the dolls in apostrophe, the speaker describes them as typical representations of femininity, with their corkscrew curls, their tinted silky hair, and their watery blue eyes. On the one hand, the speaker may be rejecting that childish image of woman because of its artificiality and prototypical beauty. But in contrast, she compares the dolls' effect with that of a healthful glass of orange juice for the person with a fever.

The phrase *el embozo de mi fiebre* is particularly suggestive. A person with a fever would need to stay under the covers, to keep warm so as to break the fever. Therefore, the "embozo," the hem of the top sheet on a bed, would come right up to one's neck, the source of the voice. Given that the speaker's fever can be an emotional one, the evoked presence of these dolls soothes and warms the speaker's throat and thus helps repair or recuperate her poetic voice. The poet may reject the former importance she and others placed on physical beauty to privilege her imagination, her poetic voice, now that she feels agitated by inspiration. As we see in the next stanza, now the positions are reversed: The speaker learns to adopt different identities, aspects, or stances toward her identity in her use of imagination.

> Casi humanas y mías, mi juego de otro tiempo,
> soy vuestro juego ahora, casi vuestra y humana.
> Esto quiere la vida: más vida poseída,
> vivida, incorporada.
> Entregada a vosotras, pudierais trasladarme
> para siempre a los años del cine de la Shirley.
>
> (vv. 7–12)[22]

The inverted parallel phrases placed at the beginning and end of the first two verses of this passage function as mirror images. Particularly effective is the placement of the adverb *casi*. Because the dolls were hers and became almost human because of her vivid imagination, the speaker now feels that, even though she is a human being, a subject, she has almost become an object of the dolls' imaginations. But rather than converting her into an inanimate, nonindividualized object, she feels even more human thanks to the multiple possibilities she now discovers through poetry. If before she was a woman formed in masculinist, patriarchal images (like the dolls), now, having formed them in her image, she sees how they allow her to create her own image—a woman's image of a woman, of herself.[23]

For that reason, the declaration "Esto quiere la vida: más vida poseída, / vivida, incorporada" is paradoxical. It plays on the word *vida,* which can mean fate or destiny, something beyond the control of the subject, imposed on her from without (her physical beauty, her biological destiny), but also more individuality and agency insofar as she is the one who incorporates these images. Again, the verb is paradoxical: She literally embodies these physical attributes while she also decides to lend them less importance, to favor her internal attributes, her imagination and her poetic voice, which she also embodies figuratively. Both truncated verses punctuate the speaker's discovery of this paradox inasmuch as she sees herself reflected similarly and differently in the image of the dolls.

In the final two verses the imperfect subjunctive *pudierais* sustains this equivocality. On the one hand, the speaker may be posing a hypothetical situation: "If I were to hand myself over to you . . ." In that case, she expresses an aversion to a childish, artificial image of her identity as a woman, just as actresses—especially child actresses like Shirley Temple—may be typecast by filmmakers and audiences. The past imposes limitations on the present possibilities for a woman's roles. But on the other hand, she may be positing a surrender to her imagination. Now that she has realized the potential of these images of the past, she has learned that she, like an actress, has the ability and the imagination to adopt any number of roles, personalities, and identities that will enrich her life and lead to lasting fame. How we (poet and readers) read these images makes all the difference. The play of similarity and difference lies in the image of the dolls reflecting the speaker.

Although sharing and offering multiple possibilities for the speaker to emulate as she delves into her past in search of herself in others, in comparison with "Muñecas" "Mujeres de casa" is apologetic. Through the variety of functions these household servants performed for the speaker as a child, these figures stimulate the now adult woman to appreciate varied aspects of her personality that can enrich her writing because of her more informed perspective. We receive a sampling of those services in the opening stanza.

> Si alguna vez pudieseis volver hasta encontrarme
> (bordados trajes, blancas tiras, encañonados
> filos para el paseo, palomas de maíz,
> 28 de noviembre, calle del Ángel, 1),
> mujeres de la casa,
> cómo os recibiría, ahora que os comprendo.
>
> (vv. 1–6)[24]

At first, the catalog of items in parentheses may appear to be random. Upon reflection, however, it appears that the speaker is evoking a custom or ritual for her family. On that day, 28 November (the poet's birthday), the family would traditionally go for a walk. Coinciding with the North American celebration of Thanksgiving to reflect on a bountiful harvest, this date falls at the end/beginning of the Catholic liturgical year. The embroidered dress of the women— a hint of textuality and creativity—the white shoulder straps of their apron-uniforms, and the piping on the edges of their clothing all suggest an attention to detail, a cleanliness and exactitude that would be paraded through the streets in ceremonial fashion. Paradoxically, that which distinguishes these women in the speaker's memory also tends to negate or render null their individuality and specificity.

The phrase *palomas de maíz* therefore functions ambivalently. The speaker may be referring to another custom of this occasion, eating popcorn, which would leave sensory traces in the speaker's memory that she always associates with these women. But the phrase may also metaphorically describe the anonymity and abnegation of these women in their white, embroidered dresses: Like pieces of popcorn, they all look alike; none is noticeably different from the others when they are all gathered together in memory as well as in reality. If they are so indistinguishable, then why does the speaker call them forth in this evocation of the past?

Just as in "Muñecas," the speaker has posited a hypothetical situation in which she addresses these women in apostrophe. She may not be able to recall specific, individual faces and names, but they hovered around her and protected her like guardian angels—implied in the specific, local place name *calle del Ángel, 1*. The speaker remembers their ministrations when she awoke from a bad dream.

> Quebraba vuestro sueño con sobresalto súbito,
> y espantabais mi miedo deslizando las manos
> por mis trenzas tirantes, me limpiabais los mocos
> y endulzabais mi siesta con miel de Frigiliana.
> Dejadme ir a vosotras, que quiero, blandamente,
> patear como entonces vuestro animal regazo.
>
> (vv. 7–12)[25]

Again she focuses her attention on sensory imagery: the sounds of her cries that would startle the caregivers, their hands on her head and hair, wiping her nose, and giving her a spoonful of honey to soothe her back to sleep. These repeated details—note the imperfect verb tenses—adopt symbolic proportions because of the split between the child that was and the adult speaker reminiscing, another implication of the stanzaic break (cf. Rosalía's poem discussed in the introduction). Ironically, her bad dream interrupted their sleep. Dreaming, then, again refers to the imagination and poetic inspiration. The speaker's braids also evoke a textual weaving of words in one's head, while the women's act of shooing these bad dreams away suggests a physical danger, such as a rooster or a dog, being chased away to protect the child-speaker. The wiping of her nose indicates that she has been crying but that the caregivers not only clean but also comfort and reassure: They take away what is messy and flowing beyond control.

Because the speaker specifically mentions Frigiliana—a town in the province of Málaga famous for its honey—she calls attention not only to the honey's warmth, sweetness, amber color, and syrupy consistency but also to the place name itself as a signifier. Indeed, the alliteration in these verses adds significantly to the soothing and calming effect of the women. Here, the fricatives /f/ and /g/, the echoing /l/, and the repeated vowels function sensorially. But we can also extrapolate other signification from this word: "frágil"; "liana"; "frígido" (cooling as opposed to the child's feverish agitation); "fricativo." And the related image of honey calls forth mountain flowers, fresh air, blue skies, and droning bees.

The return to the present tense in the final couplet instantiates these figures. The command "Dejadme" also echoes the final couplet of the poem of that name, where the speaker wishes to return to her mother's warm breast. Here we can read her act of kicking these women's laps either as her playful romping with them (climbing up onto or down from their laps) or as a return to the womb. Even though these women were not literally her mothers, now that she herself has had children, she understands the communication and exchange involved. By returning to their wombs figuratively, she will be able to draw from their abilities and to individuate them more as if they were her own mothers. Whereas sadness pervades this poem because of what the speaker perceives she has lost, determination also emerges. By dint of her imagination, her memory, and her act of textualization, the speaker can recuperate traces and fragments that, thanks to her own experience, she can now amplify, flesh out, and so use to discover more about herself, especially that part of herself that seeks poetic inspiration and stimulation. By drawing on the past in section 2 of *Marta & María,* the speaker has found new resolve within herself because she has come to terms with the passage of time and the outlet that poetry provides for the anxiety of that transience and anonymity. This advance in her return to encounter her creative personality then leads her to consider the conflict and the incompatibility between the two sides of her self in the poems of the third and final section.

The page-as-mirror functions most obviously when the poem portrays a well-known female figure, someone clearly other than the poet who seeks her own individual voice and identity. While, in accord with Adrienne Rich and Alicia Ostriker, the poet strives for a "re-vision" of inveterate patriarchal images as represented by these well-known figures, the other also allows the woman poet an interchange with this figure in the process of re-vision. That is, the poet can project herself onto the other in the mirror, lending her own attributes to the established type. But in the process she confronts, rejects, modifies, and fathoms her own personality. The process is not unidirectional: The poet does not merely revise the other according to her ideals or her politics. The other also allows the poet as subject to address herself as other (in fact, as object of her-self), but she does so by way of her own female gaze. The poem-as-mirror is therapeutic, re-visionary, liberating, creative, and empowering because, through interaction and exchange with the other, the self achieves greater *self*-reliance and independence from predetermined, patriarchal norms. This type of interaction is nowhere more profoundly felt than in the third section of *Marta & María*.

Krieger's concept of the natural ekphrastic sign, the feminist revision of a traditional female figure, and the concept of the poem as mirror all converge remarkably in Atencia's "Ofelia." Shakespeare's Ophelia is most notable for her dependence on Hamlet's approval, and when she fails to attain that approval, she goes mad and drowns (either by suicide or accident). Two principal aspects of Atencia's poem undermine this representation of woman. The first is the issue of address. It is not clear whether the poet adopts the mask of Ophelia and addresses herself and/or the audience through that mask, layering, superimposing, and confusing self and other, or if the speaker addresses Ophelia in apostrophe, marking a separation and distance between them. Even though the poem is written in the first person, one gets a strong sense of duality in the voice. Just as in *Hamlet*, Gertrude's presence on stage is momentarily supplanted by the immediacy of the scene she reports (Ophelia's drowning), so in the poem the mask of the character adopted by the speaker wears thin. It is a surface that becomes transparent, a signifier that presents the illusion of disappearing to reveal a signified. This confusion replicates the duality in the title of the collection and the figures of Martha and Mary, the domestic and the aesthetic.

In conjunction with this dichotomy, the second aspect that attracts our attention is Atencia's choice of the future tense for the majority of the verbs. The futurity emphasizes the action at the same time that it defers completion. If Ophelia is speaking, she describes her intentions, which evidently went very awry, or she is clearly mad. In the first case, the reader (like the poet) would be compelled to sympathize with the character and accept that her death was a regrettable accident. In the second, we would tend to distance ourselves from a character who evidently has little or no control over her actions. In these options we encounter the play of sameness and difference that is reversed on the other side of the coin. If the speaker-poet is addressing Ophelia in apostrophe, she may on the one hand be revealing her excessive naivete, unaware of the fate that awaits her. But if we attribute to the speaker the maturity of the poet herself, this possibility rings ironic.

On the other hand, the use of the future tense could indicate the speaker's resolve to transform Ophelia's outcome by showing her a different way of dealing with her frustrations. The poet's way of doing that is to write, of course, as she is doing in this very poem. It is again ironic that she cannot undo the past: She cannot be the young

Ophelia; she is an adult woman who, like Ophelia, has lost certain opportunities. Yet she can recuperate a sense of the lost self by projecting into the future. To regain a sense of futurity is to recuperate the past, just as to return to the past is to create a future.

"Ofelia" is a major statement in *Marta & María*. A detailed examination of the poem reveals the ironic interplay of self and other, possibility and impossibility, loss and gain in the figure of Ophelia. The first stanza posits Ophelia's response to Hamlet's rejection of her love, but the blank first hemistich of the fourth verse suggests a deviation from the expected course of action.

> Recorreré los bosques, escucharé el reclamo
> en celo de la alondra, me llegaré a los ríos
> y escogeré las piedras que blanquean sus cauces.
>   Al pie de la araucaria
> descansaré un momento y encontraré en su tronco
> un apoyo más suave que todas las razones.
>
>   (vv. 1–6)[26]

Although the prefix *re-* of the opening verb may seem insignificant (*recorrer* in itself means simply "to walk through"), the implication is that the speaker (Ophelia and/or another) will retrace steps she has already taken. If she found solace in the forest on other occasions, perhaps this time she will again be able to alleviate her sense of loss and abandonment. Such an excursion proposes an empathy between inside and outside. In the case of Ophelia, this means that the lark's song and the white stones—washed clean by the streams and then returning their whiteness to the purity, transparency, and innocence of the water—are external, natural factors that have helped her to unburden her grief in the past. For the speaker-poet, words help perform the same cathartic, cleansing process. The vocal act *reclamo* and the emblem of the songbird subtly reinforce the metapoetic dimension. Notice again the prefix *re-* and the echo heard in the future morphemes *recorreré* and *escucharé,* further indications of the speaker's insistence and persistence in her return to writing. That the lark sings "en celo," however, speaks to the problem that needs to be confronted. In one sense, "en celo" concerns the search for a mate: Ophelia pines for Hamlet; the poet for the lost other, the aesthetic side of her identity. But this expression refers to the intensity, enthusiasm, and release that draw the self-absorbed speaker out of herself. Just as the lark pours out its song, the speaker releases her own pent-up emotions; the poet is inspired to pour forth her emotions in her words.

The rivers and the stones afford further evidence of a duality between self and other. The archetypal river is an ambivalent image of the passing of time and the eternal present, whereas the stones create turbulence but also purify the water through aeration. The color white evident in the verb *blanquean* suggests both a loss (of color) and a clearer insight, turbulent foam and cleansing aeration (venting). These stones are found in the beds of the streams, emblematic of the course of one's life in which difficult experiences are those that most affect and change us, purify us.

It is at this point that Atencia inserts a white gap of silence in the poem. Rather than truncating the verse at the end of the line, she has interrupted the course of her thoughts and her words. If there is already tension between two dichotomous positions, this hiatus underscores the divergence of possibilities. Recall also that Atencia interrupted her poetic career, suggesting that the duality between Gertrude and Ophelia parallels that of the now older Atencia with her younger self, just as Atencia compares and contrasts herself with Ophelia in this interaction of self and other (cf. Rosalía's poem).

The "araucaria" is an evergreen tree, associated with immortality and upward movement. In fact, a tree outside Atencia's study in Málaga may have inspired this image. The speaker is reclining at its foot opposing transcendence and verticality with earthiness and horizontality (metaphor vs. metonymy). The prefixes of the verbs *descansaré* and *encontraré* accentuate the irony. In Spanish, to rest is literally to become un-tired. One regains energy by replenishing loss. The *en-* of *encontraré* reiterates the following preposition and calls attention to the root *contra*. Leaning against the rough bark of the trunk, the speaker finds solace because the trunk represents flow and growth (the sap in the interior, the vertical thrust similar to but different from the river's horizontal movement). This natural, unheard, life-giving flow in itself is more soothing than the logical, rigid, rough surface of reality. This comment on the natural sign and on the act of writing adds further dimension and purpose to language.

Hence we can see that the speaker-poet separates herself from Ophelia at the same time that she recognizes their similarities. This interplay is reversed and intensified after the stanzaic break, another interruption, silence, hiatus, blank, whiteness, and moment of stasis in the flow of words and thoughts.

> Prendida de sus ramas dejaré una corona
> y el agua por mil veces repetirá su imagen.
> Adornará mi pelo la flor del rododendro,
> inventaré canciones distintas de las mías
> y cubriré mi cuerpo de lirios y amarilis
> por si el frescor imprime templanza a mi locura.
>
> (vv. 7–12)[27]

Echoes of fairy tales pervade these poems. Here a reference to the prince, the "knight in shining armor," represents the fulfillment of traditional heterosexual expectations based on ideal situations. First we note that hyperbaton inverts the opening sentence of this stanza, again deviating from an established pattern (personal and societal). This procedure allows her to emphasize the final word of the verse, *corona*. This word could refer to Ophelia's renunciation of the queen's crown since she will not marry Prince Hamlet. But *corona* could also be a funeral wreath. Atencia has commented on the death of her parents, and we know that three poems of *Marta & María* are dedicated to her late friend, Blanca, a personification of her own youth. Hanging a wreath/crown from the araucaria, symbol of death and immortality, counterposes two ambivalent images, both then again placed in juxtaposition with the river. Does the river repeat the image of the crown or of the tree? Which aspect does it reflect, mortality or immortality? One also thinks of the concentric circles formed by dropping something in water. Several paintings of Ophelia contain this dizzying swirl as an image of her madness.

The motif of madness surfaces explicitly in the final word of the poem. If, however, we consider madness as a metapoetic allusion to the poet's inspiration and her need to write, we view the intervening actions ambivalently. The syntax of verse 9 confuses subject and object, so that the speaker's hair (metonymically, her head, her thoughts, her identity) enhances the flowers as much as these adorn her head. Paradoxically, inventing new songs unlike her own—as Shakespeare's Gertrude reports that the drowning Ophelia "chanted snatches of old lauds"—subverts the speaker's identity. Is she Ophelia or Atencia, the implied author? When she adopts the mask of Ophelia, does the poet lose or negate her own self, or is the opposite true: that she separates herself even more acutely and discovers her own self in contrast with the adopted personality?

The same is true of the final image. When the speaker says that she covers her body with flowers, she implies that she has stripped away all other clothing. Now she wants to see if the flowers will impress their freshness and coolness on her heated, troubled self. The verb *imprime,* only the second present tense in the poem, also alludes to writing, printing, and publishing. And if her madness is tempered, it is no longer madness. Does carrying through with the act of writing and publishing one's poetry quench the thirst for satisfaction, or does it heighten and urge one on? By covering her body (defining herself with her poetry), the speaker reveals her nudity and vulnerability (provokes greater desire). In comparison with Ophelia, the speaker realizes that she possesses the same desires, but her method of dealing with those desires is quite different. Both women have experienced loss, but Ophelia lets herself be drowned by her emotions. In contrast, while still acknowledging her loss (both literally in the death of loved ones and figuratively in her own youth), the poet pours out those emotions in her words. She chooses to "hang her hat" (the *corona*) on the tree of life (the araucaria), the production of her poetry. The future tense used throughout and the persona of Ophelia thus pull together sameness and difference, stasis and change, mortality and immortality in enigmatic, ambivalent (oxymoronic, catoptric) imagery. The poet is determined to continue her writing even though it may look as if she is drowning in the very process of writing, controlled by her "madness," her compulsion, her calling.

Significantly, "Ofelia" is placed between "La moneda" (The Coin) (two sides of the same persona, the domestic and the aesthetic) and the third poem dedicated to the deceased friend, "Casa de Blanca" (Blanca's House). If in the first section of *Marta & María* the poet vacillates, questioning the possibility of reviving her aesthetic activity, and in the second she begins to give voice to her inner self by returning to the past, in the final section she feels the irresistible urge to write and affirms her commitment to her inner voice. This decision does not preclude a tension between the two spheres of her life—the domestic and the aesthetic—but rather intensifies the relationship between them. In "Casa de Blanca," the third in this series of poems based on the motif of the dead young woman, the speaker portrays the emptiness and meaninglessness of life without the imaginative, creative spirit and decides to occupy the empty space left by the other's death. In this way she can revivify her imagination and give meaning to her life.

> No llamaré a tus puertas, aldaba de noviembre:
> el árbol de las venas bajo mi piel se pudre
> y una astilla de palo el corazón me horada.
> Porque tú no estás, Blanca, tu costurero antiguo
> se olvida de los tules, y el Niño de Pasión
> va llenando de llanto el cristal de La Granja.
>
> (vv. 1–6)[28]

The speaker's refusal to knock at the young woman's door again suggests a variety of readings. She may want to avoid a literal entry into Blanca's house because the memories are too painful, and so she passes by without knocking. She cannot, however, avoid entering via her imagination. She may therefore feel no need to knock because her intimacy and familiarity with the setting and its former inhabitant preclude the formality of knocking. Both of these interpretations posit an additional element of the transgression of a forbidden space, a descent into and return from the underworld to rescue a lost love (cf. the myth of Orpheus and the children's tale "Goldilocks and the Three Bears").

Like many other images in Atencia's poetry, the specific mention of the month of November may appear to be only a trivial detail. But a closer consideration of such minutiae illuminates subtle nuances of meaning related to the aesthetic act. Whereas November is a month when we contemplate the bleakness and grayness of life and the imminent approach of winter (death), it is also a time when we seek warmth and color indoors. While we may anticipate a time of scarcity and hunger, we also give thanks for the harvest stored away. In the Catholic tradition November begins with a remembrance of those who have died and those who have become saints; one both laments a loss and finds consolation in pure and saintly models. The speaker of the poem recognizes the passage of time and the apparent emptiness of her world.

> Tiene el regazo frío tu silla de caoba,
> tiene el mármol tu quieta dulzura persistida
> y bajo tu mirada una paloma tiembla.
> Perdidamente humana pude sentirme un día,
> pero un mundo de sombras desvaídas me llama
> y a un sueño interminable tu cama me convoca.
>
> (vv. 7–12)[29]

Seeing her life ebbing away ("el árbol de las venas bajo mi piel se pudre"), the speaker is pained by the passage of time and the death of others, especially this young woman ("y una astilla de palo el corazón me horada"). By addressing the other directly, she creates a mirror image of that part of herself that she feels she has lost. Without the other the aging poet as dressmaker has no need for wispy, fanciful cloth with which to delight her imagination. The reference to "el Niño de la Pasión," pained by a thorn and presaging Jesus Christ's suffering and premature death as innocent sacrificial lamb, echoes both the young woman's death and the splinter digging into the speaker's heart. Moreover, the crystalline tears are so pure that they become imperceptible in "el cristal de La Granja," famous for its clarity. This anecdotal detail again adopts symbolic proportions of the poem as beautiful artifact that contains purely distilled emotions. The alliteration of the phrases "va llenando de llanto el cristal de la Granja" and later "y bajo tu mirada una paloma tiembla" adds to the perception of beauty and intense emotion in an apparently transparent and desolate scene.

Even though the seat of the young woman's chair is empty and the marble surface of her table may be cold to the touch—both images of death—the dark mahogany adopts a richness and life of its own. The implicit personification of the chair in the word *regazo* may be an image of the adult woman's capacity to (re)produce and, perhaps, of the loss of that capacity (cf. "1 de diciembre"). Similarly, the marble retains the young woman's "quieta dulzura," possibly another visual image. Is the speaker sitting silently at the other's dressing table, looking into the mirror and recalling the young woman that was herself as well as the other?

Feeling "perdidamente humana," that is, painfully and hopelessly conscious of her transience because of omnipresent reminders of death, the speaker feels drawn by "un mundo de sombras desvaídas" into "un sueño interminable." By occupying Blanca's bed, she can close her eyes to life's brevity and find consolation and solace in the recuperation of a dream world of revivified emotions. These emotions may not necessarily be positive, however, for we note that this dream world consists of "sombras" and that the poet is preoccupied with the passage of time and the imminence of death. Then again, if the shadows are faded (*desvaídas*), writing represents a way of dissipating unhappiness, a cathartic experience that adds warmth and color to a vapid, vacuous life. Does the "sueño interminable" refer to death? Or to the transcendent, timeless ecstasy of participation in the aesthetic act (through writing or reading)? The perception of the emptiness of her life impels the speaker to join Blanca and to dream, to write, and thus to awaken her dormant inner self, the imaginative, percipient young woman she once was, a young woman who has not died but has only been asleep. Ironically, writing as sleeping/dreaming becomes a means of awakening (resuscitating) the inner self.

The eponymous final poem of *Marta & María* affirms the poet's commitment to the other side of her self that has been relegated to the interior shadows for so long. Here we cannot be sure if the speaker is Mary or if it is the poet, the implied author. This confusion influences our perception of the identity of the addressee also because it could be either Jesus or the poet's husband, both of whom represent poetic inspiration. The religious overtones are an important aspect of this poem, but the first stanza modifies the intertextual context.

> Una cosa, amor mío, me será imprescindible
> para estar reclinada a tu vera en el suelo:

que mis ojos te miren y tu gracia me llene;
que tu mirada colme mi pecho de ternura
y enajenada toda no encuentre otro motivo
de muerte que tu ausencia.

(vv. 1–6)[30]

Whereas in the biblical version Mary is seated at Jesus's feet, here she imagines herself reclining at the other's side, making their relationship reciprocal. The exchange of their glances, emphasizing the equality of the woman's gaze, supports this reciprocity. Therefore the nouns *gracia* and *ternura* express the woman's experience of pleasure and adopt sacred as well as secular connotations, recalling Atencia's admiration for the poetry of the Spanish mystic, San Juan de la Cruz.[31] By interpreting the other as poetic inspiration, we discern a contrast between these two levels paralleling the contrast between the physical and the intellectual, the domestic and the aesthetic, the immanent and the transcendent. The speaker can rest easy—either in this life or the next—if the other reciprocates her love. Without her spouse/faith/poetry the speaker will die even though she continues to live. With them she will survive even beyond death.

The abrupt run-on line and the truncated verse at the end of the stanza heighten these tensions. "Muerte" thus becomes the well-known conceit of sexual climax in addition to its literal meaning. Ironically, the absence of the other (her husband or Jesus) is the cause of ecstasy as well as intense grief. This ambiguity could be an allusion to the topos of death and resurrection, but it also comments on the nature of the sign. In spite of the sign's presence, it marks the absence of the referent. This play is the exciting part of writing/reading, in that it induces/seduces writer and reader to find significance in the words on the page. It is this aspect that the speaker announces in the opening verse as "imprescindible." Like her spouse and her faith, poetry is a necessary part of the speaker's life, and she questions what will become of her in the event of death.

Mas qué será de mí cuando tú te me vayas.
De poco o nada sirven, fuera de tus razones,
la casa y sus quehaceres, la cocina y el huerto.
Eres todo mi ocio:
qué importa que mi hermana o los demás murmuren,
si en mi defensa sales, ya que sólo amor cuenta.

(vv. 7–12)[32]

The first sentence of the stanza, which is pivotal to the interpretation of the poem, is remarkable for its neutral punctuation, opening it to a variety of meanings depending on whether we read it as a question or an exclamation. In the next statement the phrase that interrupts (*fuera de tus razones*) is included within the syntax, but it describes an outside condition. More ambivalence in this phrase complicates interpretation. *Fuera de* could mean "except for" or "if not for," but it could also mean "outside of" as in "anything not included in." Likewise, *razones* could refer to explanations or reasons that logically support or reinforce. Or figuratively and colloquially, it could define a purview or sphere of influence, a reach or an extent.

In this stanza the truncated verse emphasizes the word *ocio* and the ambivalence of this statement. This word can mean recreation and idleness (writing poetry), but it is also a form of relaxation and enrichment. As both secular and sacred activity, poetry can be considered a waste of time and the most important aspect of one's life because of the enriching experiences it provides. The *qué* introducing the penultimate verse echoes the opening of this stanza and again contrasts interrogation with exclamation. The sister to whom the speaker refers could be Martha, the dutiful, practical, domestic woman who contrasts with Mary and criticizes her for her idleness, her disregard of "feminine" activities (home, meals, children). Atencia may suspect that other women in her society and specifically of her age group will criticize her for pursuing her aesthetic interests rather than following a traditional path. Atencia, it should be remembered, is writing at the end of the Franco era and contrary to the image of woman advocated by the regime.

But the other whom she addresses here comes to her defense. Literally, she could be referring to her husband and his encouragement of her artistic career. But on another level, she may be asserting—for herself as well as for others—that her poetry is good; it stands on its own and justifies her writing because she puts her whole self (*amor*) into it. This word *amor* is another open signifier that suggests a variety of interpretations, secular and sacred, eros and agape. Artistic production is in itself a form of love and an inheritance that the poet can bequeath to her children and to younger poets. By writing, this woman achieves an independence that in no way impinges on but rather enriches the unity of husband and wife, the domestic and the aesthetic, the transient and the transcendent. The traditionally female management of a household has no meaning or purpose without the other. Without the significant other, everyday life—regardless of what it involves—seems vacuous and meaningless. The speaker's spouse/faith/poetry give meaning to life's trivial circumstances.

Along with the gazes in the previous stanza, these dualities form the concept of mutual recognition that Jessica Benjamin discusses in *The Bonds of Love* as the foundation of intersubjectivity.[33] Mutual recognition is necessary not only for the differentiation of the self and the definition of subjectivity but also for the dissolution of domination. This duality entails a fundamental paradox, as Benjamin explains: "at the very moment of realizing our own independence, we are dependent upon another to recognize it. At the very moment we come to understand the meaning of 'I, myself,' we are forced to see the limitations of that self."[34] Consequently, the other addressed in this poem can also be the poet herself who stages an intrapsychic dialogue between ego and alter ego, Mary and Martha, blurring the distinction between inside and outside, self and other.

With this poem Atencia affirms her commitment to writing and justifies Jesus's words to Mary in the biblical story. By choosing this parable as the basis not only of the final poem but also of the collection in its entirety, Atencia has defined a tension that resides within her between her role as domestic partner and her identity as artist/poet. These two roles are in conflict with one another, but they also work reciprocally and synergistically, one enriching and informing the other. However, we should recognize a significant difference between these two titles: the conjunctions y of the poem and $\&$ (*et*) of the book. The ampersand between the names of Martha and Mary in the title of the book succinctly emblematizes the uneasy relationship between these two spheres. This sign of intertwining spaces, an inverted and reversed figure eight, is the site of imbrication and liminality that both unites the two women and marks a separation and opposition between them. This symbol is both visual and linguistic, a quick, common abbreviation and a symbol derived from a Latin conjunction, further illuminating Atencia's dialectical and ekphrastic poetics in *Marta & María*. In contrast and comparison with the $\&$, the Spanish conjunction y equally unites and separates the two names and the two female figures of Martha and Mary. These two conjunctions are as ambivalently alike and different as the two women and the two spheres of activity they represent. One joins and separates, the other separates and joins. Which is Martha, which is Mary? Which is the true self of the poet-speaker?

In her first work after nearly fifteen years of poetic silence María Victoria Atencia confronts the tensions latent in the imbrication of two different spheres of her life and personality: the domestic and the aesthetic. This process can be seen clearly in the three poems— one in each of the three sections—dedicated to a young woman named Blancanieves who has died. The figure of the young woman enables the poet to reestablish contact with her creativity and imagination, the fanciful side of her personality which she wishes to recuperate and revitalize, that part of herself that will not be denied or taken from her, that part of herself that hears inspired words. If we consider the figure of Blancanieves in these poems as a mirror image of the speaker (or a part of her self), at least two possibilities for revisiting the tale of Snow White obtain. On the one hand, the now adult Snow White looks at an image of herself in the mirror and (perhaps bitterly) laments the time lost when she was asleep under the spell of the jealous Queen. On the other hand, the Queen may now regard the image of Snow White as the necessary, indispensable, lasting part of her life and regret her repression of that other part of her self. In the lament for lost time and opportunity the two figures of the Queen and Snow White overlap and find common ground though they approach that space from different, even conflicting, perspectives. This seeming reversal of both roles epitomizes the paradoxical relationship between two spheres of life and between two disparate aspects of the poet and contemporary women in general, particularly a woman of Atencia's generation in post-Franco Spain. The return of the repressed poetic voice and the concept of the poem as mirror is highly evident and effective in María Victoria Atencia's *Marta & María*.

2
Playing Dress-Up in Funhouse Mirrors: Ana Rossetti's *Los devaneos de Erato*

For many years Ana Rossetti has been involved in the theater, a fascination that carries over to her poetry. According to the concept of the page as mirror, Rossetti enjoys playing dress-up, disguising herself in diverse costumes and identities reminiscent of theatrical performances in the poems of her first book of poetry, *Los devaneos de Erato* (The Musings of Erato, 1980).[1] In keeping with the theory of play, however, a duality is perceptible in the voice of these poems that gives evidence of the awareness of pretense and of the seriousness beneath the surface of the costume. This duality (or what Mirella Servodidio has called Rossetti's "double-voiced discourse") has its origins in the concept of theater or dressing-up as play.[2] In her acclaimed study Mary Ann Doane discusses the related concept of masquerade. While masquerade allows a woman to resist patriarchal positioning, serves as an acknowledgment that femininity itself is constructed as a mask, and effects a defamiliarization of female iconography, dressing-up is a more appropriate description of what occurs in Rossetti's poetry.[3] We might even say that Rossetti is parodying the concept of masquerade.[4]

In *Homo Ludens* Johan Huizinga has defined play as "a voluntary activity or occupation executed within certain fixed limits of time and place, according to rules freely accepted but absolutely binding, having its aim in itself and accompanied by a feeling of tension, joy and the consciousness that it is 'different' from 'ordinary life.'"[5] In support of this concept the British object-relations psychoanalyst D. W. Winnicott argues that transitional objects provide an individual with an intermediate space of play. This intermediate space is an overlapping of subjectivity and objectivity, of sameness and difference, and is directly related to the formation of identity: "It is in playing and only in playing that the individual child or adult is able to be creative and to use the whole personality, and *it is only in being creative that the*

64

individual discovers the self."[6] This early play later manifests itself in cultural production, including the writing and reading of poetry.[7]

Dressing-up constitutes a cardinal aspect of play. Huizinga affirms that "the 'differentness' and secrecy of play are most vividly expressed in 'dressing up'. Here the 'extra-ordinary' nature of play reaches perfection. The disguised or masked individual 'plays' another part, another being."[8] In spite of this adoption of another being's identity, "the consciousness, however latent, of 'only pretending'" is never absent, another component of the relationship between sameness and difference.[9] Still further, Huizinga emphasizes that play and seriousness are integrally interrelated. Even though "play is the direct opposite of seriousness . . . the contrast between play and seriousness proves to be neither conclusive nor fixed . . . for some play can be very serious indeed."[10] Finally, play is just good fun![11]

These components of the concept of play aptly characterize the poems of Rossetti's *Los devaneos de Erato*. Other critics have mentioned various aspects of these poems that fall within this definition, especially Rossetti's similarities with the *novísimos* who came to prominence in the 1970s.[12] In these poems Rossetti dresses-up, adopting different characters as if she were an actress in a play and looking at herself in a distorted mirror, like ones found at a carnival or in a funhouse. Whereas these distortions cause us to laugh (or at least to see caricatures), in Rossetti's poetry they also serve to exaggerate, call attention to, and thus parody traditional (masculinist) distortions of both men's and women's roles and sexuality. This approach allows us to see the interrelatedness of self and other, interior and exterior, sameness and difference, play and seriousness.

Three categories or types of poems characterize these relations in *Los devaneos*. First, Rossetti avails herself of several traditional female identities, including personages from classical literature or mythology (e.g., Cybele, Diotima, Artemis, Nike), literary characters (Juliet and Isolde), and historical models (Lindsay Kemp and Lou Andreas Salomé). Each offers the poet an opportunity to explore and often to subvert the accepted or commonly held view of these figures to see what they offer her as a contemporary woman. The second category ironically involves the adoption of male personalities. These characters are as diverse as the historical-epic Paris, the religious figure of St. Sebastian, the morally despicable Gilles de Rais, and the poet's contemporary, the novelist Javier Marías. The third group consists of poems in which the poet adopts a contemporary voice to present possible scenarios in today's society. In these poems the figure is often a representation of the poet-speaker herself as a child or at another point in her life, or they entail the speaker imagining herself as another type of woman or man. This wide range of characters embodies the varied *esperpento*-like presentations that remind us of dressing-up and standing before a funhouse mirror. In this chapter I examine the female figures that Rossetti employs in the page as mirror.

Even in the equivocality of the title of *Los devaneos de Erato,* the poet adopts the identity of Erato, the muse of poetry, but her usage of the word *devaneos* and the ambiguity of the genitive *de* create distance as well as identification. "Devaneos" entails a number of contradictory definitions. The *Collins Spanish-English English-Spanish Dictionary* states that *devaneo* means (1) "delirium" and so figuratively "ravings, non-sense, absurd talk"; (2) "time-wasting pastime, idle pursuit"; and lastly (3) "affair, flirtation."[13] On the one hand, then, we can read this title as the ecstatic visitations of the muse of poetry, resulting in the poems contained in this text. In this sense the poet sees herself as Erato, being occupied by and assuming the identity of her poetic inspiration. But in another sense we can see her distancing herself from and mocking these ravings. Her distance could be a reenactment of the masculinist reader's disparagement of these poems, but also playful self-irony. In either event, play underlies the title of this collection. As Huizinga affirms, "Frivolity and ecstasy are the twin poles between which play moves."[14] Given that these are the musings of Erato, we can read them as both tongue-in-cheek and having a quite serious purpose. Rossetti mocks the poetic tradition and herself as poet, at the same time that she joins that tradition and includes herself within it. She is both playful and serious.[15]

The first type of poem involves the portrayal of a traditional, usually familiar, female figure as the alter ego of the speaker-poet. "Cibeles ante la ofrenda anual de tulipanes" (Cybele Before the Annual Offering of Tulips) is one of the most well known of Rossetti's poems. Indeed, Rossetti specifically chooses this poem and this figure to define her poetics:

> Al hablar de la primavera, es más eficaz poner a Cibeles, que como diosa de la tierra siempre implica fertilidad y renovación. El título además me posibilita la tercera persona. Pues está hablando Cibeles, yo no. . . . Es una manera de poner una máscara, o de distanciarme, o de no desnudarme demasiado. Por ejemplo, cuando he escrito de verdad usando la tercera persona formalmente, ha sido cuando realmente estaba más implicada en el tema. . . . Busco una fórmula para no sentirme demasiado implicada y observarme como si yo fuera otra.[16]

As others have pointed out, the title alerts us to a duality, for the proper name *Cibeles* refers to two different levels. In classical mythology Cybele was "[a] Phrygian goddess, often called 'the Mother of the Gods,' or 'the Great Mother': she governed the whole of nature." According to Pierre Grimal, "Cybele's major importance lay in the orgiastic cult which grew up around her and which survived to a fairly late period under the Roman Empire."[17] In fact, her attendants were known as the Corybantes, who are traditionally associated with revelry and ritual. Huizinga comments that "in all the wild imaginings of mythology a fanciful spirit is playing on the border-line between jest and earnest."[18]

On another level, Rossetti is describing a familiar landmark in Madrid, the Plaza de Cibeles and the fountain in front of Madrid's main post office at the intersection of the Paseo de Recoletos, the Paseo del Prado, and the Calle de Alcalá. This site is a traditional meeting place for inhabitants of the Spanish capital, especially for celebrations. This setting thus encompasses both the secular and the sacred, ordinary reality and a special place apart, that characterize play. The site itself is representative of the poem as transitional space.

The offering of tulips is similarly ambivalent. On one hand, it refers to the cyclical renewal of nature in the spring, over which Cybele presides. But on the other hand, it may also refer to the customary municipal landscaping in the garden areas of the plaza. The poem will go on to describe the attitude of Cybele toward these tulips: She is both appreciative and disdainful, admiring and disparaging, humble and haughty. The baroque language employed by Rossetti—a characteristic noted by almost all readers—heightens these dualities by joining seriousness with play.

> Desprendida su funda, el capullo,
> tulipán sonrosado, apretado turbante,
> enfureció mi sangre con brusca primavera.
> Inoculado el sensual delirio,
> lubrica mi saliva tu pedúnculo;
> el tersísimo tallo que mi mano entroniza.
>
> (vv. 1–6)[19]

Obviously, the description of the tulip's flowering metaphorizes the erect male member. Its "funda" is the foreskin, whereas the "sonrosado, apretado turbante" describes the glans penis. The key phrase in the opening sentence is "enfureció mi sangre." Has the speaker been titillated with sexual excitement? Or is she angry? The adjective *brusca* modifying *primavera* provides a clue that will be elaborated later in the poem. The description here is of the abruptness of the arrival of spring (the male erection), but the word *brusca* connotes roughness and curtness, a limited degree of manner or speech. These traits may characterize a male's approach to sex and love that values merely the moment of copulation and ejaculation, whereas a woman is more stimulated by foreplay, tenderness, and the protraction of ecstasy. The female speaker is excited by the possibilities before her and frustrated, thwarted, and angered by privileged male attitudes, desires, and (in)capabilities.

This duality continues in the introductory phrase of the second sentence. Does *inoculado* mean that her delirium is "pricked" by what she (be)holds, stimulating her excitement? Or does it refer to protection or immunity? One could also read a description of the orifice as eye and of being stimulated by the close observation of the genitals. The etymology of the word also suggests the grafting of a bud onto another plant, implying that the speaker anticipates the union between these two human beings through coitus. This union obtains in the language of the poem where the two levels come together: the sensual appreciation of nature in the tulips and in the penis. Likewise, *pedúnculo* describes the flower's stalk and the shaft of the penis. That the speaker lubricates this shaft with her saliva may mean that she is drooling over the beauty of nature (dewdrops?) or that she is performing fellatio. Furthermore, the verb *entroniza* ironically exalts the phallus because the speaker's hand places the tulip on high. Some may privilege male sexuality because of the erect penis, but this woman is disdainful and dismissive of that privilege. Thus duality confuses seriousness with play, high with low, a metapoetic self-referential allusion to the poet's use of language.[20] This tension augments in the latter half of the poem.

> Alta flor tuya erguida en los oscuros parques;
> oh, lacérame tú, vulnerada derríbame
> con la boca repleta de tu húmeda seda.
> Como anillo se cierran en tu redor mis pechos,
> los junto, te me incrustas, mis labios se entreabren
> y una gota aparece en tu cúspide malva.
>
> (vv. 7–12)[21]

The imperatives *lacérame* and *derríbame* express violence, but as imperatives, they are ambivalent. The speaker may be pleading for intense lovemaking or challenging, defying, urging the male to do his best, already fearing that his performance will be unsatisfying. Her mouth is already filled with desire, and she is rising to a moment of high excitation that should culminate in orgasm. Unfortunately, when the female speaker expects to take the penis into her vagina (the half open lips not those of her mouth), before she can move (and be moved) to the next level of intensity, the male puts forth all he is capable of producing. The speaker calls this production "una gota," a droplet similar to the dew, that undoes the male's erection, leaving the speaker disillusioned.

Most readers admire the mere representation of sexuality from the female perspective using baroque imagery as the beauty and daring of this poem. Even more interesting is the speaker's affirmation of the superiority of women's sexuality. Men can ejaculate but once and then have to wait to regenerate an erection. Women, in contrast, are capable of multiple consecutive orgasms. All the tulips in the Plaza de Cibeles and the gardens of the Castellana and the Paseo del Prado cannot satisfy this goddess-woman. Contradictorily, she pleads with the male to satisfy her, suggesting perhaps that her satisfaction is contingent upon her partner's ability to perform. But female sexuality is superior to the male's because of her seemingly unlimited capacity for pleasure in both foreplay and coitus. The speaker smugly criticizes male sexuality as she validates her own powers; she is attracted to but disappointed with her partner; and her tone is both playful and serious.

Assuming the identity of Cybele in the poem enables Rossetti to criticize male sexuality and affirm female sexuality playfully—tantalizingly! Her purpose is serious though her tone is light-hearted. Nonetheless, an implicit challenge or verbal sparring is in evidence, what Huizinga would call a contest or "slanging match," lending more credence to the concept of play: "Contest means play."[22] Moreover, the exaggerated imagery and the ambivalent language elevates the tone while simultaneously describing quite physical and earthy actions. As Huizinga states, "In play we may move below the level of the serious, as the child does; but we can also move above it—in the realm of the beautiful and the sacred."[23] By adopting the role of Cibeles, the speaker of this poem dresses up and exaggerates her stance as if looking at the issue of sexuality in a distorted mirror. The comical, ludic aspect underscores rather than diminishes her serious intent.

In another poem from *Los devaneos,* "Triunfo de Artemis sobre Volupta" (The Triumph of Artemis over Volupta), Rossetti explicitly mentions a mirror. Here the Greek goddess provides the speaker with an ambivalent identity, for Artemis is the protectress of virgins and the provider of the transition between youth and adulthood, innocence and sexual knowledge. Although at first the title seems to define the result of a contest between two female figures in which virginity wins out over sexual pleasure, in effect the speaker as Artemis triumphs over the hypocrisy of men. The presence of the mirror in this poem signals a paradoxical and ironic relationship between different aspects of women as they are embodied in the figure of Artemis. The opening lines, which the speaker will repeat midway through and at the end of the poem, establish an exchange of glances from different points of view.

> Edad inimitable, a tu espejo interrogo
> en cuál de mis innumerables
> alacenas está la máscara de diosa
> que de oscuro los mármoles cubría.
> Vuestro fervor, tan obsesivo éxtasis,
> la hizo hermosa y distante y la proclamó única.
>
> (vv. 1–6)[24]

Three different entities engage one another in these verses. First, the speaker addresses herself as "tú" as she looks at herself in the mirror and apostrophizes the other as an "edad inimitable." She is looking for a goddesslike mask but is unable to locate it, suggesting that she has aged (physically and/or emotionally) since the last time she looked in the mirror. At this point we can read the opening phrase only univocally as a stage in the speaker's life that is unique and incapable of being repeated. It is not entirely clear, however, whether Artemis addresses Volupta or vice versa. Does the virgin address the experienced woman or vice versa? In truth, the two are inseparable parts of the same person, but the "yo-tú" relationship also distances one from the other. The image of the cabinets where the masks are stored suggests some inner part of the speaker herself that she cannot locate. For that reason she interrogates the mirror, the image of herself in the mirror. The third entity in this exchange of glances appears in the word *vuestro* and in the *mármoles* over which the mask casts a shadow. This plural group later turns out to be a masculinist view of women that exalts virginity and places it on a pedestal.[25] But at this point we could also read it as the structure of society itself and so an internalized masculinist vision that the speaker has of herself as she gazes into the mirror.[26] The disentanglement of these contradictory, overlapping, or nested gazes comprises the gist of the poem.

The next verse marks a change in direction, but also has a sarcastic ring to it: "¡Sin embargo, tantas veces os maltrató!" (Nonetheless, how many times did he abuse you!) (v. 7). From here until the next exclamatory statement "¡Pero cuánto la amáis!" (But oh how you love her!) (v. 27), the speaker recounts the ways in which the exalted idealization of woman has teased men. Her tongue was as sharp as a whip: "Su lengua tan cruel como un látigo era." When she spied on him from a hidden location on her balcony, she would gossip about the desires she observed or heard expressed by men, but she would shy away from men if she suspected their interest in her. Her position on the balcony suggests her superiority to and distance from men and other women as well as her voyeuristic vantagepoint.

In verse 12 the speaker begins a series of negatives that build in force. Ironically, her negations simultaneously reveal hidden sensuality. For example, she details what happens behind the closed door of her bath.

> Ni pudisteis, a través de una cerradura,
> mirar cómo parsimoniosamente se desvestía
> haciendo crecer su desnudo desde la bañera.
> Vaho de enredadera gris. La mano recurriendo
> a la esponja. Y la fragante espuma, reptando
> por su cuerpo, en él se introduce
> instalando su invisible dominio.
> No bebisteis tampoco en las sabrosas fuentes
> que anegaban los turbios laberintos
> que una maligna virginidad clausuró.
>
> (vv. 14–23)[27]

This scene echoes the account of Artemis surprised in her bath by Actaeon and the dire consequences of that event, adding to the mythical overtones of the sacred nature of virginity. By mentioning the keyhole, the speaker invites a voyeuristic fantasy enhanced by the tactile and olfactory imagery of the mist, the sponge, and the fragrant bubbles of the bath snaking their way sensuously over her body. One might recall images found in pornographic magazines or even the representations of women bathing in a tub in nineteenth-century paintings. The references to hair titillate curiosity and desire in the next verses, and the unexpected entry of the speaker in the first person increases the sense of prohibited, arcane knowledge.

> Ni las sombrías axilas, ni la frondosa concha
> de la pelvis, ni la entrelazada cabellera
> supieron del amable tacto de esos dedos
> que conozco tan bien. ¡Pero cuánto la amáis!
>
> (vv. 24–27)[28]

The shift to the present tense in both *conozco* and *amáis* not only brings the poem back to the present (the woman looking at herself in the mirror) but also calls attention to the contrast between men and her. Men love that image of woman, but for her that image has been lost as she lost her innocence. Yet the memory of that image still assaults them, and they continue to seek it in the speaker: "Mas el recuerdo de ella, precipitándose, / os asalta y en mí la buscáis" (But the memory of her, hurrying, / assaults you and you seek her in me) (vv. 31–32). Once again the three distinct gazes—Artemis's, Volupta's, and the male's—meld into one. The speaker knows, however, that her former innocence is lost forever. When she then returns to the opening verse and image of the poem, we sense that a profound change has taken place and that her language has bifurcated.

> Mas el recuerdo de ella, precipitándose,
> os asalta y en mí la buscáis. Qué terrible
> e inimitable edad. Siempre a tu espejo interrogando.
> Intento renacer, antigua identidad
> que os fascinaba, aquel cuerpo tan desconocido,
> si es que es posible tal metamorfosis.
>
> (vv. 31–36)[29]

Alterations in the original statement define the changes that have taken place. First we note that the speaker has added the adjective *terrible* to *inimitable,* and then that she has fragmented the act of looking and added the adverb *siempre.* She has also not punctuated the phrase beginning with *Qué,* making it either an interrogative (rhetorical or straightforward) or an exclamation. She knows that a change has occurred, but she also wants to know exactly what the ramifications of that change are. She needs to discover in herself what those changes entail for her as a woman and how she will respond to them. She may have lost something in the process, but what has she gained? This is the interrogation that she makes in/of the mirror. She recognizes that she is now distant from her former self in the phrases "*antigua* identidad" and "*aquel* cuerpo." But she questions why that identity fascinated others. This verb expresses both attraction and distance, and the speaker realizes that she herself did not know who she was.

Now that she knows more, she might like to go back to the former self to know her better, but of course that is impossible. Because she cannot undo what has been done, she feels nostalgia for a past that cannot be recuperated. And yet it is only through losing it that she knows she has lost something. In losing her innocence, she has gained knowledge of herself. In gaining knowledge, she knows that she has lost an opportunity for deeper knowledge of herself. Even though she may try to resuscitate that former self ("Intento renacer"), she knows that such a metamorphosis is irreversible. The reference to metamorphosis evokes the myths recounted by Ovid, especially the myth of Apollo and Daphne and the theme of elegiac lamentation for loss.[30] By adding the adjective *terrible* to modify *edad,* the speaker bifurcates the language. Now "inimitable edad" not only refers to the lost self that can never be recuperated but also acknowledges the transition through which she has passed. She has reached a new stage in her development as a woman and must understand where she has been and where she is now. She realizes that in the past it was the masculinist gaze that defined her identity as it continues to define her even after this tremendous and irrevocable change. She discovers male hypocrisy in the following verses, but questions how men can expect her to be what she is not (something she did not realize before).

> Ahora soy costumbre,
> invadida patria de rutinarias delicias.
> Al poseerme perdisteis mi belleza interior
> y se os han desvanecido los deseos.
> Mas si me ayudáis a buscar
> en los armarios las túnicas olvidadas
> y a rescatar la máscara propicia,
> si me vuelvo arrogante, ¿os podré convencer?
>
> (vv. 44–51)[31]

In the words *costumbre* and *rutinarias delicias* she recognizes that because she has lost her virginity, men are no longer enticed by and interested in her in the same way. As an invaded country (a typically masculinist image for women), she has been pillaged and supposedly divested of her inner beauty. Men's desire for her has disappeared, but what they do not realize is that they caused the loss of the "belleza interior" that they were seeking to possess. They want her to remain virginal even though they caused her to lose her virginity. Now they may help her look for her tunic and her mask, but she is aware that these things are merely superficial accoutrements and that it would be false of her to put them on, to play the part of the virgin for the pleasure of men. Volupta triumphs over Artemis because the speaker accepts the transition that has taken place in her and rejects the role of the virgin where men would like to keep her confined and innocent (without knowledge). Her experience, however, will not permit her to accede to that submissive role.

Tan sagaz es la experiencia
y tan indestructible su mandato
que os sobrepasé largamente.
Incluso os instruiría. Y me lo reprocháis.

(vv. 52–55)[32]

Because of her experience, the speaker now knows more than the men who experienced her, more about them and about herself. By calling her knowledge "indestructible," the opposite of her virginity, she realizes that their very act of destruction resulted in a permanent gain, a knowledge that cannot be destroyed, only increased. Now she has gone beyond them and is capable of teaching them: The tables have been turned. That men now reproach her for her knowledge illuminates their hypocrisy and their desire to keep her in a state of innocent ignorance and so impose an identity on her that is inconsistent with her concept of self. In the final verses of the poem she reiterates that view by recurring to the opening verse, but she then rejects that falsity definitively.

Edad inimitable,
donde los dioses habitaban y era
la admiración el tributo único
que a mis pies esparcíais.

No me pidáis que vuelva,
pues la inocencia es irrecuperable.

(vv. 56–61)[33]

In comparison with the opening verse, the speaker breaks off after the comma, changing an apostrophe to an even more distant description. That age is now as distant as the Greek and Roman gods, and the speaker sees them as an ideal but false world. She is nostalgic but disillusioned, even sardonic. The final two verses are separated from the rest of the poem, signifying the speaker's rejection of the image of herself that men had imposed on her and of which she was ignorant. Though she has lost something (her virginity) and may regret it, she also accepts that loss as part of the transition she has made thanks to Artemis. Men, on the other hand, would still like to have it both ways: They would like her to be innocent as well as experienced. The speaker clearly rejects that stance and thus criticizes a double standard. She has been able to separate the two images of herself by recognizing Artemis's other characterization as the champion of women's transitions. In this sense Rossetti provides a re-vision of the traditional figure of Artemis as the patroness only of virgins. This concept parallels the refunctioning that Margaret Rose deems the principal aim of parody.[34] In this case the mirror serves to diminish an accepted characteristic of the persona and to highlight another.

Among the various identities Rossetti assumes in *Los devaneos* is that of Diotima of Mantineia. This literary-historical character appears in Plato's *Symposium* and is described by Socrates as "a woman wise in [love] and in many other kinds of knowledge" and as his "instructress in the art of Love."[35] Socrates relates at length the substance of several conversations they had when he was still a young philosopher. This contrast between the older, wiser, more experienced woman and the younger, less skilled, more innocent male receives ironic treatment in Rossetti's "Diótima a su muy aplicado discípulo" (Diotima to Her Most Dedicated Disciple). Although the basic relationship remains the same, Rossetti's poem deals with the physical, sensual aspect of love in contrast with the philosophical, metaphysical exchange reported in the dialogue.[36] Rather than forming an ethical and philosophical understanding of love, Rossetti's poem shows the female teaching the male through practice.[37]

The title announces that the speaker in the role of Diotima will address her words (the poem) to her disciple, but who exactly is that disciple? We might assume from the intertextual context that it is Socrates. Because Socrates is not mentioned specifically, however, the identity of the addressee is vague. It could be any young man learning from a wiser woman. The poem thus serves exemplarily as instructions to another woman who observes how Diotima constructs and controls the situation. By extension, it could also be that Diotima instructs the reader of the poem in poetry as play and sacred ritual, using the amorous situation metapoetically.[38] Throughout the poem the speaker calls attention to subtle sensorial details that are essential to seduction. The opening verses create an atmosphere of sensuality and invitation.

> El más encantador instante de la tarde
> tras el anaranjado visillo primoroso.
> Y en la mesita el té
> y un ramillete, desmayadas rosas,
> y en la otomana de rayada seda,
> extendida la falda, asomando mi pie
> provocativo, aguardo a que tú te avecines
> a mi cuello, descendiendo la mirada

> por el oscuro embudo de mi escote,
> ahuecado a propósito . . .
>
> (vv. 1–10)[39]

The languorous rhythm of the opening sentence fragment, and the extended and detailed description of the second sentence stretch out time and lend a decadent aura to the scene. It is almost as if the speaker were painting a picture in the style of Delacroix's *Death of Sardanapalus*. Several details add a rich texture to the scene: the afternoon, the orangish tint, the delicate sheer curtains, the aroma of tea and the roses past prime, the striped silk of the ottoman. Even the choice of the adjective *primorosos* to describe the sheers has a figurative meaning of neat and skillful design, suggesting the speaker's setting of the scene (mise en scène) in theatrical terms.

Even the posture of the protagonist, whose voice does not enter definitively until verses 6–7, reclined in her chair, wearing a dress with a low neckline, directs the other's gaze and points to the studied character of the scene. Also, the choice of the verbs *aguardar* and *avecinarse* indicate that the speaker is choosing her words carefully. *Aguardar* expunges the doubt or hope of arrival that *esperar* might connote, and *avecinarse* is more personal and intimate than either *aproximarse* or *acercarse* would have been. The second run-on line that results in "a mi cuello" shows how Diotima is in control of every detail of the encounter. Her neckline funnels or channels the other's gaze to the cleavage of her bosom and entices the other to a closer inspection of intimate places. She has let her dress hang loosely open "a propósito." All of these elements serve as a sort of wink in the reader's direction as she skillfully seduces us to continue reading. The next sentence provides a transition in which the actual contact begins.

> Sonrójome
> y tus dedos inician meditadas cautelas
> por mi falda; demoran en los profundos túneles
> del plisado y recorren las rizadas estrellas
> del guipur. . . .
>
> (vv. 10–14)[40]

The speaker announces that she is blushing, but does she blush from demureness, or is she flushed with passion? The archaic (though poetic) usage of placing the reflexive pronoun at the end of the conjugated verb accentuates and rhythmically alters the phrase, allowing for an ironic reading. The touch of the other, nonetheless, is highly stimulating. Given that he has come up to her neck and can look down the front of her dress, we would assume that he is caressing her inner thigh, along one of "los profundos túneles / del plisado." The detail of the pleating adds to the sensation, whereas the images of "profundos túneles" and "rizadas estrellas" heighten the erotic aspects of the contact. The stars to which she refers could literally be the delicate lace of her undergarments, but they could also describe the intensity of her reaction. Curiously, the word *guipur,* taken from the French and literally meaning "lace without any ground mesh, having the patterns held together by connecting threads," derives etymologically from words meaning "to cover with silk" or "to wind," but is akin to "to whip." This contact leads to the climax of the poem where insistent commands, alliteration, and anaphoric repetitions predominate.

> Apresúrate, ven, recibe estos pétalos
> de rosas, pétalos como muslos
> de impolutas vestales, velados. Que mi boca
> rebose en sus sedosos trozos, tersos y densos
> cual labios asomados a mis dientes
> exigiendo el mordisco. Amordázate,
> el jadeo de tu alto puñal, y sea tu beso
> heraldo de las flores. Apresúrate,
> desanuda las cintas, comprueba la pendiente
> durísima del prieto seno, míralo, tócalo
> y en sus tiesos pináculos derrama tu saliva
> mientras siento, en mis piernas, tu amenaza.
>
> (vv. 14–25)[41]

The commands seem to be caused by her desire, but they also have the effect of inciting the male's desire. By comparing her lips with the pure thighs of vestal virgins, the figure of Diotima tells the male what he wants to hear, but it may not necessarily be the truth! Indeed, her mention of a love bite ("mordisco") and of the tongue ("tu alto puñal") that serves to gag their panting is ironic. She also urges him to undo her clothing and to take her nipples into his mouth as part of the foreplay. The final word of the poem again rings ironic. She wants to feel his erect penis against her legs and to know that he is excited, but she describes it as a threat so that he will feel more powerful and masculine. She feigns demureness, surrender, and desire, all the time knowing what she wants and manipulating the male. She, after all, has the experience, the learning, whereas he is still a novice. Diotima is playing with the uninstructed Socrates. The female has turned the tables on the male without his suspecting it.

In the *Symposium* Diotima deconstructs the binary opposites of fair and foul, good and evil, wisdom and ignorance with regard to love. In her manipulation of the scene and the sexual encounter, the speaker of Rossetti's poem shows that women are not as innocent and weak as men would like to think they are. As Socrates uses the account of his experience with Diotima to prove his points in the dialogue concerning the nature of love, so Rossetti adopts the identity of Diotima to instruct young men and women in the art of love. In this way she gives her female listeners an advantage over men because men are merely interested in the surface. She implies that most men are not capable of discerning the irony in this poem, so they will not realize that *they* are being seduced. Unless one knows who Diotima is, the poem has only surface meaning. Once one is informed or initiated into the codes, the irony becomes apparent, and the traditional concepts of love are deconstructed. The figure of Diotima is yet another instance of the way that Rossetti is playing with identity, dressing-up in costume, and playing a part. This theatricality enables her to deflate masculine ego and demonstrate that men are not the only ones capable of seducing. Ironically, the act of dressing-up and adopting a role discovers false attitudes and misconceptions that have become part of the male imaginary.

In "Escarceos de Lou Andreas Salomé, a espaldas de Nietzsche, claro" (The Flirtings of Lou Andreas Salomé, Behind Nietzsche's Back, of Course) Rossetti appropriates the persona of this feminine figure to explore the similarities and differences between Salomé and her, and to comment on certain masculinist images of women. The poem consists of two parts titled "Al bien" (To Good) and "Al mal" (To Evil), respectively, a clear reference to Nietzsche's *Beyond Good and Evil.* In this work Nietzsche questions and in effect deconstructs "[t]he fundamental faith of the metaphysicians . . . *the faith in opposite values.*"[42] In this famous philosophical treatise Nietzsche dares "to recognize untruth as a condition of life . . . resisting accustomed value feelings in a dangerous way" because he believes that "a philosophy that risks this would by that token alone place itself beyond good and evil."[43] Likewise, Rossetti deconstructs feminine images that men consider good and bad, making a ludic commentary on contemporary social relationships by adopting the persona of the female intellectual Lou Andreas Salomé.

In 1996 Ana María Moix published a collection of brief biographical sketches called *Extraviadas ilustres: 10 retratos de mujer.*[44] Although Moix attempts to deflate the bohemian aspects that have aggrandized Salomé's life, these aspects still predominate the general understanding of this woman. Born in Russia in 1861, Salomé was an extraordinary woman for her time, one of the few women to pursue advanced intellectual studies. Her enrollment at the University of Zurich, one of the few institutions that admitted women, allowed her to move in intellectual circles and put her in contact with some of the most renowned thinkers and writers of the era, including Nietzsche and the poet Maria Rainer Rilke. Because of her keen interest in human psychology, she became a disciple of and collaborator with Freud. She was later widely known for her books and articles. Nonetheless, her belief in personal liberty and the pursuit of knowledge for women led her into scandalous situations for the times.

Her marriage to Friedrich Carl Andreas was one of convenience, coerced by his threat of suicide. (He had held a knife to his chest and threatened to plunge it into his heart if she refused.) Reportedly the marriage was never consummated. Moreover, Salomé was frequently seen with other men and often traveled alone or with male companions. Largely for the purposes of her intellectual advancement she engaged in a series of ménages à trois from among the philosophers Nietzsche and Paul Rée, the psychoanalyst Tausk, and Rilke, who accompanied her and Andreas on a trip to Russia and was her first lover. Because of these preferences in lifestyle Salomé is largely known as "una *femme savante,* brillante, decadentemente *snob* y célebre entre las elites artísticas e intelectuales de Roma, París y Berlín, como *coleccionista de celebridades.*"[45] But Moix adds that she was "una mujer que no solo se adelantó a su época por el hecho de convivir con poetas y filósofos de renombre antes, durante y después de su matrimonio, sino que poseía un talento y una inteligencia excepcional que no quiso sacrificar amoldándolos a la vida encorsetada y constreñida de la sociedad burguesa de su tiempo."[46] It is not surprising, then, that Rossetti should choose this "feminista *avant la lettre* y ferviente practicante del amor libre" as one of the personages for her poems.[47]

The dualities in the character of Lou Andreas Salomé permeate the poem. Beginning with the title, *escarceos* can literally be a prancing or playful nervous movements, or amorous posturing and attitudinizing—figuratively, flirting. This fusion of play and seriousness is reinforced by the phrase *a espaldas de.* Is the speaker making funny faces behind the back of the philosopher? Or is she, too, involved in serious intellectual endeavors of which he is unaware? Does she have to accomplish these efforts out of the public eye because this type of endeavor is not expected of women—"claro," as the speaker says? A further complication arises in the subtitles, "Al bien" and "Al mal." In both sections of the poem it seems that the poetic voice is speaking to a man she finds extraordinarily attractive. But the subtitles could indicate that the speaker personifies good and evil as handsome men.

According to Walter Kaufman, Nietzsche's *Beyond Good and Evil* "represents an effort to rise 'beyond' simpleminded agreement and disagreement, beyond the vulgar faith in antithetic values, 'beyond good and evil.' . . . He asks us to shift perspectives, or to perceive hues and gradations instead of simple black and white."[48] If this is true, Nietzsche obviously contradicts himself in light of his denigrating comments about women in §232 of that book as well as those in *Thus Spake Zarathrustra,* a book heavily influenced by Nietzsche's contact and disillusionment with Salomé.[49] Rossetti recognizes that inconsistency and plays with Nietzsche as well as with his deconstruction of binary opposites and his resistance to the simple dualities of good and evil.

The opening verses of "Al bien" present a contrast between the brilliant aura of Good (I personify this figure) and the emptiness and lack the speaker finds in her life.

> Despiadada belleza, me aniquilas.
> La luz roza en tu carne mi desierto,
> mi camino de sed, mi pasión incesante
> de hermosura. A escondidas te admiro.
> Aterrada contemplo el universo
> que me excluye de ti.
> Carente de ternura al caminar irradias
> y no miras a quienes, de verte, se hermosean.
>
> (vv. 1–8)[50]

According to the speaker, Good is totally aloof and lacking in pity for those whom he passes and affects. She characterizes him as "despiadad[o]" and "carente de ternura." His beauty annihilates and terrifies her because he is so completely unaware of the effect he has on those around him. He irradiates brilliance whereas she dwells in hiding. In one sense we can read these verses as the description of a celebrity who lives in a totally different atmosphere from others and cannot conceive of his impact on his admirers. But in another sense we can see that the speaker is in awe of his goodness, an abstract concept that she would hope to attain to enrich the desert of her life. She idolizes and desires this figure, as "mi sed, mi pasión incesante / de hermosura" suggests. But she also recognizes that an enormous gulf lies between them. The choice of the word *excluye* in lieu of *separa* increases the sense of a barrier. Yet, this abyss only whets her desire. We therefore perceive a reversal of roles: Good is haughty, disdainful, distant, and cruel, whereas the self-effacing speaker receives our sympathy for her great desire to attain a higher state of being.

In both sections of this poem, verse 9 forms a chiasmatic turning point. In this first part the parallel phrases "Imposible placer, implícito deseo" (Impossible pleasure, implicit desire) are parallel but incongruous. Both begin with negative prefixes, but the meaning of the prefixes changes from "not possible" to "inside (im-) as opposed to outside (ex-)." This ambivalence calls into question the meaning of the phrases. "Imposible placer" could mean either that it is a pleasure never to take place or that it is a pleasure one is unable to bear. Likewise, an "implícito deseo" is one that is hidden and so lacking in reality (only a fantasy) or one that, though hidden, is undeniably felt. What would happen if we were to invert the order of the nouns: *Imposible deseo, implícito placer?* Do these phrases describe Good, or are they the reactions of the speaker to Good? Are they cause or effect? This nodal point of inversions is a meditation on and criticism of Nietzsche's concept of difference.[51] It is ludic play and serious questioning. These phrases lead into the next verses of the poem where the inversions, ironies, and dualities intensify.

> Límites míos
> en tu desconcertante armonía dilúyanse.
> De tu amor desvestida permanezco
> en el páramo extraño a tu lluvia seminal,
> ya que a ti mismo engendras y fecundas.
> Aún incluso desdeñas al obediente espejo.
> Mas ¿qué es de tu poder sin el sumiso esclavo?
>
> (vv. 10–16)[52]

The "pie quebrado" (truncated verse) imposes a limit that immediately dissipates in the flow of the next verse, abetted by the rhythm and the placement of the reflexive pronoun after the verb. Note also the paradox of the conceit *desconcertante armonía:* His harmony, goodness, and beauty disconcert everyone around him, so how can he be good if he has this negative effect on others? Besides that, her inhibitions evaporate, so that she can approach a better state of being because of him. Therefore, she is on a higher plateau (*páramo*), exposed, vulnerable, and undeceiving (*desvestida*), precisely because she does not receive his nourishing and fertilizing rain. The adjective *seminal* could be an erotic nod toward sexual fluids, or it could mean "of essential importance, basic, central, principal, crucial, critical, pivotal." She lacks Good's love and the nourishment it/he brings, but that abstinence elevates her spiritually. By not participating in sexual relations, Lou Andreas Salomé is able to devote her energy and attention to intellectual matters and so achieve a higher status for herself and for all women. By depriving herself or being deprived of "Good," she is ironically and paradoxically better off. By being "bad" (that is, by reading, studying, and learning), she improves herself.[53]

There is a suggestion of Good's narcissism in the phrase *ya que a ti mismo engendras y fecundas,* but that idea is immediately negated in the next verse. Good engenders more good, of course. But that does not exclude the bad from becoming good. Although the speaker does not receive Good's blessings (participation in sexual arrangements would be "bad"), she becomes better. Correlatively, then, if Good engenders and fecundates only himself, he is egocentric, haughty, and conceited—"bad." But if he disdains his own image in the mirror, which will reflect him truthfully, he must be either very humble or very confident of himself. In either case he is self-sufficient: Good is sufficient unto itself. But then the speaker questions if Good can exist without evil, "sin el sumiso esclavo" who admires him and strives to be like him. This reference to the slave alludes to the Hegelian dichotomy of master and slave, another of the indispensable differences that Nietzsche finds so intrinsic to life. Without the slavish admiration of the masses, Good would not exist. He is beautiful only in comparison with evil and because of the admiration of those who would like to resemble him.

The speaker of this poem, supposedly Lou Andreas Salomé, deconstructs Nietzsche's arguments through the skillful reasoning of her own intellect. If we consider this "disguise" as a representation of the contemporary woman, we can see that the poet is questioning supposed male superiority and privilege represented in the dichotomies male/female, science/nature, reason/emotion, mind/body, good/evil.[54] What can we expect, then, from the second part of this poem which bears the subtitle "Al mal"? At first we might anticipate another reversal, but the second part is a continuation and a repetition of the first part from the opposite angle, undercutting sharp distinctions between good and evil, positive and negative, subject and object, beyond what Nietzsche had imagined. Again the first eight verses lead up to a paradoxical nodal point in the ninth line, but by beginning this section with the conjunction *Y,* the speaker signals a continuation rather than a reversal.

> Y te adoro, te adoro a ojos cerrados,
> tú mi extravío, tú todo mi vértigo.
> En la aterciopelada encrucijada
> de tus piernas se pierden sin remedio mis ojos.
> Me turbas. Aun cuando disfrazado
> repites voces que conozco bien,

te elevo y me entrego seducida
cuando averiguo todas tus celadas.

(vv. 1–8)[55]

Repetitions in the first two verses emphasize the speaker's ecstasy and her blind attraction to Evil (again capitalized to personify). Her choice of the verb *adorar* expresses much more than *querer* or *amar.* Her characterization of the male/Evil as an "extravío" and a "vértigo" also capture the excess of her emotions as ravings and dizziness (cf. "devaneos"). Yet, because she has her eyes closed, it is uncertain whether Evil is a real being or a fantasy. In either case the poet foregrounds feminine desire and the feminine gaze which is drawn irremediably to his crotch. Her description of that area as an "aterciopelada encrucijada" accentuates the visual and tactile aspects, but the image of a street-crossing reproduces the chiasmus that we have already observed in part 1 of the poem as well as referring to an intimate revelation. When she says that her gaze gets lost there and that it happens irremediably, she not only describes the loss of control produced by her vertigo but also implies that there is an irresistible force provoking her.

The pithiness of the phrase *Me turbas,* set off as it is from the longer phrases, could indicate the overwhelming impact of this vision. But it also undermines and abruptly halts a spiral into ecstasy. We could attribute the speaker's confusion to her state of mind as she is caught up in her contemplation, or it could be a reaction that separates her from that state and causes her to wonder what is happening, thus breaking the spell. The next sentence proclaims that she is aware of his falseness. He wears masks and costumes, he says words to her that she has heard before and that attempt to put her off, and she recognizes his hiding places and his protective defenses ("todas tus celadas").[56] Still she raises him to a pedestal and surrenders to him. Is there not a note of irony in these verses? If he is evil, why does he hide from her and try to mislead her? Is she the evil one who disregards the other's protests? Is she seduced, or is she the seducer? Is his mask really a deceit, or is she imagining how delightful it would be to seduce him? She seems relentless and insistent on forcing herself on him. In retrospect, isn't her opening statement, *I adore you,* just a little exaggerated?

If we read this section as if the speaker were addressing Evil personified, we might think that she is talking to herself. (We are reminded of the preceding sentence from the first part, "a ti mismo engendras y fecundas.") The speaker mockingly calls herself evil because she dares to admire this man, because she dares to gaze at him as an object. If she is evil for doing so, what about men? Just as in part 1 the poet criticizes the binary opposites that impose limitations on what women can do with their lives, so here she attacks a double standard that negates feminine desire. As rebel, as "la tarasca rusa" (the Russian shrew), as a feminist *avant la lettre* (in Moix's words), Lou Andreas Salomé defends the rights of women as individuals, as desiring subjects. In other words, she does adore Evil because being "evil" in this rebellious sense is to be a subject, to be what she wants to be and do what she wants to do.

This reasoning brings us to the crucial ninth verse of the poem, which in this case is reinforced by the parallelism and binary contrasts of the next verses: "Noche voraz, oscuro precipicio, / me absorbes y me imantas / mientras que, de gozo, sobrecogida tiemblo" (Voracious night, dark precipice, / you absorb and magnetize me / while, because of pleasure, I tremble in a seizure). We could consider the image of night as a metaphor for Evil or for the speaker's emotions. She may be questioning the step she is about to take, what the future holds for her, the appropriateness of her daring rebellion. But the adjective *voraz* and the dizziness of height in the visualization of the precipice are tinged with erotic excitement and abandon.[57] Characteristically ironic, the speaker is both attracted to and fearful of the new trail she is blazing. This evil attracts and absorbs her, threatens her with destruction and yet irresistibly pulls her forward. The verbs *absorber* and *imantar* imply a contrast of water and metal, liquid and solid, fluidity and rigidity, softness and hardness, pliancy and resistance. Even the hyperbaton and the punctuation of the phrase *mientras que, de gozo, sobrecogida tiemblo* heighten the sense of resistance playing against surrender, whereas the speaker could be trembling seriously or ironically from either joy or fear. In deconstructing these binary opposites, the poet stresses the tension between them. This *antilogia* or double reasoning continues in the final verses of the poem.[58]

> Me arrojo a ti, me enjoyo, me asesino.
> Y si mi pie se apoya en el abismo tuyo,
> no obstante, rectifico, tú me has de esperar fiel.
> Nada esquivarte puede, nada te desarraiga.
> Al final siempre vences, y al final te ovacionan.
>
> (vv. 12–16)[59]

To seduce Evil, the speaker must make a spectacle of herself, throwing herself at him, adorning herself with glittering jewels; but this is being false to herself. The reference to suicide may be an ironic, humorous, or playful allusion to Friedrich Carl Andreas's threat to get Lou Salomé to marry him. Nonetheless, the hyperbolic tone and the insistent repetitions suggest that the speaker may have "killed" her own chances to be "bad" by her outrageous behavior. But then, being "bad" is ultimately what enables other women to attain prohibited goals, so it is really "good." Has the speaker been false to herself and so failed to achieve her ambitions? Even if she has, taking such chances is the only way to learn. The contradiction between resting her foot on an abyss (something not there, so not permitting her foot to find solid ground) could be an amusing metaphor for her attempt to "play footsies" with this unresponsive man who thinks she is capriciously and frivolously throwing herself at him. Or it could be a very serious consideration of her missteps, the risks she has taken, which she attempts to rectify immediately. In effect, Rossetti has placed the following sentence of Fleur Jaegg as the epigraph of this poem: "Puede decirse que mi mayor placer es equivocarme" (One could say that my greatest pleasure is in making mistakes). Her assurance that he will wait faithfully for her may be either the self-delusion of her fantasy or a confidence that she will eventually attain the knowledge she seeks—a knowledge that others call "bad" for a woman but that she considers "good."

Once again the final two verses present parallel phrasing that is both similar and contradictory (the *antilogia*). The verbs *esquivar* and *desarraigar* iterate the hard/soft dichotomy, representing the proverbial conflict between the irresistible force and the immovable object. But which is which? If this evil is actually good for women, the attainment of the speaker's goal is inevitable. Unfortunately, however, the public at large will often consider *her* victory as *his* conquest. Joanna Russ has specified the masculinist skepticism of a woman writer's accomplishments in her book *How to Suppress Women's Writing:* "She didn't write it. She wrote it, but she shouldn't have. She wrote it, but look what she wrote about. She wrote it, but she wrote only one of it. She wrote it, but she isn't really an artist, and it isn't really art. She wrote it, but she had help. She wrote it, but she's an anomaly."[60] A biased, masculinist society will cheer when the daring, rebellious woman attempts to achieve brilliance and fails, succumbing to Evil. In that atmosphere Evil will always triumph and ironically be lauded for that triumph. As we have seen, Rossetti appropriates not only the identity of this nineteenth-century personage but also Neitzsche's reasoning process. In this way she again deconstructs traditional concepts of good and evil, especially with regard to masculinist images of women.

In the poems examined thus far, Rossetti has playfully assumed the persona of a female figure with whom she identifies to at least some extent so as to make a serious point. The relationship between speaker and persona may oscillate between identity and difference, acceptance and rejection, play and seriousness, but the voice that passes through the female mask "sounds" appropriate. It is in fact this oscillation that determines the give-and-take of the contemporary poet and the character she takes on. Another way of attaining a similar effect obtains when the speaker adopts a male persona. "De repente, descubro el retrato de Javier Marías" (Suddenly I Discover a Portrait of Javier Marías) contains a double reflection (an image and a meditation). In this poem the speaker looks back on an image of herself at a certain period in her life, as indicated by the persistent use of the imperfect tense. But she discovers herself (perhaps her heterosexual orientation) in her discovery of a portrait of Javier Marías, a contemporary novelist who was born just one year after Rossetti. The older, wiser speaker sees herself in both the portrait of the male artist and the younger image of herself (perhaps a character in one of Marías's books), making her tone ambivalent. She ridicules herself at that younger age and yet celebrates the moment in which she recognizes her potential by seeing it in another member of her generation. This poem is curiously reminiscent of a sonnet, but one that becomes awkward and misshapen because it has two different endings. These dualities invert the traditional poetic topos in which a female figure serves as the muse for the male artist. We first discern this interplay in the poem's title.

In addition to the presence of the first-person speaker found in the verb *descubro,* the reference to a portrait evokes the presence of a frame. The portrait in question may be a photograph found on a book cover or in a popular magazine or newspaper. But clearly the speaker announces a framing of the image. In the first stanzas of the poem, however, Javier Marías does not appear. In fact, there is no male figure explicitly represented but an image of the speaker herself at a younger age. The margins of the page on which the poem is printed thus form another type of frame that contains an image of the speaker. The first two stanzas present the speaker when she was younger in the hyperbolically melancholy and romantic image of the heroine of Dumas's *La Dame aux camelias.* The play between the historical figure Alphonsine Plessis, who adopts the pseudonym of Marie Duplessis and then becomes the fictional heroine Marguerite Gautier, who is known as "La dame aux camélias," assumes new dimensions in Rossetti's poem.

> Cuando yo era de raso y de camelia,
> Duplessi jadeante, boca llena de rojo

tras los pálidos labios como pálidas cintas,
mis dedos insistían en los Nocturnos.

Cuando apartaba el rostro del manchado pañuelo
mis pómulos copiaban los búcaros más blancos,
porcelana rarísima de los raros países,
y atado a mi garganta había un guardapelo.

(vv. 1–8)[61]

The speaker adopts the identity of Duplessi, but there is the additional aspect of herself as a younger woman. The scene before us in these verses is extraordinarily romantic and melodramatic, but the speaker presents it to us tongue-in-cheek, mocking her own over-dramatization. Seated at the piano, playing nocturnes à la Chopin, pale and innocent as a camellia, the speaker portrays herself as the typical romantic heroine yearning for love. Her emphasis on detail points to her sensuality and her desire. Her mouth is a bright red behind her pale lips, which are like two pale ribbons, and her breath is "jadeante"—is she panting with desire or melodramatically "consumptive"? When she withdraws her kerchief from her eyes—even her carrying a kerchief in her hand is extravagantly outmoded—we can imagine that not only her tears but also her consumptive blood have stained its white purity, creating a contrast between passion and purity. This theatrical gesture reveals the porcelain whiteness and smoothness of her skin. That her cheekbones have the shape of vases hints at the superficiality of the image she is developing because they are "art-ificially" idealized. And true to form, she wears a locket tied around her neck, that is, it is obligatory (both socially and amorously). The Spanish word *guardapelo* alludes to the again outdated fashion of saving a lock of the beloved's hair or his portrait in this tiny receptacle that hangs over the heart, symbolizing profound affection.

The parallelism of verses 3 and 7 suggests more than mere artistry, although that is one aspect of the quatrains. In each case there is a chiasmatic inversion of the position of the adjectives (*pálido* and *raro*) along with a change in the grammatical genders. The repetition of the adjectives themselves highlights their equivocality. The speaker is gently mocking the romantic conventions of paleness and exoticism at the same time that she idealizes her heroine/herself in the past. Yes, she laughs at herself, but she does so tenderly, remembering how beautiful she looked at that time. Rossetti "no ha renunciado a la ironía, a la comicidad sin subrayados, a la propia burla implícita de sus héroes, a los que—como tanto sucede en la vida—no puede evitar

tomarse en serio y algo a broma al mismo tiempo."[62] The *tercets* which
follow continue to focus on the locket.

> Minúsculo sepulcro, amuleto dorado
> de la adorada imagen desprovisto:
> tú no existías.
>
> Tú no existías, no, mas no por ello
> eras menos hermoso, ni por mis predicciones
> más amado.

(vv. 9–14)[63]

Characterizing the locket as a tiny tomb and a golden amulet continues the idealization contained in the romantic motifs of death and
magical love charms. Just like the chiasmus in the parallel phrases of
verses 3 and 7, here a play between *dorado* and *adorada* hints at the
superficiality and hyperbole of these images because the heroine has
not come across her beloved. For that reason her amulet is empty,
and she melancholy. When she addresses the other as *tú*, we would
assume that she is talking to the idealized lover, in this case Javier
Marías (or perhaps one of his protagonists), as professed in the title.
But the speaker could also be addressing herself as the other portrayed in the poem. The empty locket and the silence produced by
the "pie quebrado" (truncated verse) and the stanza break point simultaneously to the absence of the beloved and the emptiness or
shallowness of the heroine's life and identity. They disclose her sadness but also the falseness of the life she is leading and the romantic,
melancholic image she has adopted for herself. Similar to the gold
plating on her locket, the protagonist has assumed a melodramatic
persona lacking in depth and substance.

Repetition of the phrase "tú no existías" at the beginning of the
second tercet provokes another chiasmatic inversion, reinforced by
the parallel syntax that follows. The speaker addresses both the idealized male and the idealizing heroine. Because she was still in the
process of becoming and had not yet found herself, she had not yet
realized her ideals. But that does not negate the importance of her
fantasies. Notably, the insistent negation in the repetition of the word
no three times in a single verse emphasizes the duality of fantasy and
reality. The chiasmatic relationship between her ideal lover and her
ideal self (or her self's ideal) is underscored in the contrasts between
"por ello" / "por mis predicciones" and "menos hermoso" / "más
amado." Her idealization does not corrode and diminish reality when
it arrives, but rather provides the goals for which she strives and that

she is sure of attaining. We might see this paradox in the poet's attempt to write a sonnet in which the tercets are incomplete. Following the tercets, she affixes a couplet, two long lines that almost rhyme: "Mi muy querido rostro de pronto revelado, instante seductor, / poema inevitable, pues en mi medallón ya hay un tesoro."[64]

While *de pronto* echoes the *de repente* of the title, harking back to the figure of Javier Marías, the speaker also asserts that this is "*Mi* muy querido rostro." The face is hers even though she recognizes it in the face of another and that other is a male. The ambiguity of noun and adjective in the phrase *instante seductor* restates the chiasmus of identity just as the inversion of long and short phrases in these verses equates *instante seductor* and *poema inevitable*. This moment of revelation has resulted in a poem inspired by the portrait of a writer, another person of approximately the same age as the poet. If this other can achieve fame through writing, the speaker realizes that she too has the imagination and the ability to write. Her locket now contains a treasure, her self. Through her imagination and her play at dressing-up, the speaker discovers her own identity in that of another. Her poem commemorates (as do the medallion and the locket) this moment of discovering her potential. The ideal to which she aspired appears to her in the guise of this other (ironically a male figure), so that she is able to see the "de-idealized" ideal of herself for which she was searching. This discovery reverses the traditional masculinist view of woman as relegated to the status of object so that she can only facilitate man's actualization of his inner potential.[65] "De repente, descubro el retrato de Javier Marías" is emblematic of the poem as mirror because it portrays the poet dressing up, looking at herself in the framed image of the mirror of herself and/as others, and discovering her identity as a writer.

Because of its autobiographical context, "De repente" provides a convenient segue into those poems in which the distance between poet and speaker is foreshortened. Some of these involve the speaker reflecting (on) an image of herself when she was younger—as we observed in "De repente"—whereas others are even more contemporary. "Cuando mi hermana y yo, solteras, queríamos ser virtuosas y santas" (When My Sister and I, Unwed, Wanted To Be Virtuous and Holy) looks back at the speaker's adolescence to criticize the social conventions of a time not so far removed from the present. Similar to "Advertencias de abuela a Carlota y a Ana" (Grandmother's Warnings to Carlota and Ana), which deals with masturbation, "Cuando mi hermana y yo" contains an intriguing duality because of the two female figures, the speaker-poet and her sister Carlota. This duality of what we might call "the dark sister" functions synchronically in the simultaneous but silent presence of the sister and diachronically in the turning point that occurs in the middle of the poem. As a result of this chiasmatic troping of metaphor and metonymy, the specific anecdotal situation adopts the wider scope of social criticism.

The title offers other indications of this aspect, first in the word *solteras*. Set off from the rest of the sentence by commas, this social categorization of a female has specific connotations. To be of marriageable age but unwed during the Franco years meant that a woman was obligatorily expected to be a virgin. Such a status required certain accepted and acceptable behaviors, as Carmen Martín Gaite has documented in great detail. Also, the imperfect tense in the phrase *queríamos ser* speaks to the acculturation of that era and a certain amount of rejection of those values by the more liberated adult speaker. The opening verses of the poem establish the relationship between the sisters and a young male visitor by placing them in an edenic, prelapsarian setting. Nonetheless, the speaker indicates her awareness of the dangers lurking in this idyllic situation.

> Y cuando al jardín, contigo, descendíamos,
> evitábamos en lo posible los manzanos.
> Incluso ante el olor del heliotropo enrojecíamos;
> sabido es que esa flor amor eterno explica.
> Tu frente entonces no era menos encendida
> que tu encendida beca, sobre ella reclinada,
> con el rojo reflejo competía.
>
> (vv. 1–7)[66]

Parallel to the interruption of *solteras* in the title, the separation of *contigo* with commas emphasizes a duality in the speaker's perspective between then and now. Even though these young people are in a garden, they ironically have to descend to arrive there. It almost seems as if the speaker and her sister were angels coming down from heaven to visit Adam before the creation of Eve. At this point, however, we do not know who Adam is, but we do know that he is a student (later we learn that he is a seminarian) because of his "beca." This sash, "insignia que traen los colegiales sobre el manto, del mismo o diferente color" (an insignia that students wear on their cloak, of the same or a different color), immediately identifies the male privilege of advanced education and academic insignia that later in the poem will contrast with a woman's education.

Although the speaker specifically uses a stereotypical language of flowers, these allusions are subtly ironic. The apple trees evoke the Tree of Knowledge of Good and Evil, the Fall, and original sin. In like fashion the heliotrope is a symbol of eternal love when used in Christian iconography. Moreover, the myth of Clitia and Apollo and the movement of the (female-gendered) flower following the (male-gendered) sun shows a wavering between temptation and resistance, between the profane and the spiritual. As Chevalier and Gheerbrandt note, this flower symbolizes the overpowering influence of passion, and its aroma induces a mystical inebriation. That all three of them blush could indicate either their innocent embarrassment in the company of members of the opposite sex or the revelation of their shame for knowing too much and having lewd thoughts.

The verb *competía* explicitly introduces the concept of play and contest, an aspect that emerges more clearly in the following verses. Here the social accoutrements and the exchange of gifts form the gist of the interactions between young men and women of that time. The speaker clearly sees these details as a form of play in which she participated at the time but which she now disdains.

> Y extasiadas, mudas, te espiábamos;
> antes de que mojáramos los labios en la alberca,
> furtivo y virginal, te santiguabas
> y de infinita gracia te vestías.
> Te dábamos estampas con los bordes calados
> iguales al platito de pasas
> que, con el té, se ofrece a las visitas,
> detentes y reliquias en los que oro cosíamos
> y ante ti nos sentábamos con infantil modestia.
>
> (vv. 8–16)[67]

Several aspects of this description inform the speaker's irony with regard to the social conventions of the time: the indirect way of observing those of the other sex, their ecstatic silence, the play between the profane and the sacred in the sensual drinking of and blessing with water, the comparison of their holy cards with the plate of raisins, the protective device of the "detentes," and finally the phrase "infantil modestia." The "alberca," a cistern or reservoir, has an exotic nuance because of the word's Arabic origin and the suggestion of a vaginal enclosure. Added to the wetting of the lips and the implication of thirst as desire, the young man's act of blessing himself and the "detentes" indicate that he needs protection—either from the sisters or from his own straying thoughts. The *DRAE* defines a "detente" as a "Recorte de tela con la imagen del Corazón de Jesús y la leyenda: «Detente, bala». Se usó en las guerras españolas de los siglos XIX y XX, prendido en la ropa sobre el pecho" (A patch of cloth with the image of the [Sacred]

Heart of Jesus and the phrase 'Stop, bullet.' It was used in Spanish wars of the nineteenth and twentieth centuries, attached to the clothing over the heart). The comparison of these gifts with wartime activity reinforces the earlier verb *competía* and again indicates play.[68]

The young women have probably decorated the "estampas" with doilies and stitched them carefully with gold thread. Likewise, the custom of serving tea and raisins was what "se ofrec[ía] a las visitas." These actions were socially prescribed as proper for young women, as was seating themselves with "infantil modestia." The adjective reduces these females to childlike beings who supposedly knew nothing of sex. In comparison with the knowledge acquired by the young man (both academic and practical), these details are demeaning, making the exchange between them subliminal and erotically charged. Even the apparently innocuous detail of the pierced doilies connotes female lacy undergarments and penetration. The speaker's tone has become increasingly ironic, leading to the turning point in the next verses.

> Mi tan amado y puro seminarista hermoso,
> ¡cuántas serpientes enroscadas en los macizos de azucenas,
> qué sintieron las rosas en tus manos que así se deshojaban!
> Con la mirada baja protegerte queríamos
> de nuestra femenina seducción.
> Vano propósito.
>
> (vv. 17–22)[69]

Not only does the speaker enter in the first person singular in the possessive adjective *mi*, but now she identifies the young man as a seminarian. What might have been (and might still be) a typical social encounter between young people now adopts additional proportions. As a person studying for a commitment to the celibacy of religious life, this young man may represent what is described in Catholic seminaries as "forbidden fruit," more enticing because less available given the vow of chastity. He also adopts symbolic proportions: Men in general were to be regarded as priests in need of protection from alluring, sex-obsessed vamps.[70] The string of adjectives *amado, puro,* and *hermoso* overinflates the attraction of this young man as he represents all that was superficial, false, and conventional in social relations between men and women when the speaker was younger. Her exclamations are ironic, but again they refer to the sublimated feelings of the young people in this difficult environment. The serpents recall the edenic setting, the flowerpots are emblems of tawdry artifice, and the lilies and roses have erotic connotations. Because of the injunctions placed on them, the young women swoon while watching the young man "deflower" the roses.

From this point forward, the poem takes a turn toward the darker side as the speaker lets her true emotions pour out, now that social restrictions have loosened. We might read the final verses as sarcastic venting, but we can also read them ludically. The future tense signals this change and its subsequent duality.

> Un día, una turgente púrpura,
> tu pantalón incógnito, de pronto, estirará
> y Adán derramará su provisión de leche.
> Nada podrá parar tan vigoroso surtidor.
> Bien que sucederá, sucederá.
> Aunque nuestra manzana nunca muerdas,
> aunque tu espasmo nunca presidamos,
> bien que sucederá, sucederá.
> Y no te ha de salvar ningún escapulario,
> y ni el terrible infierno del albo catecismo
> podrá evitar el cauce radiante de tu esperma.
>
> (vv. 23–33)[71]

We can interpret the shift to the future tense in these verses as the emergence—at long last—of the interior, silent dark sister finally released from the social injunctions of silence. But it is still the voice of the speaker, the more adult woman looking back on the situation from the present (the post-Franco era of the *movida*, a "strong new wave of pop music and culture associated with Madrid in the early 1980s," around the time when these poems were written).[72] Although their voices seem to be united, overlaid one on the other, the future tense is disconcerting and illuminates a rift or split with the past. Curiously, the speaker's explicit references to a phallocentric erection and ejaculation, grossly figured as a mollusk that ejects purplish ink, is undercut by the presence of a vaginal opening. The repeated verse "Bien que sucederá, sucederá" with its internal repetition replicates this aperture, this orifice, because it is in these verses that we recognize the speaker's presence most clearly. Likewise, the phrase "Nada podrá parar tan vigoroso surtidor" can refer to phallocentric potency, but it bespeaks an ineluctable rupture in the veil of silence beneath which women had lived.

The speaker's prediction is already a reality at the time she makes it. But a doubt still exists as to the fate of the specific young seminarian of this anecdote. The future tense is literal and probable, already fulfilled and still pending, incomplete. That the speaker-poet can quite overtly mention erections, orgasm, ejaculation, and sperm is indicative of the emergence of the dark sister, a woman's formerly suppressed desire. The phallocentric is thus subordinated to the gynocentric, and the former prohibitions, represented by the scapular and the catechism's warnings of eternal damnation, will not and do not prevent the repressed woman's desire from emerging. The mollusk's ink is replaced with a luminous sperm presided over by the woman's lips and her writing (vagina, mouth, words, language).

Rossetti adopts one of her most playful stances in "Cierta secta feminista se da consejos prematrimoniales" (A Certain Feminist Sect Gives Itself Prematrimonial Advice). The first line of the poem becomes a repeated refrain that serves as a rallying cry or indeed a war cry of radical lesbian feminism: "Y besémonos, bellas vírgenes, besémonos" (And let us kiss one another, beautiful virgins, let us kiss one another). At first the bilabial alliteration of the phrase might seem to be a call for love relationships between women because the reflexive pronoun of the command reinforces that of the title and could be read reciprocally. Moreover, the contrast between *consejos* and the emphatic imperative is contradictory. Does the sect offer advice, or does it advocate a specific political agenda of which the poem is a manifesto?

Whereas this reading is possible and Rossetti's open attitude toward same-sex relationships undeniable, a contradiction exists between this interpretation and the adjective *prematrimoniales* in the title. Until recently it seemed illogical that radical lesbian feminists would marry.[73] It is certain, however, that Rossetti is playing with that point of view, appropriating the same intensity for heterosexual women to debunk traditional double standards regarding premarital sex. Consequently, we can also read the reflexive as recognition and validation of Luce Irigaray's understanding of a woman's genital labia constantly producing pleasure by rubbing together.[74] This phrase thus becomes a call to women to let their imaginations go and not be restricted by societal limitations or ideals of what the good girl or virgin should be.

Throughout this poem Rossetti employs war imagery. In spite of the violence and aggressiveness implicit in this imagery, Huizinga has convincingly shown that, even in war, play is a central factor. Indeed, this imagery contains a double entendre as we see in the first stanza.

> Y besémonos, bellas vírgenes, besémonos.
> Démonos prisa desvalijándonos
> destruyendo el botín de nuestros cuerpos.

> Al enemigo percibo respirar tras el muro,
> la codicia se yergue entre sus piernas.
>
> (vv. 1–5)[75]

First the verb *desvalijar* is based on the noun *valija,* a suitcase. To ransack, rob, or clean out as in a wartime plundering of another's valuables is equated to unpacking a suitcase. One could say that the speaker is calling for women to get rid of the cultural baggage that hinders them and prevents them from experiencing the same sexual freedom as men.[76] Her call to destroy "el botín de nuestros cuerpos" does not advocate feminine masochism, but rather a change in the supposed exchange value of that body as defined by society and especially the phallocratic hierarchy.[77] Instead of investing the virgin body with value, the speaker wants the body to have value not for the invader but for the woman whose it is. The enemy on the other side of the protective wall may be men or the negative forces and influences that place a woman's body under siege.[78] When the speaker states that she hears the enemy's heavy breathing and knows that his greed is growing between his legs, she recognizes the other's rapacious desire and aggression. Of course, the abstract greed is the male penis, but also a lance and an invasive attitude that poses a threat to women. To counter this menace the speaker argues in favor of self-masturbation, thereby wresting mastery away from the male and reclaiming control over her own body.

> Y besémonos, bellas vírgenes, besémonos.
> No deis pródigamente a la espada,
> oh viril fortuna, el inviolado himen.
> Que la grieta, en el blanco ariete
> de nuestras manos, pierda su angostura.
>
> (vv. 6–10)[79]

Again the language employed by Rossetti is equivocal. The addition of the adverb *pródigamente* could alter the reading to either "Don't be so generous with men" or "Don't give yourselves wastefully or recklessly to men; don't squander this precious gift ('el inviolado himen')

on them." Although she describes a woman's hands as a battering ram (*ariete*), this hand is not a phallic substitute. Because of the concavity in *grieta* and the modifying adjective *blanco,* the hands seem more to scoop out, to widen the opening. In his discussion of masturbation and infantile sexuality, Freud states that, when masturbating, girls often close their thighs to achieve "a certain previously-formed pressure reflex." In contrast, boys prefer the hand, which indicates "the mastery impulse."[80] The syntax is also ambiguous, so that rather than snatching away something, the hands gently cause the orifice to relax and widen. Even the construction beginning the sentence with *Que* (meaning "Let it happen thus" or "May it happen thus") softens the action in contrast with the negative command "No deis."

The war imagery adopts epic proportions in the fourth and fifth stanzas with its allusions to the Trojan War or the rivalry of the Punic Wars. The mock-heroic tone of these verses urges women not to succumb to the victors' agression.[81]

> Y besémonos, bellas vírgenes, besémonos.
> Antes que el vencedor la ciudadela
> profane, y desvele su recato
> para saquear del templo los tesoros,
> es preferible siempre entregarla a las llamas.
>
> Y besémonos, bellas vírgenes, besémonos.
> Expolio singular: enfebrecidas
> en nuestro beneficio arrebatemos
> la propia dote. Que el triunfador altivo
> no obtenga el masculino privilegio.
>
> (vv. 16–25)[82]

The terms *ciudadela* and *profanar* figure female virginity as the innermost and most sacred part of herself as the city under siege. Rather than have a man desecrate this sacred space, this seat of being, she says it would be preferable to set it aflame. These flames could be the passion of sexual stimulation that destroys virginity, but flames are also regenerative. As such, the vagina in flames would change its nature without destroying it. Note that the speaker uses the verb *entregar*, which means that she does not surrender it to the male but to her own passionate desire. In contrast, a man would "desvel[ar] su recato," that is, he would remove the veil covering it but simultaneously destroy it. She characterizes this act saying that he would "saquear del templo los tesoros." If the veil is a metaphor of the hymen, this imagery also exposes the double standard that men have imposed upon women. They disrespect a woman's modesty and sexual reserve when it is they themselves who have demanded that women adopt this attitude.

Modifying the noun *expolio,* the adjective *singular* is similarly ambivalent. The woman herself does this plundering, and therefore it is unusual, rare, infrequent. In like manner the adjective *enfebrecidas* can refer to her amorous passion or to her revengeful short-circuiting of male privilege. Although dowries per se are highly infrequent in contemporary Western society, the concept of the woman's virginity serving as dowry is still widespread.[83] Ironically, the speaker urges women to snatch back from men that which already belongs to women themselves. This act, she notes, would be beneficial in two senses: First, it is much healthier for women to recognize that their bodies belong to them; and second, if they are in control of their bodies, they will enjoy themselves much more. Again she warns against male privilege and a double standard where men can possess infinite experience in sexual matters while women are supposed to remain virginal. If earlier the *Que* beginning the phrase about the battering ram softened the urging to women, here by dint of repetition it adopts a pleading, imploring, insistent tone underscored by the phrases "triunfador altivo" and "masculino privilegio."

The penultimate stanza contains a telling alteration in the stanzaic structure that Rossetti has employed in this poem. The third verse is split into two truncated verses, indicative of the woman's self-deflowering, of her own act of breaking the hymen in opposition to the phallocentric manner. Moreover, the references to classical mythology exaggerate the contrast between men and women, intensifying the play element.

> Y besémonos, bellas vírgenes, besémonos.
> Con la secreta fuente humedecida
> en el licor de Venus,
> anticipémonos,
> de placer mojadas, a Príapo.
> Y con la sed de nuestros cuerpos, embriaguémonos.
>
> (vv. 26–31)[84]

By placing the mythological characters at the ends of their respective lines, the poet contrasts the majesty and elegance of the female figure with the comic and diminutive Priapus. The truncated third verse highlights the verb *anticipémonos,* another ambivalent command that could mean that women should get a head start on sexual awareness by using their imaginations before Priapus arrives. They may or may not actually participate in sexual relationships with other women. The important thing is to prime the pump through the invention of their own imaginations. This anticipation would require women to break through the restrictions placed on them by society, restrictions that deny women fantasies, desires, gazes—in short, their own sexual interests. In her urging women to become inebriated on the "licor de Venus," the speaker encourages women to let themselves go, to free themselves from the sobriety imposed on them by a patriarchal society. The result of this change in attitude and redefinition of women's sexuality provides the conclusion of the poem.

> Y besémonos, bellas vírgenes, besémonos.
> Rasgando el azahar, gocémonos, gocémonos
> del premio que celaban nuestros muslos.
> El falo, presto a traspasarnos
> encontrará, donde creyó virtud, burdel.
>
> (vv. 32–36)[85]

If we return to the title and remember that these verses offer prenuptial advice to women, the outcome will be that on their wedding night men will discover that women are just as experienced in sexual matters as they. Such an arrangement would level the playing field. With women having as much experience and as much desire as men, males would no longer keep women in the inferior position of sex object over which they have control; rather, women would assume an equally active role in sexual engagement. If men now go to brothels to obtain their experience—again taking advantage of women and maintaining another double standard (virgin versus whore)—they will recognize and even be surprised by their brides' expertise.[86] In "Cierta secta feminista" Rossetti appropriates an element of radical feminism to make a case for feminine sexuality. The speaker's relish in presenting this argument is playful and suggestive even though her intent is quite serious.

Given her penchant for ludic dressing-up, Ana Rossetti has such a firm understanding of who she is that she is not afraid to explore and to discover still unknown areas of her self. She does so by adopting an enormous variety of possibilities, playfully adopting different costumes and roles, looking at herself in funhouse mirrors that distort and exaggerate different aspects, and making funny faces at herself and those who observe her—we readers. Through losing herself in the identity of the other, she finds herself ever more clearly. That which identifies her most definitively is her willingness to play and her inventiveness with it. But as demonstrated, this play leads to quite serious discoveries and makes a commentary not only on identity but also on the act of (reading and writing) poetry. Ana Rossetti challenges her own and society's accepted images, inhibitions, and fears. Her theatrical extravagance makes her challenge entertaining and palatable and has insured her place in the history of twentieth-century Spanish poetry.

3

The Shattered Mirror: Grief, Madness, and Identity in Blanca Andreu's
De una niña de provincias

Like a good detective investigating a mysterious crime, the literary critic must pay attention to clues offered by the text (the scene of the crime) to formulate theories and hypotheses about the events and the motivation underlying the signifiers of a text. The accumulation of clues in Blanca Andreu's *De una niña de provincias que se vino a vivir en un Chagall* (A Girl from the Sticks Who Came to Life in a Chagall) suggests that a crime has been committed, prompting the writing of these poems.[1]

Characterized as neosurrealistic and making frequent reference to drug-induced hallucinations, *De una niña de provincias* has mesmerized readers since its publication in 1981. Many see this cult book as a reflection of the intoxicating abandon of the post-Franco transition. Sylvia Sherno provides keen insights into this work by elucidating the patterns of imagery. Other critics—John Wilcox, Sharon Keefe Ugalde, and Candelas Newton—have drawn attention to the clues offered by the text; but the picture with which they leave us is still incomplete.[2] To put this text in a new frame of reference and rearrange the textual puzzle into a cogent picture, a keen-eyed detective could build a hypothesis on the critics' "lab analyses" and valuable insights as well as point out some of the clues they have overlooked or slighted. Andreu's *De una niña de provincias* is an elegiac text whose fragmentary nature, repetitions and intertextualities, and ambivalent surrealistic imagery replicate the shattered mirror that both destroys identity and enables its recreation.[3]

As Peter M. Sacks has argued convincingly in *The English Elegy*, the stance of the elegist is often a conflicted one. In some cases the mourner feels guilty at having survived the deceased or is angry with the deceased for having abandoned him. At other times he profits from the death of the beloved by writing the elegy or is in an uncertain relationship of inheritance with regard to the poetic tradition and the conventions of elegy. Whatever the cause, the elegist adopts a variety of stances that exacerbate and intensify the grief at the same time that he seeks consolation. Ironically, these very stances allow the mourner to work through grief.[4]

Following Sacks's lead, other critics have contributed pertinent insights into the elegiac genre. In *Poetry of Mourning* Jahan Ramazani demonstrates that twentieth-century poets modify elegiac conventions through their inventive reworking of conventional tropes and topoi. But in keeping with a modern and postmodern skepticism of the efficacy of these conventions, they sacrifice a certain degree of consolation.[5] Kelly Oliver also asserts that "The relation of women to language, and therefore poetic language . . . sets up a double-bind for women in relation to language." As a result, "in *Black Sun* Kristeva argues that women can never even enter into a proper mourning for the maternal let alone work through this mourning."[6] Finally, in *Beyond Consolation* Melissa F. Zeiger maintains that contemporary women poets may never reach the same degree of consolation that men attain given the psychological differences produced by the oedipal process.[7] These issues may coincide with personal, social, and political moments of transition: the ego may be in the very process of asserting itself, and many diverse and discordant forces may press on the mourner from the outside. Thus the reparation of the shattered ego required by the elegiac process becomes a monumental task.[8] But the elegy often results in a highly distinctive and poignant work of poetry. *De una niña de provincias* renders just such an instance.

Much has been made of the literal ungrammaticality of the title and its spurious origin.[9] The equivocality of the preposition *en* where we expect (and subliminally hear) the preposition *a* alerts us also that the "niña" can be read as the speaker describing herself. She does so, however, in the third person ("vino") positing the presence of an other or the self as other. Indeed, the speaker narrates her relationship with a girl in her "colegio"—the "niña rusa" identified as Olga in the final poem.[10] *De una niña de provincias* is an elegy written out of psychic necessity because of the loss of that friend, the other who both is and is not the speaker. Typical of elegiac verse, the loss of this good friend throws the speaker-poet's identity into disorder, suggesting that the hallucinatory imagery and the fragmented poems of this work function as the broken mirror of psychic dysfunction.[11] But as Sherno has pointed out quite astutely, the images of fire and water that pervade *De una niña* symbolize both destruction and creation.[12] In effect, fire and water are equally destructive and regenerative, creating a chiasmus of tension in and between the imagery. Therefore, the speaker-poet's writing, her destruction of the image in the mirror, is therapeutic because it allows her to reconstruct her own identity, or in elegiac terms, to reaffirm her narcissism and reconstruct her ego.

Because of the psychoanalytic dimensions of elegy, especially an elegy written by a woman, Julia Kristeva's concepts of the abject and of the *sujet-en-procès* (the subject in process/on trial) are consonant with this template for reading *De una niña*.[13] The female body of the other, the "niña rusa," has been defiled and corrupted not only by her suicide but even more so by the event(s) that provoked it. Assuming that the speaker identifies with the other, her mirror image or soul mate, she has transferred that abjection to her own body and sense of self. The work of mourning for this young woman, then, involves separating herself from the other, reformulating her notion of the *corps propre*, a body clean and proper but also "a body of her own," and then reestablishing her sense of narcissism.[14]

The separation from the lost friend reiterates the separation from the mother as primary other and the establishment of an individual identity while at the same time identifying with the (m)other as female. Drugs and intoxication in one sense numb the speaker, who searches for a way to avoid and protect herself from her intense feelings of grief. Ironically, these anodynes intensify her grief, bringing her face to face with her loss, just as language—the sign—substantiates presence even though it signifies the referent's absence.[15] If the loss of her friend shatters her concept of self, throwing her psyche into disarray, the additional smashing of those fragments represented by her words allows her to destroy an old self and create a new one through the act of writing and the work of mourning. The elegiac process and especially the use of repetition—a prominent feature of *De una niña*—aim to suture the wound of grief through the veil of language.

By reading *De una niña de provincias* as elegy, we see that the death of a valued school companion has shattered the speaker's world, thrusting her identity into turmoil and threatening her sanity. The chaos of the shattered mirror is a crucial phase in the work of mourning, the narcissistic repair of the elegist's ego, and the formation of a new identity. Though she may ultimately reject consolation and compensation for the loss of innocence (or at least rail against such a steep price), the poet explores a variety of emotions in her confrontation with loss. *De una niña de provincias* allows Andreu to inscribe herself within the elegiac (poetic) tradition at the same time that it depicts a rite of passage, reflecting a personal, social, and aesthetic portrayal of the *sujet-en-procès*.

Assuming, then, that a crime has been committed and that the loss of a close friend has thrown the speaker's psyche into chaos, we find more clues to support this hypothesis in the poems. In accord with Kristeva's concept of intertextuality as thetic rupture, a movement between signifying systems that requires continuous rearticulations (elegiac repetitions) that call into question the unity of both subject and object positions, we first encounter paratextual clues.[16] The text's epigraph, "Hey, shouted Will, people are running as if a storm had arrived! It's arrived, shouted Jim, the storm is us!" is taken from a novel by Ray Bradbury titled *Something Wicked This Way Comes,* another intertextual allusion to Shakespeare's *Macbeth.* Bradbury's sci-fi, rite-of-passage novel deals with two friends, the Jim and Will mentioned in the epigraph, who encounter evil in the form of a sinister troupe of circus employees and sideshow freaks (reminiscent of *Macbeth*'s witches). They discover, however, that the possibility for evil resides within them, within their own characters. Andreu's appropriation of this intertext points to a similar discovery on the part of the two female friends, the speaker and the "niña rusa."

Two central images from Bradbury's novel also provide insight into the speaker's dilemma. One is a merry-go-round (a traditional symbol of childhood innocence) that, when speeded forward, ages those riding it; but when run in reverse, it undoes the passage of time. Unfortunately, the effects are only physical, so that the rider ages or rejuvenates superficially but retains the same sensibilities and emotional maturity. It seems that the speaker and her friend have undergone an inverse process, aging in one sense while still being too young to handle the knowledge they discover. This incompatibility between two perspectives—innocence and knowledge—held within the same person creates a conflict underlying these poems.

The second image from the novel is a maze of mirrors in which one loses a sense of the difference between representation (multiple reflections) and reality (integrated identity). In addition to the commentary on the meontic nature of language discussed by Sherno, the mirror is particularly apt, especially since Jim in the novel saves himself and his father from losing themselves in the illusions of the maze by shattering the mirrors with a rock.[17] In effect, destruction of the illusion in the mirror—its shattering—becomes a way of saving the self from being swallowed and lost.

In one sense the opening poem, "Di que querías ser caballo esbelto," is the conventional invocation to the absent muse for inspiration.[18] However, the insistently repeated *Di* is equivocal, serving as both a plea and an aggressive challenge.

> Di que querías ser caballo esbelto, nombre
> de algún caballo mítico,

o acaso nombre de tristán, y oscuro.
Dilo, caballo griego, que querías ser estatua desde hace
   diez mil años, di sur, y di paloma adelfa blanca,
que habrías querido ser en tales cosas,
morirte en su substancia, ser columna.

(vv. 1–7)[19]

We cannot be sure whom the speaker addresses—herself or another (or herself as another), or even the reader. This equivocality destabilizes the discourse and makes the meaning indeterminate (dialogical), capturing the speaker's psychic distress. She both desires to confront her dilemma (for that reason she writes) and to avoid the pain and difficulty of working through her grief. The second person in the command and in the repeated imperfect verb *querías* establishes the presence but distance of another, or the excision of the ego into self and other.[20] Her aggressive sarcasm mocks the former perspective she must acknowledge as hers at the same time that she pleads with the absent loved one's voice to return, even though she fears or even knows this may be impossible.

Reinforced by the contrast between the commands and the past verb tenses, the imagery of this opening stanza represents an idealized vision that the speaker has regretfully lost and simultaneously derides and repudiates. At one time the addressee had hopes of taking flight and achieving mythical immortality commemorated in a statue or a stele. This utopic vision is further evident in the sequence of images in verse 5: "di sur, y di paloma adelfa blanca," images of light, soaring, and whiteness. Ironically, the adjective *blanca* is also the poet's first name, equating *paloma, adelfa,* and Blanca in their innocence and purity. The progression from *caballo esbelto* to *mítico* and *griego* and then to *estatua* and *columna* indicates the desire to rise and soar above ordinary reality and to remain forever incarnated in the work of art: "ser en tales cosas, / morirte en su substancia, ser columna."[21] The futility and disillusionment of this desire, hinted in the verbs *querías* and *habrías querido,* becomes more blatant in the second stanza.

Di que demasiadas veces
astrolabios, estrellas, el nervio de los ángeles,
vinieron a hacer música para Rilke el poeta,
no para tus rodillas o tu alma de muro.

(vv. 8–11)[22]

The tone changes definitively in the final verse and in the contrast between the *tú* and the (again ideal) figure of the poet Rilke, who wrote the *Duino Elegies* on the occasion of a young girl's death.[23] One perceives a touch of exaggeration and sarcasm in the angels' visitation of Rilke with their "astrolabios, estrellas." "El nervio" may be a synecdoche for the vault of a gothic cathedral (ascendancy) and thus as metaphor for the sky and the poet's pathway guided by the stars. In contrast, the speaker is on her knees, praying for inspiration, and can only relate to the walls around her, which produce a sense of enclosure and suffocation. When she subsequently turns to marijuana, it is uncertain whether she does so to gain inspiration or to insulate herself against her feelings of discomfort (physical and mental).

> Mientras la marihuana destila mares verdes,
> habla en las recepciones con sus lágrimas verdes,
> o le roba a la luz su luz más verde,
> te desconoces, te desconoces.
>
> (vv. 12–15)[24]

Because of the ambivalence of the color green as both hope and sickness (cf. Lorca's "Romance sonámbulo" [Sleepwalking Ballad]), the three exemplifications of the drug's effect are equally equivocal.[25] To distill green seas could be to purify them and make them clear, or to make them a nauseating green, for example. Hence the repeated phrase that closes the poem, in addition to the elegiac convention of placing the veil of language between the poet and her grief, underscores the duality and equivocality of the speaker's state of mind. It speaks to both a process of self-estrangement and self-alienation that enables the speaker to sedate her pain, and a heightened awareness of the disorientation resulting from loss and grief. It is, in short, cause and effect, process and product, simultaneously. If the speaker's psyche is a shattered mirror, she takes drugs to soothe the pain, with the ironic outcome that she is more aware of her distress and the radical change that has occurred in her outlook on herself and her identity.

The poet reinforces and develops these themes in the second poem, "Cómo me parecerá extraño el aire." Again availing herself of the elegiac convention of repetition and the apostrophe of the absent other, the speaker expands on her confused state of mind. Notice especially the equivocality of the word *Cómo*.

> Cómo me parecerá extraño el aire que me envuelve,
> cómo será así extraño,
> cuando tú ya no estés,

la catedral del día,
el claustro que condensa la gran edad de la luz
y el carácter de las tormentas.

(vv. 1–6)[26]

Because *cómo* can function as either an exclamative or an interrogative, the significance of the future tense and the relationship between interior and exterior are thrown into ironic doubt.[27] As a rhetorical question, the phrase *Cómo me parecerá extraño el aire* negates any change in the speaker's attitude, whereas the exclamation anticipates change as ineluctable and inevitable. In fact, it is so vivid that the speaker already experiences it, even though the rhetorical question denies it. This paradox replicates the conflicting emotions of the speaker in her dilemma: She denies the loss of the other at the same time that she suffers its impact.[28]

Likewise she attributes her own feelings to the air around her. Here again the *tú* in the phrase *cuando tú ya no estés* is disorienting, referring to the lost other and to the self as other. Just as the speaker experiences the loss of her friend, so she projects those feelings onto the air when she herself will die. But if she is dead, she will not be able to perceive the effect her death causes. Hence the speaker now feels inept given that she is incapable of sharing these powerful emotions with her dead friend. This dilemma produces her claustrophobic feeling. Thus even the great cathedral of day (an echo and elaboration of the "nervios" in the previous poem) seems to her to be as suffocating as a cloister that reduces ("condensa") one's vision of the world to either "la gran edad de la luz" or "el carácter de las tormentas." These images in themselves deconstruct the positive and the negative. A beautiful day seen from the limitations of the cloister will be just another day, monotonously the same or beyond one's reach and enjoyment (what is positive is actually negative). But on the other hand, a raging storm will interrupt the monotony and in its violence produce excitement, strong sensations, ironically restoring the beauty of a calm, sunny day.[29] The religious overtones of the cathedral, the cloister, and by extension the sky as God reveal the speaker's fluctuating emotions.

The second stanza introduces a leitmotif that the poet will repeat elegiacally throughout the remainder of the poems. This phrase has a provocative intertextual resonance that the preceding religious context may foment.

Amor mío, amor mío, tú sin día para ti,
enjambrado entre espejos y entre las cosas malas,

muerta la plata trascendental
y las ya antiguas anémonas de égloga,
muerta esta versión que ahora oscuro, y declino, para leerla, más joven.

$$(vv.\ 7\text{–}11)^{30}$$

The phrase *Amor mío, amor mío* is a variation of Jesus's words on the cross: "Dios mío, Dios mío, ¿por qué me has abandonado?" (My God, my God, why have you abandoned me?). Whether the one addressed is the self or the other, the themes of suffering and abandonment are prominent elegiac topoi. The *tú* as the dead friend is no longer able to see the daylight; she lives in perpetual night. Identifying with her because of her grief, the speaker also has no day, no light, no joy, precisely because of the absence of the loved one. Death (absence) and memory (presence) both cause her such pain that she feels accosted "entre espejos y entre las cosas malas." In other words, her only two options seem to be either to confront herself (to look into the mirror, to see herself and/or the loss of the other) or to flee from herself by participating in unhealthful activities. Her values ("la plata trascendental") and her illusions ("las ya antiguas anémonas de égloga") have died, so that mirrors represent illusions and the "cosas malas" become a way of denying (albeit temporarily) her pain. This version (of herself and/or of the other) has died. But she is not—perhaps wisely so—ready to take the step into a more mature version of herself. She needs to wallow in her grief in order to heal, yet she also refuses to allow herself to feel grief, reverting instead to a more childish attitude. These contradictory emotions are especially prevalent in the maternal imagery of the final verses.

Amor mío de nunca, afiebrado y pacífico,
versos para el pequeño pulpo de la muerte,
versos para la muerte rara que hace la travesía de los teléfonos,
para mi mente debelada versos, para el circuito del violín,
para el circuito de la garza gaviota,
para el confín del sur, del sueño,
versos que no me asilen ni sean causa de vida,
que no me den la dulce serpiente umbilical
ni la sala glucosa del útero.

$$(vv.\ 12\text{–}20)^{31}$$

Beginning with repetition of the phrase *Amor mío* and the antinomical adjectives *afiebrado y pacífico,* the elegiac anaphora and the catalog of images lead to a powerful tension between separation and connection. Anaphora, as repetition, has the elegiac purpose of fixing in memory the one who has died at the same time that it draws a veil of language between the mourner and her grief. This duality of purpose is consonant with the attraction/repulsion aspect of the abject.[32] According to traditional elegiac theory, every loss entailed in the death of a loved one recapitulates the original experience of separation and individuation from the mother figure, the first human experience of loss, and the concomitant acquisition of language.[33] While still the topic of debate and investigation, the female version of this process differs from the male version. Consequently, we can expect a woman poet's participation in the elegiac process of seeking consolation to differ from the male elegist's. Here the speaker's verses perform a contradictory purpose: They celebrate female sexuality and yet reject identification with the maternal.[34] Because of the intensity of her grief, the speaker may be questioning her own sexual identity, at once affirming and denying her feminine sexuality. This contradiction may be due to the circumstances of her friend's death, which are never fully revealed to the reader, and the speaker's emotionally complex relationship with her dead friend: The "Amor mío" may also be sarcastic. In sum, the speaker is resisting consolation at the same time that she seeks it, writing her elegy.[35] The catalog of images in this second poem attests to the diverse fragments of the shattered mirror—the speaker's identity.

The final poem in this opening sequence, invoking/defying the muse, "Amor mío, amor mío, mira mi boca de vitriolo" (My love, my love, look at my vitriolic mouth), is a self-conscious reflection on the speaker's own words. This short, two-stanza poem shows that the speaker prefers the brutal, rebellious, and equally youthful Rimbaud of *A Season in Hell* and "The Drunken Boat" to the urbane, eloquent Rilke. The figure of Rilke offers another clue to the elusive anecdotal basis of *De una niña*. As a youth Rilke was enrolled in two military schools by his parents, clearly an inappropriate decision that had deleterious consequences for his health, requiring his withdrawal from the second. Rilke always saw himself as a misfit in those schools, long after he had left them and begun his literary career. The speaker makes reference to his *Letters to a Young Poet* in the final verse of this poem.[36] Hence, the repeated imperative *mira* may be read either sarcastically or invocatively, sustaining the contrast between the two poets' visions and the speaker's conflictive emotions. One further aspect of this poem is crucial. Making a bridge between the two stanzas, the speaker states:

> mira los árboles como nervios crispados del día
> llorando agua de guadaña.

Esto es lo que yo veo en la hora lisa de abril,
también en la capilla del espejo esto veo . . .

(vv. 5–8)[37]

Availing herself of the objective correlative of a sympathetic natural scene (a trope frequent in elegy), the poet equates the rain dripping from the trees with her tears.[38] While Sherno is correct in assessing that this phrase "joins two disparate nouns on the basis of their phonetic similarity, even as the juxtaposition imparts its own poetic logic," the phrase should not be reduced to its phonetic surface.[39] The scythe metonymically evokes the figure of death (the proverbial Grim Reaper), making the water of the tears an image for sap, the life-blood of plants. The shedding of tears and of blood is commingled in the elegist's production of her words. More importantly, she perceives these emotions not only when she looks at nature, but also when she looks in the mirror. Her recurrence to religious imagery (calling the mirror a chapel), the ambivalence of the poem as mirror, and the reflection in the mirror as self and other—all reinforce the irony of her elegiac project. Looking in the mirror (or recognizing her emotions in the objective correlative) both irritates and alleviates her grief. The image she sees—that of the deceased other—repulses and pains her, yet she must seek it to restore her sense of identity and serenity.[40]

Starting with the next poem, the speaker begins to offer more clues as to the anecdotal basis of her grief. The epigraph quoting a verse of Cesare Pavese announces the ghostly return of the other via the speaker's memory: "Vendrá la muerte y tendrá tus ojos" (Death will come and will have your eyes). The choice of Pavese is highly appropriate given that the Italian poet committed suicide (another clue to the anecdotal basis of *De una niña*), that one of his most assiduous themes is loneliness, and that his book *Verrà la morte e avrà i tuoi occhi* (written in 1950, the year of his death and published posthumously the following year) contains several passages that remind us of *De una niña*.[41] Even here the second person is equivocal, referring to the lost loved one and to the speaker, since it is through the speaker's eye of memory that the image of the other will emerge. Our first glimpse of her comes in the final stanza of this poem.

Colegio: *niña que bebía los pomelos*
directamente en labios de la noche,
que juraba acostarse con el miedo en la cama de nadie,
que juraba que el miedo
la había violado hasta doscientos hijos.

Amor, la niña rusa
que comulgaba reno asado
y bebía liquen.
Amor, la niña rusa que leía a Tom Wolfe.

(vv. 14–22; original emphasis)[42]

Whatever else we can say about this "niña," it is obvious that she had a vivid imagination and a captivating way of expressing herself, attributes that undoubtedly attracted the speaker to her. Repetition of the word *amor* evokes the leitmotif and links "la niña rusa" with the one addressed as "amor mío." In addition to her daring tales of prohibited sexual imaginings, this young woman was highly irreverent, asserting that she substituted grilled reindeer and lichen for the body and blood of Christ in the Eucharist. On one hand, the speaker may have been shocked by this sacrilegious talk, but on the other, the outrageousness and hyperbole of it were seductive.

A similar ambivalence can be found in the mention of Tom Wolfe. Does this refer irreverently to the novelist Thomas Wolfe, author of similarly hyperbolic novels describing his family romance and sexual involvement (e.g., *Look Homeward, Angel* and *You Can't Go Home Again;* also cf. Bradbury's *Something Wicked This Way Comes*)? Or does it refer to the popular culture, drug culture, fanciful novels of the author of *The Electric Kool-Aid Acid Test,* which Andreu read as a teenager?[43] The poet conflates high and low culture, serious and comic, fantasy and reality as characteristics attributable to her friend, "la niña rusa." In fact, we might even question whether this girl was Russian or if the speaker compares her outlook to the paintings of Marc Chagall (a Russian-born artist), so that the speaker considers her exotic, mysterious, and enigmatic.[44]

This presentation of the other, the lost friend, leads directly into one of the major statements of *De una niña,* the poem introduced by Saint-John Perse's line, "Corónate, juventud, de una hoja más aguda" (Crown yourself, youth, with a sharper leaf). Like Andreu's imperatives, the *Corónate* of Perse can be interpreted as a hortatory or cynical injunction, and the crown may be of thorns or of laurel.[45] These dualities are again consonant with the speaker's work of mourning, her grief and consolation, her disillusionment and her emerging new self, surviving the death of the other and coming to terms with her own mortality even as she survives.[46] Thus "Hasta nosotros la infancia de los metales raros" (Until us the infancy of the rare metals) describes the speaker's frustration and disillusionment with the world as she searches for values to assimilate and models to emulate. Again the speaker defines the ideal expectations that adults have of her generation by alluding to Bach and Rilke. Yet the music of Bach, especially his pieces for his young wife, Ana Magdalena, has been reduced to girls singing popular music on records; and Rilke is no longer as moving as he once was, as the superficial reference to a page number rather than a specific poem or passage might indicate:

> como una cinta que naciera en un cuaderno de Bach el Joven
> y viniera a morir aquí,
> en las niñas que anidan en los discos,
> mientras Rainer María ya no es tan joven como en la página 38,
> no es ni siquiera un joven muerto,
> un infante difunto sin pavana . . .
>
> (vv. 3–8)[47]

In the remainder of this stanza the speaker continues to complain about the times that have befallen her and her generation, even though she recognizes their advancement over the previous generation. Therefore her incorporation of Perse's verse has a double edge to it (pun intended, given that *hoja* means a knife blade as well as a leaf).

> y no desfallecemos entre sexos cerrados como libros cerrados,
> pero desfallecemos
> . . . .
> Ay, bostezamos ante tazas de azul de metileno,
> aspiramos con aire distante el amoníaco,
> nos hastiamos frente al alto sonido del vitriolo,
> nos coronamos de veronal,
> pues no encontramos hoja más aguda.
>
> (vv. 10–11, 16–20)[48]

While her generation may not be as sexually uninformed and innocent as the previous generations under Franco's rule, they have felt the need to turn to drugs.[49] The double edge of the final line here depends on the conflation of cause and effect. On the one hand, youths may have turned to drugs because they can find no more vivid way to exist in their drab society. Drugs heighten their perceptions but are also a form of self-inflicted abuse or damage. Drugs are a type of blade ("hoja") for slitting one's wrists or throat. On the other hand, because other means of achieving higher standards and goals seem to be out of reach, drugs provide at least one means of rising above the dullness of existence. Drugs, then, allow young people to rebel and in that way achieve notoriety, recognition, or attention. However, reading the word *hojas* sarcastically, these drugs may merely be herbs in the form of teas taken to soothe women's nerves! The verbs used are effective in capturing this duality as the speaker wavers from *bostezamos* to *aspiramos*, from *nos hastiamos* to *nos coronamos*. The implication of this declaration is a lamentation for the lost friend (who represented a truly fresh and unusual perspective, but who was suppressed for that very reason), an accusation, and a complaint as well as defiance, rebellion, and a means of self-assertion in the face of criticism.

When the speaker refers to her "brother" in the next stanza, she describes what she observes the boys of her age doing in response to life. Her comparison of him with Heliogabalus—the Roman emperor infamous for his insanity, his gluttony, and his cruelty—is far from flattering. Some of them prefer a papal crown, that is, a career in the church; others—perhaps melancholic poets—whom she calls "estos pequeños cíclopes enfermos del pulmón" (these little cyclopses with sick lungs) crown themselves with a mauve-colored cypress (a color that does not exist, according to the speaker). This image suggests that these young men have grandiose but unwarranted, overinflated, and melodramatic opinions of themselves and their suffering. Their only escape is to get drunk or stoned, somewhat harmless choices that make them parodies of "ningún caballero andante" (no knight errant). Wine fills their veins and their heads with false bravado that falls far short of Don Quijote ("el vaivén de sus cuerpos es vano y terrible" [the swaying of their bodies is vain and terrible]). Obviously, unable or unwilling to aspire to more, "no han encontrado un árbol más agudo" (they have not found a sharper tree). The change from a leaf to a tree contrasts the tea taken by women with the cypress tree, a tall, pointed tree associated with death and resurrection because it is an evergreen frequently found in Spanish cemeteries. These consumptive cyclopses depend on the tree as a crutch rather than using it as a knight's lance. This does not say much for their ability in lovemaking! First, they are egocentric—they have only one eye; and then they are lame—sexually incapable because of the wine they have drunk.

The disparaging portrait that Andreu paints of her generation is a negative self-portrait. Searching for some image that will return a reflection of her own identity, her own self, she finds only falseness and insipidity, which she rejects through her sarcasm and distorted imagery. The poem's extensive third and concluding stanza confirms that the speaker's postloss vision of her world is as vacuous and arid as her infantile mythological fantasies.

Como en mi medieval historia,
cuando ardían las piedras colegiales
para las brechas en la frente
y el cuerpo me dotaba de opio recién nacido,
la hora propia nos confunde,
nos hace himnos o hijos del antiguo caballo mitológico
y de una niña triste con la vena extendida,
de una aguja levantada por nieve increíble
por amarillo de palomas persas . . .

(vv. 35–43)[50]

Just as when she read medieval history searching for some breach in the rigidity and confinement of the school's claustrophobic atmosphere, the present moment (after the loss of her friend) offers her empty hymns or myths. Whereas in the past her own body brought her relief (perhaps through masturbation), now she receives a sedating injection (perhaps cocaine—*nieve* and *caballo* are both slang for drugs) to alleviate her sadness. However we interpret these disorienting images, the juxtaposition of past and present leaves a gap or emptiness (prefigured by *brechas*) where the lost friend momentarily enlivened existence.

The absence of the other in these fragments of images reflects the speaker's inability to define herself except as lack, as gap, as void. Ironically, that gap is what also allows her to find and define herself through this language, apparently lacking in concrete reference. Should we gloss the phrases "de una aguja levantada por nieve increíble, / por amarillo de palomas persas" as the cooling effects or the sunny, uplifting disposition that the sedatives bestow on the distressed speaker? The psychological disturbance implicit in these shifting emotions takes the form of an investigation of the speaker's family dynamic in the mention of the "caballos padres" and "vena madre" in the following verses. However, the use of the subjunctive *hablemos* as a command is again ambivalent.

hablemos de los caballos padres,
hagamos alusión a los cascos secretos que nos darán la paz
y a las bridas ningunas,
a las futuras crines delicadamente angustiadas,
hablemos de los caballos padres que nos traerán la muerte y de la luna de
    anfetamina,
hablemos de la vena madre que nos traerá la dicha del fin,
hablemos de la virgen bebida extrema . . .

(vv. 44–50)[51]

The *nosotros*-form of the command could have a coaxing tone, encouraging the shaken speaker to express her deep concerns, or a snide, cutting edge, expressing her skepticism concerning "the talking cure." The "caballos padres" may allude obliquely to sexuality, especially the primal scene or more specifically to men and their "free rein" in sexual relations as opposed to the effect this imbalance of power has on women. In that case the switch to the negative construction in the poem's coda is a contrast but *not* a contrast because the negative ("no hablemos sino") becomes a positive substitute.

> no hablemos sino del litoral y las vertientes de la locura
>   que posee a los hombres en los parques y ordena,
>
> sino del puñalito que coronará la arteria coronaria como
>   diadema suma
> con la hoja infantil del metal más raro y más agudo
>   del mundo.
>
> (vv. 51–56)[52]

The "puñalito" could be the hypodermic needle that sedates, or it could be the phallus. The semantic play of "coronará la arteria coronaria" sustains the equivalent tone of the imperatives and leads to a reworking of the opening image and the epigraph from Perse. The diadem that tops off the experience consists of that infantile leaf, a thorn or blade of a rare metal, the "espuma" (sperm? sexual fluids?) that both pains and delights, crucifies and resurrects. This leaf—sexuality? poetry?—has become the pathway to destruction and creation, but does the speaker accept or reject that option? The transition from *hablemos* to *no hablemos sino* reveals a gap or breach between possibilities where the speaker locates herself, in the absence of language, present in substitution for the absence of the lost loved one.

In portraying the options available to her generation, the speaker excludes herself (her reflection disappears from the mirror), while it is painfully clear that she feels trapped in the roles society prescribes for her. Her unwillingness to accept those options, even when in her friend's death she has seen the effect such a rejection can have, has been converted into a criticism of society. Andreu frames her individual experience in a wider scope, realizing a tension between the personal and the social that defines her era.[53] Her protest differs from Ana Rossetti's in that she is much younger, has less confidence in herself and less experience, and is less playful; but it is taken up more blatantly by Luisa Castro and Almudena Guzmán five years later, as we shall see.

In an attempt to find a space for her voice and her identity to assert themselves, the poet-speaker repudiates her former imagery in favor of a sharper and rarer metal/mettle. In the following poem, "Escucha, escúchame" (Listen, listen to me), she acknowledges the futility of language and poetry as the only means of attaining a hearing, although her sarcasm and concession to the established order belies her intent. This poem lays out Andreu's poetics in a pair of succinct statements. First she states that her impulse to write is an inveterate one that characterizes all poetry.

Escucha, dime, siempre fue de este modo,
algo falta y hay que ponerle un nombre,
creer en la poesía, y en la intolerancia de la poesía, y decir *niña*
o decir *nube, adelfa,*
sufrimiento,
decir *desesperada vena sola,* cosas así, casi reliquias, casi lejos.

(vv. 4–9; original emphasis)[54]

But then she turns poetry into a weapon as she uses it to distance herself not only from her grief and pain but also from the subject position assigned to her by society. Interrupted so as to disguise her intent, she states that her reason for writing "no es únicamente . . . / para mi soledad . . . hecha párvula muerta, / sino porque no hay forma más violenta de alejarse" (it is not only . . . / for my solitude . . . become a dead girl, / but because there is no more violent form of distancing oneself) (vv. 10–12). Again her reference to the "párvula muerta" could be a mention of her dead friend or of the speaker herself and the change in perspective that has beset her. Poetry as a form of violence distances her not only in elegiac fashion by placing words between her and loss (absence, lack) but also from the insipid, limited choices afforded by society. Poetry (writing, language) thus becomes a form of subversion.[55]

These declarations lead her into a series of poems in which she defines her position by adopting the persona (or at least trying it on for size) of the Babylonian queen Semiramis. Here we can reinterpret Sherno's reading of the ungrammatical use of the adverb *así.* The steps from one poem to the next in this series on Semiramis clearly indicate that the repeated adverb establishes a comparison elaborated by the images that follow. The fourth verse of the poem "Los labios impacientes de la noche te sanan" (The impatient lips of night cure you) emphatically asserts "es tu hora es la noche" (it is your hour it is night), ensued immediately by a pair of stanzas beginning with *así.*

The next poem introduces the figure of Semiramis predicated on elegiac repetition of *así* in verses 1, 4, and 15, and on other anaphoric concatenations. The final stanza of "Así morirán mis manos oliendo a espliego falso" (Thus my hands will die smelling of false lavender) concludes with a combination of architectural and musical imagery that segues with the appearance of Mozart two poems later, another poem beginning with the adverb *así*. The metonymic logic of the text could not be clearer, although the metaphors employed in this structure work against that logic, in accord with the speaker's subversive poetics. The choice of Semiramis as a female figure with whom to compare herself is as fortuitous as it is pointed, for it enables the speaker to unleash her anger in the healthy work of mourning. Because of her position of power, Semiramis vented her anger by decapitating her generals—an image of castration, divesting men of their power. Through her identification with Semiramis the speaker effects changes in herself manifest in her physical appearance and in her relinquishment of femininity.

> Así morirán mis manos oliendo a espliego falso
> y morirá mi cuello plástico de musgo,
> así morirá mi colonia de piano o rosa tinta. . . .
>
> . . . .
>
> así mi pelo que antes fue barba bárbara de babilonios
> decapitados por Semíramis.
> Por último mis senos gramaticalmente elípticos
> o las anchas caderas que tanto me hicieron llorar.
> Por último mis labios que demasiado feroces se volvieron . . .
>
> (vv. 1–3, 7–11)[56]

This inventory of female body parts describes her fragmentation, but also articulates her transformation. No longer will she use sweet-smelling perfumes or sachets; no longer will her hair be long and disheveled; no longer will she fret over the size of her breasts or hips. Sherno has accurately signaled the superficial alliteration of the phrase *barba bárbara de babilonios*, which communicates the speaker's disdain for the long flowing locks which, like a man's facial hair, equate—in society's view—gender with social role and power.[57] The alliteration (also apparent in the phrase *Así morirán mis manos*) is a form of repetition that adds to the elegiac veil of language.

The fascinating transition from the last stanza of "Así morirán mis manos" (Thus my hands will die) and the final verses of "Así, en pretérito pluscuamperfecto y futuro absoluto" (Thus, in the pluperfect preterit and the absolute future) attests to the transformation the speaker is undergoing. She compares her body with the bow of a violin that discordantly has no key in which to play (does not fit into any predetermined social role) but makes music of the passage of time. She characterizes this music as "verde música sacra con el verde del oro" (green sacred music with the green of gold), simultaneously sacred, golden, and atonal music. The repetition of the adjective *verde,* remitting us to the marijuana visions of hope and sickness in the opening poem of *De una niña,* is related then to Mozart's premature death. The intensity of the poet's abandonment to her expression, like Mozart's burning himself out in the intensity of his life and his music, is both sad and glorious, destructive and productive.[58]

The speaker's identification with Semiramis in this sequence enables her to release pent-up emotions connected with the death of her friend, especially her rage and her guilt. This healthy work of mourning takes place in the beautifully lyric poem "El día tiene el don de la alta seda" (The day has the gift of high silk) and in the extensive recapitulation "Cinco poemas para abdicar" (Five poems for abdicating). The former sets up various contrasts: between past and present, self and other, and two different perspectives, one innocent and the other disillusioned. These contrasts are especially evident in the repeated but altered phrase "El día *tiene* el don de la alta seda" and "El día *tuvo* el don de la alta seda" (my emphasis). This phrase may refer to a poem written by the speaker and read to/by her friend.

> El día tiene el don de la alta seda,
> pétalos desandados por el pie de la noche,
> monedas en corolas, eso dije.
> Pero se izó la nube de magnolia hasta llegar al núcleo ahogado,
> estambre eléctrico y pistilo triturado de amor,
> monedas deshojadas por el terrible cheque templario,
> o bien las brujas vírgenes prudentes
> y la plomiza nada milenaria.
>
> El día tuvo el don de la alta seda,
> amor mío, amor mío, y por eso aún escúchame,
> por eso te repito el pesado poema. . . .
>
> (vv. 1–11)[59]

The speaker mocks her former optimistic outlook expressed in the brilliant sheen of reality she perceived then but does not perceive now: the sensuality of silk, the personification of night's shadows slipping off flower petals, and the richness of the golden centers of buds.

The speaker's intrusion ("eso dije") and the change to the preterit in the repetition undercut these images. Repetition is manifest throughout the poem: not only in the phrases *amor mío, amor mío* (with its intertextual allusion), but also in the accumulation of images, again producing a vivid contrast. The progression in the first stanza from *la nube de magnolia*—the pervasive sweet aroma of the fleshy pink flowers of this tree—to *[e]l núcleo ahogado* to *estambre eléctrico, pistilo triturado de amor,* and *monedas deshojadas* focuses attention on the cloying details of sexuality disparaged again by priests and nuns (the Templar and witches to whom the speaker refers) and an emphasis on the eternal damnation to which the sensual appreciation of life leads: "la plomiza nada milenaria." One gloss for the word *cheque* would be a restraint or rein on the speaker's perspective on reality, making the connection between the repeated *monedas.* The second stanza also introduces the presence of the other in the second person, either the other girl or the self as other.

> amor mío, amor mío, tu voz que amé y que cruza
> las pupilas moradas de los puentes,
> y tu olor habitado, azul, y todo
> lo que ahora abandono y abandonas
> —este perfume fijo—,
> no sé con qué propósito,
> ni sé de qué manera clandestina. . . .
>
> (vv. 12–18)[60]

When the speaker states "te repito el pesado poema," she equates those words with "tu voz que amé." In other words, her friend inspired her perspective and encouraged her poetic expression. She recalls that voice and that perspective sadly, nostalgically, as the voice "cruza / las pupilas moradas de los puentes." Again the repetition and contrast of "abandono y abandonas" emphasize sameness and difference, presence and absence. The poem then concludes with a healthy expression of anger on the part of the speaker.

> ahora, mientras yo rompo
> la idea de tu rostro
> y continúo ignorando
> qué invierno,
> qué arteria barroca del diciembre aquél,
> qué orden despierto es el tuyo
> mientras yo vivo sola, y duermo, y te detesto.
>
> (vv. 19–25)[61]

Is "la idea de tu rostro" only a memory, or might it be a photograph, another type of mirror image? When the speaker tears up this photo (cf. the shattered mirror), she anticipates the open declaration of her anger in the final phrase of the poem, *te detesto*. This expression of anger is a sign of the healthy work of mourning through which the elegist must pass in order to restore her ego. In this regard, the other may indeed be the self as other: It is necessary for the speaker to reject and destroy her former concept of self to create a new self out of the shattered, torn pieces—or the very act of shattering and tearing, that is, of writing her rage. The final contrast between *despierto* and *duermo* expresses both the barrier between self and other and the hope of awakening to that other order. This interpretation is borne out by the elegist's guilt. The anger expressed abets the healing process of mourning but also makes the elegist aware of her guilt. She feels guilty not only for her anger, but also because she has survived and even profited from the death of the other through the production of poetry.[62]

"Cinco poemas para abdicar" (Five Poems to Abdicate) forms a significant turning point in the speaker's trajectory in dealing with her grief and coming to terms with her identity. First, we should ask what she wishes to abdicate. Given the intensity of her grief, pain, and desperation, we can assume that she is contemplating suicide, following the death of her friend. This abdication of life, however, would leave no one to maintain and proclaim the memory of her friend. After contemplating suicide, the speaker rejects (abdicates) that option. The structure of "Cinco poemas" reflects this turnaround. Following a prolonged introduction, the poem consists of five parts in the form of a parabola. The first and last poems are brief: The first is only part of a stanza (vv. 17–18), while the last rounds off the entire poem (vv. 95–101). The second and fourth poems are united in their dedication, "para mi amor," and consist of verses 19–29 and 70–94, respectively. The third and center section (vv. 30–69) is the lengthiest and the most crucial for the speaker's change of heart. The symmetry of this structure is not perfect, but with the introduction a near balance exists between the parts flanking the crucial third poem. Because of the length of this sequence, I will select specific passages from each moment to illustrate the speaker's trajectory from a desire to commit suicide (to abdicate life) to the rejection of suicide as a viable option (an abdication of abdication). The introduction announces the speaker's original intent: to leave a testimony of her reason for committing suicide. She defines her purpose at the beginning and end of the introduction as:

Cinco poemas para abdicar,
para que sean un destello terrestre en mi tránsito . . .

. . . .

Cinco poemas como cinco frutos cifrados
o como cinco velas para la travesía

(vv. 1–2, 15–16)[63]

The images of light in "destello" and "velas" marking the path of her "tránsito" or "travesía" suggest the image of a shooting star that blazes momentarily and then goes out, an emblem of the speaker's life as well as of her friend's. In contrast, her body will undergo a sense of relief from her suffering.

mientras el vaivén de mi cuerpo me dote de viejo sueño y tenga un altar
    adornado,
mientras mis ojos suspendan la aspersión del líquido más breve,
abandonen su aire lacustre y la ligereza de la lágrima cóncava en donde
    beben grullas
y otras zancudas con pie de bailarina

(vv. 3–6)[64]

The "vaivén de mi cuerpo" could indicate that she plans to hang herself (images of hanging are scattered throughout *De una niña*), creating an hypnotic effect perhaps repeated in the back-and-forth movement of her coffin down the aisle of a church to the "altar adornado" and the spiritual tranquility/repetitious monotony of a religious rite. Her eyes will no longer be filled with tears, where again the word *aspersión* resonates with the priest's hyssop sprinkling a coffin with holy water. This inversion of mourner and mourned elevates the speaker's grief to a ritual at the same time that she assuages grief by her own imagined death (another elegiac topos).[65] The perplexing images of the waterfowl drinking from the lake of her tears and their graceful, dancelike movements again connote serenity and a release from the pain (the fowls' beaks piercing her eyes). Ironically, the speaker uses marriage imagery to represent this passage from one state to another.

Cinco poemas para la marcha en el paisaje de sábana de hilo,
un páramo es encaje antepasado,
iniciales bordadas hace ya tres mil días
y alguna mancha de amor.

(vv. 11–14)[66]

These images imbricate the nuptial sheet and the winding sheet, procreation (the beginning of life) and death, as they allude to textuality. The sheet as blank piece of paper is edged with lace—the anecdotal trauma that initiates writing—and stained by blood—the friend's death and the poet's ink.

Whereas the first abdication is dedicated to "Virginia"—presumably Virginia Woolf (a great deal of whose work Andreu had read), but also a reference to virginity—"porque amó a las mujeres" (because she loved women), the second poem transfers both the love and the protest of Woolf's writings to the lost friend and their close friendship.[67] This second movement is a masterful example of repetition. The anaphora consisting of "sé bien" (I know well) and "encima de mis/tus heridas" (on top of my/your wounds) leads to the final iteration of the entire phrase "Pero cuando me duerma ya no te querré" (But when I go to sleep I will no longer love you). The beauty of repeating but varying the repetition by changing the line arrangement is prefigured by variations in the imagery and the split and oscillation between "*mis* heridas" and "*tus* heridas." Simultaneous with the suturing and healing action of the repetition, there is a widening of the rift, so that the equivocality and interchangeability of the final phrases capture the contrast of similarity and difference in self and other. Thus "me duerma" refers to sleep and death, the involuntary and the voluntary (suicide), that which is desired for rest/alleviation and for release/surrender. In this way the poem briefly recapitulates what has brought the protagonist to this moment of wavering as she contemplates imitating (repeating) the action of her friend.

In this regard, the third movement or "poem" is pivotal. This section revolves around the presence of another female figure, "una institutriz" (an instructress) who imposes and wedges herself between the two friends and even invades their private thoughts. The speaker pleads, "Dile que no se meta en los salones / y los llene de gafas estrujadas. / Ay, dile que no espante los espejos de mirada niña" (Tell her not to go into the parlors / and to fill them with crumpled eyeglasses. / Ay, tell her not to frighten the mirrors with their childish gaze). The portrayal of this woman suggests a comparison with Bernarda Alba. Bernarda had internalized the predominant patriarchal attitudes toward sex and pleasure in general, leading to the suicide (by hanging) of her daughter Adela and her denial of that fact.[68] In contrast, the speaker sees that if she too commits suicide, she will be denying her friend's death and succumbing to the forces that resulted in that event. But significantly, the speaker vehemently asserts her separation from this woman's attitudes when she repeats, "Yo no dije: ¡silencio!" (I didn't say: *silence!*) three times. (Curiously, Bernarda

Alba and Blanca Andreu share the same initials: B. A.). Therefore, when she returns to addressing her friend in the fourth movement, paralleling the second movement, she modifies her repetition in a remarkable way:

El cuarto es para mi amor.
Amor mío, amor, amor, amor,
sé bien que no te escupirá mi sueño y que tu cuello no será sajado
por el filo último de mi sueño,
que no te insultará el hiriente corazón de mi sueño,
porque si duermo ya no te querré.

(vv. 70–75)[69]

Here she says "*If* I sleep" rather than "*When* I sleep." The confrontation with the possibility of her own death, by her own hand, illuminates the treachery and the cowardice of that act, and she resolves to continue fighting for what her friend represented for her.

Y por eso voy a asesinar
con la virgen cuchilla barbitúrica
la muchedumbre de heroicos locos que entonan para mí la pesadilla y el
   bostezo,
amor mío, sin asomar por la ventana
fuegos viejos, frescas cenizas,
familias errantes de soles.

(vv. 80–85)[70]

By recuperating and recontextualizing through repetition (especially the repetition of the phrase *Sé bien*), the speaker signals the change that has occurred in her. She has not lost her grief, but her grief has taken a new direction:

Sé bien que galoparé en negro
porque negro es el color de los sueños,
negras las manos de la intimidad,
y sin espuelas, y sin bridas,
porque las espuelas son el poder, la aberración, estrellas
de tijera y abismo.

(vv. 89–94)[71]

The final section of this dynamic poem is "para mi caballo" (for my horse), that is, the speaker's poetry, which will not "take wing" on the death of her friend and of her former self: "esqueleto de mi antigua paloma" (skeleton of my former dove). "Cinco poemas para abdicar" is a pivotal moment in the speaker's work of mourning where she rejects suicide. This rejection is subtly reinforced by a brief reference to the Romanian philosopher E. M. Ciroan in the following poem. Cioran has written extensively on life, death, and suicide and in general seems opposed to suicide.[72]

Rejecting the idea of her own suicide does not exempt the speaker from dealing with her friend's death. On the contrary. Now she must come to terms with that event in spite of the pain and anguish she experiences upon confronting it. But submitting to that process will also strengthen her. The final half of *De una niña* is divided into three stages. The first is introduced by the poem "*Maggio,*" which initiates an emphasis on time throughout the first and third of these divisions. The second consists of the two poems—clearly one unit—separated from the other by epigraphs from Virgil and Quevedo. The final section returns to an emphasis on time and concludes with the openly elegiac "Para Olga." However, this progression is *not* linear. As the elegiac repetitions indicate, the speaker undergoes several fits and starts as she attempts to gain control of the emotions provoked by the absence of her friend.

Kristeva's concept of the abject dovetails with the elegiac model at this point. If in the loss of the loved one the mourner reenacts the initial experience of separation and loss of the (m)other, to a certain extent the (m)other's body becomes the idealized *corps propre* and the child adopts the role of the deject. Because of the equivocal nature of the female phenomenon of separation yet identification, the girl sees her own body ambivalently as both *corps propre* and abject. She at once exalts in and despairs of that discovery, in accord with the definition of identity as sameness and difference. The implications for the speaker are that, as a female, she must participate vicariously in the death of her friend, with all the physical and sexual horrors involved, yet as an individual, she struggles to assert her individuality. Both positions thus entail the *corps propre* and the abject in a complicated chiasmus of sameness and difference. The enigmatic poem "*Maggio*" exemplifies this dilemma.

In the elegiac tradition the month of May is the quintessential topos of spring renewal and flowering rebirth, the natural cycle that restores life and fecundity.[73] In the Catholic tradition it is the month of Mary, the mother of whom Kristeva has written.[74] But the Italian title undercuts these idyllic visions. In its stead the cycle described is menstruation. If the events underlying these poems took place while these girls were at school, it could be that the speaker experienced her first menstrual periods there. During this time her friend and confidante would have been much more sympathetic and celebratory of her entry into the adult reproductive cycle than the intrusive, policing nuns would have been. It is at this crucial moment, however, that her friend disappears and their friendship effectively comes to an end. In addition, the speaker's awakening to adult sexuality in her own body is closely related to the death of her friend. Menstruation is abject. Eros and Thanatos, like the *corps propre* and the abject, co-exist in each of the two young women, the self and the other. We can perceive these forces at play in the opening stanzas of the poem.

> Muerte en el tiempo grávido de palomas marchitas,
> en el lacrimatorio que me ofrece la maloliente tinta de mayo.
> Agonía del cauce en mi cintura y en la cintura de veleros negros,
> agonía de una ojiva de agua,
> mayo, mayo, poema oval, resplandor y salto al vacío
> una estrella de nervios que no tiene piedad.
>
> Mayo con astas locas, mayo ciervo de fiebre,
> mayo hocico de piélago me mordió el cinturón de la temperatura,
> mayo de fiebres malvas y ciervo emborrachado de glóbulos celestes
> en el sol tembloroso del ventrículo,
> pequeño ciervo solo que devoto bebió
> toda la sed dorada en las arterias.
>
> (vv. 1–12)[75]

The jump-cut from the title to the first word of the poem immediately establishes tension and destabilizes the readers' expectations of May. Death here refers to the sudden absence of the trusted friend and to the onset of menstruation. The "palomas marchitas" are the girls, perhaps exhausted by the rigors of the academic year and a lack of sunshine during the winter. In a similar vein "la maloliente tinta de mayo"—alliteration also functions as elegiac repetition—could be the teachers' red ink, correcting student work, or menstrual blood. The stress of both facets of her life (the external and the internal), compounded by the absence and therefore the lack of moral support of her rebellious friend, brings the speaker to tears and agony (physical and mental): "una estrella de nervios que no tiene piedad."

The concatenation of images introduced anaphorically by the word *mayo* not only sustains the tension between vitality and fear of death but also captures the feverish, dizzying maelstrom of interaction between the speaker's mind and body. The speaker feels overwhelmed by the very real physical effects of this new situation as well as by the confusion and lack of comprehension it generates emotionally (hormonally). Note the proliferation of images describing her disorientation: *agonía, salto al vacío, astas locas, fiebre, temperatura, fiebres malvas, emborrachado, tembloroso, la sed dorada.* In one sense these images depict the arrival of spring after a long winter: warmth, sunlight, sap rising in the plant life, an itching to romp and play, an excess of energy. But excess in the imagery pushes the tone over the edge.

In her work of mourning the speaker must confront the sequence of events that have led to her current need to seek consolation. "*Maggio*" is the beginning of that sequence, entailing several factors that have a bearing on the speaker's psyche. She even welcomed illness and the possibility of death as a way of escaping from her loneliness by accentuating it. The next three stanzas begin with the phrase "Quise una enfermedad" (I wanted illness) and the repeated "Quise la muerte" (I wanted death). The finality and even violence of the preterit tense emphasizes her desperation as she tries to cling to some stability ("un áncora cierta" [a sure anchor]) in the chaos of her world. Her reference to Bach here has multifarious meanings. While his fugue is a dizzying display of his musical (mathematical, conceptual) skill, the speaker wishes to flee, to stop the crazy confusion. Bach also evokes previous mentions of Ana Magdalena, his wife, for whom he wrote simple compositions to instruct her in music, but also of the many children they conceived, an ironic allusion to fecundity and the frequent sexual activity required by this patriarch and pater familias. The speaker then enters upon a series of images of eyes and the gaze. This passage serves as a bridge into the climax of the poem.

> Quise la muerte para unos ojos sin norte,
> para unos ojos de brújula sacra,
> para los ojos jóvenes que se izan
> a leer la estrella agreste de las diez.
>
> Ojos, los ojos míos,
> o bien ojos litúrgicos agrandados de antorchas,
> los ojos que grabaron con iniciales góticas
> en el alma guerrera de un niño de diez años,
> ojos de lirio helado en alfileres:
> clavados en el mar de los taxidermistas.
>
> Pero hablemos de ojos que desvanecen
> las lámparas sin ti. . . .
>
> (vv. 21–32)[76]

As many psychoanalytic theorists contend, "the gaze is a fundamental part of the formation of subjectivity. . . . We constantly seek the gaze of some other . . . in order to confirm our sense of presence. . . . [T]he theory of the gaze . . . involves not simply looking at, but also the idea that the viewer is looked at and positioned in a certain way."[77] Because these eyes may be both the speaker's and the other's in the mirror, it is clear that the speaker is seeking confirmation of her self at this time. She desires to latch onto an assurance of the *corps propre,* but her eyes are "sin norte": She cannot locate her direction in the eyes of the other.[78]

Andreu's metaphoric sequence ends in an enigmatic duality where it is unclear if *ojos* or *lámparas* is the subject of the verb *desvanecen.* This ambivalence also leaves the prepositional phrase *sin ti* dangling: Is it that the speaker is unable to accomplish this feat without the aid of the other; or does she in fact achieve it in the other's absence? Do her eyes overpower the light of the lamps, or are they overpowered? Is the *corps propre* formulated or dissolved, incorporated or rejected? This subjectivity, "defined, determined, and disputed," is accompanied by the speaker's act of writing:

> hablemos mientras piso descalza en esta línea novicia y con ojeras,
> mientras escribo versos como algas votivas,
> como alambres de lágrimas, mientras siento tu noche y dinastía.
> (vv. 34–36)[79]

Each of the three phrases introduced with *mientras* includes a contrast: innocence versus awareness, water versus fire, absence versus dominating presence. The final stanza then reaches a crescendo of images that can be read as either exaltation or dejection. The stanza opens with an echo of the "Amor mío" motif of death and resurrection, presaging other repetitions and recontextualizations in these verses.

> Amor, he roto el níquel de tu palabra desventurada y perfecta.
> Amor, dolidas crines de arcángeles caballos se peinan con colonia
>   de tristeza,
> porque es mayo, mayo poema oval, mayo muerte levante . . .
> (vv. 37–41)[80]

Instead of or besides addressing her absent friend, the speaker could also be addressing Eros, the personification of love and of her ego. Along with the contradictory adjectives *desventurada y perfecta,* the act of breaking and the contrast between the metallic and the intangible quality ascribed to *palabra* could be announcing a breakthrough, a triumph over her grief, a first step toward consolation. But she could also be expressing her frustration and impotence. The reprise of the winged-horse imagery could be a regression to sterile, infantile, self-deluding perspectives, or the reinscribing of that original impulse in a more mature, poignant expression. May—and the poem "*Maggio*"—turns back upon itself in a parabola rather than the sterile, perfect circle; and it is simultaneously "mayo muerte levante," death and resurrection, *corps propre* and dejection, as the lack of punctuation indicates. Even the final verses, after and including the emphatic repetition of *muerte para,* loops back to the beginning verse of "*Maggio.*" But does it achieve stasis or a breakthrough?

> muerte en el tiempo grávido de palomas marchitas,
> muerte para sus travesías delicadas,
> y para la tormenta loca como una abadesa loca,
> muerte para la ropa íntima que estremecía a Baudelaire,
> muerte para el desnudo vino verde,
> para la piedra en celo y el menstruo celeste de mayo
> y el grito equino de las madrugadas de mayo,
> muerte para la angustia caligráfica ahogada
> en el lacrimatorio que me ofrece la maloliente tinta de mayo.
>
> (vv. 46–54)[81]

While she has repeated, the speaker has also recontextualized, similar to the child Freud observed playing with the spool and substituting the words *fort* and *da* for his absent mother and thus gaining control of his emotions. The verses intervening between "muerte en el tiempo grávido de palomas marchitas" and "en el lacrimatorio que me ofrece la maloliente tinta de mayo" as well as those intervening between the first statement (vv. 1–2), interrupt, separate, form an abyss between the speaker and her friend at the same time that they expand, substantiate, and individuate the poet as subject.[82]

This motif becomes insistent in the passing and the stasis of time throughout the final poems. Following "*Maggio,*" the next poem begins with the repeated *Agosto, agosto,* the pivotal month in which the speaker learns of the other's suicide, as the reference to Ophelia in the next poem suggests. The speaker then moves forward to September and oscillates back to August, although we learn that only if we look at the table of contents. Time advances and then loops back upon itself to recapitulate the major theme.

The poem "Muerte pájaro príncipe, un pájaro es un ángel inmaduro" (Death bird prince, a bird is an immature angel), along with its introductory companion piece, stands out from the text visibly and tonally. Separated from the rest of the poems by framing epigraphs from Virgil and Quevedo, these poems represent the only moment of vulnerability, resignation, and release in the entire collection. It is in effect a poignant lament, a paean not only for her friend but for all the youth like her friend and herself who must experience loss—of a friend, of their own life (suicide), or of innocence.

The opening line and much of the subsequent imagery maintain a double edge, but here sincere grief triumphs—with irony—over sarcasm. The progression "Muerte pájaro príncipe" equates the three terms because of the lack of punctuation. A prince evokes a fairy-tale setting; and given the sexual innuendoes pervading the entire text, equating death with a prince posits just the right degree of sarcasm and disillusionment. It elevates the loss but also speaks of disillusionment (cf. the prince who comes to the rescue of Sleeping Beauty). Yes, the silly prince Death has come, but the outcome is not a happy one: They do not live happily ever after.

The same ambivalence resides in the beautiful phrase "un pájaro es un ángel inmaduro." A bird is capable of flight (of rising into the air) and has a beautiful song (to praise God), but it is still earth-bound, not quite attaining the status of an angel, as her friend will never attain adulthood. The conversion of the dead friend into a bird with the positive marks of flight and song (release and joy) represents a typical elegiac convention of metamorphosis into a natural context. The light touches of sarcasm in the words *príncipe* and *inmaduro* modify the traditional convention, personalizing it and saving it from sentimentality. The following verses then extend the speaker's lament to all of her generation.

> Y así, hablaré de tus manos que se alejan y de las manos de lo
>   hermosísimo ardiendo,
> pequeño dios con nariz de ciervo, hermano mío, héroes de alma
>   entrecortada,
> niñas de oro hipodérmico que nunca creen morir
>
> (vv. 2–5)[83]

First, the duality of *héroes* and *niñas* (later *madonas*) will reappear as an inclusive gesture that gathers all the others under the "sign" of her friend. The opening progression expands into another unfolding of imagery from "tus manos" to "lo hermosísimo ardiendo," "pequeño dios," and "hermano mío" (still the prince/bird/angel) to encompass the other boys and girls. What stands out, though, are the future tense and the image of hands as wings. The speaker commits herself to proclaiming (through her poetry and through the living of her life) and confronting the events of life, whatever may befall her. It is ironic, nonetheless, that the future defers those actions. The speaker is determined but places in doubt the completion of that confrontation. She undercuts her determination as she declares it, thus questioning the efficacy of words and her resolve. Again, this adds just the right note of duplicity to prevent her resolution from sounding like a crusade.

The image of the hands will be taken up again in the following poem. "Hundiré mis manos aquí, en este mar que no existe" (I will immerse my hands here, in this sea that does not exist), where the poet reaffirms her commitment. But here the hands belong to the dead friend and are comparable to the wings of the bird and the angel. This multifarious trope (at once synecdoche, metonym, and metaphor) refers to the work accomplished by a life. The powerful effect that the lost friend had on the speaker was like the wings of the bird and the blazing brightness of an angel. The mention of the nose of a deer gently demystifies the image of the little god but also, in keeping with the abject, adds a note of tender reality that prevents the *corps propre* from seeming too ideal. For the speaker wishes to convince her contemporaries of the need to confront these issues of disillusionment, death, loss, and disappointment. If she idealizes the loss too much, she will only justify, intimidate, and provoke her peers' escape into alcohol, sex, and drugs. Capturing the right tone to persuade them of her viewpoint requires a delicate balance. The next verses in the poem elaborate on this idea by repeating and varying the opening verses.

qué aguda la pupila y el filo de los dedos encendiendo la muerte mientras
    un ángel sobrevuela y pasa de largo
con el pico de plata y de ginebra,
labios del mediodía resuelto en ave sobre tus manos que se alejan y mis
    manos
y las manos del pequeño ciervo de aire griego salvaje, hermano mío,
y las manos sin venas de los héroes, de las madonas amnésicas.

(vv. 5–13)[84]

Softened by the lack of exclamation marks and by the chaining of this sentence with the previous one, the description of loss and the pain of seeing one's hopes or happiness escape like a precious bird is sad and beautiful. Knowledge is both illuminating and painful ("qué aguda la pupila"). The sight of it pains the eyes, the gaze, and the sound of its song, compared with silver and capable of making one drunk, is metaphor for the lips whose warmth slips away ("mediodía resuelto en ave"). The repetition with variation of the phrase *sobre tus manos que se alejan*, the image of the deer, and the boys and girls give the sensation of holding onto that which slips away. The elaboration of the image of the deer hints at the myth of Actaeon who surprised Diana in her bath and was pursued to death by his own hounds.[85] The gendering of the traditional myth may seem inappropriate since *De una niña* seems to reverse the positions: The lost friend learned too much and was hounded to her death, but the speaker only hints at the parameters of the myth so as to convince not only other women but also men of the pervasively human nature of these events.

Moreover, the phrases *las manos sin venas de los héroes, de las madonas amnésicas* are ambivalent and reinforce the earlier instances of these images. For example, if at first the heroes have an "alma entrecortada," here their hands are "sin venas." Are their souls (their spirits) split in two, totally riven by disillusionment and disappointment? Or are they brought up short, not yet fully developed? Are their hands without veins, lacking blood, dead and worthless? Or are they innocent, not careworn, but young and smooth? The images describing the "niñas"/"madonas" are equally ambivalent and slightly ironic. Are these girls totally blank-faced, ingenuous virgins? Or are they capable of future motherhood that will help them forget the painful events of the past? This ambivalence transfers to the speaker in the final verses.

Mis alas de dolor robadas por tus manos, amor mío, corazón mío pintado
    de blanco,
mis alas de dolor con botellas agónicas y líquidos que disuelven la vida,
y los labios que te aman en mí y en la convulso,
y la música en trompas delgadísimas, trompetas peraltadas, columnas
    niñas, qué
sobreagudo el do,
la mirada más alta y la más alta queja,
muerte pájaro príncipe volando,
un pájaro es un ángel inmaduro.

(vv. 10–20)[86]

Are her wings painful because they were taken away when the other left, making her life seem worthless and incapable of action and soaring elation? Or has the other now taken away the speaker's pain by dint of the very characteristics that made her loss so painful? By forcing herself to accomplish the work of mourning, the speaker has become more like the other; she has assimilated those characteristics that the other brought out most strongly in her, and she has surpassed the other. Both her pain and her strength proceed from the other, but they are and have always been within her, her own (*corps propre*).

When she then employs the imagery of the music, the phrase *qué / sobreagudo el do*, echoing the earlier phrase *qué aguda la pupila*, is ambivalent. Inasmuch as the eyes (*pupila*) and the ears are marginal orifices, they pertain to the abject. The speaker builds her own sense of self (the tonic *do*) on the absence of the (m)other, her female friend. If the sounding of the tonic is sharp (rather than flat, in the musical sense), it is because of the pain of loss and the exaltation of finding the self, as the fanfare of the trumpets announces. Recall that *do* may be found at the top or the bottom of the scale and represents both the starting point and the end point of a musical composition.

The very last verses are a masterstroke of elegiac repetition with variation. First, *mirada* is juxtaposed with *queja*, but the adjectival phrase *más alta* reverses position. Thus both phrases are duplicitous and equivocal: A high gaze expresses the loftiness of one's goals and the impossibility of attaining them; the loudest complaint is the most painful and the most consolatory. Then, when the poet repeats the opening verses, she closes the poem in a circle as she opens it in a spiral by means of the variations. She adds the gerund *volando,* indicating both that which slips away and that which soars, and she breaks the line into two verses. In this way, she instantiates change, rupture, brokenness, separation, as well as continuation, growth, transition, and new insight. Insofar as she is able to reach out to others and offer herself as a model, she has internalized the *corps propre* of the other, affirming their sameness. But in her rejection of suicide and her continued grief, dejection, and the work of mourning, she asserts difference.

An epigraph from Quevedo introduces a sequence of three poems where the image of the sea predominates and the temporal emphasis resumes before culminating in the final poem, "Para Olga." The choice of Quevedo is an interesting one because of his ability to write either stinging sarcasm or profound, heartfelt meditations on love and death. This duality is indicative of the speaker's newfound ability to embrace both the *corps propre* and the abject without synthesis but constantly in immanent but tolerable conflict (the *sujet-en-procès*). This particular quote speaks of comfort provided for "tu mudo pueblo" —the speaker's generation—by honoring distant seas. If we read this image as the traditional symbol of death (cf. Manrique and the elegiac tradition), we understand that the speaker can expect to receive consolation by confronting the death of her friend as an inevitability. This recognition marks her entry into an adult perspective on life. As she says and repeats in the first poem after Quevedo's words, "Hundiré mis manos aquí, en este mar que no existe. . . . Hundiré mis manos en noche que no existe sobre un mar que no existe" (I will immerse my hands here in this sea that does not exist. . . . I will immerse my hands in night that does not exist above the sea that does not exist). We can gloss this sea as her memory of the lost friend and/or as the source of new life.

As already noted, this poem reinstates an emphasis on temporal progression from "abril" to "agosto" and finally to the quintessentially elegiac month of "noviembre 1981."[87] Because of its importance in the elegiac context of *De una niña,* "En las cuadras del mar duermen términos blancos" (In the stables of the sea blank/white terms sleep) warrants attention. This poem is another that relies largely on repetition and a circular/spiral structure for its effect. Its structure is more balanced and symmetrical in imitation of the speaker's balance between grief and consolation. The first, third, and fifth stanzas all begin with a similar phrase: "En las cuadras del mar" and "En las caballerizas del mar, el mar se ahoga con su métrica ardiente" (In the stables of the sea and In the stables of the sea she drowns with her ardent metrics). The second and fourth stanzas begin with the preposition *Entre,* and there is a progression from bird imagery in the second to the angel in the fourth. All these stanzas are approximately the same length (five verses), with a slight irregularity in the final two.

As a result of this structure, we can see that the "stables of the sea" are the verses of poetry itself where the poet-speaker pours her grief, but from which she receives consolation and new life. This is also a proclamation of her poetics: She fits her expression within the traditional parameters of elegy, but her words are not the sterile repetition of *términos blancos* but a much more fluid and dynamic entity, as she informs us in the first stanza.

> En las cuadras del mar duermen términos blancos,
> la espuma que crepita, la droga hecha de liquen que mueve a olvidar:
> en los establos del mar reina la urraca, la intriga y la discordia,
> nueva versión del agua y del bajo oleaje,
> nueva versión del agua derramada desde todas las tierras y las tapias del
>   mundo.
>
> (vv. 1–8)[88]

The "new version" she announces is not a drug that urges one to forget one's pain, but is ruled by "la urraca, la intriga y la discordia." The magpie is a scavenger that feeds on carrion, the remnants of death, to sustain its life. The poet insists on building her expression on intrigue and discord, the primary motives that she will pick apart with her verse. The water of this sea derives from the rain that falls universally—the tears of grief. Again, this use of natural imagery to describe grief is conventionally elegiac, but the speaker's images of spilling (*agua derramada*) and the barriers separating one person from another (*tapias*), especially those of death, are rich and fresh.

When the next stanza begins with the word *Entre* and comes between the framing first and third stanzas, it is apparent that the speaker probes more deeply into herself to find new images. Yet, her employment of the verb *callar* defines through negation.

Entre los muros del mar callan los abedules que poseen los símbolos del
   mirlo,
la última voz del bosque,
calla la yedra bárbara que envenenaba ciervos leves como navajas,
el roble boreal,
arrendajos dormidos como libros celestes, incendios y lechuzas de la grava
   marina.

(vv. 6–13)[89]

The poet's song silences the birches and the ivy because of their control over the "mirlo, / la última voz del bosque" and the tendency to poison "ciervos leves como navajas, / el roble boreal, / arrendajos . . ., incendios y lechuzas. . . ." These natural elements may seem to produce negative expressions, dark, raspy, cold, but stifling these voices is counterproductive. The poet validates these voices—and her own; even though they speak harshly, their words are absolutely necessary and even celestial. The word play in *celestes* describes the jays' color but modifies *libros,* a self-referenciality. Other examples of the poet's original use of language appear in the next stanza.

En las caballerizas del mar, el mar se ahoga con su métrica ardiente,
la flora, las ojivas y las bocas del mar,
concilio de castaños en vilo verdeherido,
y alguien desde muy lejos abdicando, andando desde lejos a morir entre
   lejanas ramas empapadas:
alguien desde muy lejos esperando la flora, las ojivas y las bocas del mar.

(vv. 11–18)[90]

If the sea is an image of death, death drowns in the acceptance of death. The "alguien" is the lost loved one who finally finds a home and rest because the mourner is willing to surrender to the work of mourning. The masterful repetition in the last verse links the second and fourth verses of this stanza in a fractal-like repetition of the link between the second and fourth stanzas and forms a turning point from the negative to the positive. That trope illuminates the positive aspect of the images in the next stanza.

Entre noviembre y cascos y corolas
el ángel de los remos camina ensangrentado con olor a madera,
con pupila de pájaro el otoño gravita,
acecha el ángel de los cables y las oscuras verjas, los reductos malignos,
y el ángel de la arcilla, matriz de zarza,
polen y estela de placenta que en otoño florece en muerte.

(vv. 16–23)[91]

This stanza consists of six verses, an overspilling of the consolation and alleviation of the poet-speaker as mourner, and what a final line that spills over! But first, "el ángel de los remos" is the inspiration that impels the poet-mourner to express her grief. The angel is bloodied, but with the aroma of freshly cut wood, redolent of sap/life. Passing through a series of transformations or revelations of different capacities, this angel is the autumn that "con pupila de pájaro . . . gravita," "el ángel de los cables," and "el ángel de la arcilla." These three images descend from flight (height, the superior vantagepoint of the bird), through the cables uniting high and low, down to the clay of the earth. But this decomposition—the death of the loved one—produces a flowering. Yes, the plant that flowers is a thorny one (*zarza*), a characteristic captured visibly and auditorily in the alliteration of *matriz de zarza*. But in typically elegiac imagery—the pollen, the wake of the placenta, and the flowering of autumn—the cyclical movement into winter (*muerte*) foretells the coming of spring. This image subtly addresses the immortality of the loved one through the poetic expression in addition to the rebirth of the mourner through the work of grieving as a new person, a new subjectivity and individuality, and as a poet, symbolized in the image of the robin, a songbird. The relationship between life and death is as problematic as that between the *corps propre* and the dejected person, between the female child and her mother. Note in the final stanza the magnificent alternation of *en* and *entre* as well as the reprise of earlier images and verses.

En las caballerizas del mar se ahoga con su métrica ardiente.
Entre los muros del mar callan los abedules que poseen los símbolos del
    mirlo avisador.
En las cuadras del mar, como en la muerte,
duermen términos blancos.

(vv. 22–27)[92]

In this repetition of the opening verse of stanza 3, the comma has been omitted. Whether intentional or not, the absence of the comma suggests a more fluid transition and a more permeable interface between life and death, death and life. The repetition of the opening verse of stanza 2 includes the variation of the additional adjective *avisador*, pointing to the importance of the poet's function. And the final verse returns to the first of the poem, but inserts the phrase *como en la muerte* and breaks the line in two parts (cf. "Muerte pájaro príncipe"). This marvelous exhibition of the poet's skill interacts with the rest of the poem in a play of similarity and difference. Ironically, there is no allusion to the fourth stanza. But that is precisely the point. Unless the poet addresses death, loss, and grief by delving into the depths of herself, transgressing the norms of society, she will not attain immortality.

The fragments of the mirror have a new pattern! Still shattered, the mirror now reflects a different image. While the mirror as other may reflect the self, the speaker-protagonist reminds us that one always has the power to manipulate, to (re)arrange, and to change the shape of the image. Concomitant with the declaration of her poetics, the poet-speaker defines her personal identity.

Appropriately, the volume closes with a return to a reflection of/on the other in the mirror in "Para Olga," the final poem. The choice of this name provides a convincing clue for the comprehensive interpretation of *De una niña*. This name may be an oblique allusion to the oldest daughter of Nicholas II, the last tsar of Russia. In his novel *La flaqueza del bolchevique*, Lorenzo Silva summarizes the significance of this character. The narrator posits the situation of the Grand Duchess Olga when he ponders: "Siempre me he preguntado qué sintió aquella niña, ya muchacha, cuando vio al primer mujik con un fusil irrumpir en sus aposentos para joderle la nube de tul en que había estado viviendo hasta entonces" (I have always wondered what that girl, already a young woman, felt when she saw the first mujick with his rifle break into the rooms to defile the cloud of tulle in which she had been living until then).[93] In addition to prefiguring the death of a young woman in Silva's novel, "la nube de tul" to which the narrator refers is also applicable to the innocent world of the speaker of Andreu's poems and to her friend Olga. It seems, then, that the name Olga is symbolic of the loss of innocence and the death of a former self caused by the violent clash between two radically different worlds.

The first half of this poem is an extensive stanza predicated on the repetition of the word *niña* as a type of invocation of the other (the lost friend and the former self) and variations of commands "to speak," particularly "dilo," the same command that appears in the first poem of the collection. This stanza functions as a rejection of what is past/passed/passé. The second half of the poem consists of an alternation of the repetitions *Definitivamente* and *Y así*. These two halves invert the concept of a split in the self in each half.

The undivided extension of the first stanza and the word *niña* that imbricates self and other, old self and new self, in truth draws the line between past and present, self and other, and underlines the concept of identity as sameness and difference. The hyperbolic imagery of the opening invocation has a decidedly sarcastic thrust.

> Niña de greyes delicadamente doradas,
> niña obsesión de la cigüeña virgen
> con mechones de plumas de damasco
> que salpicaban muerte,
> de la cigüeña loca con alones
> de estricnina dorada
> que viajaba dejándote un corpóreo perfume,
> un pulcro olor a lilas, y a dorados y rudos sueños.
>
> (vv. 1–8)[94]

Repetition of the word *dorado,* the sumptuous sensorial quality of *mechones de plumas de damasco,* and the overblown evocation of the elegiac commonplace of lilacs provide insights into the speaker's sarcasm. This may even be a depiction of the deceased's funeral, attended by a chorus of angels and haloes (*greyes delicadamente doradas*), the Virgin Mary (*la cigüeña virgen*), and the deceased's grieving but hypocritical mother (*la cigüeña loca*) who, it seems, exaggerates the dead girl's innocence and tragedy in her excessive grief. The contrast creates a false image with regard to the speaker's remembrance of her friend. When she subsequently refers to Selene, she highlights the ambivalence. Selene (also called Artemis and Diana) is goddess of the moon, a virgin goddess of the hunt, fields, and forests, but also the patron of fertility, childbirth, and women's transitions. If the speaker's friend could play the sonatinas of Clementi, she also read "malévolos libros de Tom Wolfe." The speaker's invective increases in the following verses, evoking the opening poem.

> Niña de inexistente concierto,
> niña de crueles sonatinas y malévolos libros de Tom Wolfe,
> o de encajes de brujas para vendar las llagas de los corzos heridos,
> de ciervos vulnerados asomados en los oteros místicos,
> en los sitios así.
> Niña pluscuamperfecta, niña que nunca fuimos,

dilo ahora,
dilo ahora tú, ahora que es tan tarde,
pronuncia el torvo adagio alarido,
pronúnciame la lágrima caballo,
la saliva morada de la yegua,
la vergüenza del potro que se tendió a tus pies despertando la espuma.

(vv. 12–26)[95]

Although the phrase *Niña pluscuamperfecta* may refer to the girl's death, it also can mean a "has been": The speaker mocks the overblown innocent image of her friend. Her inclusion of herself in the plural verb form *niña que nunca fuimos* implies both her rejection of the false image and her identification with her friend. Because of her bitterness and her revelation of hypocrisy, her commands to speak sound like a challenge as much as a plea, inverting the relationship found in the first poem, where she says, "Di que querías ser caballo esbelto." The juxtaposition of *lágrima* with *caballo,* the adjective *morada* modifying *saliva,* and the word *vergüenza* sharpen the speaker's "dig" and her rejection of the abject. Her mockery becomes bitter in the following verses.

Declama abandonada las palabras de antaño,
sombra de Juan Ramón: *Soledad, te soy fiel.*
Declama desdeñosa las palabras de antaño,
pero no aquella estrofa cortesana,
no hables de reinas blancas como un lirio,
nieves, y Juana ardiendo,
y la melancolía entretejida
del querido Villon,
sino los verbos claros donde poder beber el líquido más triste,
jarros de mar y alivio, ahora que ya es tan tarde,
alza párvula voz y eco albacea y canta:
Dile a la vida que la recuerdo,
que la recuerdo.

(vv. 24–37; original emphasis)[96]

Here she quotes Juan Ramón Jiménez's cloying verse ("Soledad, te soy fiel" [Loneliness, I am faithful to you]) and rejects the fairy-tale figure of Snow White ("no hables de reinas blancas como un lirio, / nieves") and the martyr Joan of Arc or the grieving queen Juana la Loca. She then frames the two female figures with another poet, François Villon, whose "Testament" is an *apologia pro vita sua.* In contrast with her rejection of those false, shallow, outdated (male) expressions of sadness and options for females, the speaker then urges her friend "*Dile a la vida que la recuerdo / que la recuerdo.*" Three aspects of this declaration stand out. First, the speaker insists that the other speak, but the other then urges her (the speaker) to say these words. Who is self, who is other? There is separation and distance as well as complete identification and fusion! Next, the pronoun *la* is ambivalent, referring to *vida* and *niña*. The referent is either equivalent to *vida* or names something quite different. And finally, the repetition "que la recuerdo": Although the words are exactly the same, the meaning changes entirely because they shift from one mouth to the other. Does the speaker hope that her friend remembers her? Or does she wish to let her friend know that she (the speaker) remembers her (the friend, her former self whom she has divested or is in the process of divesting from herself). This phrase marks the threshold into the second half of the poem with its four stanzas and its alternation in mirror image.

Whereas the first half of the poem is one seamless stanza yet stresses difference through rejection, the second half is fragmented by stanzaic breaks yet defines similarity and the embracing of the other (the *corps propre*). In the very act of lamenting the inadequacy of her words (or anyone else's), the speaker tells us who her friend was and that she has introjected that image.

> Definitivamente se extravía en un bosque naciente esta muerte pequeña,
> el brote del cometa detenido,
> esto que nadie salva,
> joven volcán de huesos y ráfaga novicia
> hecha de pájaro y de párpado y de ola pensante
> que ningún libro estela,
> ningún libro estofado de oro solar de Italia,
> ningún libro de lava
> viene a sellar por mí.
>
> (vv. 37–46)[97]

In an astounding series of images the speaker describes her friend as a "bosque naciente," "cometa," "volcán," "ráfaga," "pájaro," "párpado," "ola," "estela," "oro solar," and "lava." Although she insists that no book can leave even a "trace" (*estela*) of these characteristics, no book can serve as a "stele" (*estela*) to substitute for the lost friend, the speaker has left this mark, these words, this book, and she even feels stimulated by the impossibility of her task.

> Y así la muerte tantas veces escrita
> se me vuelve radiante,
> y puedo hablar

del deseo y del lacre rubio y ciego en los faros,
del cadáver quimera de la tripulación.

$$\text{(vv. 46–50)}^{98}$$

To write a new elegy when so many other voices have already done so seems like an impossible task for the poet, but that is exactly what she has accomplished. It is ironically thanks to so many other elegists and elegies that she has been able to compose her own. Because she asserts her individuality, she joins the others. She is the same as they because she has dared to be different.

The final two stanzas invert the repetition in mirror-image fashion beginning with "Y así la muerte" and "Definitivamente," respectively. First she shows that she has converted the death of her friend into myth.

Y así la muerte
se convierte en historia de los niños marinos
encerrados en urnas floriformes,
o aquella niña muda que se ahorcó
con las cuerdas boreales del arpa
porque tenía en la lengua un veneno nupcial.

$$\text{(vv. 51–56)}^{99}$$

Here we have probably the most straightforward statement of the circumstances of the friend's death. Apparently, she preferred suicide to a forced marriage because of pregnancy ("niños marinos / encerrados en urnas floriformes"). The urns represent both the womb and the tomb. By making the implement of her suicide "las cuerdas boreales del arpa," the speaker suggests the mythical proportions of the topos. The last stanza then presents an incredible example of repetition and variation.

Definitivamente me extravío acunando camadas de raros epitafios,
niña de grey dorada,
diré a la vida que la recuerdas,
diré a la muerte que la recuerdas,
que recuerdas sus líneas conjurando tu sombra,
que recuerdas sus hábitos y su carácter solo,
su laurel ácido, su profunda zarza, su descarado error
   y sus hordas dolidas,

. . . .

diré a la vida que te recuerde,
que me recuerde,

ahora,
cuando me alzo con cuerdas capilares y bucles
hasta el desastre de mi cabeza,
hasta el desastre de mis veinte años,
hasta el desastre, luz quebrantahuesos.

(vv. 57–65, 67–73)[100]

The switch from *Definitivamente se extravía* to *Definitivamente me ex-travío* and then the ambivalent *niña de grey dorada* makes the speaker and her friend one and the same. She may be addressing her friend as "niña," or she may be stepping back from herself and seeing herself as one of those angels singing the praises of her friend as she reflects on her writing of this epitaph. Then she shifts from the command "di" to the future "diré," and she varies the phrase substituting *muerte* for *vida,* creating a chiasmus of self and other, sameness and difference. By telling life that her friend remembers it (another repetitive reversal), the speaker promises to live her own life according to the ideals her friend represents for her. By telling death that she herself (the self as other) remembers it, she declares her resolution to remember her friend's experience. The phrase is both constative and performative. It is necessary for her to remember what happened to her friend so that the same thing will not befall her. The twin phrases "su laurel ácido, su profunda zarza" replicate the chiasmus of the "hoja más aguda," as do the phrases "su descarado error y sus hordas dolidas." Her error was both "full of shame, shameful" and "innocent, shameless"; it appalled while it caused sorrow.

The next variation is a combination of the command and the declaration when she repeats and modifies "diré a la vida que te recuerde, / que me recuerde." The speaker will do what she was told to do, but she will also tell others to do the same. She will become a model for others, as her friend was a model for her, but she will write poetry, she will not commit suicide. The adverb *ahora* becomes another turning point in the chiasmus, meaning "right now" and "sometime in the immediate future." The speaker performs and postpones her obligation in the act of writing and in the conclusion of that process. The final phrase of the poem, "luz quebrantahuesos," refers to her act of writing these poems and the illumination (an elegiac topos par excellence) she has received about herself and also the effect her words will have on future readers, painfully illuminating the facts of life and the best way of dealing with them: by facing them rather than avoiding them through opiate pleasures or death by suicide.[101] A woman's elegy provides an ideal genre for exploring the poem as mirror.

4
The Female Eunuch: Luisa Castro's
Los versos del eunuco

WINNER OF THE PREMIO HIPERIÓN FOR 1986, LUISA CASTRO'S *Los versos del eunuco* (The Eunuch's Verses) vehemently protests a hegemonic, phallocentric social structure, especially as it concerns a woman's desire to write and publish. Following what she describes as an ideal childhood during which she experienced a great deal of autonomy, Castro was disillusioned by her encounter with the "real" world when she went out on her own. She begins her criticism of that world in her first work, *Odisea definitiva. Libro póstumo* (Definitive Odyssey: Posthumous Book) (1984) and continues her protest in *Los versos del eunuco*.[1] With specific regard to forging a breakthrough into the publishing establishment, Castro makes a telling comment in her interview with Sharon Keefe Ugalde:

SKU: Do you think that within the literary world subtle prejudices against women still exist?

LC: I think that they do and that they are not subtle. The prejudices are patent and the greatest one . . . comes from the group of writers (male and female) already settled in their places as authors. As all of us who are writing are too young in their eyes, I feel that for them it has a stigma of threat. . . . Or rather, I see that the writing of young people is not well received. And if you are a woman, worse yet, because it has the additional stigma of throwing in your face that your success is due to your being a chick, and if they don't brandish the excuse that they've published your work because you are a woman, they say that you have gotten to publish thanks to someone or other. It seems sordid to me, and it exists. It is a pressure with which I have lived for the past year, with which any number of colleagues of mine has lived, a pressure that surely many have had before beginning to publish something. It is a situation that is not normal in any way and depends so much on the fact that you are a woman as much as that you are young. They are two things that in some way impose on people who are already enthroned.[2]

In *Los versos del eunuco* Castro sarcastically rails against the Freudian concept of woman as castrated male, as a female eunuch, but she ironically appropriates this concept as a useful tool for asserting her poetics/identity politics. She accomplishes this feat in her poetry through a metonymical dislocation of metaphor.

Diana Fuss compares Jakobson's classic distinction between metaphor and metonymy with Lacan's between the phallus and the penis.[3] Fuss notes that "in theories of language, metaphor has long dominated over metonymy" and that "we see this dominance played out in Lacanian psychoanalysis where the phallus stands in a privileged metaphoric relation to the body (it 'stands for' sexual difference), and where the 'paternal metaphor' emerges as the privileged signifier."[4] Although she does not directly deduce the parallelism, these binary oppositions reflect the privileging of masculine over feminine drawn by Hélène Cixous.[5] Fuss does point out, however, that the relation between the penis and the phallus functions both metaphorically and metonymically, as does Irigaray's trope of the "two lips" of female genitalia. Whereas Irigaray privileges the metonymic aspect of her figure over Lacanian "phallomorphism," Fuss asserts that "what is important about Irigaray's conception of this particular figure is that the 'two lips' operate as a metaphor *for* metonymy; through this collapse of boundaries, Irigaray gestures toward the deconstruction of the classic metaphor/metonymy binarism. In fact, her work persistently attempts to effect a historical displacement of metaphor's dominance over metonymy; she 'impugns the privilege granted to metaphor (a quasi solid) over metonymy (which is much more closely allied to fluids).'"[6]

Castro employs a similar strategy in the figure (as both body and trope) of the eunuch, a castrated male in charge of the harem in Oriental cultures, in *Los versos del eunuco*. As a male, in the hegemonic social structure he had more status than the women in the harem. But he was incapable of functioning sexually as a man and thus similar to a woman, making him an ambivalent figure because he can be considered both male and female. As such, this figure destabilizes and subverts the rigid, fixed categories of gender. Miriam Brody confirms the destabilizing force of this figure with arguments that are consonant with Castro's appropriation of the eunuch in her discussion of Quintilian's classic text on good versus bad writing. According to Brody,

> ambiguously gendered figures seem to assail stable notions of the language system itself, based as it is in categories of phonemic differences. These categories are prototypes of the conceptual differences, like gender,

with which we organize our understanding of the world and our place in it. . . . The eunuch blurs categories and merges oppositions, destroying the correspondence between language and world. The eunuch is disorderly because he implies the vagueness of conceptual borders, a confusion of place, the woman having invaded the man.[7]

The eunuch held up as a reflection for the speaker in the page as mirror is an apt foil for the young woman writer trying to make a place for herself in the literary milieu. One of the key elements in this process is Castro's image of the "falo de plástico" (plastic phallus), an appropriation of the writer's pen as phallus. If the pen represents the phallus and phallogocentrism, the "falo de plástico" is a phallus as pen, an artificial phallus or dildo. This image is therefore both metaphor and metonymy. As a young woman writer, Castro wishes to demonstrate that the acquisition of the "falo de plástico" is precisely that: an acquisition, not a quality inherited along with or because of one's anatomy. Through the figure of the eunuch, Castro subverts the binary opposites of metaphor/metonymy, nature/culture, sex/gender, self/other, and masculine/feminine. Being a writer means possessing the phallus, but the phallus is not equivalent to a penis.[8]

Another important aspect of this process concerns the author's working-class origin. To become a writer, one does not necessarily have to be part of the learned upper class. Castro thus sees herself as multiply marginalized: She is young, she is a woman, she is from Galicia (one of the provinces, where a regional language is spoken), and she is from a working-class family. Yet she is convinced that she can be a writer because she can acquire a "falo de plástico" like anyone else. She adopts the identity of the eunuch to subvert preconceived notions that would prevent her from achieving her goals. By sarcastically acknowledging that she is a woman, that is, a "castrated man" (a eunuch), she asserts her "author-ity"—a social construction—and opens a space for herself within the prevailing literary ambience.

The first indication we have of this ironic subversion can be found in the text's epigraph, a lengthy quote from Terence's *Eunucchus*. In this passage Gnatho is talking to a man of his same social status whom he considers "dirty, sick, a mass of rags and antiquity." This man has spent all his money, so everyone disparages him. Even Gnatho says that he feels contempt for him. It turns out, however, that the other is not false to himself, a yes-man like Gnatho, so he receives no gifts, no perks. Consequently, this passage problematizes which is the eunuch: Gnatho, who makes himself subservient so as to receive the gifts of those more powerful than himself? Or the man who stays true to himself but has nothing? In other words, this passage presents the dilemma of the young woman writer: Should she bow and scrape, make herself subservient to the hegemonic literary community so as to be published and respected as an author? Or should she remain true to herself? Which option makes her more of a eunuch? Which makes her more of an individual? In either case she defiantly accepts the position of eunuch, of castrated man, of woman. But by recognizing and exposing the double bind in which women are placed by the hegemonic (social and literary) establishment, she also subverts and extracts herself from that situation. *Los versos del eunuco* depicts this process.

DEFINING THE EUNUCH

Castro has divided the poems of this work into five sections. The first of these, "Devociones," defines the environment in which the speaker writes and the goals to which she commits herself. The three poems of this section are written mostly in prose, although the speaker breaks into brief moments of verse at the end of the first prose poem. The use of prose could be interpreted as the "prosaic" environment from which the poetic voice emerges, but we could also see it as a rebellion against standard poetic forms. Suzanne Guerlac suggests that the contrast between prose and verse entails those of realism and idealism, the grotesque and the sublime, irony and lyricism.[9] Castro is making similar parallels revolving around the figure of the eunuch (and its various manifestations), the humble, working-class origins of her family, and woman as castrated male in contrast with the literary establishment as masculine, cultured, and sublime as opposed to grotesque. However, Castro also deconstructs these dichotomies in her use of irregular verse forms, sarcasm, and irony. Later, the use of different typefaces for two antiphonal voices—hers and the eunuch's —forms part of her subversive discursive strategy. In this way, she questions what "poetry" is.

Along with the duality prose/verse, the speaker presents us with the first instances of a metonymic slippage of metaphor, including the image of the eunuch, which designates divers characters in these poems. At first it seems that the speaker's father is the eunuch. The opening verses also provide the title for the poem, confusing center and periphery.

Quiero contaros la historia del Eunuco.
    Mi padre se moría como con ganas y dormíamos con la luz calva del anochecer haciendo eses, dibujitos cortos para ser buena. Dormíamos

apretadas a la ola como con miedo y poca tela y mi padre que no sabía nada se moría como con pena de albañil transoceánico.

Quiero contaros la historia del Eunuco, que es triste. El eunuco que es triste normalmente habita en los bosques de hoja caducifolia; el otro, el que no es triste y se lo pasa bien, abunda y es fibroso y hace su nido en la copa del invierno.[10]

After beginning with a declaration that she will tell us the story of the Eunuch, the speaker moves directly to a description of her father, in effect equating him with the Eunuch. Note also that she capitalizes the word *Eunuco* so that he adopts a specific identity thanks to the proper noun. Her use of the word *historia* also lends weight to this account; it is not fictional but actual historical truth. But none of these assumptions is necessarily totally accurate. The father's death merely sets the scene (thus the imperfect tense), and the capitalization of the proper noun converts this figure into an overarching theme. For we cannot be sure that the father to whom she refers is literally her biological father or if it refers to a time in history when patriarchal culture dominated. It might even include the patriarchal, dictatorial reign of Franco in Spain, so that her father's (literal or figurative) death is the beginning of her own story of becoming.

Several of the images in these verses are similarly ambiguous, and some, though metaphors, are subtly displaced by metonymic devices. First, the phrase *como con ganas* picks up the thread of the narration where the title leaves off. This phrase may mean "as if" he wanted to die or that it was inevitable. The scene then shifts focus to those on the periphery, the *we* of the verb *dormíamos*, later defined as female in the adjective *apretadas*. These peripheral figures are contiguous with the dying center and in that sense metonymical. Moreover, the personification of the light as "calva," as belonging to the "anochecer" (a liminal time between day and night), and as making esses is equivocal. Is this a displacement of a characteristic of the father (his baldness) onto the light, in which case it would be metonymical? Does it mean that just as her father's life is hanging by a thread, so the light of day is scant? Or does it mean that his death is certain, ineluctable, because it was as plain as his bald head?

The fluid flickering of the light converts the dying of one day into the emergence of a new one, but it is also compared with the act of "haciendo eses" and with "dibujitos cortos." The first of these is both a visual and an auditory image, again destabilizing the synaesthesia with environmental (metonymical) phenomena. Both images suggest writing, and the girls (young women) are involved in this action "para ser buena." We might infer that they are scribbling or doodling or even practicing their pen*man*ship (their entry into the symbolic) to pass the time and to keep out of trouble; but they are nonetheless engaged in putting pencil or pen to paper. In that event, the description of the light is a displacement of the action of the characters in the scene, providing a metonymic bridge from dying father to flickering light to the beginnings of poetic inspiration and writing. This process continues in the next sentence that anaphorically picks up the thread by repeating the verb *dormíamos*. Then we see a gathering momentum of anaphora in the repetition of the title and the phrases *como con miedo* and *como con pena* in the next sentence, to be followed shortly by the repetition of the opening sentence, "Quiero contaros la historia del Eunuço." Although the speaker is writing prose, these elements begin to characterize her production as poetry. The relation between metonymy and metaphor is thus called into question.

The images of the sea and the ship reinforce this tension. It is as if the speaker and her companion(s) (her mother and her sister?) were on a ship with its deck rocking with the movement of the waves. Her allusion to "poca tela" may mean that there is little wind in the sails: little hope of her father surviving, his labored breathing; or only a hint of (poetic) inspiration, with no clear cut direction and purpose to their lives. Or it could be a reference to their poverty and lack of blankets (warmth and comfort). The image of the "albañil" may characterize her father as a laborer, someone who worked with his hands to keep the ship (his life and his family) afloat, or her own awkward attempts to write, to make her way through life (the sea). The carpenter is a lowly figure, decidedly not as powerful as a captain, suggesting that the speaker discerns a certain similarity between herself and her father (they are both eunuchs in a way), at the same time that she sees his struggle ending and hers just beginning.

When she repeats the opening sentence, then, the identity of the eunuch is ambiguous, as the change to the lowercase indicates. However, she also tags another phrase onto this sentence, making it both similar to and different from the opening sentence and metonymically transferring the sadness from the story itself to the specific characters. The eunuch's story is a sad one, but should we attribute this sadness to her or to her father? Does he feel sad that his life has not been more meaningful? Or does she feel sad because the same fate could await her? The adverb *normalmente* points to this ambiguity, for we cannot be sure if it modifies the preceding verb phrase *es triste* or the subsequent "habita." For that reason we call into question the image of the "bosque." A forest is a place of life, vitality, and growth but also a dark, mysterious, and threatening space. Likewise, the "hoja caducifolia" could suggest dying but also resurrection, an autumn that will eventually lead to spring. These images refer to the death of the father and to the emergence of the daughter's life (the "hoja" as the blank page), as well as the historical context, simultaneously. It may be that the speaker would like to show her venerable father that she is a worthy heir and do something that will make him proud of her, but she may also feel overshadowed by the past and prevailing expectations (both as a woman and as a member of a society in transition).

At the end of this passage the speaker sets up a contrast of otherness, reminiscent of Terence's eunuchs. The other goes through life easily; his life is not sad. In comparison with her father, the other has a comfortable life. The verb *abunda* could mean that many others enjoy this privileged life, or it could mean that his life is productive and prosperous. In like manner the phrase *es fibroso* could mean that he is tough but flexible, and that he produces abundant texts. That he makes his home "en la copa del invierno" connotes his aloofness and coldness, his insensitivity to the type of life led by the speaker's father. This other provides a metonymic contrast with the father by dint of contiguity.

The next two paragraphs again shift the focus to the first-person speaker. Again the poet avails herself of anaphora and metaphoric slippage, devices connected with metonymy. Even her alliteration is metonymic in that it emphasizes the sequential rhythmic and sonorous aspects of the signifiers rather than their more abstract, metaphoric signifieds.

> Yo tenía un aspecto augusto de algo amargo, yo tenía unos zapatos
> con fervor y tenía un agujero en la oreja y tenía un paraguas color
> hierro que les gustaba mucho a los vecinos.
> Yo tenía muy grandes las manos y de lejos olíamos a patata.[11]

Looking first at her father and then at the other in contrast in the previous verses, the speaker now assesses herself. Like the other, she recognizes that she was even then somewhat aloof and disdainful of others. Her pride in her shoes perhaps plays on the Spanish idiomatic expression "más contento que un niño con zapatos nuevos" (happier than a child with new shoes). But if her shoes make her proud and therefore "masculine" (does *niño* mean little boy or the generic but masculine "child"?), her pierced ear identifies her as feminine and even subject to the patriarchal order. Pierced ears, like all piercings and tattoos (and one would have to include castration in this category), pertain to the abject.[12] One could say that piercings are like tattoos in that they can imply marginal or deviant subcultures connected with those, like the eunuch and the poet in this text, who choose to live beyond the norms of society. These outlaws can assert their nonconformity to conventional middle-class attitudes and values, according to Arnold Rubin. In fact, we could say the same of piercing that Rubin says of tattoos: "Tattoo is one way of reassuring, or reinforcing, the ego under pressure. It provides an expanded, alternative, volitional identity: one *can* come to terms with the psychic constraints of the slot(s) one occupies in society. One *can* escape to a simpler time and more straightforward values."[13]

She vacillates again, however, when she mentions her umbrella. This apparatus serves to protect one from the rain, and because hers was the color of iron, it connotes the strength of her character and her ability to defend herself. When she says that her neighbors liked her umbrella (her stolidity, her boldness), she again expresses her pride as well as the approval and admiration of those who knew her. The shoes, earrings, and umbrella are all tangential elements that serve to characterize the speaker. They are therefore metonyms that function metaphorically, in consonance with Irigaray's usage of the figure of "two lips."

The speaker's confusion about her position is evident when she swings back in the other direction in the next paragraph. Her overly large hands signify that she is from the working class, and the odor of potatoes that she and her family exude from afar attests to the limitations of their diet because of economic conditions. How are we to read her opinion of these additional metonymic traits? She seems on the one hand proud but on the other embarrassed by her social status as both worker and woman. These dualities and ambiguities reflect the speaker's mixed emotions at this moment of transition. She recognizes certain traits in herself that distance her from her father and her societal milieu, but she is also quite proud of her heritage and of the capabilities that help her strive to overcome external limitations. The tangential fragments that she uses to characterize herself are metonymies that function as metaphors, metaphors for metonymy.

As the poem develops, the speaker continues the contrast between a general description of the times and her own personal experience and attributes. The slippage continues in the image of the eunuchs (whose identity constantly shifts), in the displacement of adjectives and adverbs, and in the metonymic twists given to metaphor. Note also the change of address and the anaphora in the following verses.

La historia del Eunuco es para que veas: Había todas las tallas a elegir para probarse; era un tiempo preñado de eunucos y despertadores. Era un trasiego incesante de botellas vacías y divinas inmolaciones diarias, máculas en mi nombre desprovisto de linternas, máculas en la frente de

los chóferes que traían impecables visitantes, máculas en el calendario
empeñado de la memoria; era un tiempo respetable de eunucos sin
florituras, camisa blanca y poder, deber y claudicaciones.

Yo, que descifraba las agujas del reloj con mi sudor, conocí las piernas
del eunuco desde lejos, pantalones a rayas con un cadáver dentro y un
falo de plástico en la mano por amor al honor y devoción al cielo que
nos mira.[14]

When the speaker slides from the plural address to the singular, we
might assume that she is not only addressing the reader more indi-
vidually but also herself. Nonetheless, her didactic purpose has not
changed: She wishes to demonstrate what she has gained from these
experiences. This time period offered a variety of possibilities and
identities that people could try on as if they were suits or dresses of
different types. But what is the speaker's tone? On the one hand,
it seems that the options are limitless and the possibilities endless,
giving people a great deal of hope. But on the other hand, she may
be sarcastic because of the superficiality and pretense of choosing
one's identity in this fashion. The surrealistic imagery of "un tiempo
preñado de eunucos y despertadores" abets this sarcastic reading,
especially the word *pregnant*. In the context of eunuchs, this word is
obviously ironic even though it does express anticipation, optimism,
and the expectation of new life. Now it seems that everyone wants to
be a eunuch, that is, the type of person described in the epigraph
from Terence: the yes-man, the flatterer, pretentious and false. The
alarm clocks are wake-up calls. Again this image is metonymic: It creates the vision of someone having to get up early in the morning to go
to work, to assume responsibilities, get ahead in the world through
hard work. The tangible object of the alarm clock is peripheral and
concrete, but it evokes the abstract concept of the attitudes that were
emerging at that time in history.

The next sentence picks up the verb *Era* anaphorically and then
slips to another repetition of the word *mácula*. Again the images are
ambivalent. First, "un trasiego incesante de botellas vacías" could
mean that people were draining the last drop of excitement and intensity out of life or that they were wasting their time because they
had already emptied the bottles, decanting what was already empty.
Further, the word *incesante* could mean "nonstop" or "laid off," that
there was no work available, that their efforts were futile. The daily
sacrifices that people made are described as "divinas," which could
mean that they were altruistic, ennobling, and uplifting, or that they
were exaggerated to seem like noble enterprises but were really very
common and ordinary (*diarias*, quotidian, banal). The speaker's tone

is simultaneously hopeful and sarcastic. Is she returning to the past to relive and revive those emotions as she felt them then, or is she retrospectively expressing her disillusionment?

The insistent dactylic stress of the repeated *máculas* emphasizes the speaker's disappointment as well as her sarcasm as she fails to reach the goals she has set for herself. These blots on her reputation (her "name") result from her failure to attain recognition.[15] The "linternas" are flashlights that focus on something or someone in the surrounding darkness but also the light of a lantern that will illuminate all around it. She has not earned the reputation she sought. These blots also appear on the faces of the chauffeurs who bring distinguished guests for visits. One might imagine government officials or dignitaries who make tours of the provinces. These distinguished visitors are "impecables" in that they are by comparison without sin, or neatly and cleanly dressed in the latest fashion. The contrast between the chauffeurs and these dignitaries points up the class distinctions that still pervade society and make the chauffeurs ashamed of their subservience and their inability to find other work. The third instance of the blots marks the calendar: specific dates, deadlines, holidays, or anniversaries that pass without celebration. The unusual adjective *empeñado* describing the calendar suggests that a certain period of time has elapsed but that a goal has not been attained. Literally, the pawned item has not been redeemed, and figuratively, those who have needed to pawn their things have not been able to take advantage of that time period to earn or advance (in either money or esteem). Again, these images entail tangential, contiguous, and metonymic (perhaps synecdochic) elements that characterize the historical period.

The figure of the eunuch again undergoes alteration or slippage, coming as it does at the end of these anaphoric metonymies. Now we might see them as hardworking people who maintain their sense of dignity and their self-respect in spite of hard times. They have no frills (*florituras*), no white shirts (shirts without stains, literally and figuratively), no power, only debts and aging; they are just eking by. In spite of their pretensions, in spite of their attempts to put on a bold front and to get ahead in life, in spite of the great promise that the era held for them at first, they have not been able to get ahead. The adjective *respetable* is again displaced to characterize the historical period rather than the eunuchs themselves. This metonymic indirection sarcastically removes respect from those who perhaps deserve it or sharply criticizes those who put on airs and set their sights too high, not realizing that the status quo would prevent them from succeeding and attaining their goals (cf. Terence). But it also expresses a heartfelt concern for those disenfranchised and downtrodden classes who can only eke out the merest existence. The ambiguity of these images and the multifarious interpretations to which they lend themselves reveal the effect of metonymic slippage.

When the speaker subsequently enters in the first person, setting herself up in contrast and comparison, the figure of the eunuch again undergoes a transformation. She has been working hard, putting in long hours, sweating, but is still goaded and stung by the hands of the clock (the passage of time). Because of her effort, she has become perceptive and incisive, as the verb *descifrar* implies. She is therefore able to recognize what she describes as the ridiculous figure of the eunuch when he approaches her. Even though she may not have seen him before, she is astute enough to be chary of him. This gnomelike figure has spindly legs made even more ridiculous by his striped pants. He would seem to be a buffoon, a burlesque or comic figure, except that his colorful and loud pants contrast with his cadaverlike appearance. This trait suggests that he is starving because he doesn't have enough to eat, but he still wants to dress in a way that will call attention to him.

Most notably, this eunuch carries the indispensable "falo de plástico" in his hand. In lieu of a potent penis, this character carries a pen "por amor al honor y devoción al cielo que nos mira." We might infer from these images that he has his eyes and heart set on high ideals, that his pen is divinely inspired, and that his writing is a way for him to attain respect (*honor*). But this characterization could be either admiring or sarcastic. The image of the sky looking down on them could mean that some higher power is watching over them and guiding their steps, or that they find themselves in a highly inferior position with regard to their aspirations. At first glance the portrayal of the eunuch may not be very flattering, but that may be an indication of the speaker's skepticism when she first sees the eunuch approach. In the next paragraphs we see why she may be so skeptical of him.

> Había también los Grandes eunucos con el falo de plástico mejor, con color y un poco más erguido, pero mi voz no alcanzaba sus tímpanos aún y ya sabía sus casas de telón y comadreja con perros a la puerta y detrás oficios raros.
>
> En la mano la cartera con magia y cuchillos de repuesto y un falo de domingo por si alguna emergencia para no improvisar.
>
> Pero allí mi soledad como una lona azotada. Pero allí mi piel que habría de venderse por un diente de elefante. Allí el miedo, el terror de los conejos ignorantes que caminan horas y horas con los ojos abiertos sin esperar a nadie que llegue con una estampa.[16]

This passage presents the contrast between the life lived by the "Great eunuchs" and that of the speaker. These personages are undoubtedly well known, frequently published, canonical authors who can afford expensive pens. They even carry elegant spare pens in case of emergencies. As metonymies, these pens may refer to what they have already published or to texts in reserve in the event that they may need some ready "cash" (name recognition). The houses to which the speaker refers may be their publishing houses. Behind the curtain of their publicity (a stage curtain with all its connotations of theatricality and bombast) weasels with dogs (underlings and posted guards) protect them from the scrutiny of the outside world. Meanwhile, they make sordid deals to get their work published or to control what is published. As a matter of fact, in their billfolds these people carry large sums of money used for bribery as well as a handy supply of knives for stabbing their enemies or critics in the back. Having the same shape as pens (phalloi), these "cuchillos de repuesto" may be their invective, their ability to wield words sharply and critically.

In comparison with the grandeur of these magnates, the speaker feels so inferior and miniscule that her voice cannot reach their ears. Perhaps she has submitted a manuscript to editors (or dreamed of doing so), but since she is an unknown author, her voice, her text, her verses cannot penetrate the publishing house structure to make a dent in the eardrum of the Great eunuchs. The series of anaphora of *allí* demonstrates her vulnerability as a young woman writer. By describing her solitude as a piece of ragged canvas and as her skin, the speaker alludes not only to her need but also to receiving no support (practical or moral) from anyone around her. She has no one on whom to rely for help: no models, no support system, no tradition (literary or social), no women's network to counter the old boys' network. That she wears canvas attests to the coarseness of her life and the toll that the winds have taken on her already. She is willing to sell her poetry (her very skin, her solitude) for any amount, for what can one do with "un diente de elefante"?

Instead of legitimate offers to publish her work, she feels only terror because of the types she runs into. She describes these types as "conejos ignorantes" (an image that has traditional connotations of excessive, lewd sexuality), who idly seek to be literary agents for anyone, provided they can take advantage. Their avid eyes are wide open, yet they do not find anyone with real talent. If one has only mediocre, banal, trite talent similar to that of mass-produced religious cards, they are ready to pounce. They are incapable of recognizing anything that resembles good art, and as soon as trouble arises, they disappear, go underground. This sarcastic description paints a disparaging, unflattering picture of others in addition to showing the vulnerable speaker's distrust.

In the final passages of the poem she intensifies her criticism, but an eruption of poetic verses asserts her identity as poet. Here again the figure of the eunuch shifts slightly, in keeping with the slippage of this image throughout the poem.

> El Gran Eunuco bombea el mundo pero no conoce mis manos en el barro.
> El Gran Eunuco duerme tranquilo y no piensa en mi corazón que bajo tierra sabe todos los nombres del odio.
> El Gran Eunuco bebe en las fiestas del verano con su prole de palo alrededor
> sonriendo
> y no me ve entre la gente que frecuenta las piscinas, en los paseos largos que la ciudad pisotea, en los altos teatros que se llenan por la noche de familias.
> Pero allí mi soledad haciendo un sitio para algún mensajero sin cara.
> Pero allí mi soledad.
> Vomita las cenas, deshace las camas
> hace tiempo que no sueña nada grato
> y presiente el final.[17]

The slippage in the image of the eunuch has proceeded from possible identification with the speaker's father to a plural form to the partial capitalization of "Grandes eunucos" and then back to the singular but capitalized "El Gran Eunuco." All of these have been subsumed under the general title of "Historia del Eunuco." We can now see that the "Eunuco" represents patriarchy, the phallocratic hegemony in general. In this most recent avatar, El Gran Eunuco represents God, the Father par excellence, or Man in general, who bombards the world with his works, his image, and his importance, but who is totally oblivious to how hard the speaker has been working just to survive. But the Gran Eunuco could be Franco (the mythologized image of Franco as the father figure of contemporary Spain).[18] He is able to sleep tranquilly because he feels that his conscience is clear, while in contrast the speaker feels "lower than dirt," having been accused hatefully just for being true to herself and her emotions ("mi corazón"). Her heart lies "bajo tierra" because of all the contumely that has been heaped on her in spite of her efforts. Thinking specifically of Castro, we understand that she might feel multiply marginalized. But the contrast between the speaker and the permutations of the eunuchs emblematizes the contentious relationship that exists between women and men in patriarchal societies in the Western world.

The speaker's contempt and ridicule reaches a peak in her portrayal of the high life enjoyed by El Gran Eunuco. While she is working year round, the Great Eunuch spends his summers attending fashionable parties and sipping drinks at poolside, surrounded by his smiling but stiff admirers. By describing these admirers as "su prole de palo," the speaker suggests that they are his protégés or those who pattern themselves after the Great One, but that they are lifeless, stiff, artificial. Inasmuch as the Great Eunuch does not see her, she offers several possible explanations. First, it may be that she is too inconsequential to be noticed by the Great Eunuch; second, it could be that she is there but that He is absent from among the common people; a third possibility would be that she is *not* there because she is not one of His groupies; and finally, she may not be there because *she* does not get to go on vacation given that she is always working, trying to make a living.

She does, however, call attention to her absence by way of her "semiotic" eruptions into verse, even in the description of the Great Eunuch.[19] First, the word *sonriendo* is set off from the rest of the paragraph as an announcement not only of the falseness of the Eunuch's admirers but also of her own presence-by-absence, sardonically deriding those who fawn over and adulate the Great One, a foreshadowing of Hélène Cixous's "laugh of the medusa" below.[20] Then, when she returns to the motif of her solitude, retrieved from the previous segment of anaphora, she again ambivalently and evasively uses the image of "haciendo un sitio" to suggest her presence/absence. The anonymous messenger for whom she clears a space is absent, just as the space that she clears is empty. Yet her act of clearing that space and of anticipating the arrival of some still unidentified source of inspiration, of messages, of words, testifies to her expectations and her agency through her activity.

The final four lines of this prose poem are again in verse and express ambivalent feelings of anticipation and exasperation. In her loneliness/solitude (*soledad*) the speaker may not be able to eat or sleep because she is so dissatisfied with the status quo. If she dreams at all, her dreams (her aspirations) are not optimistic because of the discouragement and disillusionment she has experienced. We might even read the last verse, "y presiente el final," as a foreboding of suicidal thoughts or at least a discontinuation of writing, a haunting evocation of the poetry of Plath.[21] However, we could also infer that her disgust with her life and the social environment for young women in particular has reached a point of such frustration that she is on the verge of breaking out. It is not insignificant that the verbs of this passage are in the third person, presumably attributed to her "soledad." Given the ambivalent meaning of this word, we can also imagine the speaker finally reaching the point where she becomes self-reliant through her writing in solitude and her acceptance of her identity as a young woman writer.

After dismantling the poem by segmenting it into sections, we can see how its subtle structure functions. A slippage in the different conceptions of the eunuch and the affirmations in the first person of the speaker herself show the fluctuations and seething of the speaker's identity vis-à-vis the (phallocratic) society around her, which also happens to be in flux at this time in history. In each of the portrayals of the eunuch, with their shifting, destabilizing slippages as if along a fault line, the speaker discovers facets of herself through comparison and contrast, a play of similarity and difference. In this initial poem in the collection, she posits her tense, volatile anxiety as a young woman writer trying to break into a hitherto exclusive or even prohibitive field of endeavor or social structure (the editorial world).

Castro's metonymic distortion of metaphor sharpens her criticism and allows her to circumvent a counterattack, thus protecting her vulnerability. In the past critics might have called this maneuver "avoiding sentimentality." However, if we look at the comments made by Ramón Buenaventura in his anthology *Las diosas blancas,* we can see that Castro and he did not get along well and that Buenaventura could very well represent this editorial hierarchy and be another manifestation of the Great Eunuch.[22] At the same time, we have seen how Castro appropriates the figure of the eunuch, embracing it sarcastically and defiantly so as to deflect and reflect its characteristics onto a patriarchal society that wants to keep women in a subservient role by calling them "hommes manqués." She is about to show that anyone can possess the phallus/pen and that possession of this "quality" is determined by one's willingness to adopt certain attitudes. To possess the phallus is—for men or women—a state of mind, not a question of anatomy.

The first section of *Los versos del eunuco* posits the poet-speaker's struggle to identify herself as a writer. She envisions the figure of the eunuch as her alter ego and as other, as a mirror reflection, so that she can explore the similarities and differences between them. Both are defined as rebels in an uprising against the patriarchal-literary establishment, but one is a man-woman and the other is a woman-man. Which is which is impossible to assert with certainty, for indeed each continually changes places with the other, just as metaphor and metonymy slip from one side to the other of a Moebius strip. The language employed by the poet is therefore equivocal, slippery, difficult to pin down, constantly in flux. In this process she again blurs the distinction between metaphor and metonymy. She positions herself in an intermediate space that challenges preconceived notions of masculine and feminine writing. In "The Laugh of the Medusa," Hélène Cixous defines this space as "writing (in) the in-between":

> To admit that writing is precisely working (in) the in-between, inspecting the process of the same and of the other without which nothing can live, undoing the work of death—to admit this is first to want the two, as well as both, the ensemble of the one and the other, not fixed in sequences of struggle and expulsion of some other form of death but infinitely dynamized by an incessant process of exchange from one subject to another. A process of different subjects knowing one another and beginning one another anew only from the living boundaries of the other: a multiple and inexhaustible course with millions of encounters and transformations of the same into the other and into the in-between, from which woman takes her forms.[23]

While returning to prose and progressively becoming shorter, the remaining two poems in this section focus on the arrival of a new eunuch who will become the speaker's illicit "lover," her alter ego, and the image of herself in the mirror. In general, we can gloss this figure as the poet's inspiration, but we cannot minimize or negate the narcissistic and erotic overtones of this relationship, especially as concerns society's reaction. Public outrage and censure centers around the speaker's attempt to transgress the limits of the female role, and there is even a hint that the speaker is a lesbian or, in Spanish terminology, a "marimacho." Describing her adoption of "masculine" attributes as a love affair with the grotesque image of the eunuch, the speaker invents a narrative. This metonymic device allows her to define the internal changes in her along with the censure she receives from society at large.

In the second poem the speaker describes herself as a soldier or a warrior (a traditionally male role) who does not receive recognition for her efforts to defend herself and her principles. But she also recognizes that to achieve her goals she will have to pay her dues as an author. If she is dedicated to writing (what she sees as a philanthropic endeavor—literally, an act done for the love and betterment of humankind), these are the sacrifices she has to make. The accusations of lesbianism, of illicit love with a "defective" lover, and the rotten sustenance she receives for her efforts call into question the concept of philanthropy. Ironically, in her desire to give of herself in the way she deems most appropriate, the speaker receives only criticism, ostracism, and abuse.

As its title indicates, the third and final poem in this crucial introductory section of *Los versos del eunuco* proffers an invitation we might be hesitant to accept. In "Ábreme el muñón a ver qué tiene dentro" (Open My Stump to See What It Has Within) the eunuch prompts, challenges, even commands the speaker (and the reader) to examine the site of castration. On the one hand, this might be the scar where the male genitals were removed, but on the other, it may be the female genitalia. In either case, the title encourages the speaker (and the reader) to go beyond the surface, to explore the interior, and to ascertain how hidden qualities define identity. From a feminist point of view, the title urges people not to judge women solely on their anatomy or superficial beauty. In light of the poem as mirror, this challenge is consonant with the oxymoronic relationship between surface and depth, interior and exterior, self and other. The eunuch again provides the edge to this process because the invitation to explore a site of male castration (a scar) as well as a vagina might be repulsive, whereas it might also be erotically charged and arousing. The opening passage of this poem relates another encounter with the eunuch in which violent and painful imagery both attracts and repels the speaker and the reader.

> Mientras una piara de culos rosa nos espía detrás del mundo rojo de la tarde, a ver qué tiene dentro, me dijo, ábreme, a ver, a ver toma la copa rota, a ver qué tiene dentro.
>
> De modo que me dispuse a entrar con vidrio y vimos caer la sangre blanca al suelo blanco del lavabo y conocimos los ojos del dolor de los que no aman.
>
> Aquello cerró en pocos días; el eunuco no vino a verme en dos semanas.[24]

The emphatic intensity of this urging on the part of the eunuch is offset by the speaker's disdain for the "piara de culos rosa" spying on their tryst. Usually applied to a group of hogs or pigs, "piara" debases the voyeurs. In addition, their faces are compared to rosy butts or assholes, not a flattering portrayal of those who would like to interfere with this encounter. But this image also suggests putti, the rosy (asexual) cherubs or cupids who guard over idealized scenes of love. In contrast, the image of the broken cup and "vidrio" connote violence and the possibility of injury. In spite of its ambivalence ("let's see" or "in order to see"), the repetition of the phrase *a ver, a ver* underscores the reciprocity. Does the eunuch urge the speaker to explore his genital area or her own? Certainly, the prohibitions against masturbation, especially by females who for many years were assumed not to masturbate, might pose a barrier against this investigation, accounting for the sense of repulsion. But this probing also implies a better understanding and greater knowledge of self that becomes the basis for poetry.

At first the image of the white blood spilling on the white floor of the washroom seems to be redundantly insignificant. However, Cixous states that "there is always within her [woman] at least a little of that good mother's milk. She writes in white ink."[25] The spilling of blood on the white floor figures the act of writing with blood, of pouring out oneself onto the blank page. It is also a commonplace of mystery stories and of children's literature that milk is invisible ink that can be made visible by putting the sheet of paper over a warm light bulb or a candle. The heat of the bulb makes the milk visible, revealing the message heretofore invisible. The parallels with the reader's need to decipher the poet's codes are patent. That this action takes place in a "lavabo" connotes a cleansing, purifying process. All of this flows from the site of castration, the vagina, often associated with menstrual flow. It therefore pertains to the code of life and the capacity for (re)production. But the violence of the broken glass may also conger up images of slitting one's wrists, attempting suicide. What writing thus involves for the author is a spilling of one's guts, a spilling of blood, an intensity that is painful but powerful. When the speaker participates in this encounter with the eunuch, her poetic inspiration, she imagines seeing "los ojos del dolor de los que no aman," the reaction of readers who are incapable of following her beyond the bloody, violent, repulsive surface to appreciate the ecstasy of poetry as love. Again we see instances of the indirection of Castro's imagery where metonymic elements (like the basin in the washroom to evoke water as both destructive and regenerating, or the white blood as mother's milk and ink, the life-giving power of writing) modify traditional metaphors.

This first section of *Los versos del eunuco* forms the starting point for the rest of the collection and is an important statement of the young woman writer's frustration in her attempt to break into publishing circles. The remaining sections relate the poet's constant endeavor to overcome these obstacles through her contact with the eunuch and a deepening of her poetic ability. A major difference, however, is noticeable: In all but one of the following sections the poet uses free verse rather than prose. Only in the fourth section does she revert to prose. These four sections bear the following subtitles: "Versos para ver o El osario de las horas" (Verses for Seeing, or the Ossuary of Hours), "Los versos del eunuco" (The Eunuch's Verses), "Aclaraciones" (Clarifications), and "Poemas pirotécnicos" (Pyrotechnic Poems). By following her progress through the remaining four sections, we will see how the poet explores the alterity of the eunuch, to "work (in) the in-between," and to subvert the connection between having a penis and having the phallus, between equating anatomy with the writer.

EXPLORING THE SELF

The second section of *Los versos del eunuco* also consists of three poems, though now the form shifts from prose to verse, advancing the poet's acquisition of her own poetic voice. In conjunction with the first three prose poems, these three establish a pattern of similarity and difference because of the tripartite structure. A pattern of three-three thus appears and will be repeated. It is important to recognize this pattern because in this second section of the text the poet will strive to loosen her expression. Using metonymy (especially parallelism and anaphora) as her starting point, she now begins to experiment and to explore the options available to her. The shift from prose to verse is the first indication of this process. In addition, the verses she employs vary in length from one syllable to "versículos," long verses more similar to her prose utterances. She also experiments with the placement of words on the page, with the ambivalent placement of adjectives, adverbs, and other words, with odd line breaks (ending with a preposition or a conjunction), and nonsense syllables, to mention only the most obvious elements. Having established a pattern (a conformity), the poet then transgresses, subverts, and reworks it in search of her own individual style, her own voice. Unfortunately, she is dissatisfied with the results because they still do not meet her expectations.

Another indication of the poet's experimental attitude can be found in the title of this section: "Versos para ver o El osario de las horas." Her playful approach to language is manifest in the repetition in the first half of this title, especially in the truncating of *versos* to produce *ver.* Her tone could be nonchalant, as if to say, "Let's see what happens if. . . ." But as we saw in the chapter on Rossetti's *Los devaneos de Erato,* play has a serious underlying intent. We could imagine the speaker saying, "You want to see what I can do? Well, take a look." In the second half of the title, a subtitle within a subtitle, the repetition of the vowel /o/ along with the word *osario* portends that all this experimentation will result in nothing of worth (a big, fat zero).

The ossuary, however, also connotes getting down to the "bare bones," the pith of language and the self after all the external trappings and disguises have been stripped away. Also, mention of the hours points to a motif and structural element of this section. At the end of each poem the speaker specifies the passage of time with a prepositional phrase, beginning with *a las cinco* (at five o'clock) and proceeding hourly to *a las diez* (at ten). The hours she spends in this endeavor will be thrown into the ossuary, indicating on the one hand that she has wasted her time, but on the other that she has made progress on which she can build. By highlighting the physical attributes of language in the ludic repetition, she marks the way in which she will depart from and modify metonymy to attain other means of expression, adding to her metonymic distortion of metaphor.

The first poem, "Cae impenitente una lluvia de falos. Una virgen se lamenta" (A Rain of Phalloi Falls Impenitently. A Virgin Laments), relies on repetition and anaphora, establishing the rigidity with which the poet will break in an attempt to free up her expression. She is the virgin, the novice poet who needs to gain experience. Here we find a chiasmus because the words *impenitente* and *se lamenta* are ambivalent. If one is impenitent, it may be because one has done something wrong without regretting it, but there may also be no need for penitence because one has done *nothing* wrong. Does she lament that she is a virgin or that the rain of phalloi is falling? The two phrases thus play off one another with positive and negative connotations. The opening stanza makes a telling statement: This experimentation takes place at night while the eunuch is sleeping. The poet does not want to depend on her "male muse."

> De noche cuando el eunuco
> duerme
> soñando con mi tercera muerte y mi corazón
> divide el oro de la sangre
> un pequeño temblor me habita la boca.
>
> (vv. 1–5)[26]

Lack of punctuation and awkward line breaks make these verses disorienting. Because the verb *duerme* is isolated by itself after an abrupt enjambment, it is ambivalent. It may be that the eunuch is truly asleep or that he is not vigilant, not watching what the speaker is doing. This implies that she is doing something, some subversive activity, behind his back. The placement of the phrase *soñando con mi tercera muerte* without punctuation makes us question whether it is the eunuch or the speaker who is dreaming, as well as whether the dreams are unconscious images or conscious daydreaming. Likewise, it at first appears that *mi corazón* is the compound object of the preposition *con* until we read the next line. Then it becomes the subject of the verb *divide* and part of a compound clause. Along with these confusions, the imagery is ambivalent. That the action occurs at night could indicate that the speaker herself is in the dark, disoriented, uncertain about her steps, but night also abets her surreptitious activity. The image of "el oro de la sangre" suggests something precious, but dividing it could diminish and disperse that wealth (time, life) but also dole it out in a steady rhythm (the pulse, equivalent with music and poetry). Finally, the trembling that the speaker feels could be for fear or joy, and we cannot be sure if it is just entering her body by way of her mouth or if it lodges and concentrates itself in her mouth as the stimulus for speaking/writing poetry. Metonymy prevails in the next stanza as the speaker-poet begins to write.

> Pulsar útiles arpas
> entonces,
> templar cálido hierro, cerrar
> sobre algún sexo las manos aún gritando
> sólo puedo morir, sólo puedo morir,
> quizás signifique
> estar cerca
> de mi soledad con un nudo.
> Quizás signifique verter fotografías en una zona
> a menudo extranjera
> golpeando una arena cimentada.
>
> (vv. 6–16)[27]

The consecutive infinitives *pulsar, templar,* and *cerrar,* the anaphoric repetition *quizás signifique* plus more infinitives, and even the repeated phrase *sólo puedo morir* all indicate rigidity and structure even though the images within this structure are unusual. A repetition of the single isolated word on the second verse even links this stanza with the preceding one, further setting the structure in place. *Entonces* is also ambivalent, for it is unclear whether it functions metonymically or metaphorically. Does it refer to that time when the eunuch is asleep, creating metaphorical simultaneity? Or does it mean *luego* (then, next), as a consequence of the first scenario? This word influences our reading of the infinitives, making them express present events ("in doing these things") or future, potential action ("if one were to do these things"). The anaphoric *quizás signifique* is ambivalent on two counts: The adverb literally denotes doubt, as does the subjunctive of the verb, but this phrase reinforces the contrast between present and future. Is doing the things expressed in the infinitives equivalent to "estar cerca de mi soledad"? Or is it the result of that action (cause and effect)? Is it process or product? The knot attributed to the solitude could indicate a puzzle needing to be solved or that the solitude is made fast, secured, instantiated. And obviously, the word *soledad* is ambivalent. Does the parallelism of the anaphora equate or elaborate on "estar cerca de mi soledad" and "verter fotografías en una zona"? Within the structures formed by anaphora and parallelism, the poet is making a space for her free play with language, just as night is both disorienting and productive.

Of paramount importance in this stanza is the repeated phrase *sólo puedo morir.* Given that the repetition is included on the same line, these phrases replicate the pattern we saw earlier of three poems followed by three poems. Here we have three beats, separated by a comma, followed by three beats. In the next stanza we will see the poet alter and vary this arrangement so as to create more space for herself as a poet within the limits of language and the poetic tradition. But we should also notice the phrase's inherent ambivalence, signaled by the repetition. This may be a cry of despair or determination. The speaker may fear failure, or she may be defying it. Is she lamenting her lack of poetic skill now that she has eluded the eunuch's supervision? Or is she casting a straw to the wind, willing to do anything, take any risk, even that of failing? The next stanza continues these trends.

> Pero cuando duerme o se empeña en la venta de
> mis bienes,
> en mi rostro sobre el palo,
> sólo queda
> morir, sólo
> queda morir, lo doloroso
> es la mañana con himno y camareras,
> lo doloroso
> es mi cuerpo con andamiaje de ola como edificio
> de
> aire.
>
> (vv. 17–26)[28]

Several characteristics of these verses draw on previous threads as the poet modifies and stretches their possibilities. The first verse not only returns to the opening of the poem where the eunuch is sleeping, but also to the subtitle of this section in the conjunction *o*. Are these two alternatives, or are they equivalent, the second defining the first? Are they metaphoric or metonymic? Also, the preposition dangling at the end of this verse modifies the abrupt line breaks of the previous stanzas and will become a major technique of the work. When the eunuch sells her goods, is it for her benefit or to her detriment? Is he her agent or her pimp? Does raising her head on the end of a stick promote her identity, her celebrity, or does it mock her?

The poet reprises but modifies the parallel phrases of the preceding stanza: "sólo queda / morir, sólo / queda morir." In addition to the change in the verb from *puedo* to *queda,* she changes the rhythm from three-three to two-two-two. At the end of the poem, which follows immediately, it seems that she prefigures the mention of two hours at the end of each of the three poems of this section. Although she deviates from this structure as well as the initial one, the mere positing of these parallels demonstrates her creativity and capacity for variation. The substitution of *queda* for *puedo* is equally equivocal in that it restates the ambivalence of the first instance (despair versus determination) and also reshapes it, tempers it, moving from potential to outcome. The change is not only semantic but also grammatical as the verb changes from the first person to the third. In addition to the fragmentation and the realignment of accents and axes, this shift ironically distances the speaker from that which she finds stifling.

There is, however, a vacillation as the speaker tries to widen the space in, of, and for her voice in the anaphoric repetition of the phrase *lo doloroso.* Yet, within these boundaries she inserts her metonymic imagery. Mornings are difficult because they remind her of orthodox participation in religious ceremonies (hearing church bells, going to daily Mass) and of the need to straighten her living space (morally as well as literally). These early morning activities interrupt her rest and joy in her achievement (her lovemaking with the eunuch, her poetry) and may even be an allusion to her superego. The maids, female figures who perform traditionally female tasks, represent a set of values that the speaker is challenging. In like fashion, the hymns are highly traditional types of poetry that can be original but also quite stale. Again we can question whether the parallelism of the anaphora is metaphoric or metonymic. We can easily perceive the contrast between solidity and fluidity in the contrasting images of "andamiaje" and "edificio," "ola" and "aire," respectively, compounding the similarity and difference of the parallel phrases. After attempting to write without the eunuch, the speaker experiences mixed emotions of disappointment and exhilaration, falsity and substance, dependence and autonomy. She then concludes with parallel phrases about the passage of time and her progress or lack thereof:

> A las cinco se llena de mujeres como
> un parque.
>
> A las seis un viento que oscurece
> lo recorre como un
> sable.
>
> (vv. 27–31)[29]

Even though she begins this poem using the phrase *De noche,* this marking of the hours does not tell us if it is morning or evening. When her body "se llena de mujeres," does the speaker experience a multitude of voices seeking expression in her poem? Or does she see her poetry as commonplace and criticized by other women? We can assume here that the subject of *se llena* and the antecedent of *lo* in the next sentence refer to the most immediate noun, the speaker's body, but again, the connections are tenuous and deliberately ambiguous.

Whereas the wind could be inspiration, it obscures and penetrates her body like a saber. This implement is shaped like a phallus, and penetration is implicit in the verb *recorrer.* According to Chevalier and Gheerbrandt, a sword "separa el bien del mal, hiere al culpable" (separates good from evil, wounds the guilty one). Moreover, they associate the sword with both fire and water (both symbols of destruction and regeneration). These dualities are consonant with the speaker's mixed emotions. But Chevalier and Gheerbrandt also trace a link between writing and the sword. As poetic inspiration, "la espada es . . . la luz y el relámpago ya que su hoja brilla" (the sword is . . . light and lightning given that its blade shines).[30]

The speaker picks up this thread in the next poem, one of the most original and intriguing in the collection. Throughout the first part of "Una virgen se debate pulsando con martillos el cuerpo inquebrantable" (A Virgin Debates, Beating with Hammers the Unbreakable Body), Castro inserts the interjection *zas,* onomatopoeically reproducing the sound of the slashing sword. This nonsense syllable provides yet another example of the experimentation by which the poet stretches language, enriches her expression, and individualizes her voice. Through the mention of the virgin, "pulsando," and the body, the title links this poem with the previous one. But it also extends the metonymic process of defining the poet's voice. Besides the repeated *zas,* she continues to experiment with the arrangement of the verses on the page, anaphora, and parallel phrases. Instead of three separate stanzas to begin the poem, she condenses them into one long stanza, but she fragments this unit with odd line spacing. The first sentence is fairly regular, ending with a single word isolated on the line.

> Mi cuerpo que el mundo tocó con sobresalto,
> que creció con sus huesos derechos
> a las ramas zas, que se fue conquistando
> para alcanzar zas el techo blanco de las casas zas en que vivió
> desposeído.
>
> (vv. 1–5)[31]

Not only does the interjection *zas* surprise us on its first appearance. Each time it appears it follows specific mention of striving for higher aspirations in the "ramas," the verb "alcanzar," and "el techo blanco." This placement truncates the striving for higher goals in addition to placing those actions within the (social) framework figured by the anaphoric repetition of *que* in the three clauses and in the image of the houses where the speaker lived "disenfranchised." Literally and paradoxically, the speaker's body was evicted from these houses in which she dwelt. There is also a progression from birth to childhood to the growth spurt of adolescence, but all funnels into the abrupt, run-on, truncated line. As a female, she was dispossessed of her body (her sense of self) by societal (patriarchal) expectations and traditional roles that stunt and limit her. It is also significant that she objectifies herself as "Mi cuerpo" and distances herself from her body as her identity, perhaps another indication of the effects of societal biases. The *zas* thus becomes the site of conflict between what she strives to attain (her physical and intellectual growth, her sense of wholeness) and the limitations imposed on women by societal norms. The next segment begins with an anaphoric repetition of *Mi cuerpo,* but this phrase is indented so that it follows directly after *desposeído.*

> Mi cuerpo
> que ardió
> y fue
> de los pobres muchachos delgados malvestidos de las
> letras zas y la tuberculosis
> que lo amaron con
> pústulas zas y fiebre tantas zas veces.
> Aquí está zas.
>
> (vv. 6–13)[32]

The image of "los pobres muchachos delgados malvestidos de las letras . . . y la tuberculosis" pokes fun at the stereotypically romantic image of the poet. That they have tuberculosis bears witness to their weak poetic skills: Lack of breath is equivalent to lack of inspiration or sustained elocution. Besides that, they have repulsive pustules and are feverish, sickly, both physically and intellectually. It may even be that they have venereal diseases (cf. Bécquer). However, these pustules and the fever may be on the speaker's body, suggesting that poets are so obsessed with the representation of the female body in their art that they either include such disgusting details or erase them in their fervor.[33]

Another curious aspect of the interjection *zas* is that each time it follows a word that ends with -*as*. This echo augments the sarcastic humor of this portrait as well as erupting at unexpected times, especially after the odd line breaks following the article *las* and the preposition *con*. The detached verse "Aquí está zas" adds more dimensions of ambivalence. On the one hand, it could be an offering, however ironic or literal, of her body. Or on the other hand, she could be mocking their excited discovery of another female body. The *zas* thus becomes her slashing at them as well as their insensitive, grotesque machinations with women's bodies. As stated above, the interjection is the site of contention, erupting "semiotically" (in Kristeva's terms) to show the violence of what is perpetrated on women's bodies and the bitter self-defense of the speaker's indictment. The next segment ends with the parallel phrases that Castro has been turning in different directions and probing from different angles.

> Se ve que odia con su nombre y
> un número próximo en la cola del dolor
> que pregunta zas una zas, dos horas zas
> cuánto tiempo, cuánto tiempo.
>
> (vv. 15–18)[34]

Like the other repeated statements in the preceding poems, the phrase *cuánto tiempo* is ambivalent because it could be either a rhetorical or literal questioning, betraying the speaker's inveterate suffering at the hands of these men or her exasperation and rebellion against it. The speaker feels dehumanized in that she is little more than a commodity sold to the next person in line with a number, or that she has gotten in line for suffering like so many women before her (now it is her turn). Not only does she ask hour after hour, but also her questions come more rapidly, as indicated by the repetition of *zas* three times in the space of a single line. However, these interjections could also be the patriarchy's quick response to any attempt on her part to challenge the status quo.

These three segments crowd together the three stanzas of the preceding poem and play off the three poems of the first section and the three poems of this section, suggesting a mise en abyme or a fractal structure. At this point, the poet returns to the hour motif, propelled forward by the verses we have just read. Based on the already established pattern, we would expect to see two more hours pass at the end of this poem. But the poet once again pushes the envelope by adding a third hour here rather than reserving it symmetrically for the next poem. The first two hours are parallel in their description of an arrival. But in the added hour the poet recurs to anaphora to indicate her feelings of limitation, but also struggles to overcome these obstacles with unusual and ambiguous imagery, stretching the limits of language:

> A las nueve habita mi corazón
> el musgo y el guardabosques viene
> y
> viene
> un tendero con cajas de fósforos para incendiar
> el crepúsculo en mi oreja y arder la sangre
> de las nueve
> de mi cuerpo
> como
> plástico.
>
>   (vv. 24–34)[35]

Just when it seems that the poet will fall into another iteration of frustration, she pushes herself over the edge. This transgression is most apparent in the distribution of the words on the lines: the isolation of single words and the elongation of the utterance. Also, we have to question the grammar of the first two verses. What is the subject of the verb *habita*—"mi corazón" or "el musgo"? Which inhabits the other? Which is within, which without? This duality is repeated in the inversion of subject and verb in the phrase "y el guardabosques viene / y / viene un tendero." Are these two different figures, or does the second elaborate and explain the first by adding new information? How is a game warden (or forest ranger) similar to and different from a shopkeeper? Both take care of something, but one works outdoors and the other indoors. One is alone in a natural setting, whereas the other mingles with people in an urban scene. Yet both of these individuals supply inspiration for the poet. The woodsman dwells in, guards, and protects a sacred space in solitude, and the shopkeeper, as the speaker tells us, brings boxes full of matches which he is willing to "sell" to anyone. These boxes of matches are figures for words, signifiers full of the potential of striking and producing flaming signifieds. Because they are phosphorous, they possess devilish nuances, and they can destroy and regenerate simultaneously.

Indeed, the shopkeeper intends to "incendiar / el crepúsculo" in the speaker's ear and to make her blood burn. This phrase could mean that he will destroy the light, plunging the world into darkness, or that he will set the sky ablaze with color. In fact, *crepúsculo* can mean both dawn or dusk, just as the phrase *a las nueve* refers to both morning and night. His action could either delight or anger the speaker. As images of the poet, the shopkeeper and the game warden posit possibilities for the speaker, but since they are both men, she is ambivalent about this input. Saying that her heart is made of plastic and that it will burn, the speaker reminds us of the "falos de plástico" that are pens/penises. Is this an artificial "dildo"? Or is the ink in her pen burning as easily as plastic? And it is her body that melts. The reference to the body remits us to the central motif of this poem, the topic of the opening segments, "Mi cuerpo," and to the title "Una virgen se debate." Poetry is a riddle (like the riddle of one's sexuality or identity) and a series of variations on a theme (as sexuality and identity are in constant flux over time).

The third poem in this sequence further develops characteristics we have observed in the previous two: the use of anaphora, experimentation with the arrangement of the lines on the page, ambiguous and ambivalent imagery, and the inclusion of the hour in the second half of the poem. Therefore, it will not be necessary to analyze this poem in detail, but there are several aspects worth mentioning. First, the bipartite structure of these poems, with the second half consisting of a progression of time from five o'clock to ten o'clock, reinforces the two-two-two pattern in contrast with the three-three arrangement. These patterns function on several different levels of the text, suggesting a fractal and reinforcing the tension between these levels, the fragmentation of structure, and the appearance of chaos.[36] However, the speaker is attempting to make a space for herself, expanding the envelope of language semantically, syntactically, phonetically, and structurally beyond accepted limits. We can even see that although six hours pass in the course of these three poems—lending them a two-two-two distribution—the poet has deviated from the expectations she herself creates. The vacillation between two poles (three-three versus two-two-two, prose versus poetry, long versus short verses, etc.) and the occasional aberrations in this pattern, along with the indeterminacy of the images, show that the poet is involved in a struggle to make a space for herself in the social, cultural, and literary environment.

The next aspect that deserves attention is the title, "De una virgen despechada. Labra rosas en el pubis y cultiva ajos en la sangre" (Of a Discouraged Virgin. She Carves Roses in Her Pubis and Grows Garlic in Her Blood). Again the title makes reference to a virgin, pitting these three poems against the predominant theme of the eunuch in the first section. This juxtaposition recalls the basic premise of this study: That the poem functions as a mirror in which the poet compares and contrasts herself with an image represented in the mirror. Now we are in a better position to understand that if Castro sees herself as a eunuch, it is undoubtedly because that is the image a hegemonic patriarchy has imposed upon her. Rather than reject that image outright, she defiantly accepts it with the express purpose of repudiating, distancing, and remaking it. This process is nonetheless a struggle in that the poet must deny that she is a eunuch by separating herself and thus achieving independence.

In this particular title the tensions of this struggle are paramount. First, the word *despechada* is highly suggestive. If we read this word literally, taking into account its etymology, it describes the amputation of the breasts (*des* + *pecho*). Is this an allusion to St. Barbara, the virgin and martyr whose breasts were amputated because she would not submit sexually to the king? This hagiographic intertext serves as an allegory for the poet's relation with the literary and social establishment. In truth, the word *bárbara* means "awful, frightful, bold, and daring," all adjectives that characterize this young woman. Moreover, *despechada* refers to the weaning process, the moment in development that separates and individualizes all human beings in relation to the mother: The poet is seeking to establish her individual poetic voice. Figuratively, also, *despechado* means "angry, indignant, spiteful, and disdainful," descriptive of her attitude toward the limitations (the definition of woman as castrated male, as eunuch) imposed by a patriarchal society. Further ambivalence resides in the preposition *de* which can indicate that this poem is about her as well as emanating from her. As we saw in Blanca Andreu's *De una niña de provincias* in the previous chapter, this ambivalence splits the identity of the speaker. In addition to the Lacanian concept of the individual as fundamentally split, this differential between self and other, subject and object, mirrors the tension we have observed in these poems.[37]

The second part of the title contrasts the verbs *labrar* and *cultivar* as well as *rosas* and *ajos, pubis* and *sangre*. The binaries contrast art and nature, sweetness and acridity, exterior and interior, respectively. To carve something is to make a work of sculpture or some other artifact, but it does so crudely. To cultivate the land is an "earthy," physical, laborious experience, but one that is the foundation of civilization and culture. Likewise, the smell of roses can be cloying, and garlic adds intensity, pungency, and flavor to other foods. The carving of roses on the pubic area may sound angelic, but refers to masturbation. And as we have already seen, blood is an image of the mother's milk (cf. *despechada*) and the poet's ink, defining the speaker's sarcasm and bitterness. The word *labrar* in the title and the redefinition (or re-vision) of the image in the mirror (woman as eunuch) reemerges later in the poem in the section on the ten o'clock hour.

> A las diez un equipaje equivocado llega
> y lo vestimos con el odio en el encaje
> y a la piel le salen disyunciones por el forro
> pero no hay sal, ni porvenir, ni
> público
> esperando.
> Los recién llegados observan cómo me desnudo sin razón.
> Es una condena. Opero sobre mi cuerpo. . . .
>
> (vv. 31–38)[38]

With the arrival of the wrong luggage (cf. arrival of the tide, train, game warden, and shopkeeper previously), the speaker as representative of women tries on different clothing. The speaker seems to put on this clothing because it is expected of women, but she obviously hates the feminine quality of the lace, and the lining sticks out, showing that these clothes are ill-made. She obviously rejects this "labeling" or "uniformity." She does, however, use the plural form of the word *vestimos* to show that many women try on these feminine trappings. Even though others think that she does so "sin razón," the speaker rejects that identity when she states "me desnudo" because she knows that such an image of herself not only is false but also has no future and will not attract an audience for her poetry. Her statement "Opero sobre mi cuerpo," while alluding to castration or mutilation (amputation of the breasts), explicitly remarks her efforts to redefine her identity, her image in the mirror.

One more aspect merits attention before moving to the conclusion of this poem. Just before the entry of "A las diez" the speaker mentions—among other things—a "caja de los vientos." This phrase resonates intertextually, but it entails an ungrammaticality. At first Pandora's box comes to mind, a sexist myth that blames all women for the evils of the world because of her curiosity. But in the *Odyssey* Ulysses receives a bag of stormy winds from Aeolus so that he can travel safely over the seas toward Ithaca. His greedy crew, however, thinks the bag contains gold, and they unleash the winds, leading to disaster for their ships. This conflation of two distinct episodes equates women's curiosity with men's greed, canceling them out. If we assume that both men and women are capable of instigating disaster (even though their motives may be different), then we cannot characterize one group more detrimentally than the other. This subtle combination of male and female figures again demonstrates the speaker's re-vision of the image in the mirror.

In the next stanza, indented and altering the visual presentation of the poetry on the page, the speaker begins with a one-word sentence: "Comienzo." Here we are at the end of the second section, having read six poems, and the speaker is only beginning! I would suggest, therefore, that these two sections have been a preliminary backdrop that has served to establish the speaker's position with regard to many things: society in general, the literary hierarchy, her own image in the mirror, different possibilities for defining identity, the language she employs in her poetry, and the reader. When we then note that the title of the next section is the same as that of the entire collection, and when we remember that there are five sections, the fourth of which is a return to prose, the pattern of the three remaining sections continues the mise en abyme pattern. The third and fifth sections are the most substantial in the collection, and they are separated by a single poem in prose related to the opening section. Let us now look at these three sections to see how the poet effects the transformation of her (self-)image.

Separating and Incorporating the Eunuch and the Self

The center section of *Los versos del eunuco* is composed of sixteen poems, five of which are printed in all uppercase letters and are supposedly poems that the eunuch writes on the wall of the speaker's house while she is away. But of course we know that Castro has written all the poems. The antiphonal exchange between these two voices may at first seem totally random and chaotic. On closer perusal, however, the poems are arranged quite deliberately. Again the poet establishes a pattern only to modify and elaborate it. The arrangement of these poems begins with three poems in the speaker's voice, followed by one in the eunuch's (all caps). This grouping of three that we have observed in the previous sections provides the basis for the next progression of one, two, and three poems in the speaker's voice, each followed by one in the eunuch's. The entire section then concludes with an additional poem in the eunuch's voice. The increase in increments from one to three after the initial positing of the pattern emblematizes the emergence of the speaker's voice in juxtaposition with the eunuch. Here the interplay between self and the other in the mirror, the speaker and the eunuch, similarity and difference, comes to the fore.

Consequently, we might regard the ending of this section as a chiasmus. The final speaker's poem, "Ad urbe condita," consists of two parts designated by Roman numerals (the only such poem in *Los versos*). The poem immediately following, in the eunuch's voice, bears the title "Post urbem conditam," an obvious sequel and response. But the additional eunuch's poem suggests two different endings to the section related to the two sections of "Ad urbe condita." In this reading the progression from one to three poems opens a space for the speaker's voice in a chiasmatic relationship with the eunuch. The poet forges and "writes (in) the in-between" by "learning to speak otherwise."

Castro opens this section with an epigraph in Latin by the poet Tibullus: "Quis fuit horrendos primus qui protulit enses?" (Who was the first to make this terrible sword?). Whether the sword refers to the phallus or to an instrument of castration, the answer to this question would seem to be "Freud." In this section Castro will distance herself as woman and as writer from Freudian phallogocentrism. Again she employs a number of metonymic devices that enable her to open a space in language. One of the most notable, of course, is anaphora. The first two poems are structured by dint of anaphora. The following abbreviated quotation from the first poem shows how anaphora leads into the second poem.

> Un eunuco me escribe versos, versos
> de muerte, versos de palo,
> versos de almendro para jueces y palestras.
>
> Un eunuco me escribe versos verdecidos
>
> . . . .
>
> Un eunuco me escribe versos y yo
> lo amo . . .
>
> Un eunuco me fatiga desde siempre con sus versos.

Yo lo amo como una salvedad de piedra
florecida, como un impuesto de sangre, como una cicatriz
que no poseo.

(vv. 1–4, 9–10, 17–20)[39]

The concatenation of anaphora as a structuring principle has two possible intentions. One is to emphasize the repetition and the speaker's weariness with these gestures: The eunuch becomes tedious in his persistence, and his verses limit and stifle the speaker-poet. But another interpretation would recognize the impulse and forward drive of metonymic repetition (perhaps emblematic of sexual engagement) that leads the speaker to ecstasy. Her fatigue in this case would be a pleasant exhaustion and a feeling of accomplishment (sublimity) after vigorous activity (sexual or textual). On the one hand, the eunuch's verses threaten to suffocate the speaker's voice because of the stiff restraints they impose. On the other hand, they stimulate her, heighten her knowledge of self, and lead to a greater individual profile, as demonstrated in the *yo* dangling at the end of the third repetition. This sequence leads from mere "versos, versos" to "versos verdecidos" (either moldy and outmoded or renewed and refreshed) to the emergence of the phrase *yo / lo amo*. We can read this last phrase as sarcastic or genuinely intense.

These observations help prepare the way for the second poem of this section in which a reversal and dislocation of metaphor take place. Here the poet begins with an epigraph by the absurdist Antonin Artaud: "Un uso que no conoces, al que jamás has asistido" (A use you don't know, that you have never attended). We will return to this marginal, paratextual element shortly, but first let us examine the opening verses. Following anaphorically from the previous poem, these verses set up the situation that the poet will reverse at the end of the poem.

Versos como incendiarse en lechos, hundir
la espuela y dame
la trinidad oscura de tu alma,
el cajón extraño de tu cuerpo, y alta
parábola de ti . . .

(vv. 1–5)[40]

Although the speaker leads us to believe that a series of infinitives will now function metonymically, suddenly she switches to the imperative *dame* and a series of three images. We do not know, however, whether these images function autonomously, describing three different items, or if one elaborates and defines the previous one, equating all three. The parallelism of body and soul along with the syntax of the phrases is both comparative and contrastive. In total, they represent both the container and the contained. The comparison of writing with sexuality shows that these acts demand intensity and commitment if they are to be successful. Read in the context of the previous poem, elliptically "[El eunuco me escribe] Versos como incendiarse en lechos," the dualities of rape and love, destruction and passion, dominance and surrender are still prevalent, but the comparison of a noun (*versos*) with a verb (*incendiarse*) dislocates the metaphors. This change in emphasis continues in the next verses, where the poet experiments with the arrangement of words on the page while she simultaneously returns to anaphora.

> y
> yo
> que vivo al otro lado del incendio
> ausente y silenciada
> y cantando cosas tristes, yo
> tan lejos del herrero y sin alma
> y un cuerpo amargo para enmudecer
> tendré que decir bueno, así es, mi amor,
> así es . . .
>
> (vv. 6–14)[41]

The poet retrieves not only the anaphoric *y yo* but also the *incendio* from the first line of this poem. Does she speak in contrast with the eunuch, or is she emphasizing her presence even though she is on the other side of the fire? Does the fire separate them? Or is it that she has gone beyond it? Is her being beyond the fire an escape from it, a reluctance to enter it? Or has she passed through and is now far beyond it? Even though she says that she is absent and silenced, she is singing. A typically masculine figure, the blacksmith is someone who forges iron. He may make tools, but also swords. Further retrieval of the body/soul dichotomy pulls together various threads, but the points of reference are ambiguous. We should also add that this poem consists of only one, long, convoluted sentence, making intelligibility even more elusive. In these various ways—through anaphora, the connection with the previous poem, the weaving together of various threads of significance, experimentation with the spacing on the page, and ambiguity—the poet creates aporia, gaps in the text in which to insert herself, in which she can speak otherwise by writing (in) the in-between. Her repeated assertion "así es" thus rings ironic, indicating both resignation and assertion. The speaker then reprises the opening verses of the poem but with significant changes that mark the dislocation of metaphor.

> y   quemarme en lechos, hundir
>   la espuela y darle
>   la trinidad oscura de mi alma,
>   el cajón extraño de mi cuerpo,
>   mi parábola más alta,
>   esas cosas que no conozco
>   y callo.
>   (vv. 15–21)[42]

The changes in pronouns reverse the relationship between the eunuch and the speaker. If at first he made demands as the one who controlled the action (sexual or textual), now it is she who gives, not because he has asked but because she controls the action. As participant in this sexual/textual politics, the speaker has turned the tables and become a subject in her own right. She is the one who "digs in the spur." She assumes the active position in these acts. She gives her soul and her body not in surrender but assertively, even aggressively, as a manifestation of her agency. Now we can see that the prepositional phrases *de mi alma* and *de mi cuerpo* are ambivalent in that she can open parts of herself in this exchange but still retain control over other aspects. Her giving of herself is voluntary rather than obligatory. As a result, she herself discovers new aspects of herself that she had not known previously.

Here a return to the epigraph is signaled in the verb *conozco,* significantly altered from the second person to the first. This additional indication of agency involves risk as well as the excitement of discovery. Even her final statement "y callo" points to her agency in that she is in control of what she silences (cf. "silenciada") or what she reveals. But in doing so, she also extends that same privilege to the other—the eunuch or the reader, the reader as eunuch—who then has the same freedom to interpret what the poet has said. This simultaneous affirmation and surrender of the self by granting the same possibilities to the other recalls the reciprocity of Luce Irigaray's commentary on Emmanuel Levinas's philosophy. For Levinas, eros is

> on the "threshold" (*le seuil*) of need and desire, marking the limits of the dwelling, separating the subject from the world, creating a boundary behind which the subject can withdraw from the public gaze and into the clandestine twilight of the lovers' embrace. Halfway between sense and

nonsense, between clarity and obscurity, eros evinces not so much a duality as a thoroughgoing ambiguity. In eros, the truths and certainties of the world, the will to mastery and control, are suspended.

The effect of eros, then, is to recast a subject who has learned to control its world, who has achieved mastery of itself, back into a state of flux where the borders of self and other, between the I and the world, are no longer so clear, where the gap between the I and the other is not so well-defined, nor so easily grasped.[43]

Because of the dislocation of metaphor and the metonymic devices that produce slippage, this definition of eros is also applicable to Castro's poetry in *Los versos del eunuco,* as her own comparison of sexuality and writing suggests. The definition of the subject, according to Levinas, always involves a dissymmetry and inequality, for "Any equality between myself and the other is dependent on the originary experience of the other as one who transcends me, approaches me from a dimension of height, or puts me in question."[44] Through her "face-to-face" encounter with the eunuch, the other in the mirror who is her reflection (according to Freudian and patriarchal definition), the speaker experiences that dissymmetry and discovers her own identity. "The identity of the I itself—the being of the I—is given through the other."[45] The poems of this first part of the center section of the collection not only establish the pattern that the poet will modify and vary but also prefigure the modifications and variations themselves.

The third poem in this section is one of the most moving and gripping of the entire collection. In its thrust toward transcendence and universalization, it affirms the poet's highly individual poetic voice. This poem also introduces the arrival of the eunuch's writing on the walls of the speaker's house. These poems will serve as the alter ego of the speaker, as she observes herself in the figure of the eunuch who writes them, and will allow her to modify that image. For these poems provoke the speaker's emergence as an individual who no longer depends on the other in the mirror even though the other is indispensable. This short third poem is framed by the eunuch's presence, but in the in-between the speaker's voice pours forth independently. The opening of the frame describes the end of an encounter, a reciprocal exchange between poet and eunuch.

> Me amamanta con sencillez. Recoge su lengua,
> olfatea mis víveres y se va.
> Vértigo y parto.
>
> (vv. 1–3)[46]

How is it possible that a eunuch nurse (give the breast to) someone? This ungrammaticality refers to the code of writing in which the breast provides milk, the woman poet's ink used for writing. The eunuch gives her sustenance and inspiration by drinking at her breast, but then he leaves, taking his "tongue" with him. When the eunuch sniffs the speaker's "víveres," it is unclear whether these "provisions" are for the speaker's use or for his. Are they her sexual parts? Are the provisions physical or spiritual? The speaker's vertigo subsequent to the eunuch's departure can be either an ecstatic or a sickening feeling, just as the "parto" is a delivery and a separation, a gift and a loss. Both refer to the speaker's feeling of independence after the eunuch's departure. She is both liberated and abandoned, so she feels great energy and great distress, fullness and emptiness. With the conclusion of their encounter with her mixed emotions, the speaker reflects on this exchange and the meaning it has for her as a poet.

> Los niños de la nieve no lo entienden,
> no entienden este lugar que dejamos para siempre
> cada día, para no volver, cada día.
> Le cedemos al lugar todo su sitio, reducimos
> cada vez incluso el tiempo, pensamos que es
> mejor así, que nunca nos pertenece, lo dejamos
> crecer, hacerse viejo, tirarse pedos en libertad
> y nos vamos sabiendo que no se puede volver.
>
> (vv. 4–11)[47]

The "children of the snow" are those people who are incapable of sharing the speaker's emotions, those emotions based on her encounter with the eunuch, her poetic inspiration. They are unaware that life is both precious and fleeting and that it is necessary to take advantage of every minute of every day. In these verses we see the slippage of metaphor into metonymy in the repetition and elaboration of concepts and images. First the speaker uses the indefinite object pronoun *lo*, but what is its referent? The eunuch? Her emotions of "vértigo y parto"? Or is it a prefiguration of that which follows, "este lugar" and all that it represents as metaphor? The contrast between "para siempre" and "cada día" as well as the repetition places in tension the passage of time. The fleetingness of time as a place to which we can never return is something that accompanies us throughout our time on earth. The repetition of "cada día" reveals its ambivalence: It refers to each specific day and to that which occurs every day. The anadiplosis of the phrase *cada día* demonstrates the repetition and the novelty, the tradition and the originaiity of its usage.

The slippage continues in the movement from "lugar" to "sitio," from "cedemos" to "reducimos" to "dejamos," from "cada día" to "cada vez," and from "lugar" and "sitio" to "tiempo." The poet then repeats the pronoun *lo* but converts it into a personification that absorbs all its referents (the eunuch, the speaker's emotions, time, space, life, the world) into one figure. Whereas at first this figure appears to undergo a normal development of growing up and growing old, it becomes a caricature because of its farting. These farts are empty signifiers, pure wind emitted from an abject orifice, "words" or "utterances" that are indistinct, ridiculous, and often malodorous, in bad taste.[48] This humorous caricature disguises the fact that it represents the human condition in general, especially if we do not partake of the same perspective as the poet-speaker in her relationship with the eunuch. This aspect is evident in the slippage from the first-person plural *y nos vamos* to the third person impersonal *no se puede volver.* The condition described is both personal and universal; it pertains to all but differentiates those who are like the speaker. It expresses similarity and difference.

A similar slippage occurs in the final two verses ("Cuando volvemos las paredes están llenas / de palabras" [When we return, the walls are full / of words]), which close the frame but also lead into the next poem, belying closure. Contradictorily, just as the speaker affirms again that we cannot retrieve these lost moments, we do return. But what we find on returning is "the handwriting on the wall," the eunuch's poems printed in all caps on the walls of the speaker's house. These poems represent the antiphonal voice that responds to, dialogues with, and opposes the speaker-poet's voice, but they are in effect written by the same person, the speaker's alter ego. That is, when we return to retrieve what was, we now find only words marking absence. If the wall performs the function of paper, this graffiti enables us to see the obvious, to see what we have missed, to know absence because of presence and presence because of absence. Similarly, the eunuch as castrated male, as female, marks an absence that is a presence. The "lack" of a penis is not the denial of the woman but a mark of her presence. Woman is a signifier, a subject, because a signifier obtains through lack, absence. As Shoshana Felman states, "Femininity, in other words, is a pure difference, a signifier, and so is masculinity; as signifiers, masculinity and femininity are both defined by the way they differentially relate to other differences."[49]

The framing of "Me amamanta con sencillez" demonstrates that the speaker is opening a space for herself from which to speak in her own voice, especially in the absence of the eunuch. When the eunuch returns in the capital letters of the next poem, we are aware of a duality. On the one hand, we hear the eunuch's voice antiphonally opposed to the speaker's. But on the other hand, we know that Castro has written all the poems in the collection, that none of them issues from another source. And the eunuch is absent; only his words are present. Therefore, these poems in all caps are highly double-voiced. Although it is not necessary to analyze all the eunuch's poems in their entirety, the first verse is worth investigating to verify this double voicing. The eunuch begins by stating "VIVO EN EL VACÍO BURDEL DE LOS BALCONES" (I live in the empty whorehouse of the balconies). Whereas the alliteration of the bilabial fricatives /v/ and /b/ at first appears to be a poetic device, the excess of repetition discloses its ludic, ridiculous nature. This stammering effect places the eunuch in ridicule because the balcony is a brothel where women are put on public display for men to see and choose. Through the babbling repetition and the modifying adjective *vacío,* we become aware of the criticism of the eunuch's point of view. Contrarily, the satirical mockery of this babbling attains the status of poetry, almost as if it were "through the back door" or a type of "back-handed compliment."

This eunuch's-appeal-to-the-speaker/speaker's-appeal-to-the-reader again relies on anaphoric chaining as it returns to the imagery of bodily secretions emblematic of writing.[50] For example, the speaker of the poem says that s/he "CAMBIARÍA MI CORAZÓN POR UNA MEADA TUYA QUE LLEVARA / TU NOMBRE" (I would exchange my heart for one of your pisses if it bore / your name). Provided that the other (the one being seduced—speaker and/or reader) responds to the seductive overtures with even the most minimal, demeaning attention (a "pissing"), s/he would receive the speaker's heart: her emotions, the total outpouring of intense expression. But the speaker realizes that this offer is insufficient: "PERO NO BASTA ESO" (but that is not enough).

A series of ambivalent anaphoric questions/exclamations culminates in a revival of the bilabial alliteration: "QUIÉN BEBE DE LA VOZ DEL VAGABUNDO" (who drinks the voice of the vagabond). As an exclamation, this sentence expresses the speaker's frustration in trying to obtain the impossible: to drink (imbibe, receive refreshment) from an intangible source (the voice) of one who is constantly on the move, unstable, rootless, unreliable. But as a question (literal or rhetorical), the speaker is attempting to find a reader, someone who will desire him/her to verify his/her identity.[51] This duality is further evident in the ambivalence of the following verses: "NO BASTA / NO / SE PUEDEN PLANTAR ENREDADERAS EN ESA VENTANA" (it's not enough / no / one can['t] plant vines in that window). The placement of the second *no* makes it point in two directions: (1) "no basta, no—se pueden plantar"; (2) "no basta—no se pueden plantar." To plant vines in a certain window is to expect them to grow. But the environment may or may not be propitious for growth. Is this, then, an effective strategy or not? Curiously, the verse itself presents an intertwining of alliterative sounds. Is the alliteration purely superficial, or does it point to the production (growth and proliferation) of meaning? Do these verses function as rhizomes or as fractal geometry patterns that appear chaotic but are in reality merely a different organization or order? Deleuze and Guattari's emphasis on heterogeneity and nonhierarchical arrangements of elements is consonant with the figure of the eunuch and Castro's dismantling of the phallocentric editorial industry.[52] Fractal structure is similar in its appearance of disorder, but chaos theorists underscore the shift in perspective necessary to discover a new concept of order. This thinking is consistent with Castro's project of realigning readership and editorial policy so that her voice can be heard.

The poems in all caps—ostensibly spoken in the eunuch's voice—function metapoetically, and there is an exchange not only between the eunuch and the speaker (the alter ego and the self) but also between the speaker and the reader. The space in-between the speaker's poems and the eunuch's in all caps, and in-between the double-voicing of the eunuch's poems continues to mold and broaden a place for Castro's emergence as a poet over the course of *Los versos del eunuco*. The exchange of antiphonal voices shifts back and forth throughout this section, subversively opening and widening a space in-between where the speaker can insert her voice and leading to the climax of "Ab urbe condita." This final poem in the speaker's voice is followed by two in the eunuch's, the first of which—immediately following "Ab urbe condita"—is "Post urbem conditam." Given that these are the only two poems in this section bearing titles, their placement at this juncture attests to their importance for the speaker's emerging voice. These two titles play against one another: "Ab urbe condita" is a set phrase in Latin, meaning "from the founding of the city [of Rome]," whereas the second is a variation on this phrase invented by Castro. The titles echo one another, but the change in the prepositions from *ab* to *post* requires a change from the ablative to the accusative case, introducing a variation. The ablative phrase looks to the past and measures the passage of time from the founding of Rome until the present moment (that is, since time "immemorial"), the lengthy time that patriarchal hegemony has ruled Western (particularly Spanish) society. In contrast, the accusative structure looks from this present moment toward the future, implying that it is time for a new order, a new structure of society to emerge.

These two titles and the structure of "Ab urbe condita" continue to enlarge the space from which the poet's voice emerges, for "Ab urbe condita" is divided into two parts distinguished by Roman numerals (the only instance of this structure in *Los versos*). Castro also continues to experiment with the metonymic juxtaposition of words at the beginning of part 1.

> Desde que fundamos la ciudad
> en las escuelas
> falos
> de pupitre y sermón
> malamados
> entre la fauna y la flora resabida de las manos operantes
> funerarias.
>
> (vv. 1–7)[53]

If this passage (it is not even a complete sentence) seems ambiguous, it may be because the poet is shuffling and interspersing different parts of the syntax in a style reminiscent of Joyce's *Ulysses* or Cortázar's *Rayuela*. Skipping every other line and going back to the beginning to complete the thought, we can reconstruct the passage. It thus culminates in a nodal point: the single word *funerarias*. This passage implies that children have been indoctrinated with stereotypical sex roles from the very beginning of their education. The "falos" here refer to the teachers who wield authority and who teach academic information that privileges the male over the female as if it were "God's truth" (the sermons). The running together of the words *mal amados* emblematizes this shuffling of thoughts and syntactical phrases and anticipates the nodal point. The final adjective pulls together three possible threads as its referents: It may refer to "las escuelas," "la fauna y la flora," or "las manos operantes." We can thus see that everything about schools contributes to the indoctrination of children according to traditional sexual models. As if embalming them, the hands of the teachers mold children along these lines, always resulting in the same stifling and deadly stratification. Via her interspersing of these verses and the incomplete sentence, the poet dislodges and thereby dislocates traditional (syntactical) logic to create a space for herself to speak otherwise. She continues this disruption of societal expectations of the sexes in the next stanza. Here she characterizes herself as both masculine and feminine, as she implies that her "castration" is as important as having one's adenoids or tonsils removed.

> Soy la novia de tacones altos
> y buques en la voz.

Ni el músculo me reconoce
ni soy su único hijo,
voy a comer con el viejo
y le dejo en el baño mi estatua y
en las escuelas
un libro de generales y otoños con mis testículos
dentro
gemelos y miserables.

(vv. 8–17)[54]

As an aficionada of high heels, the speaker recognizes her femininity, but her deep voice, sounding like the horn of a ship, lends her masculine characteristics. The "weight" of her message is what identifies her as "masculine." In spite of her deep voice, the speaker feels no obligation to fulfill typically masculine roles: She is not muscular (does not rely on brute strength to effect changes in the world), nor does she bear the responsibility of an only son to carry on the Name of the Father. Though she eats "con el viejo" (probably the Father, the "old man"), she defecates in his bathroom: Her "statue" is the food she has eaten and converted into excrement, waste that is left over after she has used the nutrition to strengthen herself. Likewise, she leaves a book containing her testicles in the master's schools as proof that the idea of the female as castrated male is outmoded. Are the words *generales y otoños* an allusion to Gabriel García Márquez's *El otoño del patriarca* and the hollow decadence of a dictatorial regime—patriarchy? The final adjectives *gemelos y miserables* may have mythical overtones of Romulus and Remus ("ab urbe condita"), of the theme of fratricide (the "weaker" of the pair is "feminized" and subjugated), and of the pain this situation has caused. But "miserables" can also express the speaker's disdain for the privileging of those male organs and the concept of woman as eunuch. In the final verses the speaker enigmatically disappears.

Soy el cónsul enfermizo de la primera vez.
Recuento con intriga. Me desmeleno despacio.

A ver, llega tan muda. Le aseo el uniforme a la desdicha
y nos caemos fatal,
presiento su breviario de viajes, imagino sus chapuzas
literarias
y desaparezco profundamente

me voy sin cobrar un duro.

(vv. 18–25)[55]

Several phrases in these verses are ambivalent, again widening the space for the poet to speak otherwise. First, in a very loose anaphora the speaker changes from "Soy la novia de tacones altos" to "Soy el cónsul enfermizo." This change juxtaposes male and female, but because the consul is sickly, he seems more feminine than masculine. This additional allusion to Remus shows that the speaker is reshaping the image of the other (Remus, women) as weaker and victimized: She recounts "con intriga" to point out the injustices and misconceptions on which Western civilization is founded. The act of disheveling her hair demonstrates her grief in a traditional manner, but the verb *desmelenar* could mean that she cuts off her hair. This other traditional expression of grief also converts the female figure into a "male" with shorn hair. In the account of her "emasculation," the speaker subversively and surreptitiously "masculinizes" herself. She plots ("intriga") a reshaping of her image in contrast with the traditional history of the relationships between men and women.

As noted above, *A ver* provides another instance of ambivalence. As an elliptical form of the phrase *vamos a ver*, it invites a closer look at preconceived notions. This colloquial abbreviation also creates a sense of intimacy, so that it could be addressed to the reader (as other) or to the speaker herself. It is as if we were overhearing her interior dialogue with herself and following her thought processes. In contrast, *a ver* could also be another way of saying "para ver," "in order to see." This usage creates more distance and logical formality. As a result, does the verb *llega* function as a command or a declaration? Does it invite the reader to approach and observe the speaker stealthily, quietly? Or does it describe the male alter ego ("animus") of the speaker, the one who wears the uniform, for whom the speaker brushes and straightens it? In like manner, "Nos caemos fatal" could be interpreted positively or negatively: These two sides of the same person may be perfectly in harmony with one another, or they may be totally opposite and antagonistic—or both. When the speaker then disappears within this otherness, is she hiding her feminine identity, or are self and other so completely consonant that they are indistinguishable from each other? Finally, when the speaker states that she disappears "sin cobrar un duro," does she mean that she deserves to be paid for the services she has rendered to this male other but receives nothing, not even a nickel? Or is she saying that she has performed her services gratis and that she does not expect or request remuneration? In other words, *cobrar* means both to charge and to receive in payment.

The reshaping of the speaker's image as eunuch continues in the second part of the poem. Here the poet deploys many of the same techniques to describe the status quo "ab urbe condita" so as to undercut and dislodge the traditional image. Once again the poet shuffles various ideas and intertwines sundry threads of signification. If the poem begins with the same verse as above, the first part of the poem is an inserted "digression," loosening anaphoric repetition by driving a wedge into the structure. Then the anaphora creates both substitution and continuation as the first verse "Desde que fundamos la ciudad" (Since we founded the city) changes to "Desde que abrimos el manual milenario / de los malos" (Since we opened the millennial manual / of evils). To open "el manual milenario / de los males" parallels the founding of the city and perhaps represents an apocalyptic vision. No one has dared to disturb this vision and the social structure that encompasses it, to question or succeed in challenging male privilege and a hierarchical system that can only lead to destruction. Now things are different, she seems to say: They have awakened together as equals, and the slow deterioration of male privilege has begun. The final sentence of this passage indicates that the speaker and the eunuch arrive at the same place, though from different directions or at different paces: "Nuestros paseos se detienen delante de las farmacias" (Our walks stop in front of pharmacies). These pharmacies represent places for obtaining that which will heal. This remedy is equivalent to the "dolor" mentioned at the beginning of this part of "Ab urbe condita" in that it also runs its course one drop at a time.

> Gota a gota vamos haciéndonos este amor malo
> desordenado y
> letal.
> Sus ojos no me miran
> de forma
> lamentable.
>
> (vv. 21–26)[56]

Drop by drop, little by little, they administer grief and remedy their love. The old form of love, privileging the male experience, is lethal, but it is also dying. Does the last sentence mean that the other looks at the speaker, but not with a lamentable expression on his face? Or does it mean that he sadly does not look at her at all? The risks involved in this transition are great, but they also promise much.

The final two poems—both written in the eunuch's voice (all caps)—offer two choices to demonstrate the gap that has opened in which the poet can write. The first of these, "Post urbem conditam," dialogues with the previous poem and contains the choices in the repeated anaphora.

SI TE ACERCAS A MI BOCA SE VE QUE ME CRECEN
SALMOS
SI TE ACERCAS A MI CULO
SE VEN SASTRES EMPALADOS
RIFAS SALVE EXPECTACIÓN
      Y LE DICES AL DOLOR
      QUÉ MAL LA COREOGRAFÍA.

(vv. 1–7)[57]

The contrast between "mi boca" and "mi culo" represents front and back, a smile and a frown, respectively. However, even though a "butt" may be negatively marked as the "rear end" of something or someone, Jean-Luc Herring has stated, "Unlike the face with its mixture of trickery and pretense, the behind has a genuine sincerity that comes quite simply from the fact that we cannot control it."[58] In other words, what may at first seem to be a smile can be a deceit, just as what may at first seem to be rejection may be the truth approached from a different angle. The image of the eunuch is therefore first appropriated and then repudiated by the speaker-poet in *Los versos*. As signifier, the eunuch appears to be a lack but is in reality the mark of absence, a presence. Emblematic of this incommensurability and arbitrariness of the relationship between signifier and signified, "rifas" can be raffles or disputes, positive or negative, outcomes or expectations. The indentation of the final two verses introduces an antiphonal voice within the eunuch's voice and returns to the image of "dolor" that dominates the thematics of the second half of "Ab urbe condita." But the final verse is ambivalent. It can be read as an ironic, sarcastic commentary about grief and pain, or as a lament. In either case, the choreography refers to learned theatrical routines, the dance of male and female in patriarchal society.

The final poem visually represents the gap in its distribution of verses into two couplets. Once again there is anaphoric repetition of the verb *soy*, and we wonder if the two terms of the anaphora are metaphorically equivalent or metonymically progressive.

SOY UN PUEBLO EN CAMISETA TRABAJANDO
PERO NO HAY ESPOSAS DENTRO

SOY UN VECINO DE SESENTA AÑOS QUE LLORA.
ESTA ES MI CASA.

(vv. 1–4)[59]

The second verse of each couplet bifurcates because *esposas* can mean "wives" or "handcuffs," indicating a matched pair. In this "pueblo" (town or people), the necessity of matrimony no longer exists, but only people (men and women) dressed similarly because all are working. The phrase *Esta es mi casa* may be the phrase that the sixty-year-old neighbor sobs, or it may simply be a declaration of the misery of life. After sixty years, one has virtually lost the opportunity to experience life in the same hopeful, joyous way that youth experiences it. But that does not mean that changes are not possible.

REDEFINING WOMAN

The death of the image of the eunuch (woman as castrated male) as a viable, tenable definition of woman's identity takes place in the fourth section of *Los versos*. In addition to the similar title "Aclaraciones," this section returns to prose, just like the first section of the collection, "Devociones." If in that first section the speaker proclaimed the reasons for her adoption of the image of the eunuch, in this section she declares that it is no longer apposite. Also, she announces the imminent death of her father at the beginning of "Devociones," and we noted the various implications of the father figure and the slippage of the identity of the eunuch there. Now in "Aclaraciones" the speaker clarifies those aspects of the eunuch that she can accept as hers and those that she discards as inappropriate.

The one poem of this section bears the title "De cómo se ama a un eunuco y cómo se muere" (About How One Loves a Eunuch and How One/He Dies). This long prose poem is divided into four segments (each beginning with a large capital letter), thus prefiguring the four poems in the final section of *Los versos*, "Poemas pirotécnicos." This structure plays against the three prose poems and verse poems of the first and second sections of the book, respectively. It continues the fractal pattern elaborating not only on the first two sections, but also on the variations of three speaker poems and one eunuch poem of the central section. In short, what appears on first reading to be a chaotic and random distribution of poems is in effect a highly symmetrical and well-planned arrangement. The original image we form (like that of the eunuch) is transformed into quite a different one, even though it consists of the very same material. As our view of the structure of the collection changes, so the image of the eunuch, of woman as castrated male, undergoes a re-vision and reformulation.

The opening passage of the poem foreshadows the eunuch's death in his jaundiced color and in the decreasing effect that his voice has on the speaker. In spite of the diminished impact on her ability to create poetry, others continue to attribute her voice to the eunuch's influence.

> Y así fue que cada día llegaba más amarillo, con aliento amarillo de vaca y los ojos colgándole sobre un fondo amarillo. Así fue que cada vez llegaba más muerto, sin palabras que decir, inconexos versos golpeándome el corazón.
> Pero nadie quería creerme.[60]

The color yellow represents the sickly and possible cowardly state of the eunuch as the enunciator of masculine poetry. This oblique intertextual allusion to Dámaso Alonso's *Hijos de la ira* (Children of Wrath) evokes existential anguish and subversion of the dominant dictatorial hegemony of the Franco regime. The female speaker now finds herself in a similarly subversive situation, but existential anguish has become a question of subjectivity and agency in a patriarchal society. Because the eunuch's verses are "inconexos" and fragile as he approaches death, they may strike the speaker's heart from the outside, may beat against her chest, but they do not motivate and pulsate within her. In spite of their conspicuous weakness, no one wants to believe that the speaker now has a life of her own and that she is capable of producing her strong statements without the aid of the eunuch.

The metamorphosis in the eunuch's appearance is unmistakable when he dies, and it is necessary to prepare him for burial. The scene of his death is reminiscent of the death of Franco. The appearance of two gendarmes adds irony and ludic humor to the scene. Whereas these two figures represent society's policing of the woman poet's activity, the French term places them in a despicable position. Charged with the disposal of the cadaver, these policemen work almost surreptitiously so that no one will notice that the eunuch has died. Described first as a child, the dead eunuch causes embarrassment for the policemen when they strip off his clothes. For the body of the eunuch has adopted "un aspecto de doncella virginal apetecible hasta para un gendarme" (the virginal aspect of a young woman appealing even for a gendarme). The speaker implies that even these gross servants of public interest are attracted lustily to the nubile beauty of the eunuch, whose face is pale, whose sensual, fleshy lips are a vibrant red, and who has feminine hips and breasts that jiggle. How ironic that the eunuch has been transformed into a female figure so attractive that even in death it provokes the lust of insensitive functionaries! Yet, even though the eunuch now appears attractive, the woman writer's poetry still cannot find acceptance and be treated demurely by the cultural police. The speaker does not even have time to shed a tear for the death of the eunuch before society accuses her of emasculating and destroying this image. Instead of welcoming this change, society aggressively accuses the poet of grotesque crimes.

In the second section of this poem, punctuated by the anaphoric repetition of the phrase *Quise explicarles* (I tried to explain to them), the speaker confronts the opposition to change. The anaphora again replicates the rigid limitations imposed on a woman poet. Society even accuses her of wishing to overthrow the family unit, a right-wing protest common wherever the "threat" of diversity and a relaxing of societal norms occur. In a scene evocative of the prostitute from the New Testament, the speaker concludes this section saying, "Quise explicar tantas cosas mientras llovían piedras" (I tried to explain so many things while they rained stones). The analogy between the crime/sin of adultery and the emergence of the woman poet's voice from her relationship with the eunuch hinges on the threat to the status quo and social order. But it also reveals the hypocrisy and ossified attitudes of society where compassion and understanding are absent and where individuals are treated impersonally and categorically.

The situation worsens, demonstrating a woman's double bind. In the first section of the book, society ostracized the speaker for her relationship with the eunuch. Here she receives mistreatment for having terminated that relationship: "Habían llegado de todos los países para verle e interrogarme y maldecirme y sepultarme a su lado con lágrimas y esfuerzo. Así se castiga a la mujer que siega un falo por estos pagos de preces."[61] Taking refuge in her house, closing doors and windows, the speaker places a sign on the door to explain what has happened. This written message (a poem within a poem) justifies their relationship, making her a witness who faithfully relays the eunuch's message in her poetry. However, society refuses to listen to her explanation. It refuses to accept the poetic expression as hers, but heaps "mierda de gallinas" (chicken shit) at her door for having usurped the eunuch's phallus.

In the fourth and final section the speaker resigns herself to her fate and decides to turn inward. She will no longer expect or hope for the public's approbation of her poetry but will hand herself over for crucifixion. Following a catalog of miracles she will perform, seeing in herself an imitation of Christ, the final sentence of this passage ambivalently accepts the outcome and disparages the Pontius Pilate attitude of society.

Es una decencia natural el olvido.

Y espero sentada el final. Sé la muerte que me aguarda. Conviene lavarse las manos.[62]

It seems as though the speaker is so discouraged with the acceptance of her poetry that she will not write anything more. But the one-sentence paragraph (a sententious statement) and her final declaration are equivocal. The naturally decent thing to do would be to forget what has happened. Should she forget her aspirations, or should society forget her transgression of its norms? Is it she who will wash her hands of poetry? Or is it that society must accept the responsibility for what it has done? Pontius Pilate wishes to foist the blame onto the assembled people, but he too bears responsibility for Christ's death because he could have released Christ in opposition to the wishes of the people. He is the ultimate arbiter, not they. Perhaps the speaker should give up; perhaps she should succumb to social pressures and deny her poetic gift. But that would be a denial of self. That might be what society expects her to do, to wash her hands of poetry, but is that what she will do? In addition to resignation, the final sentence also rings defiant: That may be what she should do, but she will not. This fourth section of the book serves as a nodal point for the speaker's conflict.

FIREWORKS

The final section of *Los versos* is titled "Poemas pirotécnicos." On the one hand, this title refers to destruction by fire, containing as it does the word *pyre* and evoking images of women (especially Dido) throwing themselves on funeral pyres. On the other hand, it suggests fireworks, brilliant displays of controlled explosions and thundering auditory impact. Castro has also placed an epigraph beneath the title, another passage from Tibullus's erotic elegies: "pomosisque ruber custos ponatur in hortis / terreat ut saeva falca Priapus aves" (And in fruit-filled garden let red Priapus stand guard / to scare the crows with a ferocious billhook).[63] The reference to the garden includes an allusion to Ceres and to ears of grain and bunches of grapes. Whereas a billhook is "a tool with a curved or hooked blade at one end, for pruning and cutting" (similar to a sword), Priapus (the phallus) merely stands guard over the abundant production of the goddess. He will scare away the crows with the ugly threat of castration, but the goddess will reap the harvest. If the crows are the critics of Castro's poetry, the poet will subversively enjoy her production beneath her cutting sarcasm.

Similar to the theme of the virgin that unifies the poems of the second section of *Los versos,* the first three poems of the final section are connected metonymically through their titles. In this instance, the second title completes the first one: "Antes de ser árbol fui cazador" (Before Being a Tree I Was a Hunter) is followed by "Pero no pude decir ni una palabra sola" (But I Couldn't Utter Even One Word). Both of these titles are included as lines of their respective poems, and the final verse of the second poem is the title of the third: "El inventario de la muerte" (The Inventory of Death). This connection creates a sense of dynamic movement forward even though all these poems deal with the speaker's self-definition. In lieu of the image of the eunuch, the speaker finally declares that she is an angel in the last poem, "Mordiendo por las calles a los hombres que se aman" (Biting in the streets the men who love themselves). This poem also includes its title within it, but it is substantially longer than any other poem of the collection. In this way, the poet subverts closure and propels herself and the reader into the expectation of future poetic production, having found her individual voice. By looking at specific moments from this sequence of poems, we can identify the tensions between the speaker's rejection of the image of the eunuch and the re-vision of her image as an angel.

The first poem is pivotal in this process given that its title establishes a contrast between a tree and a hunter. The preposition *Antes de* and the preterit of *fui* indicate that the speaker has definitively left behind her image as hunter. This image connotes someone who wanders without definite direction in search of quarry: a target, a prize, a trophy, vital sustenance. The first stanza of the poem consists of a catalog of possible prey for the hunter, all introduced anaphorically with the verb *cacé* (I hunted). The preterit tense of this verb is ambivalent insofar as it indicates an action (hunting, seeking) totally in the past, something the speaker does not do any longer (regardless of her success or lack thereof); or it can describe those things that she succeeded in "bagging." The absurdity of some of these images of the hunter's quarry defines the futility of the speaker's search as well as the rich variety and imagination of her ideals. For example, the image of the "negros caballos de río" on the one hand sounds preposterous if we read these animals literally as hippopotamuses. But on the other hand, we can read it as metaphor (not a flat, trite one, but a real metaphor) in which the speaker tries to capture a raging, fluid, galloping passage of time that leads to death. This image embodies an abstraction (time) in black horses.

Other images in this sequence function on the basis of similar ungrammaticalities. In the verse "cacé nobles dentaduras de conejo" to attribute nobility to the dentures of rabbits is absurd, but the placement and choice of the adjective jolts us into an alternative reading. Rabbits are swift and prolific, so that if the speaker can catch a glimpse of their teeth (one of the prominent characteristics that identifies them as rodents), she will have captured something special in a fleeting moment that she can turn into poetry. Likewise, the final image of the faces of mermaids ("y rostros de sirena en el culo del invierno / cacé" [and the faces of the siren in the ass of winter / I hunted]) evokes the incident from the *Odyssey* where Ulysses defies fate to listen to the sirens' song. The speaker wishes to incorporate that song into her poetry also. By seeking their face "en el culo del invierno," she dares to confront the truth even though it may be disagreeable and have a chilling effect, even though it may reside in unappetizing, unexpected, or unwelcoming situations.

The hyperbaton that isolates the repeated *cacé* on the final line of this stanza brings an end to the speaker's search for ideals. However, she uses a parallel phrase to open the next stanza, continuing the process of changing her definition of self: "Antes de ser puente fui incendiaria / y en cada cabello abrí una brecha / como un barco" (Before being a bridge I was an arsonist / and in each hair I opened a breach / like a ship). Parallel with the opening verse of the first stanza, the first verse here posits a contrast between an arsonist who destroys with fire (she states later that she knew fire) and a bridge that makes connections and brings together two opposite sides. In her act of splitting hairs, she leaves a hole as large as a ship. That she is born of a uterus of ashes with a skin beneath her skin ("piel bajo / la piel, en el útero / cenizas / y así nazco") suggests both the act of molting or shedding an old self and the phoenix arising from the ashes of its own destruction. Even the placement of the verses on the page indicates a separation and juxtaposition of old and new selves.

This birth initiates the emergence of her new voice in the final section of *Los versos*. As an animal tamer who lives in the circus, the speaker now "beards the lions in their den." She confronts those who growl and snarl about her poetry and gains their respect if not their complete submission. But the worst part of her life now is her duty to water the plantation of eunuchs who are growing up. Still beardless, these young people could be either boys or girls for whom the poet bears a responsibility through her actions, especially her gesture of writing. In spite of the fatigue of dealing with the lions, she needs to continue nourishing the attitudes she herself has worked so diligently and spoken so vehemently to establish. The "beardless" soil has yet to produce an abundant crop. Castro thus accepts the social responsibility of being a poet.

The rift between past and present conceptions of self takes the form of a contrast between conditional and future tenses in "Pero no pude decir ni una palabra sola" (But I Couldn't Utter Even a Word Alone). If, grammatically speaking, the conditional is the future of the past, the speaker's statements "Yo habría de imprimir la biografía del espanto . . . Porque habría que inventar el error" (I would have to print the biography of fright . . . Because I would have to invent error) delineate her formerly frustrated goals because of society's opposition to her project. Hence the title of this poem. She describes the others as "austeros taciturnos" (austere [and] taciturn) who "pueblan / arcos, cruzan puentes, / se acercan sin rubor a la puerta / de mi casa sostenida" (populate / arches, cross bridges, / approach shamelessly the door / of my sustained house). Although this situation is lamentable, she declares in the middle of the poem, "Esto no es el final" (This is not the end) and that she will continue to transform the perception of her own body: "sólo atento a la fiebre derribo únicamente / mi cuerpo hermoso, / mi habitáculo" (attentive only to the fever I raze only / my beautiful body, / my abode). The body is attentive only to its fever, its "illness," the negative view in which femininity is held by patriarchal society. The speaker values it and considers it the lodging of her being, so she will reconstruct its meaning.

In the final stanza of this poem, the speaker emphatically affirms that she will continue her struggle so that when she dies, she will be able to look back on her life and recognize the many changes she has effected. If she does not do so, she will not be able to face death valiantly. The poet skillfully deploys anaphora in these verses by varying the relationship between repetition and the object of the anaphora, keeping the reader off balance and in constant need of adjusting his/her understanding of these relationships. The direct address of another in the *tú*-form contributes to this effect. She drinks from the vein of the other, yet a whole people is waiting for and calling out to the other. One could argue that the *tú* is the alter ego of the speaker herself: the woman who draws from her own experience, whose mouth is worn out with proclaiming her poetry, and yet who continues to receive sustenance from her past, who is in the process of becoming someone who does not yet exist and whom the speaker may never realize fully. Nonetheless, her commitment to achieving this future self is resolute.

The third poem in this sequence, then, bears the title "El inventario de la muerte." Just as in the first two, there is a disjunction between past and present, here in the figure of an alchemist. Based on the desire to transform base metals into gold (a project similar to the poet's wish to transform language and society), alchemy is "a method or power of transmutation; esp., the seemingly miraculous change of a thing into something better." In medieval times the alchemist was both philosopher and magician, images for the poet who works with language. In the first stanza, the speaker requests that the alchemist make soldiers flee. This disappearing act would eliminate resistance to the project of those who would transform society. In the second stanza she commands that the alchemist be given fire (both destructive and regenerative). The speaker, with the aid of forces she imagines to be helpful to her, defines her commitment to destroying the status quo and building a new society. In the center of the poem, she affirms this commitment. She has dirty fingernails, indicative of her hard work, "getting her hands dirty," and the smell of her skin is a body odor indicative of her effort, whereas the strategist's shoes she mentions are metonymically related to the path she must follow. Even though her efforts may be in vain, she emphatically states she will not abandon this image of herself or the possibilities that she will create for herself and for others in the future.

The final poem of the collection is a lengthy statement in which the speaker redefines her identity as an angel. Nonetheless, she is still in search of words "para perder la vía" (to lose the way). She hopes to derail her expression from the accepted norms so that she can express her rage. However, in addition to her ardent search, she also expresses doubt that such expression is available. After all, she must employ the same language as everyone else, the patriarchal, symbolic language, if she is to communicate with others.[64] Can such a language be bought in wine shops? Is it possible to find such a delicious wine to whet her palate, to loosen her tongue, to transport her to new heights of expression? These wines, as she states in the second stanza, must be attentive to the pain in one's bones, even one's strongest and densest bones, and to the return of shoulders (again an indication of strength) or earth (the body itself) to embers that will burn and destroy but also regenerate. She continues the theme of fire in the next stanza, where she declares that she is an angel.

> Quiero saber cómo se cae a las llamas,
> cómo se cae a la hoguera alta
> y doble del
> dolor mejor de todo dolor. Yo soy
> un ángel falto de recursos, no me mires, voy
> hecho lentamente
> con el corazón pobre de pobreza de ángel,
> con la indigencia en el centro
> atento
> como un noble mensajero del error

al dolor
de los mamíferos.

(vv. 17–28)[65]

Weaving together various elements, the speaker illuminates the paradoxical situation in which she finds herself. How can one fall up, as she would like to do by falling "a la hoguera *alta*"? Her doubling of the word *dolor* hints at a mystic ecstasy arising from pain. This duality is expressed phonetically in the alliteration of the words "alta / y doble del / dolor mejor de todo dolor" and rhythmically in the odd line break after the preposition *del*. The disorienting effect of these verses after the perplexing act of falling upward replicates a sense of drunkenness as both loss of consciousness and heightened consciousness. Moreover, the speaker stresses her feeling of lack reiteratively in the echo of "pobre" and "pobreza," and in the synonymous "falto de recursos" and "indigencia." This lack, however, does not refer to her "castration" but to a sense of inadequacy with regard to the message she brings. The "mamíferos" to whom she refers in the last verse could refer to all human beings, but it could be addressed specifically to women inasmuch as nursing young at the breast is a key characteristic that identifies mammals. Women experience a double pain ("dolor"), in general as members of the human race and in particular as women. But because they do nurse all humans at their breasts, they also experience ecstasy. Even though the poet may not be overly endowed with large breasts, she can nonetheless give of herself in an enriching and nourishing, nurturing way through her poetry, her words, her message (angel = messenger).

The next four stanzas consist of the speaker's complaints about the world in which she lives. Whereas she might like to learn about other aspects of her world, such as the birds, instead she finds herself pointing out how terrible her world is because of its injustices: "Mirad, mirad, es tan terrible esto" (Look, look, this is so terrible). These injustices center around the women she has known, especially her mother and the women about whom her mother told her. She gratefully thanks her mother for showing her the plight of women, as she expresses in this poignant stanza:

> Y las mujeres que cuento en mi cabeza, que recuento,
> que olvido,
> sus vestidos azules que tendré que colgar, sus
> dolorosas manos, vírgenes verdaderas.
> Las mujeres que mi madre me abrió para que no empezase
> todos los versos con un nombre. Para que no empezase

todos los versos con su vidrio de nombre.
Todas las mujeres que
recuerdo
buscando un duro cuenco donde albergar el vientre.
Todas las mujeres que mi madre me abrió.

(vv. 62–72)[66]

In speaking of her own life, she also speaks of what she has inherited from other women. The blue dresses that she will have to hang up are the ideals that they were never allowed to attain. Their hands were "vírgenes verdaderas" because they could not write (or in any other way create) what they wanted to express for themselves as women. They never achieved their fulfillment, always remaining virgins in that sense. The variety of these other women was revealed to the speaker by her mother, and because of that multiplicity, the speaker is able to vary her expression. She does not need to repeat the same sentence structures in her writing, an act indicative of her ability to escape from the dull routines imposed on women by a patriarchal society. Beginning every sentence with a noun makes a person's (in this case, a woman's) utterance as transparent as glass, minimizing its importance by making it disappear. According to the speaker, the most vulnerable spot of these women is their "vientre," their capacity to (re)produce. If they had been able to protect this area from exploitation, they might have had time and energy to devote to other endeavors. By ending this stanza with the verb *abrió*, the speaker suggests how her horizons have expanded thanks to her mother.

After this brief excursus into gratitude for her mother and lament for the women about whom she learned, the speaker reacts as if waking from a trance to return to her purpose at this point. She asks pardon for this digression because she still has a mission to accomplish: to effect changes in the present world. The image "la noche de los gendarmes / que me araña el pezón" (night scratching the speaker's breast) is the patriarchal policing that chafes her as a woman, but also something that stimulates her breast, urging her to write with her white ink. It thus causes her irritation and consolation, pain and satisfaction. As an avenging angel, then, she expresses her hate for the situation in which she finds herself and other women. Even though her mother's stories have opened new horizons for her, she still must do battle with a society that limits what women can achieve. Then follows a description of the speaker's rage.

Mi odio espera el odio con olor a mantel
y derramado vinagre, ese odio
que se mea en el tacón de las bibliotecarias

hasta que nacen lirios
y la tierra empantana los taxis vigilando
una escuela.

$$(vv.\ 80\text{–}85)^{67}$$

The lifting of the tablecloth after a meal evokes typical women's work. The spilled vinegar attests to the speaker's bitterness. Moreover, her desire to piss on the heel of a librarian is an act of defiance in the face of those women who maintain the silence imposed by patriarchy. Her urination would be so profuse that the taxis waiting in front of schools (presumably to whisk off those who continue to promote and proselytize patriarchal attitudes) would become bogged down, stopping the commerce in such ideas. The continuation of these trends in society causes the speaker as angel to feel that she cannot soar, that her wings are weighed down with sadness and discouragement. Obviously, she is crestfallen and fatigued with her effort. That does not, however, prevent her from imagining what it might be like to live in a better world where she could experience love without submitting to the patriarchal order. She then initiates a long rhapsody of the imagination to show her vision of how happy she could be and how she would not even have to return to heaven. Before concluding the poem, the speaker provides a redefinition of her body that bears no resemblance to the eunuch. If the eunuch's body is grotesque, scarred, mutilated, this description of her body is self-affirming without being overly idealized.

Es más dulce mi cuerpo;
aquí está con medallas y
caderas, con el verbo del tabaco y la hojarasca.
Es más dulce
así
con huellas diminutas de dientes de ave viva
en mi sexo como una ropa
antigua que devora
la sal, en los pechos enanos como pruebas, retenidos
y en la cintura que ardió
con muertos, barricadas, botellas,
armaduras
y un almanaque inútil con la fecha del ocho
y los niños del valle, los perros y las cañas.

$$(vv.\ 135\text{–}49)^{68}$$

In stating that her body is composed of "medallas y / caderas," the speaker implies that it is firm yet round. She has not received medals for her beauty, but rather has pride in who she is. The "huellas diminutas" that she has on her sex, her small breasts, and her waist are wrinkles (similar to crow's feet around the eyes) and folds in her skin. She does not pretend to be an ideal, a goddess, a sex symbol, or a fashion model. She is quite simply a woman.

The images she uses to define the parts of her body function metonymically. When referring to her sex and her breasts, she uses the comparative *como,* indicating simile, but phrases following this conjunction illustrate metonymic slippage. "Una ropa / antigua que devora la sal" elicits a connection with the sea, with sails, with the expansive freedom and the corrosive passage of time archetypically associated with sailing vessels. Her sex metonymically adopts salty sea smells and a coarse sturdiness that the wind of inspiration and ecstasy swells. If her breasts are retained like "pruebas," we might imagine that they provide only a small taste, a puzzling yet pleasing sip of what is inside the speaker.

Her final statement may be interpreted in two distinct ways. "Cuánto tiempo he de esperar" (How long must I wait) can function as both an interrogative and an exclamation and expresses both desperation and defiance. In closing *Los versos del eunuco* with this repeated phrase, Castro indicates that she has worked through the issue of her identity. She has adopted the Freudian image of woman as castrated male (a eunuch), but she has done so to reshape and reenvision her identity as anything but that image. Her poetry has a social and political purpose: By presenting her own struggle with that false image of herself as a woman, the poet hopes to influence the society around her. Her vehemence and sarcasm should shock men out of false images of women and encourage others to adopt a stance similar to hers in combating and changing these images.

5

The Mirror as Male Gaze: Almudena Guzmán's *Usted*

CUT OF THE SAME CLOTH AS LUISA CASTRO'S *LOS VERSOS DEL EUNUCO* and runner-up for the Premio Hiperión to Castro's text in 1986, Almudena Guzmán's *Usted* also protests masculinist attitudes toward the young woman poet. It too makes a powerful statement about the reception of women's writing by the masculinist literary establishment. While this book consists of forty-seven brief and intense poems, Guzmán has arranged them sequentially to recount a love affair between a young woman and her literature professor. But throughout *Usted* we are left in doubt as to the cause-and-effect connections and the passage of time between one event and another. Instead, these poems privilege the female speaker's emotional responses to specific incidents and encourage the reader to fill in the lacunae. The poet thus explores the liminal space where narrative and lyric genres overlap. This no man's land corresponds to the imbrication of protagonist and poet, of sex and text. By holding the text up as a mirror and suggesting similarities between her protagonist and herself, Guzmán establishes a parallel between the sexual content of the text and her experience with the act of writing and an unsympathetic (masculinist) reader's devaluation of her work, that is, someone (usually a male but not always) who cannot share the woman writer's emotions and therefore disparages her poetic expression. The reflection in the mirror therefore represents the male gaze looking back at the woman reflected therein.

Even though the protagonist of this narrative-like sequence of poems bears the same first name as the poet, Guzmán vehemently denies that the text is in any way autobiographical.[1] Yet, of the first four books published by this young author before a long hiatus of silence, this work is the most sarcastic and bitter in tone.[2] Moreover, because of certain details of the text that I will specify, *Usted* responds to the condescending attitudes of critics and reviewers of Guzmán's poetry. An example of that tone appears in the comments of Luis M.

197

Marigómez in a newspaper article reporting on one of Guzmán's readings of *Usted*. Although in the main a favorable commentary, the reporter emphasizes the diminutive, childlike, or doll-like stature of the author, diminishing the seriousness of her poetic endeavor.[3] The tone of this commentary echoes that of Ramón Buenaventura in his introductory statements to the women anthologized in *Las diosas blancas*. Buenaventura begins with a statement about Guzmán's "adolescent mystery." For Buenaventura, her petite, little-girl physical appearance contrasts sharply with the content and expression of her poetry. Later he also denigrates her preparation as a poet, saying that she has not read widely enough. He attributes the appeal of her poetry to "el descaro con que se cuenta, la frescura con que se vive los versos, la ingenua desfachatez de sus aperturas sexuales" (the shamelessness with which she writes, the freshness with which she lives her verses, the ingenuous openness of her sexual declarations).[4] In short, until recently the attitude of male authors and critics concerning women's poetry has been disparaging and condescending, although the recent anthology *Ellas tienen la palabra* (1998) signals a change in attitude, an acknowledgement of women poets' ability and popularity.

To correlate the protagonist's sexual experience in *Usted* with the author's statement about textual politics, let us consider the representation of the female figure in each of the work's five sections. Considering the mirror as the male gaze enables us to see the speaker's attempt to change her image of herself. But ultimately she reverts to a parody of woman whose identity is determined by male expectations. We can see an early indication of this subversive attitude in the dedication of the book, "A Usted, / en obediencia." This paratextual element, like the name of the protagonist of the work, deliberately blurs the distinction between art and life. Normally, a dedication is made to a real person, someone the author knows well and wishes to honor with the dedication.[5] In addition, as with many dedications, this one is written as if it were in verse. Moreover, sarcasm predominates. To whom, then, does the speaker dedicate this book? The sarcasm points to a theme of revenge because of the rage the speaker/poet feels. In an essay ambivalently titled "Just Rage," the psychoanalyst Adam Phillips notes that

> if rage renders us helpless, revenge gives us something to do. It organizes our disarray. It is one way of making the world, or one's life, make sense. Revenge turns rupture into story. And it shows us the extent to which meaning is complicit with the possibility of redress, with a belief that losses can be made good (revenge as savagely optimistic mourning). Because tragedy

always threatens to baffle the possibility of action—our minor tragedies, that is to say, as well as real ones—revenge keeps hope alive.[6]

The first section of *Usted* contains thirteen very short poems describing the awakening of erotic/poetic desire in the speaker. Not insignificantly, the object of her desire is her literature professor, whom she idealizes as she denigrates and berates herself. Whereas she compares him to the classic Greek statue of the discus thrower, the epitome of corporal perfection and dynamic form, she sees herself as awkward, unattractive, and childish. Because of his profession as a teacher of literature, this male figure represents not only the male muse, but also the poetic tradition and the male literary establishment that judges women's writing. The speaker's first glimpse of this figure is subtly evocative of the metapoetic dimension and introduces a double-voicing in the speaker's address. The first poem also establishes the connection between writing and the woman's body.

Usted se inmiscuye en mi bufanda
desde un aura blanquísima que me reverbera los labios.

No me muevo,
no fumo—quizá a su silencio le moleste esa arruga en la nieve—;
y sólo cuando marcha me doy cuenta
de que he estado aguantándome el pis todo el rato.

(vv. 1–6)[7]

The cold weather and the snow function as more than mere anecdotal details. Instead, they allude to the poet's mental state as she sits before the blank page, ready to write. Her scarf represents a protective barrier surrounding the throat (synonymous with the speaker's voice; the barrier is double-sided, preventing escape as well as intrusion), through which the male insinuates himself. The "aura blanquísima" may be the condensation of her breath. Combined with the uncontrolled trembling of her lips, this image suggests an inchoate speech act provoked by the unexpected appearance of the male muse, the poet's inspiration.

This aspect is reinforced in the second stanza in the speaker's mention of the "arruga en la nieve" interrupting and disturbing the silence. The wrinkle is equivalent to the line of poetry written on the blank page. The shadow in the snow refers to her uncomfortable feelings inasmuch as they disturb the whiteness of the page. Unsure of herself and of her ability to write, she tries to make herself and her words as unobtrusive as possible. The speaker diminishes herself and her writing by emphasizing her stillness. She does not dare to move in the presence of this superior being, and she certainly ceases smoking. The presence of the cigarette identifies this young woman as "masculine" in that smoking was originally a masculine activity for which women were arrested if they dared to smoke in public.[8] The cigarette may also represent the pen because it is held in the fingers and smoke is inhaled into the lungs and expelled through the mouth as "words." The phrase beginning with *quizá* between dashes not only underscores the speaker's clandestine attitude toward her writing. It also introduces a double-voicing because we cannot be sure if the phrase is addressed to the male figure directly as in the first stanza or if the *su* and the *le* mean "his" and "him" ("de él" and "a él") rather than *your* and *you* ("de usted" and "a usted"). The apparently insignificant pronouns problematize the addressee because we do not know if the protagonist is addressing the male directly or if she is speaking of him in the third person. This aside or interior monologue may then be overheard by a more sympathetic audience, one that can identify with the speaker, that is, read from a woman's perspective. This ambivalence pervades the work, signaling the subversive use of language to undermine the restrictions imposed by the male gaze.

This aspect is particularly important in the final verses of the poem. The speaker has been so preoccupied with the presence of the male that she has been unaware of her own bodily needs. The double-voicing thus reinforces a disjunction between interior and exterior that has further metapoetic implications. First of all, it is obvious that while we are participating in the aesthetic experience, we lose awareness of our physical surroundings and enter the world of the text with a willing suspension of disbelief and a suspension of our awareness of the world around us. Guzmán heightens the tension and adds a psychoanalytical dimension when the speaker becomes aware of her need to urinate. In addition to the erotic overtones evoked by this allusion to the genital area, urination is a way of discharging latent, unwanted, or uncomfortable emotions. As we saw in the chapter on Blanca Andreu's *De una niña de provincias,* urine pertains to the abject and the definition of the *corps propre.* Because of the male gaze, the speaker of *Usted* considers herself a deject or a stray.[9] It can be a way of releasing tension without declaring the underlying emotions and making them clear to oneself and to others. This image reinforces the double-voicing—still evident in the ambivalent "marcha"— in its connection with writing. Has the speaker been able to express herself in her writing, in this shadowy wrinkle on the page, or has she expelled her emotions without full consciousness and awareness of what she is saying? This ambivalence points to the uncertain beginning of the poet's task of writing and dealing with inspiration, the erotic-poetic emotions stimulated in her by the male muse.

The elusiveness of these emotions appears again in the second poem, where the speaker refers to the male figure as the discus thrower. Guzmán continues to link the poetic with the erotic in this poem where the speaker masturbates to relieve the tension aroused by her desire for the male figure.

> Usted se me escapa en los pasillos como
>   un discóbolo impregnado de aceite.
> Pero todo lo que habla es una mano enguantada por mis
>   medias.
> (Desnuda, froto su voz contra las caderas de la sábana
> para no dormirme tan triste.)
>
> (vv. 1–4)[10]

The parallelisms between this poem and the first solidify the speaker's relationship to both erotics and poetics, the textual and the sexual, and begin the narrative's unfolding. The first stanza of each poem begins with the word *Usted,* placing the emphasis on the stimulus. The reflexive construction *se me escapa* again calls attention to the speaker's lack of control of this inspiration, along with the description of his body covered with oil in typical gladiatorial practice. This allusion to competition shows that the speaker-poet is struggling with her emotions and does not know how to capture them in words. Ironically, she uses the word *impregnado* to describe his body. Even though this word can mean "thoroughly saturated" or "covered," it also refers to pregnancy, fullness, and immanent arrival. The speaker as a female is projecting her own emotions onto the male figure, a practice that will increase in later poems in this section. Her contradictory emotions express fullness and the need to give birth to her emotions through language but also the frustration and inability to find words to express herself.

In her attempt to capture this elusive means of expression, the speaker hears only the male's voice as he slips out of her grasp. Hearing his voice has a sensual effect on her, making her feel as if a gloved hand were caressing her leg. The mediation of the glove and the silky stocking she wears on her leg increases her desire at the same time that it thwarts fulfillment. As a result, the speaker recurs to auto-eroticism, again displacing and projecting her emotions. Rather than stating directly that she masturbates before going to sleep, she speaks of rubbing his voice against the hips of the sheets of her bed. This displacement increases the sensuality of the description but like masturbation points to the lack of the other. If the other is only a sheet (again, an image of the blank page on which the poet wishes to write), a ghostly, elusive absence stimulates the imagination but hinders experience. The speaker may derive some satisfaction and pleasure from her fantasy, but she is still sad at not having fulfilled her desire.

Though she feels inferior and inadequate, the speaker begins to gain more confidence in her relationship with the male figure, her muse. She begins the next poem in this section by denigrating her physical appearance. But it is exactly at this moment that the male seems to notice her for the first time: "Justo el día en que llevo gafas y un jersey horroroso / usted descubre mi arriconada existencia" (The very day that I wear my glasses and a horrible sweater / you discover my wallflower existence). The speaker is obviously and painfully self-conscious about her appearance. Even the word she chooses for glasses, *gafas,* sounds harsh and unattractive, along with her "horrendous" sweater. Moreover, she refers to her life as mere existence in a corner, as a kind of wallflower. Her contradictory feelings are evident in the following statement in the repetition of her surprise: "Le hablo con la sorpresa de no sorprenderme al tocar una ardilla" (I talk to him with the surprise of not being surprised on touching a squirrel). The solipsism of being surprised at not being surprised reveals her insecurity and lack of self-knowledge. This ambivalence is reinforced in the image of the squirrel, an animal that embodies tension in its quick, unpredictable movements and its abrupt stops (defensive strategies).

In the last stanza the speaker resists the temptation to hurl herself on the neck of the male figure, with his back to her, as he places some papers in a folder. Here again the metapoetic aspect emerges in the papers placed in the folder and in the description of her desire as an "alud de labios" (avalanche of lips). On the one hand, this phrase may refer to her desire to kiss him uncontrollably on the nape of the neck, but on the other, it describes an outpouring of words that the speaker-poet is barely able to contain. As she becomes more familiar with the male muse, she is gaining more impetus to express herself—erotically and poetically—an urge that goes beyond any inhibitions she may feel.

Guzmán makes direct reference to the image of the mirror in the fifth poem, which defines yet another step in the relationship between these two figures of the poet and her muse. The trivial, rapidly sketched details of the anecdotal scene again adopt metapoetic dimensions, but the image of the mirror suggests that the speaker is projecting her own feelings onto the male.

Hoy lleva una corbata de gavilanes en mi tono preferido de azul.
Almorzamos juntos gracias a la lírica
y, llegado el café,
se me hace inevitable mirarlo por encima de la taza,
para después sonreírme flequillo abajo como la niña mala que fui:
Somos exactamente iguales. Y ninguno de los dos conoce la existencia de
    los espejos.

(vv. 1–6)[11]

Double-voicing is again apparent in the verb *lleva,* so that we cannot be sure whether the speaker is using "usted" or "él," whether she speaks directly to him (although silently) or of him, whether there is proximity or distance between them. Her focus on his tie (a traditional phallic symbol of masculine power and authority) connotes a bird's soaring flight in the blue (the poet's inspiration carrying her to greater poetic heights) as well as the (masculine) sport of falconry and the hunt—the male as hunter and the female as prey. Does the speaker fantasize about the male seducing her, or is she projecting as she tries to seduce him? It is also significant that they are lunching together because of their mutual interest in poetry.

As they are having coffee, she cannot resist the temptation to flirt with him over the rim of her cup. It seems, though, that she sees herself as she would like him to see her, "como la niña mala que fui." The preterit tense in the verb *fui* conflicts with the mischief and playfulness of her bangs ("flequillo") and her coquettish use of the cup to dissimulate and enhance her advances.[12] Continuing to fantasize, she concludes that they are exactly alike in their disdain of the mirror, that is, narcissism. Yet it seems that narcissism is exactly what informs this scene: He is flattered by her attention while she imagines that he is equally enchanted with her innocent but sophisticated allure. She is both a child and a woman, seducing as she is seduced (or so she would like to believe). According to this unreliable narrator, neither of them is egocentric, a highly innocent and limited view of both love and the poet's involvement with the muse and the control one has of one's words in the act of writing. As readers, do we identify with the speaker, or do we distance ourselves from her? The ambivalence of the reader's position parallels that of the speaker both erotically and poetically, sexually and textually.

Indeed, throughout this first section of *Usted* the speaker exhibits her insecurity in this love relationship (of the writer and the muse) as she gains more confidence in the very act of writing. We see her constantly vacillating between insecurity and control. Because she is just learning what love and poetry are, the speaker-poet vacillates between uncertainty and enthusiasm, between self-doubt and desire, between seducing and being seduced, analogous to her act of writing. A key moment in the development of this section occurs when the speaker and the male figure meet again for lunch. In this poem the speaker identifies herself as Almudena, the alter ego of the poet who both is and is not the author. The same contrast between insecurity and impulsiveness obtains, but the speaker here addresses herself, adopting a greater sense of self-affirmation and determination to fulfill her desire for love and for writing.

> Volvemos a comer juntos.
> Este hombre cada día más guapo y a ti te rebasan las ojeras.
>
> Qué importa.
> Qué importa el poco tiempo que tienes para enamorarlo,
> qué importa la sopa fría
> —no puedes permitirte el lujo
> de perderlo de vista un solo instante, Almudena—,
> si cuando vas a citar *yo siempre estoy triste*
> él se anticipa y acariciándote los ojos dice que le encanta tu alegría.
>
> (vv. 1–9)[13]

Coming together to share another meal brings the speaker and the male figure face to face over a table, reminiscent of a writing desk. At first the speaker is cognizant of the differences between them and of her "inferiority." But by addressing herself in the second person, the speaker effects a change toward a less self-conscious attitude about love and writing, eros and logos. Her insistent repetition of the phrase *Qué importa* and her naming of herself as Almudena (the poet's first name) emphasize her self-affirmation as she throws caution to the wind. If the time she spends with her muse is so short, she might as well take advantage of it. Ironically, her loss of self-consciousness is both self-affirmation and disregard of self, but we perceive a change in her outlook. Formerly, she protected herself from herself (cf. the scarf) by worrying about her deficiencies. Now she values herself enough to forget about herself. Letting her soup get cold, she now establishes her priorities: Writing is more important and sustaining than food.[14]

This reversal in her attitudes leads to another ironic reversal in the final verses of the poem. Just as she is about to declare her feelings for the male figure by reciting a sentimental poem full of sadness and loneliness, he tells her how much he appreciates her liveliness and gaiety.[15] This compliment thwarts the expression of her inner feelings and short-circuits her self-affirmation because of the disparity between interior and exterior. His declaration overrides and suppresses hers in that she has chosen the sentimental words of a male poet to express herself. She therefore would sound ridiculous and false if she were to declare these words because they are not hers. She would be parroting, not speaking; he (the other, the audience, the reader) would see through her words, and she would appear ridiculous. Along with the direct address and the naming of herself, this poem represents a moment of illumination for the speaker as poet. The suppression of words she knows will ring hollow, will force her to seek her own words. The falsity of the image projected back to her by the male gaze frustrates but also illuminates the speaker as to her identity, that is, who she wants to be.

This first section of *Usted* concludes with three poems of disillusionment. In the first of these the speaker is seated on a bench outside and facing the window of her professor's office. Here again we see the speaker denigrating herself as she bounces her shoe on her foot. It is not enough that this activity is pointless and serves only to waste time; she also thinks her shoes look like a witch's. Does that mean they are ugly or that they lend her enchantment and allure? They—or she—do attract another male's attention, but the speaker is totally disdainful of this man for he does not measure up to her expectations: "(Otro—pensé—que tampoco tiene nada que hacer esta tarde)" (Another one—I thought—who doesn't have anything to do this afternoon). Their meeting would be transient and superficial (a type of writing she shuns). This other male is winter personified: Time has passed, but it has been a fruitless season in the speaker's life. The younger men who appear in this section function as foils for the male figure and bring out his superiority and ideality.

As she is about to leave, she spots her professor with his back to her in the window, speaking to someone else. At that exact moment her books (again, note the textual dimension) slip noisily and clumsily out of her lap, making her look foolish in his eyes as he turns around. Once again she appears inept and childish, and so she disparages herself. The male gaze catches her in an awkward moment, and she assumes awkwardness as characteristic of her identity. She sees herself negatively in the reflection of the male gaze that determines her sense of self.[16] However, she has attracted his attention.

In the penultimate poem of the section the professor impatiently and unceremoniously evicts her from his office, slamming the door behind her ponytail. This reference to her hair characterizes her as childish and is metonymically related to the professor's dismissal of her writing. The folder she carries in her hand is *mustia* (musty) an adjective that indirectly describes its contents, her writing. Moreover, this folder prevents her from pulling up her socks, another indication of her immature, bobby-soxer image—a far cry from the silk stockings mentioned earlier. Indeed, she states that she feels "muy pequeña, muy poca cosa" (very small, very insignificant) as he, "todo entrecejo fruncido" (all furrowed brow) forces her out of his office. His serious, wrinkled brow contrasts graphically with her juvenile image.

The final poem portrays their parting, presumably for a vacation, although the passage of time is ill-defined throughout this experience. Their farewell is marked by a handshake, a clear signal of the distance the male muse inserts between them. The speaker is clearly disappointed by this cold separation, which takes place in a bus shelter. This transparent, impersonal, public space is the point of departure, marking a temporary separation.

Given the absence of the male figure, the ten poems of the second section of *Usted* define a transitional period in the protagonist's development. These poems deal with her yearning for the absent male (the poet's loss of inspiration) and the different ways she has of coping with this absence. These are poems about longing but also about growth. Her maturation throughout this section is predicated on separation from the male and the experiences she undergoes on her own. The protagonist uses this time and these experiences to gain a better understanding of herself and to develop her independence from the ideal male other. A major theme of this section concerns the protagonist's coming to grips with her femininity (who she is and what she desires). At first her childish attitudes prevail. But she is keenly aware of the importance of this period in her life and of what she stands to gain. The absence of the male decenters him as the only means of making these discoveries. In the first poem, for example, she tries to minimize the absence of the other with a nonchalant attitude.

Usted se ha ido. Pero tampoco conviene dramatizar las cosas.

Cuando salgo a la calle,
aún me quedan muchas tapas risueñas en el tacón,
y mis medias de malla consiguen reducir la cintura de la tristeza
si su ausencia va silenciándome en una resaca de escarcha.

(vv. 1–5)[17]

Attempting to put up a brave front, the speaker goes out and pretends to have a good time eating "tapas" and wearing high heels and sexy stockings. It is patent, however, that she feels the absence of the other as "la cintura de la tristeza," as something limiting and binding on her. His absence also silences her "en una resaca de escarcha": Her sadness sometimes feels as if she were hung over, and the image of the frost implies a cold, bleak environment. Her attempts to deal with these feelings by going out (her reference to the "tacón" of her shoe connotes walking and activity) suggests that she is seeking inspiration by other means. She expresses both her pain and her determination to learn from this experience in the final stanza.

> O sea, que no estoy tan mal.
> Porque yo podré ser de vez en cuando un eclipse. Pero nunca
> un eclipse sin sangre de luz.

$$(vv. 7–10)^{18}$$

At the same time that she bravely, willingly, but falsely resigns herself to the other's absence, she is not happy with her role as "un eclipse." Without the light of her "sun," the protagonist feels "eclipsed," that is, empty, blank, without joy or brilliance.[19] She therefore recognizes that she is suffering as she mentions in the word *sangre* and that this suffering will lead her to illumination of new aspects of herself. She may feel eclipsed (diminished, brought low, joyless) by the absence of the other, but she is determined to learn something from this experience, to gain insight ("luz") in spite of her unhappiness. In other words, she endeavors to forge an independent view of herself, diverging her gaze from the male's.

In her nostalgia and melancholy for the absent other, the speaker at first seeks ways to soothe and assuage her loneliness. Connected with the emptiness already described, Kristeva refers to a "psychic void" that can be filled by meaningless or innocuous activities such as "wearing herself out doing housework or checking the children's homework."[20] Remembering her loss of innocence as a child, she reexperiences some of her childhood pleasures and transitions. In the second poem she compares the memory of the other to the loss of the childhood pleasure of going down the sliding board: "Su recuerdo es como la fe de aquella infancia, / rota al mismo tiempo que mis braguitas en el último tobogán" (His memory is like faith in that infancy, / broken at the same time as my underpants on the last sliding board). Her disillusionment is comparable to that moment when she realized that she was no longer a child and had to be more demure because she had torn her underwear while going down the slide. This image also evokes the moment of her first menstrual period through its metonymic proximity to the genital area and the image of something being torn.[21] The second stanza underscores this impression in its reference to short skirts and the speaker's self-

consciousness: "No duele, sólo desespera un poco, igual que esas fal-
das cortas de después de la fiebre" (It doesn't hurt, it only exasperates
a little, just like those short skirts after a fever).

In the aftermath (of her period and of his departure) she no longer
feels pain but is still concentrating on the event and anticipating further pain. She assuages these feelings by eating pastries: "Y lo rebaño
cada día con pan dulce" (And I sop it up each day with sweet bread).
Her choice of the verb *rebaño* merits attention because of its reitera-
tive prefix and the soothing softness implied by the act of bathing.
Rebañar, however, literally means "to sop up" or "to wipe clean" (another image that evokes the menstrual period).

The third poem in this sequence hinges on the extended metaphor of the children's game of stepping from one square of the pave-
ment or tile floor to another. The speaker pretends that if she can
step on three blocks, she will go to his house just to look at it from
the outside, but if not, she will go home. This childish method of making a decision is doomed from the beginning, but it gives her insight
into what she really wants. The odds are stacked against the speaker.
In the end, however, she decides to cheat. She has not stepped on
three blocks but four, and breaking the rules that she herself has imposed on her decision, she goes to his house, again in the vain hope
of catching a glimpse of him even though she knows he is not there.
The childish game and the impulsiveness of the speaker's actions represent the point of departure for her transition toward more adult
ways of dealing with absence and solitude.

The four poems in the center of this section form a key step in the
speaker's growth. In these poems she comes to grips with absence, attains greater insight into who she is, and grows in independence. The
most important event in this series entails the speaker's encounter
with another woman in the mirror of a plate-glass window. She sees
herself in this other woman in the mention of her "flequillo," but she
also recognizes her difference from her.

> Una mujer de ron y esmalte negro,
> flequillo y vagina cosmopolita,
> me abre sus piernas tras los cristales del meublé.
>
> Es la niebla.

$$(vv.\ 1\text{–}4)^{22}$$

The other woman in this scene both attracts and repulses the
speaker as she sees herself as both similar and different from her. The
focus on certain details rapidly sketches a characterization of the
other woman as Guzmán highlights a few pertinent details of the

other to juxtapose her with the protagonist. Instead of saying that this woman is drinking rum, the poet calls her "una mujer de ron," giving her a stronger personality and suggesting a certain dissipation or decadence. Her drinking rum may be a reference to her impact on the speaker given that rum is a strong, intoxicating beverage that can have an unexpected effect on the drinker. But the rum, along with the reference to her "esmalte negro," may also mean that the other woman has a dark complexion, is wearing dark clothing, or has a tough, threatening air about her. (At least the speaker feels threatened in this circumstance.) All of these would have the same effect of attraction and repulsion, intoxication as both heightened and dulled consciousness. Her dark nail polish suggests a certain decadence that allures and warns away. Fingernails are a prevalent image in *Usted* as a means of characterizing women, and polish on nails suggests defenses.[23] The modification of the woman's sexuality as "cosmopolita" implies that she is experienced in the ways of the world, perhaps because she is a prostitute. Indeed, the French word *meublé* designates a house of prostitution and connotes an exotic, French attitude toward love.[24]

When the woman in the mirror (the window functions as a glass surface on which the image of the observer is reflected and superimposed on the other) spreads her legs, she is clearly making a proposition to the speaker.[25] The final phrase of the poem, "Es la niebla," indicates the speaker's confusion. She does not know how to respond to this invitation because of the contradictions she feels. She may want to emulate the knowledge, self-confidence, and disinterested attitude that she admires in the other woman, but she marks a definite distinction between them in her heterosexual orientation as opposed to the other's offer of a same-sex encounter. The "mist" with which she describes this experience refers to her momentary confusion. A significant aspect of this brief encounter is the absence of the male. Another woman as the other decenters the male and focuses on feminine issues and perspectives as a way to constitute subjectivity. This experience then leads the speaker to a fuller understanding of her own desire, as expressed in the following companion poem.

> Veladamente,
> descorriendo pestillos,
> ha llegado hasta mi cuarto
> una pantera translúcida con la piel de diamante
> que me morderá la nuca cuando menos lo espere.
>
> Es el deseo.
>
> (vv. 1–6)[26]

Here the speaker characterizes her desire as a sleek, elegant panther that moves silently and gracefully and is able to overcome all barriers. Its translucid fur sparkles like a diamond, establishing a contrast between the brilliance of these images and the black color of a panther. These characteristics refer to the protagonist's sensuality and sexiness, creating an image of herself as a beautiful but dangerous, unpredictable, desirous woman. This contrast is in no way discordant. It softens and enhances the image of the woman in the "meublé" in the previous poem in spite of the same sense of danger and fatal attraction. In other words, these two companion poems mirror one another. In the first, the speaker discovers who she is *not,* whereas in the second she defines herself through this image of her desire. The image of the panther is one that the speaker can willingly accept of herself and her desire. Although it is unpredictable, it is highly attractive. The description of the panther evokes Kristeva's definition of the "black sun" because of its shiny darkness. We should recall that this poem is the second of a paired set. These poems thus represent a turning point in the speaker's perception of this image. However, this change is short-circuited in the later poems of the collection, and the speaker returns to the primary definition of the "black sun." The recognition of herself and her desire in these poems marks her maturation and the higher definition of her identity.

The change the speaker has undergone can be seen in the final three poems in this section. The next poem specifically mentions the mirror, and the hangover may be an indication that the speaker has had a same-sex encounter, although the poem is disjointed and the references vague. The juxtaposition of different images fragments the speaker's reality, imitating a hangover, but the mention of rum alludes to the woman in the window of the "meublé."

> Botafumeiro de espinas
> y vómitos.
>
> Ron de la noche,
> Alka Seltzer
> —¿Es que nadie va a hacerme una manzanilla?—,
> cucas portuarias insensibles al Baygón.
>
> Ácida calima de duna desarraigada en un espejo.
>
> (vv. 1–7)[27]

Reference to the Botafumeiro, the incensary of the Cathedral of Santiago de Compostela, and to the thorns lends religious overtones to what seems to be a trying experience for the speaker. But *bota-fumeiro* also means "adulation," suggesting seduction and imitation. After drinking rum, the speaker has a hangover and needs Alka Seltzer and an herbal tea to ease her headache and to calm her queasy stomach. Her statement "cucas portuarias insensibles al Baygón" may describe the other women around her (sisters? friends? roommates?) whom she criticizes for their perceived insensitivity to her physical and psychological needs. She accuses them even of being insensitive to the popular insecticide Baygón (By-Gone is a brand name) because she cannot get rid of them. The "cucas" evoke "cucarachas" or the feminine form of "cucos" (hence, bogeywomen). These images also evoke the "mujer de ron" in the previous poem who has a "vagina cosmopolita." But they may also refer to her hangover and her memories of the night before. It is only when she enters the bathroom and looks at herself in the mirror following this night of debauchery that she recognizes changes in her outlook.[28] It is possible that she has just taken a shower, which would account for the mist on the mirror where she sees herself and reacts "acidly" to the vision in the mirror. (Or it could be that her vision is blurred—literally and figuratively.) By mentioning a dune, the speaker evokes the salty, misty air of the beach and the sense of barrenness that she feels. That this dune is uprooted describes her sense of loneliness (the absence of the male figure exasperated by the experience she has just undergone) and the shifting ground of her identity as she is in the process of change. She questions her identity not only because of the male's absence but also because she is defining her own perspective, defining herself as a *sujet-en-procès*.

The final two poems of this section—also paired poems like the woman in the "meublé" and the panther poems—present the speaker in a new light. To assuage her loneliness, she has gone out with other men, but these young men only bore her. She describes the first as a "cretino" who can talk of nothing else but his experience in the military (an obligatory stint for Spanish youths). She also notes that he does so "mientras me tapa baboso la calle y la vida / con su espalda" (while he blocks me slimily from the street and life / with his back). This slimy, repulsive masculine figure, apparently drooling from desire for the speaker, limits her outlook on life and leaves her dissatisfied with the perspective he offers. Her impatience with the situation is augmented by her lack of cigarettes: She has an addictive yearning and taste for something more satisfying. The poem then ends with a rather lengthy and detailed parenthetical fantasy of her unbuttoning and removing her professor's shirt—whether he wants her to or not. This fantasy portrays her rather than the male as the active partner in the relationship.

The final poem in this pair and this section again places the speaker in a boring encounter with another man, but we learn that only at the end of the poem. Prior to that revelation, she addresses her absent ideal by telling him how boring her life is without him. She compares the passing hours with translucent lemons from which she squeezes (bitter) juice onto her wrists—her pulse—in a type of mock suicide: As she says, she drains these lemons of their juice "de una manera desesperadamente cobarde" (in an desperately cowardly way). While comparing the boring passage of time with suicide, the ebbing away of life, she participates in other experiences only as a means of preparation for the beloved's return.

Separation from the male figure allows the protagonist time to grow, so that when they are reunited in the third section, she has gained more self-knowledge and self-confidence. The intensity of feminine affect comes to the fore in this crucial section of *Usted,* which opens with another mention of the mirror. This mirror happens to be the rearview mirror of a car, and it focuses attention on the joining of hands that initiates the relationship between the speaker and her professor. The ambivalent adjective *lírica* along with the mention of the hands lends metapoetic dimensions to this moment.

> Sólo conservo
> —gracias al espejo retrovisor—
> la vaga refracción lírica
> de dos manos,
> que estrechadas frente a un desafío de tactos dispares
> se hicieron amantes.
>
> (vv. 1–6)[29]

Whereas the rearview mirror serves to locate the anecdotal scene in an automobile, it also functions as an emblem of memory, connecting with the past: the reunion with the beloved. The speaker focuses on one single element, a synecdoche of the entire moment that serves as the extended metaphor of the poem. Moreover, the poet has chosen the word *refracción* rather than *reflejo* to indicate a certain degree of distortion attributable not only to the reversal of the image in the mirror but also a skewing of the perspective. Within the frame of the mirror the union of the hands (perhaps reminiscent of M. C. Escher's well-known drawing of a hand drawing a hand) points to the act of writing and the complementary relationship between the muse and the poet. The tension in this exchange is evident in the words *un desafío de tactos dispares* and the contrasting follow-up phrase *se hicieron amantes.* The reciprocity between the writer and her inspiration is characterized both as a challenge (one to the other) and as a loving relationship. The image in the mirror also calls into question the issue of representation and the ability of language to capture the moment. This poem thus begins the speaker's love affair with her literature professor but also the poet's engagement with poetry on a new level of intimacy.

Fearing that their relationship will be banal and trite, the speaker expresses her doubts about this affair in the following poem. She even questions whether it would be better to extract herself from this situation now because of the risks involved. Apparently the lovers have tied up traffic because they have engaged in some heavy petting and have not noticed that the light has changed. The blaring of horns—certainly a common event in Madrid traffic—also evokes the idea of a discordant announcement heralding the beginning of the affair, much like a musical fanfare. This ironic as well as triumphant blare presages the eventual failure of this relationship and the pain it will cause the speaker. Again the second-person address interrupts the speaker's consideration of fleeing the scene, a rational voice in counterpoint with the speaker's feelings of love and inspiration.

> y me planteo si no será mejor
> —aún estás a tiempo—
> huir de sus ojos como quien huye del atasco,
> porque usted me vuelve loca . . .
>
> (vv. 5–8)[30]

This madness is the ecstasy of both love and poetic inspiration, but the two voices in counterpoint (similar to the double-voicing of the third-person verbs meaning "usted" and "él") also reflects the tension in the relationship posited in the previous poem. They are "Presos los dos de aquel imposible decoro adolescente" (Both prisoners of that impossible adolescent decorum), that is, caught in idealistic expectations, and they run off to their first sexual encounter "como quien va al estanco de los primeros cigarrillos" (like someone who goes to the tobacco shop for her first cigarettes), engaging in socially censored activity. The description of the foreplay in the next poem foregrounds the woman's experience of orgasm. By revitalizing inveterate imagery of a bee and a flower, the speaker decenters the phallus and privileges female sexuality.

> Exquisita pendencia la de mi boca y la suya
> por ese dedo abeja que libó entre murmullos y distensiones golosas,
> las sucesivas floraciones de mi anémona nocturna.
>
> (vv. 1–3)[31]

Although we might wince at the trite image of the bee and the flower, the erotic overtones comparing the vagina to a nocturnal anemone and the male finger to the bee turns to the speaker's advantage because the poem privileges a woman's experience during intimate relations.[32] The phallus is suggested but minimized in the metonymic figure of the finger, whereas the speaker's "murmullos y distensiones golosas, / las sucesivas floraciones de mi anémona nocturna" stresses woman's pleasure and her capacity for multiple orgasms. The bee stimulates, but the woman's responses ("murmullos," "distensiones golosas," "sucesivas floraciones") predominate over male orgasm. Consequently, this "exquisita pendencia" describes the poet's and reader's encounters with language and the power of recontextualization of traditional imagery to create intense poetic experiences. This poem evokes similarities with some of Bécquer's *rimas* in their erotic overtones, the effective recontextualization of Romantic imagery, and the release of linguistic power through compact expression.

The first four poems of this section thus establish the ebb and flow of the speaker's affair with the male figure. The tension between the two and the speaker's wavering between control and loss of control of herself continue in play throughout this section. She clearly rejects the status of muse for herself in this relationship, however. Even though she recognizes that their affair is unexceptional ("Reconozco que no somos muy originales, / nuestra historia es la de medio Madrid" [I recognize that we are not very original, / that our story is that of half of Madrid]), she refuses a traditional role. As she states, "no seré yo desde luego la imbécil que pierda su tiempo en agradar a los poetas" (I of course will not be the imbecile who wastes her time pleasing poets). Unlike other women who may be involved in this type of affair, she will not let herself be used as an object for male gratification. The future tense as definitive asseveration, the emphasis on the first-person pronoun *yo,* the interruption in the phrase *desde luego,* and the subjunctive mood of *pierda* suggesting a hypothesis that will not become reality—all these elements point to the speaker's determination not to let herself be used. She is instead rewriting her role in the relationship as a woman and as an active participant rather than an object.

The polyvalent image of the mirror reappears in the following poem. As the relationship between the two advances, the speaker acquires an image of herself that is constantly clearer and more pleasing. The mention of her eyes in relation to the gaze in the mirror is particularly important in the definition of self.

A cada contracción del espejo
se me iba poniendo la piel preciosa
mientras cumplía
—toda ojos velados—
aquella indecente promesa nuestra de las doce.

(vv. 1–5)[33]

The word *contracción* has erotic overtones that suggest a comparison between the mirror and the vagina. The speaker's increasing experience in love allows her to focus more clearly on who she is, so that her image in the mirror becomes closer and more well defined. The beautiful alliteration of the first two verses moves the place of production of the /k/ and /j/ in the back of the oral cavity to the frontal /b/ and /p/, foregrounding the emergence of the speaker's identity in her use of language. As she goes to another rendezvous with her lover, she describes herself as "toda ojos velados." On a quite literal level, we might interpret this image as her wearing eye shadow, making her more womanly and adult, more alluring and seductive, or as her eyes half-closed in erotic ecstasy.[34] But to what extent is she also trying to deceive herself? Does her keen focus on her complexion in the mirror reflect her happiness or the superficiality of the image? To what extent is she aware that this relationship is not lasting, is only superficial, and to what extent does she fool herself into believing that it will last? She fulfills a promise—to herself as much as to him—but she admits that the promise is "indecente" and tries to distance it with the demonstrative adjective *aquella*. Even the mention of the time "las doce" is ambivalent. It is not clear whether it is noon or midnight, the time of greatest illumination and insight, or a bewitching hour that deceives and casts a malevolent spell. Is the speaker aware of what she is getting herself into, or is she bewitched by her own feelings? Is she breaking away from the male gaze and establishing her own gaze, or is she still under the spell of the male's opinion of her?

This poem is followed by a series of poems that focus on the male figure, evidenced by their beginning with "Señor" and "Usted" before returning to the speaker's intense experience of orgasm. While it is true that the speaker responds to him, revealing her emotions, the male seems to gain the upper hand in spite of the speaker's struggles to maintain her autonomy. The next poem is symmetrical in its construction in that a parenthetical series of details interrupts the main sentence. However, the scene describes an uncomfortable act of fellatio (an oral act) performed in a car. The obstacles, discomfort, and dangers involved in this experience carry over into the speaker's life the next day, making her distracted and out of touch with her surroundings. Listed impersonally as "la cremallera problemática, / la mota en la lentilla, / los guardias al lado, / el frío" (the problematic zipper, / the mote of dust in the contact lens, / the guards off to one side, / the cold weather), these minor irritations make for a dissatisfying experience, though one the speaker cannot get out of her mind. Does the final phrase, *el frío,* describe the thrill the speaker experienced in this moment or the lack of passion in this act? Who is using whom in this relationship?

In the next poem the two are making love, with her on top of him. Their two bodies have blended in the exchange of sexual fluid and sweat, which would seem to indicate their fusion and loss of self in other. But it is at this moment that the speaker wants to call the whole thing off: "quisiera decirle / . . . / que no puedo más, / que voy a pararme" (I would like to tell him / . . . / that I cannot go on, that I am going to stop). Does this statement refer to the pleasure of that particular moment, which is overwhelming, or to the relationship in its entirety because of something the speaker dreads? The parenthetical phrase that concludes the poem defines the depths of passion and experience that the speaker is discovering, but also her fear and resistance: "(Era el placer como una de esas muñecas rusas que se abren / y aparece otra, / y otra)" (It was the same pleasure as one of those Russian dolls that opens / and reveals another, / and another). Is she or is she not in control of her situation?

The companion poem of this one refers to the aftermath, the day after their sexual encounter, and confuses the rain with a bath. Rain, like light, is a traditional symbol of poetic inspiration, which the speaker still experiences the day after. But does the memory of the experience continue as a sensorial, sensual encounter, or does it threaten to drown the speaker? Is the rain a traditional image used to project the speaker's feelings of drowning in sadness and loneliness, or is it enlivening, fertilizing, stimulating?

> Señor,
> la lluvia del domingo
> es una inmensa bañera
> que me sumerge a cámara lenta
> en el telón espumoso de sus rizos del sábado.
>
> (vv. 1–5)[35]

Because of the mention of Sunday we might even think of the rain as purification in the religious sense as well as tears of sadness and repentance. Moreover, the cinematographic phrase *a cámara lenta* evokes the falsity of representation while at the same time it intensifies the emotions of the scene, as does the image of the rain as a curtain that both deforms and softens the image. The extension of the poetic verse from the short two-syllable opening to the sixteen-syllable line is indicative of a surrender, but the surrender can be read as a positive giving of oneself to an emotion or the ebbing away of control and life. This duality replicates the ambivalence of the verb phrase *me sumerge* in spite of the passive position of the speaker in the grammar of this phrase.

These poems lead to another passionate encounter between the two lovers. Here the emphasis shifts back to the speaker's experience of sexual gratification and an eclipsing of the phallus in favor of the clitoris.

> Soy un racimo de uvas
> y aguanto como puedo
> este oleaje creciente de su boca
> aguijoneándome al sol.
>
> Hasta que estallo.
>
> (vv. 1–5)[36]

Grapes are a traditional symbol of fertility and metonymically are related to intoxication, the intensity of the erotic/poetic experience. The speaker describes herself as a bunch of grapes on the vine that the light of the sun spurs to growth. This image represents cunnilingus, another oblique metapoetic allusion. Particularly striking is the second verse of this poem given that the verb *aguanto* connotes resistance that heightens the intensity of the experience but that also expresses dissatisfaction that the speaker tolerates. Her male partner seems to push her to extremes that she is not ready or not willing to approach. If grapes metonymically allude to intoxication and intoxication is heightened or dulled consciousness, it is unclear to what extent the speaker feels in control of the experience by making her own choices. It is both stimulating and frightening. When in the final verse she states that she explodes, it may be from total fulfillment and ecstasy, or a breaking point that pushes her over the edge.

Indeed, the very next poem marks a change in their relationship. While they are eating spaghetti for supper (presumably in a restaurant), he says something that offends her. As usual in these poems, the details are not included, only the speaker's emotional reaction. Note also that this poem begins with the appositive *Señor*, recalling several of the poems leading up to the culmination point in the previous poem.

Señor,
si usted sabe
que yo ahora estoy celosa
por lo que me ha dicho,
tenga al menos el detalle de no hacérmelo notar durante la cena.

(Nunca en mi vida enrollé espaguetis con tanto odio.)

(vv. 1–6)[37]

Humor emerges in the last verse of this poem from the incongruent juxtaposition of the trivial act of twirling spaghetti and the anger the protagonist feels at this moment. By displacing her anger and understating it with the parentheses, the speaker imitates the male reaction to something she has said: He has trivialized it, ridiculed it, or pointed out the impracticality of the idea. Her use of the phrase *estoy celosa* indicates the male's preference or at least attraction to someone else and his diminishment or disregard of the speaker's feelings. He has not been sensitive to her feelings by bringing the matter up while they are dining. Her emphasis on the inclusion of *usted* expresses her anger, along with the precise, conventional language of her reproach in the phrase "tenga al menos el detalle de no hacérmelo notar." This mock-courteous phraseology underscores the social dimensions of the scene and bears on the metapoetic aspect. It would seem that the male figure has in some way disparaged the speaker's maturity or perhaps her idealistic expectations. Perhaps she has not been giving enough (emotionally), a critique of her ability to write with sustained passion. After all, the poems of this collection are all quite brief (although that in no way impugns their intensity). Or perhaps he does not feel the same commitment to their relationship that she is developing, in which case the intensity of her writing is not cerebral enough for him, does not attain the transcendence that he prefers, is too corporally centered. Whatever his comment, it serves as the pretext for curtailing the relationship.

Moreover, this crucial moment again forms part of the sexual-textual semiosis. For just when the woman writer feels herself achieving plenitude of expression and fulfillment in the production of the text, a masculinist reader dismisses and devalues her poetry by not taking it seriously, not understanding it, or criticizing it for its lack of depth, intensity, and/or universality given that he cannot identify with it.[38] His insensitivity causes the speaker-poet's disillusionment with the direction of her work because of the literature professor's criticism.[39]

The speaker's displacement of her anger in her act of twirling spaghetti receives a variation in the next poem. Here she is daydreaming in class about some of their encounters. Whereas details such as the loss of her earrings or runs in her nylons appear trivial, they lead metonymically to the genital area and a suggestion of loss, disillusionment, disappointment, even violence. In the midst of this reflection, the speaker's friend Mari Carmen asks to borrow a pen, at which the speaker expresses her anger openly to this other female.

> —¿Tienes un bolígrafo de más?
> —Toma, y a ver si dejas de pedirme cosas,
> que contigo al lado no hay quien coja un apunte, Mari Carmen.
> (vv. 7–9)[40]

That a pen is involved in this exchange is no mere triviality given the metapoetic implications of the text. The speaker has clearly displaced her anger at the lover onto her friend, a reflection of herself. (If Almudena is an Arabic name, Mari Carmen is clearly a Virginal Catholic one.) The speaker's anger, expressed openly and impatiently, in effect is aimed at herself, not only because she was distracted and not taking notes (copying the male professor's words) but also because it reminds her of her "failure" at writing. This section then ends with an unstable peace between the two lovers. The speaker's illusion of attaining a certain status as a woman (and) writer has definitely undergone disappointment after a promising beginning.

From this point forward the relationship and the poems take a disturbing turn. The poems of the fourth section are almost surreal in their presentation of the events because the speaker seems numb. This section recounts a trip made by the lovers to a distant city, although it is difficult to determine which city. Because of the description of the rainy, cold weather and a cathedral that they visit, we might deduce that they go to either Santiago de Compostela or to London. In light of the restriction on abortion in the Catholic country of Spain during the Franco era, London was traditionally the city Spanish women visited to have this procedure done. Even if there is no literal abortion performed on the anecdotal level of the text (as the author Guzmán maintains), the effect of this trip vitiates all life from the speaker, leaving her destitute emotionally. The effect of these poems is chilling in the portrait they present of the speaker as a woman.

The indifference and zombielike state of the speaker are evident from the very beginning of this section. The first word we read is an isolated *Nada* (Nothing), reinforced by the double negative of the second verse "No pegaba nada con tanta lluvia" (Nothing was sticking with so much rain). This hopeless mood conflicts acutely with "esa chaqueta de angorina rosa y botones de nácar / que él me regaló" (that jacket of fine pink wool and mother-of-pearl buttons / that he bought for me). The rosy pink color of the jacket, the softness of the "angorina," and the iridescent mother-of-pearl buttons seem totally out of place in this grim, rainy landscape. Note that "angorina" is an artificial angora, a "man"-made fiber that represents false tenderness. These same elements suggest innocence, and the mother-of-pearl buttons allude obliquely to a pearl, a tiny growth within the soft and irritated interior of a clam (a vaginal image). Moreover, the speaker explicitly substitutes *él* for *usted* in this passage, connoting the distance between them.

Further images of damage and loss of innocence can be found in the second stanza. Here the protagonists are prevented from lighting a candle to the apostle (St. James in either London or Santiago) when a young child bumps his head on the baptismal font. This trivial incident again shows harm being done to a child, particularly because it entails the font. Emblematic of innocence, a washing away of sins, and new life, the font and the sacrament it represents are negated by the hurt inflicted on the child. Given that this image may be figurative as well as literal, the child may represent the hopes the speaker had for the relationship between her lover (her poetic inspiration) and her. When the child's parents arrive, the speaker surrenders the child to them in contrast with her own hopes for fulfillment through the poetic act. That they were prevented from lighting a candle again alludes to the lack of hope (light) and the deprivation of saintly or divine intervention. (Note that the protagonist gives up the child.)

Because the cathedral museum (a place where relics reminding them of the past are housed when they are no longer in use) was also disappointing, they go out for a walk: "y al final un paseo dudosamente conciliador por los soportales" (and finally a stroll dubiously conciliatory along the columned walkway). Here they encounter another scene that again points out the differences between them: "—basta que a mí me hicieran gracia los punkies, para que a él lo escandalizasen—" (—it was enough for me to be tickled by the punkies, for him to be scandalized by them—). The presence of punkies would seem to be irrefutable evidence of their being in England, but they could just as easily be young Spaniards or British tourists in Santiago. In any event they delight the speaker but scandalize her lover, a contrast reinforced by the change in the form of the imperfect subjunctive. Following this incident, their choice of beverages at a bar reflects the same contrast: She asks for milk and he for "su maniática ginebra 'MG / con Schweppes de naranja, por favor'" (his maniacal gin 'MG with orange Schweppes, please'). Does she avoid alcohol because she may be pregnant? Isn't it a little odd that she orders milk at a bar? These differences in their behavior and reactions attest to the growing emotional and physical separation between them. The poem then ends with an afterthought on the speaker's part, a lack of importance signaling that it is even more telling. It is further disconcerting that the speaker addresses these comments to several others as if she were writing a letter or a postcard about their visit.

> Ah,
> se me olvidaba contaros
> que el frío fue la nota predominante del día
> y que la noche, a pesar de todo, la pasamos juntos.
>
> Espalda contra espalda.
>
> (vv. 14–18)[41]

Again the coldness of the relationship is underscored by the sympathetic image of the weather, the contrast between day and night, and of course the final statement. Even though the lovers sleep in the same bed, nothing occurs between them as they have their backs turned toward one another. Even the preposition *contra* connotes their mutual antagonism.

The imagery describing the speaker's mental state grows increasingly more ominous and violent. For example, that night she has a dream in which she sees the male figure as "un barbero borracho" whom she envisions as a fire-eater or sword-swallower in a circus. In other words, he swallows all the light (inspiration and happiness) available, but he is putting on a show. Once again, the speaker ends this poem with one of her highly effective parenthetical expressions in which she sees him sweeping her body away as if she were a dead moth fatally attracted to his flame. And he does so "silbando" (whistling), as if she meant nothing to him. In yet another poem the silence between them allows her to hear the swift fall of the guillotine blade onto the nape of her neck. The images of this poem show that the speaker feels helpless in the face of impending doom.

> Antes,
> nunca hubo el silencio necesario entre abrazo y abrazo
> para advertir el parpadeo de esta guillotina
> que hoy,
> al rozar por sorpresa mi nuca con sus manos de lejía
> me ha puesto los ojos amargos.

> Yo misma no me oigo cuando grito.
> Querría huir. Pero ya es tarde:
> las sábanas se han convertido en agua cenagosa
>   mezclada con pegamento.
>
> Y dentro de poco,
> como esa cosa horrible siga detrás de mí
> y usted continúe dormido,
> me moriré de risa ante el retrato de Leonardo que
>   tengo enfrente de mi cadáver.
>
> (vv. 1–13)[42]

These haunting images reveal the distress of the speaker. She screams but cannot hear herself, as in a nightmare, and she cannot flee because the sheets of the bed have turned into muddy water mixed with glue that prevent freedom of movement. Whether these are dream images or fantasies the speaker has while awake, they are frightening because of her lack of control over her own body and the lack of concern and awareness of her plight on the part of the male figure (who sleeps through it). Her hysteria seems truly irrational if, as she says, she will die laughing because of the portrait of Leonardo da Vinci that she has in front of her, or that she sees even though it is not immediately there. I would suggest that this portrait is that of Mona Lisa whose mysterious smile has been the emblem of feminine enigma throughout the centuries.[43] In culmination the speaker refers to her body as a cadaver rather than something alive and vital. Does she feel this despair because of an impending abortion, the loss of that part of herself that has life but will lose it, leaving her empty and "sterile"?

The climax of this section takes place in a chilling poem full of violence and torture. It is this poem that most suggests that an abortion takes place, although it may not be a literal event but rather the vitiating of the speaker's self-respect and autonomy.

> Quién es esta sombra
> que aterriza limpiamente en mi cuerpo
> como un halcón.
>
> Su garra me frena las muñecas y la huida.
>
> Su aliento de niebla va sajando despacio,
> los tersos y ahora bermejos visillos de mi vientre.
>
> (vv. 1–6)[44]

The lack of punctuation of the initial question and the image of the shadow descending like a falcon on the body of the speaker suggests a loss of consciousness through either sleep or an anaesthetic. Moreover, the falcon evokes a predatory animal associated with the masculine activity of falconry and hunting, making the speaker and her body the prey or victim. This impression is compounded by the falcon's use of its talons to restrain the speaker's wrists to prevent her from fleeing. In another surreal or dreamlike state the speaker finds herself unable to escape from the restraints imposed on her by the male figure and patriarchal society's positioning of her. If not an abortion, this scene might represent unwilling sex on the part of the female speaker, a rape that she has no power—physical or societal—to resist.

The final image of the poem repeats the dark violence of the falcon's descent upon her in the word *niebla* echoing *sombra* in the first line and in the verb *va sajando* demonstrating the effect of the falcon's talons. *Niebla* also appears in the poem about the "mujer de ron," where it represents the speaker's confusion and sense of being threatened. In fact, the talons may refer to the surgical instrument used for scraping the uterus during an abortion. By comparing her womb with sheer curtains ("visillos"), the speaker expresses her loss of innocence. If this scene represents the extended metaphor of an abortion, it shows her change in the color of the sheers. Normally, these window treatments are a gauzy translucent white, but here they become a bright, bloody red. The sadistic cruelty of the "surgeon" performing this "operation" is apparent in the adverb *despacio*. Is this a dream, an abortion (surgical or spontaneous), or a rape? In any event, the speaker feels vitiated and cruelly dispossessed of her inner self through the image of the falcon.

In the final poem of this section the speaker has returned home and emptied her suitcase on her bed. The suitcase represents her memories and her inner self, as we have seen in the poetry of Atencia and Rossetti. In contrast with those instances, Guzmán does not use the suitcase as memory in which to store things but as something she empties, trying to forget what has happened. The contents are not beautiful and treasured, but repulsive and worthy of rejection. When she describes this chaotic tumble of clothing as a "revoltijo de sapos" (a jumble of toads), she shows her disgust for herself in the repulsion she feels for slimy toads. As a result of her experiences, the speaker is obviously depressed: She becomes weary of the simple task of storing her clothes in the closet, and she is crying hysterically, uncontrollably. Significantly, she fears what her mother will think. This evocation of another female figure, and most importantly of her mother as role model and woman, represents the superego that stimulates a sense of guilt in the speaker's psyche. Her mother also represents an older generation and a different image of woman. Whether the hope for a brighter future or the criticism of the attempt to attain more freedom for women, this mother figure causes the speaker to recognize the disillusionment with her aspirations, her failure, and painfully to acknowledge her similarities and differences with this mirror image. The poet captures these complex emotions in the final image of the poem, an ekphrastic reference to Mantegna's well-known painting "Dead Christ."

> y escribiendo una y otra vez que la vida es el escorzo
> más doloroso
> que hubiera podido pintar Mantegna en sus pesadillas.
>
> (vv. 7–9)[45]

These verses refer to the painting of the dead Christ foreshortened and overlooked by his grieving mother, Mary. As the prototypical mother figure, Mary provides yet another image of the speaker as woman and mother and of her mother. To what extent does Christ represent pure innocence, life, an ideal, or the loss of a child (through senseless death)? The foreshortening (Christ is viewed from his feet) makes the scene immediate, as if the viewer were one of the grievers. The immediacy intensifies the grief, as does the phrase *en sus pesadillas*. Life is a nightmare, according to the speaker, equivalent to crucifixion.

The longest poem in the collection, the final poem is also the most disturbing because of the image of woman it presents. The image she projects as childish, helpless, superficial victim is a remaking of the self in accord with the male gaze. If we recall at this point that the book is dedicated "A Usted, en obediencia," we recognize the speaker's irony as well as her seriousness. The childish image of a woman interested solely in such superficial details as her fresh nail polish, her hair, and which miniskirt to wear embodies a prototypical patriarchal image of a woman. Yet, several elements of this dramatic monologue reveal the speaker's irony and the serious commentary beneath the frivolous surface. One consistent aspect of this poem is the combination of hyperbole with understatement. The speaker's nonchalant attitude and her focus on her fingernails reveal her ironic attitude.

> Como me aburro mucho
> mientras las uñas se secan,
> miro de reojo el calendario:

hoy es veintidós
y este domingo desde su charco de patitos rojos
me salpica la memoria:
Creo que usted cumple años,
pero no lo sé seguro,
tampoco voy a llamarlo, la verdad,
más que nada por las uñas.

(vv. 1–10)[46]

Emphasis on her fingernails points not only to the protagonist's help-lessness but also to her defensiveness and need for self-protection. She may even feel a need to disparage her feelings for her lover by placing him in an inferior priority to her nails and other aspects of her appearance, thus expressing her apparent indifference. Her bore-dom, the expression *de reojo,* her equivocation ("Creo que," "no lo sé seguro"), and finally the interposed *la verdad* are all equivocal. For example, to look at the calendar "de reojo" means both "out of the corner of her eye" (expressing her indifference) and "giving it double, repeated attention" (*re-*), doing a double-take and realizing some-thing. Even the date on the calendar, the twenty-second of the month, a Sunday, so that the numerals are in red ink, is overdetermined.

22

The number two and the pairing of them remind her of their re-lationship, whereas the red color can connote passion or pain. The trivial detail of seeing these numbers as little red ducks that pique her memory suggests a childish image and yet disillusionment. They even suggest drops of blood, the menstrual cycle, and the slipping away of the possibility to conceive a child (her "failure" at writing).

The equivocality of the language in this opening stanza belies a first, superficial reading. Rather than view the speaker as childish, in-different, and frivolous, we should recognize the rage underneath her words. The recognition of this rage indicates that the speaker still has self-respect and still hopes to overcome the obstacles placed in the way of her fulfillment. As Adam Phillips has perceptively stated,

That we can feel humiliated reveals how much what matters to us matters to us. Our rage is itself a commitment to something, to something pre-ferred. . . . Once you know who or what humiliates you, you know what it is about yourself that you ultimately value, that you worship. Tell me what makes you enraged—what makes you feel truly diminished—and I will tell you what you believe or what you want to believe about yourself. What, that is, you imagine you need to protect to sustain your love of life.[47]

The next two stanzas continue the speaker's attention on her fingernails as a means of protecting herself from other memories.

> Qué tormento,
> yo antes las tenía todas mordidas y llenas de padrastros,
> pese a las estrategias de la tata Carmen
> para que abandonara ese mi primer vicio:
> dulces, manotazos, mimitos, malas caras,
> ponerme en vergüenza delante de las tías. . . .
>
> Aunque se me secaran las uñas pronto,
> tampoco lo podré llamar
> porque he quedado a las nueve,
> ya son las ocho y media
> y aún no me he moldeado siquiera la resaca de pelo que llevo . . .
> (vv. 11–21)[48]

Recalling her nanny's efforts to keep her from biting her nails, she evokes this other female figure who tries to indoctrinate her as to what is expected of women in a patriarchal society. But the speaker also calls attention to her own stubbornness as a negative characteristic, and it is just this quality that prevents her from relenting and calling her former lover. Shifting her attention to her hair poses another barrier to phoning him, but also has more symbolic import. On one hand, her disheveled hair is emblematic of the confusion and tangle of her thoughts at this moment. On the other hand, its profuse complexity and her ability to give it shape demonstrate a beauty and talent of which she is proud. As well as recalling Medusa's snakes, her hair is a crown and a treasure. The theme that looks can be deceiving, encouraging a deeper reading of the text under consideration, continues in the next stanza with more memories of childhood.

> Es curioso,
> a veces me pregunto en qué árbol del parque me enganché la niñez.
> Sólo conservo de ella este pelo mío tan dulce,
> y el recuerdo de aquellas pistolas de agua que robaba a los chicos
> con cara de absoluta inocencia . . .
> (vv. 22–26)[49]

Whereas these memories characterize her even now, the speaker affirms traits of herself that she admires. Although she feels that she has lost her childhood innocence, having hung it on a tree in the park as if it were a jacket or her shadow (pace Peter Pan), she still has fine hair, like that of a child. Moreover, she remembers having stolen water pistols from the boys, able to deceive them with her innocent face. As phallic symbols, the water pistols (which "urinate") are appropriated by the speaker by means of her guile. Yes, she is deceitful and uses feminine wiles, but she outwits the boys and appropriates traditional symbols of male subjectivity.

The final third of the poem deals with the speaker's immediate concerns: the plans she has for this evening. Her friend Piedad is going to introduce her to "un vecino suyo guapísimo" (a very cute neighbor of hers). This thought evokes other memories from her more recent past.

> Por entonces yo salía con David
> —¡y menudos celos se agarraba la tetona de Fátima
> cada vez que nos veía abandonar algún rincón oscuro,
> con las manos pegajosas de tanta pipa tímida!—
> un amiguito que siempre se gastaba su paga en invitarme al cine los
>   domingos. . . .
> (El otro día, por cierto, me lo encontré
> y los dos nos hicimos los locos.)
>
>   (vv. 29–36)[50]

The speaker fondly remembers some of her first amorous experiences with a young man named David, a possible reference to the ideal youth portrayed in Michelangelo's statue. Her description of her competitor Fátima as "la tetona" creates a contrast with herself, indicating that physical attributes are not the only attractions a woman possesses. In another artful use of the parenthetical expression, the speaker recalls running into him again. This aside undercuts her phrase "los dos nos hicimos los locos." Beneath her frivolity and zaniness lie great tenderness, vulnerability, and a yearning for intimacy. These aspects are still evident in the final stanza, but the speaker again manifests her rage in her refusal to communicate with the outside world.

> Piedad ya está llamando al portero automático,
> pero si le abro ahora se me estropearán las uñas;
> que espere,
> total,
> así se evita el enfado
> de verme todavía en pijama
> y sin saber qué minifalda ponerme para la fiesta.
>
>   (vv. 37–43)[51]

The speaker's refusal to answer the intercom and let her friend in, along with the mention of her fingernails, echoes her refusal to call her former lover. Telephones thus inhibit communication, as the nails once again represent her defensiveness. The speaker wants no pity (her friend's name is Piedad), especially self-pity. Yet her reference to the pique her friend will feel on seeing her still in her pajamas is a projection of her own anger. She attempts to cover her anger with the triviality of deciding which miniskirt to wear, but such superficiality reveals her deep rage. This anger is evident in the offhand way she dismisses her friend's "compassionate" attempt to get her out and about, and when she says, "que espere, / total, / así se evita el enfado." The speaker is in no mood for a party. She is not eager to become involved in another relationship after she has been hurt so deeply. Again Phillips provides insight into the positive aspects of rage:

> Anger, then, is only for the engaged; for those with projects that matter (not the indifferent, the insouciant, the depressed). That is to say, those for whom something has gone wrong but who "know," in their rage, that it could be otherwise. . . . At its most minimal our picture is of something interrupted, an epiphany of obstacles. Of a creature unavoidably deflected from its aim (of satisfaction, of justice, of mastery, or "more life," of dying in its own way). Our rage speaks of intrusion and sabotage and betrayal, but also, paradoxically, of insistence and refusal and hope. . . . Rage becomes the often forlorn hope of reinstating a damaged ideal version of ourselves—not exactly making our presence felt, but keeping whatever we value most about ourselves in circulation. From a psychoanalytic point of view, growing up entails loss of status—a kind of disembodying— and then its attempted restoration. And what loses status above all in the process of growing up is the desires of childhood.[52]

Instead of a healing process, we see that the protagonist of this work is still smarting from the physical and emotional evisceration she has undergone and does not want to let herself experience the emotions of pain, grief, anger, hate, or even sympathy that may only expose her to more belittling ridicule. As a representation of the poet's experience with writing and the reception of her work by an unsympathetic audience, we see that the poet too is hurt and resentful.

Usted is a transgressive text in many ways. Through its exploration of the liminal space between narrative and lyric genres, the text causes us to question to what extent these incidents are autobiographical and to what extent they are imaginary, blurring the boundary between text and life, between the sexual and the textual. The ambivalent function of the male figure, the respectful and sarcastic use of the pronoun *usted,* and the problematization of the addressee con-tribute to this liminality. *Usted* is a sardonic, angry text, a scathing indictment of the sexual-textual politics that disparage and devalue women's writing. But ultimately *Usted* illustrates Almudena Guzmán's ability to wield language with great skill, subtlety, variety, and inten-sity of expression and shows that she is capable of turning humilia-tion into triumph because of her dedication to herself and her poetic talent.

6
The Abandoned Woman:
Margarita Merino's *Baladas del abismo*

OF THE POETS INCLUDED IN THIS STUDY, MARGARITA MERINO perhaps avails herself of the poem as mirror with the most variety and imagination. Whether by means of fictional characters, historical situations, her daughter, or the landscape, the speaker of Merino's *Baladas del abismo* (Ballads from the Abyss, 1989) sees herself reflected in the poem. Yet all of these manifestations of the page as mirror can be subsumed under the figure of the abandoned woman. According to Lawrence Lipking, this figure has a long tradition in Western literature.[1] It is ironic that the majority of this genre consists of men adopting the voice of the abandoned woman. As Catherine R. Stimpson notes, "[The abandoned woman] has often taught men how to explore their feelings; women have to construct a feeling, speaking, writing self."[2] However, when a woman poet expresses the feelings of abandonment, she often makes the reader uncomfortable, for

> if abandoned, they have, in turn, abandoned convention, decorum, control, the ordinary mind. . . . Her language becomes that of a mind and sensibility too passionate, too electrifying, for the grids of culture. Necessarily, she stands beyond the authority of the literary canon as well. . . . [This literature] would instruct us in the ways in which poetry can resist masculine authority and the cruelties toward women that authority practices and condones. Although the abandoned woman is alone, she seeks to share her feelings, including her devotion to such resistance. . . . Because she has broken codes, customs, and civilities, she cannot reassure us . . . that nature and art, imitating nature, are in harmony.[3]

This capacity relies on a fundamental duality in the word *abandonment* itself, as Lipking acutely points out. He also notes that, "Women who live in 'abandon' are capable of sudden dangerous turns. They become the objects not only of pity but envy, not only of fear but at-

230

traction. Moreover, since neither the protection nor the inhibition of the law applies to them any longer, they constitute a potential threat to a well-ordered society."[4] Indeed, Merino's poetry has received severe criticism. Even her ardent supporters at times lament her emotional and verbal excess, but such surfeit clearly identifies her as the figure of the abandoned woman in *Baladas del abismo*. The majority of the poems in this collection consists of long versicles and often extensive lucubration on the emotions of the abandoned woman. Hence they clearly illustrate what Lipking has defined as "the difficulty of accommodating the poetry of abandoned women to any received notion of poetic traditions or canons." In several of the poems from *Baladas,* Merino's identity as the abandoned woman becomes evident. These poems also demonstrate implicitly an issue broached by Lipking with regard to the poetry of abandonment and one of the central concerns of this study: "the special problems of women in finding a voice or a place in tradition and establishing their identities as poets."[5]

Perhaps the most memorable poem of *Baladas,* "Apunte sobre Emma" (Sketch of Emma) employs the prototypical abandoned woman as its intertextual reflection. The concept of intertextuality encompasses a wide range of possibilities and has been employed by writers for a variety of effects and purposes.[6] When in a woman's text the intertext entails the representation of another female figure, intertextuality can adopt an additional dimension, functioning as a mirror in which the speaker of the text in question observes an image of herself and can react to what she sees in different ways. Merino proffers such an example in "Apunte sobre Emma." Here the poet's meditation on and dialogue with Emma Bovary, the protagonist of Gustave Flaubert's classic novel, allows her to criticize a society that oppresses her and to arrive at an affirmation of herself in spite of that society. Through the different stances Merino adopts with regard to the image in the (inter)textual mirror, various contrasts arise, producing double-voicing in the language of the poem. The interplay between the poetic persona and the representation of the female figure, the varying degrees of distance between the speaker and Emma, and double-voicing reveal the relation between mirroring, reading, and writing, and the dynamics of reality versus fiction, life versus art, a paradoxical relationship that transforms the past into fiction but makes fiction a reality. The opening stanzas immediately establish the relation between the speaker and Emma, the situation in which both find themselves and the irony inherent in that situation.

Te veo, Emma, los ojos extraviados,
estás muy bella con esa tez transfigurada
por toda la revelación de tu tristeza.

Ay, Emma, tan hermosa, sutil y refinada,
luchando por huir de la tenaz monotonía
tu ambición no supo conformarse a lo vulgar
y soñaste con volar abandonando ansiosa
una cicatera ciudad que siempre ha escrutado
envidiosa, rapaz, la belleza que te estrena
cada fecha, la fulgurante palidez que te da
la amanecida cuando a la ventana te asomas
melancólica por la ausencia de la pasión
y la ternura plenas que te arrebatará
renovado y tacaño el día que comienza.

(vv. 1–14)[7]

Through her direct address in the statement "Te veo, Emma," the speaker defines a distinction and distance between herself and the other that she will emphasize by repeating Emma's name at the beginning of the next four stanzas. It is as if the speaker wished to keep the other at arm's length to observe her better. Emma's predicament reflects her own, so that her observation of Emma provides more insight into herself. On the basis of her description of Emma in the opening stanza, we might think that she was observing the painting of a saint in ecstasy because of Emma's "ojos extraviados" and "tez transfigurada" by a "revelación." Yet this beauty is caused by the sadness of having been abandoned by her lover, so that this image could be her own face in the mirror. The speaker has focused on Emma at the height of her grief, one that the speaker shares and perceives intensely. Consequently, her use of the second-person address problematizes the locution of the poem and results in a double-voicing: The speaker simultaneously addresses herself as well as Emma. The subsequent stanzas in which the speaker specifically mentions Emma present a vivid contrast between the individual and society, particularly the individual female and a provincial (patriarchal) society that limits a woman by defining her role narrowly.

Emma que querías dejar atrás la intrascendencia
de ese pueblón paleto y recatado que te abruma
para gozar una vida liviana, como saben hacerlo
las hembras deseadas que unen al grácil esqueleto
una cabeza inquisidora y aprenden obligado

el ejercicio de pensar en libertad a solas,
a utilizar—al cabo de desengaños y traiciones—
su aguda inteligencia largo tiempo postergada
al aspecto turgente de un cuerpo adivinado
bajo los pliegues del tafetán y el hilo.

Emma que disfrutaste siendo niña las cultas
disciplinas que provocan un gusto indesmayable
por la estética: la música rotunda que sacia
el ánimo dispuesto, la mística sublime
que eleva a la devoración de otras pasiones
más terrenas, el tenue mensaje que los libros
van dejando irrepetible al paso de los años,
Emma, preciosa, que tenías tu sensibilidad
despierta al claro discernimiento de las cosas.

$$(\text{vv. } 15\text{--}33)^8$$

On the one hand, Emma, "tan hermosa, sutil y refinada," is able to appreciate the finer pleasures of the intellect. The fourth stanza tells us that as a child Emma savored music and books. She is therefore ambitious and aspires to transcend her mundane surroundings ("soñaste con volar"). Emma arises fresh each day, hopeful, glowing with the rosy hue of her dreams, illuminated by the dawn she sees from her window, a symbol of her optimistic outlook. But the environment in which she lives is not conducive to her aspirations. Living as she does in a "cicatera ciudad que siempre ha escrutado / envidiosa, rapaz," "ese pueblón paleto y recatado que te abruma," Emma is suffocated by "la tenaz monotonía," "lo vulgar," and "la ausencia de la pasión / y la ternura plenas." This stinging indictment of the oppressive provincial capital as mean, envious, greedy, and yokel applies just as well to León (Merino's hometown) as to Yonville. This duality is evident in the persistent switching from past to present verb tenses throughout these stanzas. The poet not only talks about Emma but also about herself and her city. Perhaps one of the most telling ways in which this environment oppresses women consists of the clothing that entraps body and mind and prevents them from using "su aguda inteligencia / largo tiempo postergada / al aspecto turgente de un cuerpo adivinado / bajo los pliegues del tafetán y el hilo." The bourgeois provincial societies of nineteenth-century France and twentieth-century Spain privilege a woman's physical adornments and her curvaceous body at the expense of her intellect. These societies convert a woman into a text to be bound and consumed by masculinist readers, as the next lines suggest:

> De ti dijeron, Emma, que poseías ese algo
> femenino que puede inspirar todos los versos
> que se escriban, que eras "ella" en todas
> las novelas: presencia turbadora insuflando
> eternamente sentimientos de posesión
> que luego te encadenan. . . .
>
> (vv. 34–39)[9]

In short, these stanzas accuse the provincial society of a debilitating treatment of women. By keeping Emma at arm's length and focusing attention on her, the speaker has subtly and subversively criticized a stifling society and protested against the destructive situation in which she finds herself. In the next stanza the speaker omits direct mention of Emma, marking a change in her stance. Indeed, the double-voicing of the language intensifies as the speaker explicitly mentions the mirror.

> Te detuviste contemplando aquella demoledora
> imagen del espejo, enseñando a tus huesos
> motivos para la seducción y no supiste
> atender el sordo silbo de lo auténtico.
> Creíste que serías una joven perenne,
> diosa indestronable, encarnación mortal
> de la hermosura trémula. Pensabas caprichosa
> que la luna existía para alumbrar
> tu alcoba, que podrías hacerte un prendedor
> con las estrellas.
>
> (vv. 46–56)[10]

The image of/in the mirror initiates an introspective reading of woman from a woman's point of view. La Belle addresses these issues in her summary final chapter, "A Mirror of One's Own," stating (in relation to D. H. Lawrence's Lady Chatterley) that "mirroring is a phenomenon over which *she* has control. She has found a certain freedom within the glass to explore herself in terms given by her own body—rather than in terms established by the mirror as a representative of societal values."[11] Such a reading does not evade self-criticism. On the contrary, describing herself always through the image of Emma, the speaker acknowledges her errors, illusions, and superficiality; but this recognition enables her to reformulate her image of herself and to revise the reading of herself. First she chides herself sarcastically for her capricious illusions. Then her penchant for adorning herself with fine dresses and surrounding herself with knickknacks and use-less objects comes under fire in the following stanza.

> Eligiendo tu ropa con esmero, acicalada,
> rodeándote de objetos que ahora son inútiles,
> amortiguabas la falta desgarrada que nunca
> las prendas materiales habrán de relegar
> de tu intuida ausencia. Amontonando enseres,
> bibelotes que te iban quitando tanto espacio. . . .
>
> (vv. 57–62)[12]

Whereas she realizes that she was trying to compensate for an absence, an emptiness in her life, she now knows that "Para aprender a amar / hay que perderlo todo, estar ligeros / de equipaje" (To learn to love / one must lose everything, travel / light).[13] With its shift in discourse, this sententious statement marks yet another change in the speaker's position: She seems wiser and more insightful, as if she had a view superior to the Emma of the first five stanzas. Now she addresses Emma more intimately and compassionately as she becomes more introspective. Another criticism she levels at herself concerns her naiveté and her idealism about male-female relations, as disillusioned she laments:

> los torpes amantes
> que fueron poseyéndote te hicieron diestra
> a costa de quitarte el tierno afán gozoso
> que te movía pura a su querencia.
>
> (vv. 75–78)[14]

She thought she would receive as much love as she was learning to give, but she has learned that "el hombre es animal que tiene miedo / y se retrae minúsculo ante una entrega / inmensa" (man is an animal who is afraid / and recoils shrinking before an immense giving). No one had explained to her what the man's reaction would be:

> Nadie te dijo que el galanteador que alcanza
> la presa que le enerva se vuelve desdeñoso
> y ya no mima el que fuera objeto delirante
> de sus duermevelas, que todos los regalos
> con que tu amor le colma (pues tu celo
> por él tendrá añadido un deje maternal)
> él los recibirá de pronto como dueño,

> tirano por derecho. Otras damitas vanas
> habrán de parecerle el colmo de la sabiduría,
> modelos de buen tono y modales, súbitamente
> maestras singulares. No te sorprenda, Emma,
> pues el vencer la timidez y devenir experta
> resta protagonismo a quien en estas lides
> ambiciona la primera fragancia de la rosa.
>
> (vv. 102–15)[15]

This process of disillusionment culminates with a reprise of the direct address of Emma, but now there exists a solidarity between the speaker and Emma, reinforced by an intertextual allusion to Rosalía de Castro's poem from *En las orillas del Sar* commented in the introduction. As in Rosalía's poem, a wiser, more experienced woman addresses a younger, more innocent one and attempts to console her after a disappointment in love. She is of course able to do so because she has gone through the same experience. The speakers of both poems are critical of men and of a masculinist double standard with regard to a woman's experience in love. Connecting with Rosalía's text, the speaker posits solidarity with her and other women who have undergone similar experiences. Her evocation of this solidarity further suggests a reconciliation with herself as a woman—a reconciliation of exterior and interior, past and present, that leads to the binary opposition that will pervade the final stanzas of the poem: Eros versus Thanatos. The first significant mention of this intertwining of the forces of life and death comes in an extended metaphor of fire.

> Los hombres que elegiste no gustan del rescoldo,
> a semejanza de ti se extasian en las llamas
> y no ha de encenderse un fuego poderoso
> allí donde las chispas son menguantes,
> allí donde se espacia el crepitar sonoro
> de los carbonizados restos de lo que fue madera
> y que la combustión voraz ha consumido insana
> sin largueza, dejando de su aura reciente
> una escasa ceniza en el hogar, un polvo funerario
> que un suspiro levanta a su acomodo.
>
> (vv. 123–32)[16]

As symbol of both passion and destruction, fire here connotes the female speaker's experiences with men, the loss of innocence, and the passage of time. Many men prefer to have more experience in love than their partners so that they can be in control to facilitate their manipulation of women and assign them to an object status. Once a woman has taken part in "la combustión voraz" of love, all that is left of her passion is "una escasa ceniza en el hogar, un polvo funerario." In other words, according to this masculinist view, too much familiarity with "estas lides" leaves a woman less passionate and exciting than a younger, more inexperienced woman. The speaker then launches into her own opinion of what love is, a reading that differs significantly from and revises the male reading. Because the stanza that begins this re-vision consists of only three verses, it reminds us of the first stanza of "Apunte" but reverses the relationship of distance and intimacy between the speaker and Emma: "Es el amor luminoso y gigante como un cosmos, / descubre repentino el vértigo astral, / el magma alucinante que generó el comienzo."[17]

If at the beginning of the poem the speaker distances Emma by addressing her directly, here she relates to Emma with greater intimacy in spite of her impersonal language. According to the speaker, love can reveal prodigious insights into oneself; or it can serve as a distraction "para distraer la limitada mente de la especie / del horror al postrero fluir hacia el olvido" (to distract the limited mind of the species / from the horror of the last flowing toward oblivion). A man, she says, looks only at superficialities that will turn his contemplation away from unpleasant thoughts:

> El encanto de un óvalo perfecto,
> los ojos desmayados en guiños siderales
> de una mujer herida por el tiemblo del amor,
> el esplendor del cuerpo que se ofrece,
> hacen que el hombre que no sea extraordinario
> —ignorando otros ritmos—aparte la mirada
> del desgarro de tu corazón transido por la angustia,
> del presentimiento ensimismado que te asalta
> sobre la magia inasible de la felicidad
> y lo efímero del mundo, ajeno en su rotación
> a los sentidos que habrán de conocer la soledad
> del frío, el silencio, que moran en las tumbas:
> húmedos lagares del gusano, reinos de la sombra
> donde el plácido sol que reconforta
> no posará jamás sus tibios dedos generosos.
>
> (vv. 145–59)[18]

The contrasts between "sombra" and "sol" and between the tomb as "húmedo lagar del gusano" and the "tibios dedos generosos" of the personified sun underscore the contrast between Thanatos and Eros.

This image may derive from the tale of the rape of Leucothoe. Leucothoe's father, Orchamus, was furious because Apollo had deceived and impregnated his daughter, so he buried her alive (cf. the abandoned woman's death in life because of love). According to Ovid, Apollo "tried whether the strength of his rays could restore living warmth to her chilled limbs, but fate made all his efforts useless."[19] The speaker implies that a woman is capable of recognizing and facing death, of accepting death as an integral part of life and love. She can participate more fully and insightfully in love than "el hombre que no sea extraordinario" who does not give of himself completely and uses sex and women to deny death, to negate and escape from Thanatos. In short, the speaker defines a fundamental difference between men's and women's experiences of love and privileges the feminine view. A return to the direct address of Emma at the beginning of the penultimate stanza signals the conclusion of the poem and forges a new relationship between the speaker and Emma.

> Ay Emma, nada ha respetado tu desdeñada
> búsqueda de lujo, de armonía y de placer
> y todo lo has perdido. Te robaron rapaces
> tu estima, la capacidad de soportar altiva
> la vida cenicienta que te aflige,
> y al fin no lograste encontrar la voz gemela
> que supiera templar el delicado instrumento
> que tu alma enajenada hubiera hecho sonar
> vibrante y conmovida volviendo a la pureza.
>
> (vv. 160–68)[20]

Identifying with Emma, the speaker understands that Emma was searching for a life of luxury, harmony, and pleasure, and that she has lost everything in that search. Men have greedily robbed her even of her self-esteem and her ability to tolerate the monotony and drudgery of life. Does the word *cenicienta* rewrite the fairy tale ending of Cinderella since Prince Charming wasn't so charming? In these verses the speaker feels as disappointed and disillusioned with life as Emma. If in this stanza she identifies with Emma, the final stanza describes her rejection of the final image in the mirror with one significant reservation: The speaker reads Emma's death with the compassionate empathy of another woman rather than the distanced gaze of a man.

> Lloro impotente cuando te veo comer, febril,
> veneno para ratas, y una muerte espantosa
> te seduce largamente reventando tus vísceras,

las garras obscenas de la culpa vengadora
se clavan en tu garganta yerta, provocan
los estertores un vómito negruzco sellando
la boca que gemía en las coronaciones
y que aprendió a mentir en la infidelidad.
Te está colmando ahora el dolor del abandono,
recorre tu organismo corrompido el arsénico,
penetra la ponzoña negados recovecos:
los senderos recónditos que el desabrido amor
no supo conceder a la alegría.

(vv. 169–81)[21]

Even though she identifies and empathizes with Emma's feelings and the causes of her despair, the first-person verb forms at the beginning of the stanza designate a rejection of the image she sees. These verbs mark the first time since the beginning of the poem that the speaker has explicitly signaled her presence. In the first verse of the poem she separates herself from Emma, leading to a heightened perception of her own problem and a more profound introspection into herself. As a result of that process she has been able to recognize and accept her mistakes and imperfections and also to affirm her qualities in a revised reading of herself. That process has empowered her to define and affirm her own outlook on life and love in spite of the deep disappointment and disillusionment she still feels. Now when she repeats the use of the first person, she again separates herself from Emma, but she does so in order to reject the reversal of Eros and Thanatos that the masculinist outlook imposed on Emma. That view is expressed in the personification of death as a seductive lover and in the phrase "provocan / los estertores un vómito negruzco sellando / la boca que gemía en las coronaciones."

Despite that separation and rejection, the speaker cries and feels impotent in the face of Emma's death. Her tears reveal that instead of reading Emma's suicide with the detached, perhaps pitying eye of a male author/reader, she views it compassionately. For at the same time that she rejects Emma's solution—a solution imposed by the patriarchal society and which the speaker rejects by affirming her own subjectivity—she understands the feelings that have brought Emma to this pass. The final verses of the poem, which recognize "el dolor del abandono" that Emma feels, show that the speaker is experiencing Emma's death, not just observing it. She too feels the bitterness, the poison of a failed love coursing through her body, and the tragedy, senselessness, and frustration of Emma's death. We are left, then, with a catharsis that combines relief and suffering, Eros and

Thanatos, an affirmation of self and an incorporation of the other—an embracing of opposites defining the truly remarkable capacity of a woman's love.

"Apunte sobre Emma" is clearly an autobiographical text. But through the act of writing the self, objectifying herself in the image of Emma Bovary, Merino achieves profound insight into herself and the position of women in her society. The subtle changes of distance and identification between the speaker and the (inter)textual image delineate a dynamic process of knowing herself and of bringing about a change in her perspective on herself and her experiences. This rereading of herself as a woman through her interaction with the mirrored other leads to a re-vision, a correction of the narrow provincial (masculinist) reading of woman. This process demonstrates the semiotic capacity of the (inter)text as mirror.

Perhaps the most significant feature of this process concerns the dissolution of the boundary between life and art. At the same time that the poet objectifies herself, framing her experience and her past in the image in the text, she also vivifies Emma, causing her to transgress the frame of Flaubert's novel, making the boundary between life and art porous in both cases. The poet may have divested herself of her past by objectifying it and revising it in the (inter)textual mirror, but she has also created a text that will last indefinitely. She has exorcised her emotions through the catharsis of writing, but she has also made them a more permanent and vivid part of herself. By employing the (inter)text as mirror in "Apunte sobre Emma," Margarita Merino has demonstrated the ironic and paradoxical nature of this device by deconstructing and imbricating the binary terms of self and other, reading and writing, life and art.

Poets often adopt a mask or costume through which to filter and color their voices and lend special nuances to their words. If we consider the poem as a mirror in which the female poet interacts with an external, textual representation of herself, a costume or mask becomes a way of disguising and distancing herself but also of discovering greater insights into her feelings. Merino's adoption of disguises differs significantly from that of Ana Rossetti in tone and purpose. Whereas Rossetti is ludic, Merino is pathetic in the sense that "an abandoned woman must be pathetic, and elegiacs are right for pathos."[22] Whereas Rossetti makes fun of images to effect changes in society, Merino explores the image to repair primary narcissism. However, these characteristics are not mutually exclusive. The use of a disguise allows the poet's voice to emerge in a different tonality, more similar to the personae that Ezra Pound defined in his poetry. When the adopted persona happens to be a woman of the past, the historical dimension of the reflection produces intriguing effects through the interplay of temporal perspectives. Such is the case in a poem from "Baladas antiguas" (Ancient Ballads), the second section of *Baladas del abismo*. The relationship between past and present through the representation of the female figure in the textual mirror intensifies the impact of each poem through an interplay of temporal perspectives.

In "Dama en balaustrada" (Lady at the Railing) the poet sees herself as the wife of a nobleman gone off to war. As from her balcony she anticipates the arrival of winter and contemplates the absence of her beloved, the desolation and drabness of life correspond with the implied author's contemplation of a ruined castle and her identification with the woman of the past. Although she maintains a low profile and never overtly reveals her presence, we might surmise that on the anecdotal level she has visited an ancient castle in ruins. This castle symbolizes her emotions and forms an objective correlative for her life in shambles. She thereupon crosses the threshold of time, envisages herself as the lady of this castle, and meditates on the series of events that led to the destruction and desolation she finds in this scene. The first stanza unfolds slowly and establishes the mood of the poem in both its representation of the female figure and the language employed in this portrait.

> La dama suspiró mirando la rosa desvalida
> que arrancada por el insomnio al rocío
> iba desparramándose al calor de sus muslos
> en desolados pétalos, en hojas sombrías
> como la sangre seca y el néctar de las moras
> maduras, sobre sus rodillas de estatua
> de carne demudada que se aquieta.
>
> (vv. 1–7)[23]

Like the rose "arrancada por el insomnio al rocío," the lady has arisen early in the morning, unable to sleep. Her melancholy is evident not only in her sigh but also in her description of the rose as *desvalida*, an adjective that applies more appropriately to a human being than to a rose. As symbol of the transience of beauty and happiness, the rose, "desparramándose . . . en desolados pétalos, en hojas sombrías," is yet another objective correlative for the speaker's emotions and posits a mise en abyme. Whereas dew symbolizes fecundity, regeneration, and revivification, the rose has been plucked from the dew and has disintegrated, implying a loss of vitality and hope. By comparing the disintegration of the rose with "la sangre seca y el néctar de las moras / maduras," the poet suggests the image of menstrual blood and the possible depression that can result after menstruation or the advent of menopause. The speaker then compares the lady with an "estatua / de carne demudada que se aquieta." This mise en abyme of images, equating speaker, lady, rose, and statue, along with the preponderance of words describing melancholy and loss, creates a nebulous picture of the speaker's state of mind. It is almost as if the poet were looking at herself in an old, clouded mirror or through tear-filled eyes. The image is not sharply defined, and the emotions emerge in accord with the uncertain light of dawn. This scene introduces a profound meditation on the transience of pleasure. The slippage from the speaker's present to the past is underscored by a similar nostalgic evocation by the "dama" in the second stanza.

> Quiso, la dama taciturna,
> distraer su melancolía al hilo de la rememoranza
> de lejanas primaveras, cuando en su juventud
> no había reconocido, aciago,
> el acre sabor de los aconteceres en la lengua:
> "Dónde se cierne ahora la alegría
> estrepitosa como una catarata . . ."
> "Dónde se volcarán las fuentes clamorosas
> con que salpica el fresco júbilo a la dicha".
>
> (vv. 8–16)[24]

The traditional image of spring as youth emphasizes the temporal dimension of the mirror and the passage of time. The repetition of the word *Dónde* in the projected thoughts of the "dama" suggests the classical theme of ubi sunt, whereas the juxtaposition of past and present stands out in the recognition of "el acre sabor de los aconteceres en la lengua." These images instantiate the connection between the abandoned woman and the elegiac genre. Moreover, the water imagery suggests the passage of time and a loss of vitality. In contrast with the fleeting memory of happier days, the lady then contemplates the bleak, lonely winter that awaits her. In the next two stanzas the repetition of the word *invierno* introduces a series of images defining the loss of color, vitality, music, and warmth. The servants have deserted their lady, taking victuals and horses with them; weeds invade the garden. The threads of tapestries fade; blue vases (representing hope) no longer display the aromatic and promising buds of carnations, roses, and camellias. Musical instruments are silent, and there is no fire in the hearth. Winecellars and stables are empty. These thoughts are replete with symbols marking the passage of time: spider webs filling corners, woodworms eroding the "bargueño" (symbol of memory), the yellowing of pictures and the protagonist's skin. The image of the falcons also functions metaphorically on two levels, past and present.

> Es momento de conceder la libertad
> a los halcones que gozaron parejos
> sobre el puño de mi señor las monterías . . .
>
> (vv. 66–68)[25]

Falcons, used in the hunt, were symbols of the inheritance passed on through primogeniture. For the lady, releasing them would represent a relinquishment of ownership, an admission that the lord has died without heir and that he will never return. As symbols of domestication and civilization, the falcons will now return to their wild state, as will the knight's lands. Supposing that the implied author now finds the castle in ruins after many centuries, we transpose this act onto her psyche as a poignant relinquishment of the return of the lost beloved. The falcons represent her feelings for him and her surrender and release of those feelings. The speaker in the present has reconstructed this picture of medieval life, only to show it disintegrating again as the protagonist anticipates the coming of winter. This play between the reconstruction of the past and the anticipation of future destruction underlies the entire poem and leads to an ironic conclusion. The final stanza consists of only one sentence introduced by three clauses projecting into the future.

> Cuando los siglos nos ofrezcan
> brutal el espectáculo de las demoliciones,
> inferida la decadencia de las piedras,
> sanguinario el impulso de los bárbaros
> y las hordas noctívagas;
> cuando atestigüe el esqueleto desnudo
> de un castillo vencido en el asalto
> el desamparo de los artesonados
> en las llamas,
> el rigor del incendio acaecido,
> la tristeza que hereda a las pisadas
> que medían los escarpines ágiles
> dueños del espacio avasallado;
> cuando el pasado sea testimonio
> de la sinrazón, del hambre analfabeta,
> de la intolerancia, la miseria,

del ánimo siniestro, el desatino
que despiertan las guerras;
sabremos que tampoco los salones
permanecerán jamás indemnes
del toque de sentencia con que las campanadas
de los cuatro jinetes de la desesperanza
condenan al ilota y a los parias.

(vv. 69–91)[26]

This projection into the future (using the subjunctive in the verbs) coincides with and works against the speaker's retrospection into the past, creating an intriguing interplay of temporal perspectives that leads to an ironic conclusion. The lady anticipates exactly what the speaker finds. Across the span of centuries these two women meet, each finding in the other recognition and compassion. Both find destruction, loss, and emptiness. This play of temporal perspectives in the meeting of the two women across the centuries imbricates past and present, but demonstrates that time's passage heals as well as destroys.

The words *ilota* and *parias* in the final verse encapsulate this paradox. Literally, *ilota* refers to a person reduced to the lowest grade of abjection, an apt description of both female figures in this poem. The destruction and decay of the scene is related to the concept of abjection. Kristeva examines the etymology of the word *corpse* or *cadaver,* based on the Latin verb *cadere* meaning "to fall." In fact, Kristeva describes the wounded ego as "a fortified castle," similar to the castle where the speaker of this poem stands. According to Kristeva, "Abjection is therefore a kind of narcissistic crisis."[27] Both the poetic voice and the historical personage see their world in ruins because of the loss of the beloved, the absence that has caused their extreme melancholy. But this word has a historical dimension because it derives from the designation of a Spartan slave, the lowest social category in Spartan society. *Paria* presents a similar duality. Whereas it has come to signify any outcast, any person generally despised or avoided, it too derives historically from a member of one of the lowest social classes in India, a hereditary drumbeater. This sociopolitical, historical dimension demonstrates that the situation described in the poem is universal and timeless. Lipking defines "the widespread appeal of songs of abandonment: they speak for oppressed people everywhere. . . . Abandonment, that is to say, cannot be set apart from politics. . . . Abandoned women complain for everyone." In short, the poetry of abandonment functions as "a powerful social protest."[28] Nonetheless, Spartan society no longer exists nor the drumbeater in Indian society. The drum, recalling the image of the bells earlier, is another ambivalent symbol. Both instruments represent the relationship between two worlds and an inversion of destruction and creation, in addition to their metapoetic connection with rhythm, music, and the creative act. That is, they represent both death and resurrection. This duality is already in evidence in the two female figures, the interplay of past and present, self and other, interior and exterior.

In spite of the apocalyptic vision and inescapable destruction in the figures of "los cuatro jinetes de la desesperanza," and in spite of the abjection of these female figures, the poet implies that time will destroy the negative as well as the positive. By crossing the threshold of the past and by textualizing an image of herself in the lady, Merino has connected with an archetypal situation and discovered a degree of consolation. The "dama en balaustrada" stands on a liminal space that looks back to the past and out toward the future. What at first seems to be a bleak outlook on destruction also contains a glimmer of hope in the cyclical changing of the seasons. The image of the other demonstrates the historical dimension of the mirror as the poet dons a persona and speaks through a filtered voice. But that interplay with the past has ironic consequences, as writing the poem provides cathartic relief.

In "Dama en balaustrada" the poet adopts the perspective of a historical persona. By donning a costume and inscribing herself in a lyrical space delimited by the historical frame, the implied author presents us with an image of herself that reflects her present situation. The profile of that situation is only slightly perceptible, heightening the defamiliarizing effect of the costume and the temporal distance. Once we are aware of the positioning of the implied author in the present, in front of the "mirror," the play of temporal perspectives is set in motion, simultaneously delineating and telescoping past, present, and future of both the woman in the text and the implied author. This defamiliarization and redefinition of a topos through the image of the textual mirror intensifies the emotional impact of the image through the interplay of past and present. This undercurrent works against the possible triteness and sentimentality of the topos and thus continues the poetic tradition while rewriting it from a feminine viewpoint.

As improbable as it may seem, Merino even sees herself reflected in a male figure portrayed in the page as mirror. "Memento" is an elegiac remembrance of the poet's father. Through the description of this male (patriarchal) figure, the poet distances herself from a panoply of characteristics that she had inherited from the past and that are embodied in the father figure. In this radical portrayal of otherness, however, the characteristics she rejects are those that in truth define her values and show who she is. Although a patriarchal figure that still dominates the female speaker's life, the father figure contrasts sharply with the lover who has abandoned her. This duality produces an intriguing tension between sameness and difference, self and other, rejection and acceptance. Fully three-fourths of the poem is dedicated to a remembrance of the father figure and the role he played in the life of the speaker. The opening verses establish the relationship between father and daughter.

> Se han cumplido casi once años
> desde que se me ofreció tu rostro adelgazado,
> once años desde que selló tus labios
> el rigor invencible del último silencio.
> Tanto tiempo ha pasado mi vida sin ti,
> tanto tiempo la que fuera tu casa
> ausente a tu cuidado,
> que las monedas rubias del rincón,
> los elefantes menguados que llamaban
> a la suerte con sus trompas alzadas,
> las banderitas de latón,
> la tortuga de piedra,
> los pequeños repuestos para todo,
> las plumas y plumillas,
> las cajitas de pasta que albergaron tinteros,
> se han ido de tu armario.
>
> (vv. 1–16)[29]

Repetition of the time that has passed (almost eleven years) and the beautiful image of death sealing the father's lips forever emphasize the distance between the speaker and her father. Further repetition of the phrase *tanto tiempo* creates a parallel between the speaker's life and the house that was under the father's care, again drawing attention to the connection between elegy and the abandoned woman. Fanciful childhood imagery—gold coins in the corners of the room, tiny elephants heralding good luck, the flags of tin soldiers, a turtle carved in stone, pens and bottles of ink for drawing or writing— recalls a more innocent time in the speaker's life. Obviously, these illusions and fancies have disappeared along with the father figure, so that his dresser and her life are now empty and bleak. These images accentuate the distance the speaker remarks between an image of her past self and the abandoned woman of the present. The subsequent verses develop this contrast as the speaker paints a clearer picture of her father.

> Ya nunca volverás a quedarte dormido
> en el sillón de orejas que cobijó tu siesta,
> ni tampoco el despacho se nutrirá repleto
> de hermosas ediciones de libros bienamados,
> nadie volvió a guardar papel de barba
> en el cajón, y yo no encuentro
> aliciente ninguno al revolver espacios
> que ocuparon tus cosas sorprendentes,
> tus cosas que ofrecían exacta la imagen
> de un hombre bondadoso y delicado
> mientras estabas vivo.
>
> (vv. 17–27)[30]

Forceful negation of the future tense verbs *volverás* and *nutrirá* with the phrases *Ya nunca* and *ni tampoco* poignantly underscores the speaker's loss. All the characteristics attributed to the father signify what he provided for her: The chair where he took his afternoon naps displaces the sense of protection and shelter ("cobijó") the father provided for his daughter. Perhaps even the wings of this chair ("orejas" [ears]) indicate that he listened to her and comforted her, giving her peace and rest. Furthermore, the luxuriously bound books that lined the father's study allude to the way in which he whetted and nourished his children's imaginations and pursuit of knowledge. Whereas the "papel de barba" (rough-edged writing paper) may have been an idiosyncratic preference of the deceased father, its "beard" suggests the wisdom that no one has been able to replace, wisdom that only the father had stored away. Moreover, the paper itself connotes writing, personal expression in written form.

The second half of this lengthy catalog of paternal characteristics again introduces the presence of the speaker, juxtaposing self and other. Looking through the void left by the father's absence provides no alleviation for her: She finds only lack, nothing that would confirm the values and traits that her father represented. It is not merely that her father has died and left a void in her life. No one else has been able to fill that void because he does not possess the same qualities and offer the same attractions ("alicientes"), the same charisma, the same values "de un hombre bondadoso y delicado." These two adjectives define the deceased father's treatment and recognition of others and provide insight into his way of responding to their needs. Indeed, this man was an ideal paterfamilias, as we see in the tender though comic portrayal of the following verses.

> No he visto repetirse aquel desfile plácido
> de pijamas y boinas y chancletas de cuero
> en que refugiaste tu nostalgia,
> oh príncipe vestido de mendigo
> que te investías toga y chaqué
> de cuando en cuando
> para aplacar los ánimos del círculo cerrado. . . .
>
> (vv. 28–35)[31]

The last line here suggests that the father invented this comic figure to bring harmony and lightness to family tensions. He is a prince dressed as a pauper (an allusion to Mark Twain's gentler satires) whose pajamas were a toga and whose crown was a beret. By transforming her father into a storybook emperor, the speaker not only provides an example of his function within the family, but also elevates his figure to the status of myth. His presence had a magical effect on the speaker and her siblings, lending him a special aura. The poem then mentions several other instances in the community that exemplify and extend the father's influence while maintaining his special abilities to ingratiate himself by helping or pleasing others. These examples culminate in the following verses, where the speaker recapitulates a sense of loss that is not only personal but also cultural.

> Ya nadie se arrebata con sueños legendarios
> de justicia y canciones, cultura y convivencia,
> pues se durmieron—igual que tú—los otros,
> los viejos camaradas de las mitologías y la ética,
> los mismos que fuisteis asistiendo al espectáculo
> de tantos pájaros de juventud revueltos en el barro.
>
> (vv. 46–52)[32]

The phrase *Ya nadie* is elegiac in its repetition and consummates a series of negatives indicating loss, absence, and emptiness: *Ya nunca, ni tampoco, nadie, no encuentro, No he visto, Nadie, Ya no existen, Ya nadie,* and *No escucharé.* The pairing of "justicia y canciones, cultura y convivencia" displays the full range of the hero's capabilities. He is not just a dreamer, an idealist disconnected from the practical world around him, but a complete human being. Like him, a whole generation has passed away. This generation had watched their "sueños legendarios" die and fall away as new generations emerge. The "pá-jaros de juventud revueltos en el barro" may refer to their lost hopes and aspirations or to the new generation's incapacity for flight and the attainment of new heights. In any event, the speaker is clearly disillusioned and laments the loss of the ideals represented by her father that she had inherited from him. At this point, she enters emphatically in the first person to remark on the changes she sees in herself.

> Y yo, yo tampoco soy la que tú conociste,
> aquella legítima heredera,
> la díscola princesa de un reino milagroso,
> pues he sido trocada al desaliento
> por la enésima hecatombe: yo también
> —precipitado mi andamiaje en los fosos
> de légamo y azufre en los que se hundieron
> las claras torres y las águilas—he sido sepultada.
>
> (vv. 53–60)[33]

The motif of negation here takes a turn because the speaker includes herself. She rejects the image of herself as "aquella legítima heredera, / la díscola princesa de un reino milagroso." Her idealism and aspirations have been deflated, so that she bitterly mocks herself as the princess of a magical kingdom. The demonstrative adjective *aquella* distances that image of herself as forcefully as the father figure differentiates the otherness of the image in the mirror. As she was building her castles in the air and soaring with the eagles, others have tipped over her scaffolding and precipitated her into "fosos / de légamo y azufre." If the word *légamo* (muck, slime) evokes a grotesque defiling of what is pure and innocent, *azufre* connotes not only the stench of Hell but also fire and pain. In addition, the phrase *la enésima hecatombe* attests to an unending assault and mistreatment at the hands of those around her. Because we might catch glimmers of hope and regeneration in the image of fire, mud, and sacrifice, the definitive phrase that closes this sentence after the interruption still leaves the hope of resurrection as a possibility, however remote. The final verses of the poem reinstate the image of the father and ironically demonstrate the speaker's acceptance of her inheritance in spite of the defeat and humiliation she feels.

> Gimo desde este pegajoso lecho repugnante
> ante la muchedumbre embalsamada de las momias,
> pero a mis patéticos suspiros sólo

> responde un compás homogéneo de rebuznos
> desde que tú te marchaste con la túnica negra
> y me dejaste en los caminos de los insolidarios,
> padre mío.
>
>   (vv. 61–67)[34]

Even though the speaker says that she is buried, she groans and sighs, indicating that she is still alive. Indeed, the people around her seem more dead than she: She characterizes them as "la muchedumbre embalsamada de las momias." Moreover, she in effect says that they are asses given that they respond to her suffering and pathos with guffaws. Her anger toward them even carries over to her father, who has abandoned her, taking with him the black tunic. He has not left her the option of dying as he had. It is typical of mourners to express anger at the deceased for having abandoned them, and it is a positive step in the mourning process.[35] The isolation of the phrase *padre mío,* the first explicit mention of the subject of this elegy, creates a peripateia. As the speaker finds herself surrounded by unsupportive and insensitive people, she reconnects with her father and reaffirms the values and worldview that he represents for her. Ironically, through the distancing and loss of those values in the male figure portrayed in the poem as mirror, the speaker comes to acknowledge and embrace those values in herself. A radical separation between self and other becomes a committed affirmation of self through other.

The multisectional poem "Quien nunca he sido" (Someone I've Never Been) explicitly mentions the mirror, but the speaker fails to recognize the other reflected before her. The first section shows her estranged from everything in the world around her as well as the image of herself that she sees. As if in a dream world, she feels powerless and disoriented.

> Los días de mi infancia han cruzado El Umbral.
> Están ahora al otro lado del espejo. Al otro lado.
> No puedo encontrar el resorte que haga chirriar
> nuevamente los goznes de esta puerta lívida
> donde se me arrebatan para siempre
> las prendas luminosas que me pertenecían.
> No logro hacerlas regresar tampoco
> hasta la orilla aciaga donde la muerte atisba
> secándome los poros en cada anochecida.
>
>   (vv. 1–9)[36]

As the phrases *El Umbral* and *al otro lado* indicate, the speaker feels as if she, like Lewis Carroll's Alice, has stepped through the looking glass. These phrases also suggest that she feels she has died and speaks to us from the other side of the grave. However, the speaker's position is equivocal given that she sees her *past* on the other side of the mirror. Is she on the outside looking at her past and seeing her former innocence as an illusion? Or is she disoriented within the inverted world of the looking glass, observing reality from an estranged and distorted perspective? Which is reality and which illusion? The mirror as threshold evokes Lacan's definition of the mirror stage as the threshold of reality that leads to the formation of subjectivity.[37] Conversely, here the speaker finds herself questioning who she is because her view of the world has changed drastically. She has been abandoned by her image of herself based on her past. Has she lost her sense of self, or is she just awakening to it like the child in the mirror?

The repetition in the first two verses creates a discursive as well as pictorial frame for the poem as mirror. The second sentence repeats the information of the first one, with the iterated phrase *al otro lado* substituting for *han cruzado El Umbral.* This repetition then becomes the organizational principle for the poem. In the subsequent verses the negative verb phrases *No puedo encontrar* and *no logro . . . tampoco* continue this strategy and emphasize the speaker's loss of agency. Finding herself trapped in what seems to be a horrible nightmare, she gropes for a hidden magic lever that she knows is there because she has used it before: She wants to press it "nuevamente."

The image of the squeaking hinges and the livid door suggests the speaker's lack of agency and her state of mind, while the dark colors of the word *lívida* evoke brutality and violence as well as a lack of brilliance and joy. The speaker has been battered, if not literally, physically, certainly spiritually and emotionally. Moreover, her anxiety increases because she sees her "prendas" disappearing through this door. On one level, this word may refer to her clothing, leaving the speaker naked and vulnerable, while on another level, it may refer to characteristics of herself, increasing her sense of estrangement from her former self. The adjective *luminosas* reinforces the contrast between past and present as it plays against the livid color of the door. The reflexive verb form *se me arrebatan* emphasizes yet again the speaker's lack of agency and control, and her sense of loss and abandonment.

The speaker is powerless to prevent this loss or to make these "prendas" return "hasta la orilla aciaga donde la muerte atisba." Once again, the speaker's positionality is equivocal: She wants her things to return to that side of the mirror where death is spying on her. Is that *through* the looking glass where the speaker finds herself estranged from reality; or is it back from beyond the frame of the mirror, in the harsh reality where the speaker has been stripped of her former illusions? In effect, liminal spaces dominate this scene, but they represent a hermetic barrier rather than a porous interface. The speaker's pores dry up and her skin becomes a screen between herself and the outside world. This process occurs "cada anochecida," leading her irreversibly toward night and darkness, augmenting the lack of color and life-giving water and making her rigid, brittle, and blind.

Repetition continues to structure the poem and the vision it offers of the speaker's world. In addition to the anaphoric repetition of the interjection *Ay* (a shout of pain), the following verses continue to develop images of darkness, dryness, bitterness, and the loss of innocence. They then culminate in an intertextual reference to the film *Citizen Kane.*

> Ay el rictus crispando mi boca,
> el amargor de la saliva náufrago en la lengua,
> adelgazados los labios violáceos . . .
> Ay la piel trocándose en páramo,
> en cuero insensible aquel tacto cálido,
> ya toda botín del crepúsculo: "Rosebud . . ."
> (Rosebud ardiendo insignificante entre trastos.)
>
> (vv. 10–16)[38]

First, mention of specific parts of the speaker's mouth adopts metapoetic proportions, attesting to the harshness of the poet's words, caused by the pain of abandonment. The poet mixes images of suffering and death with the erotic acts of kissing and caressing. For example, *rictus* suggests pain and death, whereas *náufrago* represents the breakup of the speaker's world; and the purplish color of her lips echoes the earlier "puerta lívida." The description of her skin as a cold wasteland and a piece of leather insensitive to a warm touch advances the images of a barrier and the harshness of the speaker's existence. By metaphorizing all of this as the booty of dusk, the speaker repeats her sense of helplessness and loss.

The evocation of the last scene of *Citizen Kane* in which we see the protagonist's childhood sled going up in flames, thus explaining his loss of innocence, epitomizes a life devoid of emotional connections and loving relationships. The punctuation here is ambivalent, suggesting barriers, frames, and thresholds. The quotation marks and suspensive periods include tacit but meaningful information, but the parentheses emphasize the insignificance of the "trastos" destroyed in the fire. This image also evokes (quite obliquely) the figure of another abandoned woman—Dido—so that the flames represent passion and destruction, Eros and Thanatos, a contrast we have already encountered in "Apunte sobre Emma."

In the final verses of this section the speaker returns to the image of the mirror and the sense of loss and estrangement she is experiencing. Again, images of coldness and a lack of color as well as the speaker's great suffering appear.

> Mirad qué pálida imagen me devuelven
> las lunas de hielo en las que me reflejo
> aletargada de abandono rumiando mis recuerdos,
> lamiendo las heridas con que corona el amor
> a quienes no consienten la liturgia del manso:
> el preámbulo cáliz del expolio y la herrumbre.
> Soy ahora La Reina De Los Fríos. Poco a poco,
> mi rutilante combustión ha devenido escarcha.
> Se diluyeron en humo los días del pasado
> borrándose los rostros familiares . . .
>
> (vv. 17–26)[39]

By addressing the readers in the command *Mirad*, the speaker underscores the distance between herself and her world, those around her and the image she asks them to view. As a command, it expresses her desperate plea for recognition in the face of indifference. The image of "las lunas de hielo" is highly overdetermined. *Lunas* may refer literally to the moon and its cold, silvery light. Or it may be the quicksilver backing of a mirror. In either case the speaker's reflected image is icy and distant. Therefore, she describes herself as "La Reina De Los Fríos," representing the epitome of coldness, apathy, and lack of sensitivity or passion. She further compares herself with a star whose "rutilante combustión" has turned into frost, and her past has literally gone up in smoke. She cannot recognize familiar faces, reiterating her sense of alienation from self and others and her disorientation because she has lost her sense of identity based on what she remembers from the past.

Indeed, she feels so mistreated by love that she compares it to a crucifixion: Love places a crown of thorns on those who do not consent to "the liturgy of the meek," a preamble to crucifixion and the nails or lance wound of the cross ("herrumbre"). Because she does not consent to being a meek sacrificial lamb, her punishment is coldness and indifference, the loss of passion and so of her very sense of self. This leads her to break down in embarrassing laments that remind her of another situation in which human beings find themselves in desperate straits: "y me rompo en lamentos vergonzantes / junto a aquellos que buscan los restos de su hogar / cuando tras el terremoto quedan en pie las ausencias" (and I break down in shameful laments / along with those who seek the remains of their home / when after the earthquake only loss remains standing"). The comparison found in the final two lines culminates the portrait of the speaker and closes the frame of the poem as mirror, for they parallel the opening verses of the poem. As earlier in the image of the shipwreck, the house destroyed by an earthquake serves as an image of the speaker's life and world.[40] Looking for some shred of self, of who she is, the speaker finds only cataclysmic destruction. The only thing that remains is absence. The speaker's world has been shaken to the core, leaving her with nothing but rubble and ruin. This image evokes the scene described in "Dama en balaustrada" but also prefigures the second section of this poem where ruins are the predominant image.

At this point in this multisectional poem the structure recapitulates the framing device of the opening poem. The second and seventh (final) sections of "Quien nunca he sido" are patently shorter than the other sections (consisting of 14 and 16 lines respectively). These two shorter sections frame four sections that display a decidedly autobiographical bent as the speaker reflects on her past. The moments she chooses from the past are the fragmented ruins that she treats in the second section, opening the frame. Even though the verbs and other images are positively marked, in truth the tone of this section is sad. It seems that the speaker is trying to convince herself that her situation is salvageable: "Amo las ruinas. Entiendo la belleza / epíloga que subyace en el fragmento / donde se reducen las formas presentidas / del antiguo esplendor" (I love ruins. I understand the tardy / beauty that lies within the fragment / where the perceived forms of ancient splendor / are reduced"). The two verbs *Amo* and *Entiendo* would seem to indicate a balance between heart and head, affect and intellect. Yet the object of these verbs—"ruinas"—places that equilibrium in question. The addition of the adjectives *epíloga* and *antiguo* reinforces this countercurrent by alluding to loss and a sense of belatedness. Although the speaker, in Gestalt fashion, is able to perceive the whole beauty on the basis of the remaining parts, the fragments she observes can be considered either a condensation or a reduction of the original beauty.

A tension therefore underlies ("subyace") not only what she observes, but also the observer's credibility. It is a tension between presence and absence, loss and recovery, that adopts metapoetic proportions because of the words *epíloga* and *fragmento* as well as the ambivalence of *antiguo* ("antique," "out of date," and "former"). This tension continues in the description of some statues, ekphrastic images in which the speaker sees an image of herself.

> Busco la complicidad de las estatuas
> en sus órbitas ciegas de contemplar
> La Nada Minúscula que preside
> la espera de quien escucha alertado
> la fórmula que inspire el motor torrencial
> de la vida, el golpe con que sorprende
> la luz vertiginosa.
>
> (vv. 5–11)[41]

In the concatenation of first-person verbs, *Busco* is much more equivocal than the others, for it encompasses loss and discovery, doubt and certainty, absence and presence. In addition, the word *complicidad* is ambivalent, connoting relationship and association, but with overtones of clandestinity and transgression. Moreover, the speaker focuses on the eyes of these statues, which are blind from having contemplated "La Nada Minúscula." In describing the eyes as "órbitas," she refers not only to their spherical shape but also to a cyclical life style and the futility of the statues' wait/hope for "el motor torrencial de la vida" and "el golpe con que sorprende / la luz vertiginosa." Like the speaker, these human forms wait (in vain) to come to life, to see the light. This latter image also resonates with metapoetic implications of inspiration and sentience. If, however, the adjectives *torrencial* and *vertiginosa* imply fertility and precipitous liveliness, they also hint at destruction and overwhelming violence. The subjunctive mood of the verb *inspire* expresses hope and doubt.

In short, the speaker's relationship to the antique fragments she purports to admire is highly equivocal. She finds solace in them, but they also remind her of her loss and the devastating effects of her abandonment. If we keep in mind the title and theme of "Quien nunca he sido," we see once again that the speaker is disoriented and alienated, that her world has been reduced to chaos and destruction, and that she is attempting to discover some meaning and sense of self in the wake of her abandonment, in her "ruined" sense of self. The final verses of this section sustain the duality of her position, her distance and her self-inclusion in the possibility of revitalization: "Pero las estirpes condenadas a la soledad, / no tienen una segunda oportunidad / sobre la tierra" (But the races condemned to solitude / do not have a second opportunity / on earth). The shift from the first-person verbs in verse 1 to the more equivocal *Busco,* and finally to the sententious third-person generalization of this sentence problema-tizes even more the speaker's position and tone.[42] Does she belong to these "estirpes" who are condemned to solitude and never attain a second opportunity at life? Is she like the ruins she observes? Does she have hope that some poetic justice is still possible after life "so-bre la tierra"? Or is she highly disillusioned and cynical about life in general? Her declaration may be self-inclusive, but its impersonality and sententiousness distance and exclude her from the scene, as if placing her beyond it.

In a continuation of this ambivalence, the second section forms a frame with the final section for the four other sections that recount in autobiographical fashion certain moments in the speaker's past. These accounts are thus the fragments and ruins of the speaker's life as she attempts to discover coherence in her sense of self after the torrential, vertiginous experience of having been abandoned. Can she see the Gestalt in the fragments? Can she rearrange the shattered pieces of her self-image to construct a new definition of self? Will the image she describes in these framed sections reflect a shattered or a whole self, a valid or a false one?

Select passages from the four framed sections characterize differ-ent stages in life and depict another female figure as a reflection of the speaker. Thus we can specify the different avatars of the speaker's self as we come ever closer to the poetic voice who addresses us in the present. Section 3 of "Quien nunca he sido" returns the speaker to the almost mythical and certainly fantastic era of her earliest experi-ences with reading and the development of her imagination. Auto-biographically, Merino (born in 1952) would have attended elemen-tary school in the mid to late fifties. This section opens with a mention of "una incruenta Guerra de los Mundos," which I understand as the Cold War. The first passage for consideration here entails an explicit mention of the speaker seated before a mirror.

> Delante del espejo de mi madre,
> pude engalanarme con delicados velos de luz
> que me brindaron de sus colas los cometas.
> Asteroides melancólicos trocaban conmigo
> su radiante collar de un aura indefinible
> por canicas de vidrio y cuentas de colores.
> Un constante riesgo, una sorpresa nueva,
> alimentaban mi alborozada espera cotidiana,
> y así los muebles, los enormes sillones,

los espacios entre pared y cortinones,
los ángulos oscuros del prolongado corredor,
ocuparon el lugar del jardín que no tuve,
se convirtieron en mi alquitara en selva virgen.

(vv. 11–23)[43]

How should we interpret the speaker's use of her mother's mirror? Seeing herself as her mother suggests that she is adopting (literally putting on) the characteristics of "woman" as defined by that era. The illusions created by delicate veils and shiny glass beads is enhanced by the speaker's fantasy, as she imagines that comets' tails have formed the veils and asteroids have exchanged their brilliance for the glass beads of paste jewelry. To what extent is the illusion of herself merely a "reflection" of her mother's role in society or the imaginative fiction created by a mind nurtured on literature and fantasy? When is illusion slavish imitation and deception, and when is it generative and constitutive of self?[44]

Indeed, the speaker uses her imagination to transform the ordinary, commonplace world into adventure and surprise. The different spots she mentions throughout her house are representative of her inner space, her inner world. These places—the furniture, enormous armchairs, the spaces between curtains and walls, and the dark corners of a long hallway—have an aura of womblike enclosure and warmth, and they take the place of a garden (or yard) that she never had. In her imagination (her "distillery") she converts these spaces into a "selva virgen." These images of the garden and a virgin forest, powerful and significant aspects of feminine identity, echo the early life of Jane Eyre at Gateshead, where the protagonist of Brontë's novel would hide behind the curtains of a windowseat to read.[45] The adjective *virgen* is particularly telling. But does the speaker escape from the oppression of societal roles and positionalities? Or is her sense of self determined and constructed/constricted by false illusions?

Later in this same section, in a parenthetical aside to the reader, the speaker describes her first disillusionment as she leaves the womblike comfort of her home and her imagination and enters the world of school. She sees herself having to conform literally and figuratively to uniformity and banality, which provokes the compassion of "algunos Inmortales":

no os extrañe tampoco que se compadeciesen
por tantas tropelías que la historia ha perpetrado
sin rubor en el singular linaje de las niñas:
de las niñas que—como entonces yo—sólo aspiraron

> a disfrutar en paz su propia autonomía,
> a soñar suavizando las atroces aristas
> de la vida, a leer, pensar, cantar, bailar,
> a entregarse a dibujar un mundo excéntrico
> y celeste donde todo lo tierno tenga hueco,
> a tratar con la docta especie animal
> que tanto enseña de las cosas necesarias.
>
> (vv. 60–70)[46]

By addressing the readers parenthetically, the speaker establishes greater intimacy and emphasizes the present from which she views her past. This procedure allows her to contrast her present disillusionment with that of her childhood to highlight a pattern of injustice committed in the socialization of girls and women. There are some adults who are aware of this limiting process, whom she calls "Inmortales." The speaker maintains that girls "sólo aspiraron / a disfrutar en paz su propia autonomía," but instead they had to "ponerse adormilada[s] un áspero uniforme, / [y] unos horribles zapatones de gorila / que atenazaban los pies" (put on, half asleep, a rough uniform / [and] some horrible gorilla shoes / that bound their feet). The uniforms and ugly, clumsy black shoes restrict the expression of individuality and freedom for the speaker and her schoolmates (cf. the traditional practice of binding Chinese women's feet), all of whom attended a school for girls only.[47] In spite of or even because of the restrictions imposed on her, the mischievous speaker's curiosity does not diminish but only intensifies. However, her imagination and curiosity get her in trouble, as we see in this passage from section 4.

> Me achacaban todos los vicios concentrados:
> yo era desordenada, curiosa, no dejaba
> títere con cabeza, lo avasallaba todo,
> —y me adornaban con lindezas sobre Atila,
> su caballo, los hunos, los bárbaros, las hordas,
> el demonio, el infierno, el huracán,
> que servían para ilustrar el rosario
> de la perorata con ejemplos—.
>
> (vv. 29–36)[48]

The expressions "no dejaba / títere con cabeza, lo avasallaba todo" allude to the speaker's thirst for knowledge. Would a male child be as criticized for being disorderly and curious? Would his dismantling of clocks or motors, for example, receive condemnation? The speaker recites a "rosario" of epithets applied to her: Attila, wild horses, Huns, barbarians, hordes, a hurricane, hell on wheels. When she accuses others, she is berated as a liar.

> Cuando yo les juraba que nada de eso hice,
> cuando me rebelé un segundo a los castigos
> y grité insolidaria el nombre real
> de sus autores denunciándoles,
> desvelando impía sus ritos y sus lares,
> ellos—los otros, los rectos, los adultos—
> me llamaron el peor de los insultos,
> era una mentirosa, tanto enfrascarme
> en locas fantasías me estaba robando
> mi precaria cordura sin remedio . . .
>
> (vv. 37–46)[49]

Lying is a subversive strategy that in this case allows the speaker to fight against the restrictions imposed on her. But the adults also want to limit her imagination, accusing her of madness, another subversive strategy. The sad result of these recriminations is that the speaker lapses into silence and repression. She learns to betray herself as part of her socialization as a woman. Her madness in the passage above and her "beasts" in the following verses are keenly reminiscent of the protagonists in Charlotte Brontë's novels, particularly *Jane Eyre,* as discussed in Gilbert and Gubar's *The Madwoman in the Attic.*[50]

> Pero aprendí a callar el nombre
> de mis camaradas y mis bestias,
> silenciando sus hechos para siempre.
>
> (vv. 47–49)[51]

As the speaker becomes an adolescent in section 5, this process continues. Again she describes an avatar of herself when she sees her reflection in a store window, another manifestation of the mirror.[52]

> Sin apenas sentirlo, me alcanzó precoz
> el tiempo de crecer.
> Qué rara estaba, qué largas piernas
> tuve, con tacón. Oyendo los elogios,
> motivo ya de repentinos silencios
> a mi paso, me embadurné los labios
> de carmín, y como todas las demás
> sonreía tontamente al caminar.

> Como todas las demás, lloraba compungida
> y me alejaba de los escaparates al verme
> reflejada en el cristal, torciendo
> los tobillos al correr por Ordoño.
>
> (vv. 1–12)[53]

Even though the speaker describes herself as "rara," she repeats the phrase "como todas las demás." She may have seen herself—or may now see her former self—as strange and awkward because of the high heels she wore, the lipstick she put on, and the stupid smile she had on her face when she passed a group of boys who suddenly became quiet. But she was just like all the other girls! Ironically, the speaker flees from the sight of herself in the mirror. Obviously, her self-esteem is quite low, and she feels estranged from her image. Twisting her ankle is a means of describing a woman's debility, vulnerability, and awkwardness because of female accoutrements.[54] Whereas the name of the street Ordoño may be trivial and incidental, it also evokes other similar words: *orden* (the patriarchal order), *ordeñar* (to milk, a self-conscious awareness of her breasts), *ordo* (the calendar, the cyclical passage of time). The speaker feels caught—"framed"—in an image of herself determined by societal norms and expectations of certain age brackets, but simultaneously she tries to escape, aware of the awkwardness of her image and her objectivization by society. This description precedes further indications of her disillusionment and her loss of childhood innocence. Because of her physical growth, the speaker cannot participate in activities she enjoyed as a child. She must assume adult attitudes. To help, her mother keeps watch over her and places restrictive rules and clothing on her.

> De pronto, El Reino del Maligno se cernió
> por allí. Tomaron las aceras un tropel
> de Ejercicios Espirituales, El Pecado
> Mortal. Lo Prohibido. Entonces los pechos
> picudos y la abnegada vigía de mamá
> se clavaron en cerco y cinturón,
> y vi consumirse las horas del poniente
> desde la galería, entumeciéndome,
> adivinando los laberintos prodigiosos
> por los que—materia inguinal—arribamos
> del huevo elemento
> a este disimulado hemisferio de los castos.
>
> (vv. 35–46)[55]

Although her mother and the nuns have spoken to her about "spiritual exercises" and "mortal sin," the speaker is left to wonder about the true facts of reproduction. It seems that she has begun to experience menstruation, as the isolated phrases *materia inguinal* and *huevo elemento* imply. The mystery of her own body and the lack of information leave the speaker "entumeciéndo[se]"—literally and figuratively— in the quasi-medieval setting of a gallery. The adolescent girl finds herself isolated, quarantined, "entombed" in her own body and away from the society of others. Again, a woman's process of socialization has constricting and numbing effects on the concept of self, subjectivity, and agency.[56]

The penultimate section of this poem, the final mirror-image before the frame closes, begins with a disturbing declaration: "Quién fui después de aquello, / todavía no lo sé" (Who I was after that, / I still don't know). She also doubts whether this attempt to understand herself is worth the effort.

> No logro decidir si ha merecido la pena
> el truco de aprender a costa
> de ir mirando a lo real sin ver
> y desempolvo ensimismada el bagaje que tuve.
> Hay un revuelo de polillas en la urdimbre,
> se desploman cenicientos mis compinches
> en el desván de la conciencia destemplada
> por aquellas texturas que nunca volverán.
>
> (vv. 5–12)[57]

Now the speaker realizes that she had grown up with a great deal of baggage, but can she rescue any of the texture of those days from the devastating effects of time, the moths that have destroyed the fabric of her life? If she cannot recuperate anything of value from her past, how can she reconstitute her subjectivity? If she repudiates her past, will that enable her to reconstruct her identity in accord with her own definitions and parameters? Without her consent, the speaker has been dispossessed, not only of her toys and games, but also of her past. Her kaleidoscopes (a beautiful, colorful, fantastic vision of the world), compasses (giving her life direction), stuffed animals, and games have been replaced with shoes, face creams, perfume bottles, and other cosmetics. The image of her dolls is one of the most meaningful: "Ahora tienen las muñecas en la pupila ausente / el mercurio de los termómetros rotos / por la soledad y las fiebres nocturnales" (Now the dolls have blank pupils / the mercury of thermometers broken / by solitude and nocturnal fevers). As we have seen in other poems in this study, dolls are images of women. Here the speaker specifically mentions their eyes (similar to those of the statues in section 2 of this poem). She describes them as "ausente[s]," containing the mercury of broken thermometers. Because mercury is the equivalent of quicksilver in the backing of a mirror, the speaker sees her own eyes in those of the dolls. That the thermometers are broken "por la soledad y las fiebres nocturnales" refers to the speaker's loss of innocence and high fevers caused by erotic desires.

Having lost the vestiges of her past, including her grandparents, the speaker describes herself as the ugly duckling who will never grow up to be a beautiful swan. This "rubber ducky" is swimming in a porcelain chamberpot, an apt image of the speaker's past. She then recurs to mythical imagery as a representation of woman and of herself.

> Diana persigue un rayo de luz tenue
> de La Cara Oculta De La Luna,
> y se le escapa del peplo un pecho níveo
> con un pezón de plata derramando una gota
> de leche que se vierte en el carcaj.
> Ya nunca he de cabalgar frenética en la noche
> junto a Las Amazonas, ladra mi sinrazón,
> mi pulso se acelera presa de la nostalgia,
> escucho nítidos los cascos de los caballos
> profanando la quietud de los cementerios
> y las bóvedas se ensordecen con el eco.
>
> (vv. 44–54)[58]

The mythological figure of Diana, the goddess of the moon, the hunt, childbirth, and virginity, reflects similarities and differences with the speaker. This comparison is especially pertinent in light of a drawing Merino has made and included at the end of *Baladas*. The face of this figure resembles the photo of Merino on the frontispiece of the work and shows the woman's exposed breast along with her bow and a quiver of arrows. Amid the flames surrounding her, is Diana sinking in destruction or arising in regeneration? Is Diana's pursuit of a beam of light from the dark side of the moon a hopelessly impossible aspiration given that no moonbeams emanate from the dark side? Or is it an ideal that she strives to attain in spite of overwhelming obstacles? Her snowy breast, silver nipple, and drop of breast milk lend their whiteness to the arrows, Diana's shafts of moonlight. These arrows may be symbols of the female writer's pen and her inspiration.

The speaker is hunting for her own sense of self through her writing (cf. the verb *Busco* in section 2 above and its ambivalence).

The results of this search, however, are equivocal, as we can infer from the image of the Amazons. These mythological female figures are self-sufficient, preferring to live without men. These warriors may represent some feminist factions that advocate communities of women only. According to Pierre Grimal, "Artemis was . . . the protecting deity of the Amazons who, like her, were warriors and huntresses and independent of men."[59] The speaker realizes that she cannot form part of these factions, but perhaps she is opening a space for herself to change her thinking.[60] Via her contemplation of (reflection on) the past she explores the possibility of change and reconstitution of self.

Another important female image that arises at this point is that of Lot's wife, the biblical woman turned to salt for looking back at the past: "acaso soy una estatua de sal, / pues miro atrás desobediente y dolorida" (perhaps I am a statue of salt / for I look back disobedient and aggrieved). Nonetheless, she is already—in her view—a pillar of salt. Because of her past and her formation, she is already calcified or ossified, rigid, dry, and bitter. Evocative of the ruins she loves and understands, the pillar connotes both destruction and strength. And salt is a flavoring that enlivens and enriches the sense of taste, a person's appreciation of life. According to *Women in Scripture,* Lot's wife is one of the unnamed women in the Bible. As Lyn M. Bechtel says, "When the large cities of the plain of Jordan are destroyed because of their people's lack of discernment of good and bad, Lot's wife looks back and turns into a pillar of salt. Salt preserves her in a fixed state. Is this symbolic of her still being tied to the security that city culture is assumed to offer?"[61] In the context of Merino's poem we could infer that the speaker looks to her past because of the security it offers and the insecurity of her present sense of identity. The final image of this section returns to the image of Diana the huntress, the most positive avatar of the speaker that we encounter in *Baladas.*

> Huelo a tierra mojada, sudan las bestias
> urgidas por la espuela, disparo un dardo
> preciso a una Quimera, y grita,
> grita con un lamento atroz,
> cuando se troncha mortal sobre la hierba.
>
> (vv. 63–67)[62]

The chimera that Diana pursues and shoots with her dart may be the image of her former self, the illusion of life on which that image was based, or even an image of the lover who abandoned her. While it is true that she slays the past, where does that leave her? Without illusions or a past. In short, without an identity. But she has adopted the mythic identity of Diana on which to build a new concept of self, someone she has never been before: "Quien nunca [he] sido." The speaker is on the threshold between the past and the present, a former self and a new self. If in triumph she has left the past behind, she also faces an uncertain future, hopeful but doubtful and apprehensive.

The final section of this poem closes the frame around the image of the speaker. But have we seen a fragmented, shattered, ruined image, or does the speaker finally shut the door on her former image as if it were a photograph from the past? Perhaps the final section will provide a clue. But even here the language is extremely equivocal. In the opening verses the speaker feels passively invaded by apparitions: "Me invade en esta hora un mar de apariciones. / In Memento mis héroes que el segundero aparta" (A sea of apparitions invades me at this time. / In Memory of my heroes that the second hand sets aside). Are these apparitions the ghosts of the speaker's heroes, or have her heroes returned to her? Is she hounded by her memories of the past or inspired by the revitalization of her ideals? The lack of an independent verb in the second verse problematizes the statement. Does the secondhand—metonymic of the passage of time, the ticking of a clock—separate the speaker from her past? Or do her heroes help her put her pain and loss behind her? Then she uses the future tense, but the language is still equivocal.

> Sellaré con mi sangre el pacto revivido:
> Acaso los dioses sin poder que me alentaron
> podrán volver si les invoco, ignorando las reglas
> que impuso la legión vencedora de Los Grises.
> Temeraria rasgaré sobre el papel el humor púrpura
> inundando cada letra con todo el desamparo
> que me aflige envejeciendo los sueños que pretendí
> inmortales. . . .
>
> (vv. 3–10)[63]

The speaker as poet will write with her blood, with all the passion she can muster. But the future tense defers the action and causes us to question how definitive these actions will be. The adverb *Acaso*, the compound construction *podrán volver*, and the if-clause *si les invoco* all express tentativeness. Moreover, sealing the pact with her blood may mean that the speaker will be drained of her passion and life. Even though she is fearless, her act defined with the word *rasgaré* could mean that she will slash her wrists over the paper. She has wanted her dreams to be immortal, but are they? In the next verses the construction *Habrán de* continues this ambivalence.

> Habrán de acompañarme enardecidos
> mis dulces camaradas, se abalanzarán guerreros
> para yugular esta calma terrible que ha querido
> hacerse señora del angosto pasillo de mi casa . . .
>
> (vv. 10–13)[64]

Does this construction indicate a yearning, anxious hope, on the part of the speaker? Or does it express her certainty that they will accompany her? Is this image of warriors cutting the throat of this terrible calm a vengeful fantasy or a certainty the speaker anticipates? The "señora" who is trying to take over her house is the figure of a mature but socialized woman who epitomizes the confinement and limitations imposed on women. The speaker sees her house—her life—as a narrow hallway, an enclosed and limiting pathway through life. The final verses, closing the frame with the anaphora of *ya,* nonetheless forestall closure: "Ya adivino un griterío infernal en los tabiques, / ya las luces parpadeantes, la oscuridad preñada / de ojos vigilantes les conduce certera hasta mi puerta" (Now I perceive the infernal shouting in the boards, / now the blinking lights, the pregnant darkness / of vigilant eyes leads them surely to my door). Does the verb *adivino* describe something the speaker actually hears or something she imagines? Is the hellish shouting music to her ears because of what these shouts promise to destroy: "la legión vencedora de Los Grises" and the laws they have imposed? Or are they tormenting her with the memories of her lost past? *Grises* is Spanish slang for "police." Here, Merino uses the term to refer to the "cultural policing" of gender roles. The "luces parpadeantes" may be coming on or going off, and the darkness may be pregnant with menace and harassing vigilance or with hope and aspiration (the eyes as stars).

"Quien nunca he sido" is a profound, introspective assessment of the speaker's life. As stated above, the image of Diana is the most positive view of the speaker as abandoned woman found in *Baladas.* In the very next poem, the last of the collection, the image reverts to that of the abandoned woman, thus closing the frame of the book prior to the ambivalent image drawn by Merino to represent herself as Diana. The tension between these "two endings" of *Baladas* and the ambivalence of the framing device leaves the conclusion unresolved, but Merino's use of the page as mirror is versatile and effective.

7
Double-Voicing, Double-Vision: Amalia Bautista's *Cárcel de amor*

In *Usos amorosos de la posguerra española* (Romantic Practices in the Spanish Post-War Era), Carmen Martín Gaite recounts an incident that reportedly took place in either Palencia or Valladolid and concerns a woman engaged to an inconsiderate, verbally abusive man. In spite of the protests of friends and family, she continued her plans for marriage. After walking down the aisle, when it came time for her to respond "I do," she answered in a clear, unwavering voice, "I certainly do not." Then, turning to all those filling the church, she added emphatically, "And if I have arrived at this point, it is so that all of you may know that if I remain single it is because I damn well please!" She then strode resolutely out of the church. Martín Gaite's response to this incident is noteworthy: "If that anecdote was true, something that I could never prove, I don't understand why that woman . . . hasn't had a statue erected in her honor."[1]

It may be coincidental that Martín Gaite's *Usos amorosos* and Amalia Bautista's *Cárcel de amor* were published within a year of each other; yet each work attests to a post-Franco repositioning of feminine subjectivity. While Martín Gaite documents and debunks the Franco regime's conservative idealization of woman here and in many of her novels, Bautista's poems posit a transition from feminine vulnerability to agency, from object to subject, through the depiction of romantic involvement. Of the poets in this book Bautista is the one who has most recently begun her poetic career. Like Luisa Castro and Almudena Guzmán, she protests against patriarchal attitudes that tend to objectify women. Her tone, in contrast, is much more ironic because of its double-voicing and the double-vision of the female protagonist.

Bautista has undoubtedly taken the title of her work from the eponymous late medieval work by Diego de San Pedro, a compendium of courtly love and the epitome of male-female relationships. The novel presents the opposition of two irresistible feelings of love that over-

266

power the lovers, resulting in a hopelessness that devours the idealized woman or in the death to which her devoted but chaste admirer surrenders himself voluntarily. By adopting the title of this well-known work, Bautista reformulates male-female relationships, presenting them from the woman's point of view, ridiculing the disastrous effects of phallocentric love. Hence the double-voicing and double-vision that simultaneously portray a traditional representation and an alternate perspective.

Cárcel de amor is divided into four evenly balanced sections, each containing seven short poems, with the exception of the first section, which consists of eight. We can therefore read the first poem "Contra remedia amoris" (Remedies Against Love) as introductory. Before examining this key poem, let me outline the progression we see in the four sections. The emphasis of the first section falls on the male figure and the ways in which men objectify women. Nonetheless, the perspective is that of the female speaker(s) and defines her perplexity. On the metapoetic level, we can see the insecurity of the novice poet whose inspiration, portrayed as an egocentric male in the love relationship, deceives, disillusions, betrays, and wounds the woman poet. In the second section she describes her inspiration as "madness," a traditional image for the arrival of the poetic impulse, but one that adopts charged significance when speaking of women because of the long psychoanalytic interest in (female) hysteria. Shoshana Felman clarifies this concept, affirming that,

> quite the opposite of rebellion, madness is the impasse confronting those whom cultural conditioning has deprived of the very means of protest or self-affirmation. Far from being a form of contestation, "mental illness" is a *request for help*, a manifestation both of cultural impotence and of political castration. This socially defined help-needing and help-seeking behavior is itself part of female conditioning, ideologically inherent in the behavioral pattern and in the dependent and helpless role assigned to the woman as such.[2]

This section of *Cárcel* marks a transition in the speaker's attitudes, though her position is still inconstant and vacillating. Opening with the title poem "Cárcel de amor," the third section shows the speaker's realization of men's infidelity and of her own power, and posits the moment of rebellion against the status quo.

Although hints of characteristic female subject positions (such as Scheherazade) are evident in earlier poems, the final section consists of poems that have a female archetype mentioned in the title. Through her interaction with the images in the mirror of the page, the speaker-poet rejects and reenvisions traditional, stereotypical views of women, such as Colombine and Galatea, and establishes her own individuality as woman and poet. In spite of this assertion, sadness pervades these poems, demonstrating the mixed emotions that accompany a woman's gesture of individuation and self-assertion. In comparison with Almudena Guzmán, Bautista's ironic stance and sarcastic tone are more distant, aggressive, and overtly critical of patriarchal practices, whereas Guzmán evinces more pain and defensiveness. Hence, throughout *Cárcel de amor* a tension exists in the double-voicing, creating a double-vision of the speaker as woman and poet. A closer look at individual poems supports this reading of the page as mirror.

As stated above, the first poem—although included in the opening section, not set apart as a prefatory poem—serves as an introduction to the collection by postulating the double-voicing that controls our reading of the remaining poems. The Latin phrase "Contra remedia amoris" not only partakes of a long tradition but also problematizes the point of view. Is the speaker of this poem a young, inexperienced woman seeking the means of dealing with "the bonds of love"?[3] Or is she the wise, experienced woman who casts spells and mixes potions because she knows how to induce or distance love, to seduce or reject her lover? Does she set herself up for a fall because of her insecurity and defensiveness? Or is she clearly superior to the men who approach her?

> Yo no soy de ese tipo de mujeres
> incapaces de amor y de ternura.
> Yo sé lo que es valor y lo que es sangre,
> aunque odie el sacrificio y me repugne
> la vanidad que nace en la violencia.
> Quiero ser la mujer de un mercenario,
> de un poeta o de un mártir, es lo mismo.
> Yo sé mirar los ojos de los hombres.
> Conozco a quien merece mi ternura.
>
>   (vv. 1–9)[4]

Does the poem speak against remedies of love or invoke remedies against certain types of love? What is more, the opening statement sounds as defensive as it is assertive, as if the speaker were excusing or defending herself, as if asking herself why such things (as yet unspecified) happen to her. It also defines the type of woman she is not, distinguishing her from harsh or bitter ("frigid") women incapable of loving, at the same time that it tells what kind of woman she is. From the very beginning of the text, double-voicing places speaker and reader on uncertain ground, and we cannot say for sure how we should read the speaker's tone.

The second sentence elaborates these dualities, now from a positive stance that is immediately undercut. We are not certain of the relationship between *valor* and *sangre*. Are they synonyms or antonyms? The speaker may know what valor is, but does that necessarily mean that she possesses it? She introduces a negative phrase in the conjunction *aunque*, while the subjunctive mood of the verbs *odie* and *repugne* reinforces the doubt and equivocality of this assertion. The additional pairing of *sacrificio* with *vanidad* problematizes the previous pair, *valor* and *sangre*, and casts all in the light of violent actions. Finally, the verb *nace* has a positive connotation, but it gives rise to violence, vanity, and a useless sacrifice. *Sacrifice* thus adopts a negative connotation, suggesting "the act of giving up, destroying, permitting injury to, or foregoing something so given us," "a selling or giving up of something at less than its supposed value," and "the loss incurred." Even though the speaker asserts definitively with the phrases *Yo no soy* and *Yo sé,* these declarations are equivocal and problematic.

Her next statement specifies three types of men whom the speaker would be willing to love: a mercenary, a poet, or a martyr, all of whom are equal in her eyes. That is, a mercenary (one who sells his services to the highest bidder), a poet (one who knows how to wield words effectively), and a martyr (one who altruistically sacrifices himself for an ideal) are indistinguishable: All men are alike when it comes to love. All use their particular skills to advance their personal status: the mercenary to gain money, the poet to seduce, and the martyr to achieve ecstasy. One has to wonder why the female speaker would want to be involved with any of these men. Is it that she will profit (materially or spiritually) from the relationship? Or does she resign herself hopelessly to a vapid situation in which she is little more than the object used by these men for their own aggrandizement? Does she exercise the same control and advantage as they, or is she nothing more than a subordinate adjunct that mirrors their identity? From what position does this woman speak?

The final two verses of the poem continue the pattern of first-person affirmation in the verbs *Yo sé* and *Conozco,* and the phrases are equally ambivalent. As a reader of men's eyes, does she impose her will (through her gaze) on them by rejecting what she does not want? Or does she conform to their expectations of her expressed in their narcissistic gaze? Is she the same or different? Even though she can recognize the men who merit her tenderness, is she choosing wisely or not? Does she know what she wants? Sigrid Weigel comments on this aspect in her essay "Double Focus: On the History of Women's Writing":

Women are always defined according to male criteria as regards their characteristics, behaviour, etc. . . . Thus her self-portrait originates in the distorting patriarchal mirror. In order to find her own image she must liberate the mirror from the images of woman painted on it by a male hand.

The metaphor of the "mirror"—its reverse side and edges, its splintering and "doubling" effect—is now commonly used to describe female self-awareness controlled by the male gaze.[5]

Certainly, the types of men the poetic voice describes in the subsequent poems of this section reveal this duality. In the following poem, "El incrédulo" (The Incredulous One), the male figure doubts the sincerity of the female speaker when she declares her love for him. As a result, she questions her commitment and her view of reality. The male thus determines what she thinks and feels—or does he?

> Me dice que no estoy enamorada,
> y a veces me dan ganas de jurarle
> que olvidaría el sol entre sus brazos,
> o que quisiera estar besando siempre
> sus labios, o que no me importa el tiempo
> cuando me mira oscuro, fijo y loco.
> Pero, ¿de qué me serviría tanto?
> Sé que jamás creería una palabra.
>
> (vv. 1–8)[6]

Does the male's opinion shake the speaker's confidence in what she feels? Or does she find reassurance in her (self-)knowledge? Her description of her love is ambivalent. Is she trying to convince him "que olvidaría el sol entre sus brazos, / o que quisiera estar besando siempre / sus labios, o que no me importa el tiempo / cuando me mira"? Is she reveling in the plenitude of the emotions she feels, affirming her feelings, her experience of love? Or is she deeply sardonic? At the end of the poem does she resign herself to a lack of communication and sharing? Or does she say, "I don't care what he thinks as long as I'm enjoying myself"? Does his questioning deny her love or teasingly spur it on? Or does she know he is "playing games"?

Not only is there double-voicing in these poems; there is a double-vision of the speaker. The poetic voice simultaneously belongs to an inexperienced, insecure, disenchanted, frustrated young woman, victimized by manipulative men, and to a confident, ironic, experienced woman, aware of the pitfalls involved in love relationships and the treachery and cruelty of some men. The voice and vision are double because the speaker has been a victim in the past and speaks from a knowledgeable position to other women who are victims now.[7]

Another instance of the relationship between male and female can be found in "Enigma." The structure and narrative quality of this poem funnel the reader's attention toward an epiphanic revelation. The "enigma" to be solved at first seems to be the profession of the female speaker's lover, to whom she addresses her words in apostrophe. But another enigma confronts the speaker after she solves the first one.

> El primer día que salí contigo
> dijiste que era extraño tu trabajo.
> Nada más. Sin embargo, yo sentía
> que mi piel se rasgaba hecha jirones
> cada vez que tus manos me rozaban,
> y que tus ojos eran como aceros
> que hacían que los míos me dolieran.
> En adelante siempre fue lo mismo:
> tú te enorgullecías de tu arte,
> más sutil y directo cada día,
> y yo no comprendía nunca nada.
>
> (vv. 1–11)[8]

Through the use of past tenses and a withholding of information, the poem creates suspense. Because the situation is presented from the point of view of the female speaker, we learn little about the male other in the first seven verses. Emphasis falls instead on the experience and feelings of the speaker. Her vivid sensations when the male runs his hands over her skin and looks at her with a penetrating gaze could, on the one hand, describe the intensity and sensuality of her reaction to him. On the other hand, the violence of the verbs *rasgaba* and *dolieran,* the expression *hecha jirones,* the onomatopeic repetition of the /rr/ and other fricatives, and the coldness communicated in the word *aceros* express foreboding. The discomfort imbricated on the sensuality might even suggest a masochistic stance which, according to Jessica Benjamin, many women adopt under the restraints of a phallocentric structure of domination (a lack of mutual recognition).[9] In addition, the laconic, distant presence of the male contrasts with the speaker's sensorial descriptions. He tells her only that he has a strange job: "Nada más." She in contrast provides a description rich in semantic and phonic texture.

The male's diffidence is echoed at the beginning of the next verses. The inexpressive "fue lo mismo," his superiority, his increasing pride in his skill, and his relentless lovemaking, the contrast between *tú* and *yo,* and the negatives associated with the woman's comprehension show that she is overwhelmed, immobilized, rendered passive. Attentive to the few clues offered her, the speaker finally solves the riddle of her lover's profession: "Ahora lo sé. Conozco ya tu oficio: / lanzador de cuchillos. Has lanzado / contra mi corazón el más certero" (Now I know. I know about your profession now: / knife thrower. You have thrown / the most accurate one at my heart). This revelation explains the ripping sensation on her skin, his steely eyes causing her eyes to ache, and the improved accuracy of his ability to sweep her off her feet. Moreover, his "knives" may be his words, which have both a pleasing and a painful effect on the speaker. This discovery, this solving of the enigma of his profession, is not, however, the end of the poem. A second enigma arises in the final sentence: If this guy is such a good knife-thrower, how is it that he has hit her in the heart? Metaphorically, of course, he has succeeded in enamoring the speaker. But the violence of the image and the incommensurability of the literal and metaphoric levels confirm the conversion of the female into the object of male subjectivity, ironically equating love with death, Eros with Thanatos, masochistic pleasure with a painful loss of agency.

We can view the male figure in this poem as representative of the masculine poetic tradition. The female admires that tradition, finding it stimulating and attractive. But if she remains in the position assigned to her by that patriarchal structure, it can be stultifying and destructive. Of course, one could argue that all poets face this dilemma. But Bautista's gendering of the positions calls attention to the particular problems confronted by female writers. Precisely because of the female point of view and the additional sentence after the first revelation, the enigma becomes how and why this has happened and whether this situation can be altered. Once again, however, we should recognize the split perspective, the double-vision. The past tense verbs and the narrative nature of this poem, along with the narrator's withholding of information, distance the speaker from the protagonist. The expert has flung a knife at her heart—but he missed! Perhaps the knife has had no effect precisely because she is informed and experienced in this man's ways, rendering his knives/words/ploys ineffectual. The final verse thus marks the end of their relationship: She retains no feelings for him.

The final poem of this section reverses the power dynamics between male and female, but leaves the woman in an equally unsatisfying situation. With echoes of the relationship between Semiramis and her generals or between Queen Elizabeth I and Sir Walter Raleigh, here the speaker is a queen against whom her subjects have attempted a rebellion. Because of her anger, she presents herself as a stereotypical "castrating bitch" inasmuch as decapitation metaphorizes castration or the enervation of phallic potency.[10]

> Aquel motín, sin duda imperdonable,
> merecía la muerte, uno por uno,
> de todos los que en él participaron.
> Mi cerebro y mis ojos, impasibles,
> contemplaron decenas de cabezas
> terribles, desgajadas de los troncos.
>
> (vv. 1–6)[11]

This unpardonable threat to the queen's authority causes her to contemplate and even to effect the decapitation of the guilty rebels. According to cold reason ("Mi cerebro y mis ojos, impasibles"), she knows that this punishment is the proper course of action. On a less allegorical level, we can assume that these men in some way work for or are under the leadership of a woman in a position of power (perhaps in the business world). But her authority and political wisdom are short-circuited by the arrival of another.

> Pero llegaste tú. Con tu mirada,
> descarada y valiente, hiciste inútil
> toda la autoridad de mi corona.
> Tú, más fuerte o más débil que los otros,
> mereciste el indulto y mereciste
> ser el capricho de tu reina, y siempre,
> mientras que yo no ordene lo contrario,
> deberás ser mi amante. . . .
>
> (vv. 7–14)[12]

Instead of including him in the general slaughter, the queen is swayed by her heart ("el capricho") because of this man's gaze: "tu mirada, / descarada y valiente." This gaze confuses her, so that she does not know if he is "más fuerte o más débil que los otros." Is his willingness to admit his fault a strength or a weakness? As a strength, is it positive or negative as far as the queen is concerned? Does it make him attractive or dangerous because deceitful and untrustworthy? As a weakness, does it make him more or less desirable as a lover? Consequently, even though she takes this man as her lover, it is always with the proviso that she can change her mind if more trouble arises. Given the ambivalence of her feelings for this man, however, her decision leaves her troubled.

A veces pienso
que esto es mayor castigo que la muerte,
y no sé si conspiras en silencio
o si tu abnegación es cobardía.

(vv. 14–17)[13]

In spite of what seems to be the queen's vulnerability, by making her the narrator of this situation and placing her in the position of power, the poet has inverted and defamiliarized the power relationship. As a result, she becomes an unreliable narrator. Because women are usually in the subordinate position in a patriarchal society, the poem gives a warning that women may also subvert the power relationship. By admitting to her own blind spot, the speaker indirectly signals the blind spot of all positions. Shoshana Felman comments on this situation:

> Psychoanalysis precisely teaches us that every human knowledge has its own unconscious, and that every human search is blinded by some systematic oversights of which it is not aware. . . . The unconscious means that every insight is inhabited by its own blindness, which pervades it: you cannot simply polarize, oppose blindness and insight. . . . [This] attitude only *reverses* the polarization but does not restructure, undermine, the illusory polarities.[14]

This suggests that any position of power and authority is tenuous and thus destabilizes the masculinist position of control, a foreshadowing of the changes to be realized in the following sections of *Cárcel de amor.*

The second section serves as a transitional section where madness plays a key metaphoric role. As both hysteria and poetic inspiration, madness opposes and undermines masculine ideals of reason, logic, and objectivity. As Felman states,

> If, in our culture, the woman is by definition associated with madness, her problem is how to break out of this (cultural) imposition of madness *without* taking up the critical and therapeutic positions of reason: how to avoid speaking both as *mad* and as *not mad.* The challenge facing the woman today is nothing less than to "reinvent" language, to *re-learn how to speak:* to speak not only against, but outside of the specular phallocentric structure, to establish a discourse the status of which would no longer be defined by the phallacy of masculine meaning.[15]

The poems of the second section of *Cárcel de amor* seem illogical—and even depressing—if read without irony and without the double-vision that characterizes Bautista's writing in this work. Picking up the thread of the argument from the final poem of the previous section, "Las antiguas llamas" (The Old/Former Flames) initiates this section by questioning psychoanalytic and therapeutic practices with regard to female hysteria. Psychotherapy and the transference process become the basis of a lie that at first seems to keep the speaker locked within (patriarchal) cultural definitions of madness.

> No pude confesarte dónde había
> estado tanto tiempo, ni explicarte
> mi vuelta inesperada. Sólo pude
> hacerte sospechar que en aquel año
> te había sido infiel impunemente.
> Y era mejor así. Volví a rendirme
> ante tus ojos y ante tu perdón.
> Me olvidé de que estuve en aquel centro
> para enfermos mentales. Volvió todo
> a ser como fue siempre antes de irme.
> Volvió el amor desgarrador y dulce,
> y la pasión nociva, y en mi pecho
> volvieron a encenderse sin clemencia
> aquel dolor y las antiguas llamas.
>
> (vv. 1–14)[16]

The psychoanalytic concept of the return of the repressed receives double emphasis in this poem, not only in the repetition of the verb *volvió* but also in the speaker's return from the mental hospital. As she returns, she revives the relationship with her lover and the emotions she experienced in that relationship. However, she does not confess where she has been, but instead invents the lie about being involved with someone else. Repetition of the verb phrase *No pude* and *Sólo pude* implies an attempt that has not been carried out, but also to a certain extent a stubborn refusal to admit the truth. By making her lover suspect that she had been involved in another love affair (an allusion to transference and the therapeutic process), she leads him to believe that she is repentant and aggrandizes his feelings of forgiveness in taking her back. Thus she would seem to place herself in an inferior, subordinate position in the male gaze ("Volví a rendirme / ante tus ojos y ante tu perdón") and to reinstate the conditions that lead her to the mental institution in the first place!

Parallel but contrary to this reading, the final verses suggest that the speaker has returned to exact her revenge; hence her lie: It is more effective to wound the lover surreptitiously so as to turn the tables on him. It also allows her to come into contact more keenly with her feelings. Her love for him is indeed "desgarrador y dulce," but she also recognizes *now* that it was harmful, pitiless, and destructive, as the phrases *nociva* and *sin clemencia* and the image of the flames indicate. It is just as appropriate, however, to attribute those characteristics to her love as well as his. Now she is the one "sin clemencia," and the destructive flames are regenerative as well. The speaker is now able to recognize and to utilize her pain so as to alter the dynamics of the relationship because of her psychotherapeutic experience.

The relationship is truly conflictive and ambivalent: She seems to love him but also to insist on a change in the dynamics so that they become more equal and equitable. This process continues to unfold in "El mensajero" (The Messenger). Traditional wisdom advises us not to kill the messenger just because he brings bad news. That the speaker of this poem does precisely that encourages us to expect a reversal of our initial impressions and accepted reasoning. On the surface it would seem that the woman who addresses us has surrendered her autonomy to her lover. Like the slave in Hegel's configuration of domination, the speaker of "El mensajero" says that she would do anything her lover might want.[17] She readily admits that she sees things only through his eyes, so that his every whim annuls her free will. She depends on him to call for a date; his kisses manipulate her emotions.

> Haría cualquier cosa que él quisiera
> porque ya sólo veo por sus ojos.
> Mi voluntad se anula a su capricho.
> Me sigo entusiasmando si me llama
> por teléfono y dice que salgamos.
> Sus besos me enternecen o me excitan,
> pero nunca me son indiferentes. . . .
>
> (vv. 1–7)[18]

It would seem that this woman has capitulated unconditionally to patriarchal power. The only positive aspect is the enthusiasm with which she describes her pleasure. But we should not rush to judgment and condemn her yet. Almost as an afterthought she lets us know that she is getting ready to go out (presumably because her lover has just called) when a friend comes to visit. While she gives her visitor a beer to keep him occupied, she continues to get dressed. In the interim, the visitor, his tongue loosened by the beer and perhaps jealous of the other male, fulfills his role as messenger by giving the speaker "una pésima noticia: / 'él no te quiere; siempre te ha engañado'" (the worst news: / 'he doesn't love you; he has always cheated on you'). The clipped sentences of the speaker's response attest to her anger, which we might assume is directed toward her lover as she learns this troublesome news: "Termino de arreglarme. Me perfumo. / El me espera. No puedo llegar tarde. / Acabo de matar al mensajero" (I finish getting ready. I put on perfume. / He is waiting for me. I can't arrive late. / I've just killed the messenger). Benjamin defines this process as "attunement" or an "intersubjective view" which requires "mutual recognition."[19] The speaker still intends to keep her date in spite of the news she has received. Is her perfume an attempt to cover up the disagreeable news? Is she trying to hide the truth from herself? To mask her feelings? Is she going to ignore what the messenger has told her?[20]

Just as earlier we learn coincidentally that her lover has called out of the blue and that she is excited about going out, at the end of the poem she matter of factly reveals that she has killed the messenger. We might explain her behavior as a refusal to acknowledge the truth, but the extremity of her response and the understated, terse language shock us into an alternate reading. The speaker's action indicates that she has control of the situation, that she is the active proponent, the agent of her destiny. Because she enjoys her lover so much, she will not let anyone or anything stand in the way of her desire and pleasure.

In comparison with the speaker of "Enigma," who is the passive recipient of male desire, the speaker of "El mensajero" actively deflects, rejects, and negates the masculine vehicle of signification (the messenger) to affirm her agency, her search for pleasure. She appropriates Thanatos in the service and to the advantage of her Eros. The same can be said of this poetry. While using a traditional hendecasyllabic meter, Bautista structures her poems around an anecdote where the (metonymic) narrative of the male-female relationship functions metaphorically. The flat, direct language seems proselike, even conversational, even though it is the meter of the sonnet, the epitome of poetic form. Moreover, the withholding of information on the part of the speaker manipulates the reader and creates an ironic tone that subverts the surface meaning. The poet seduces us readers, and through her double-voicing creates a double-vision of the image of the woman she presents in these poems. The absurdity (madness) of "killing the messenger" as if it were nothing at all defamiliarizes and subverts the situation.

One might say, following Freud's analysis, that what is perhaps most uncanny about the uncanny is that it is not the opposite of what is canny but, rather, that which uncannily *subverts the opposition* between "canny" and "uncanny," between "heimlich" and "unheimlich." In the same way, femininity as real otherness . . . is uncanny in that it is not the opposite of masculinity but *that which subverts the very opposition of masculinity and femininity.*[21]

The speaker's project in this section of *Cárcel de amor*—the transition she proposes—involves divesting herself of former attitudes and habits and acquiring new perspectives. As indicated in the image of "Las antiguas llamas," this process is simultaneously destructive and regenerative. "La renuncia" (The Renunciation) presents a similar duality as the speaker decides to effect major changes in her lifestyle. Here her renunciation of makeup is particularly indicative of these modifications.

> Estaba acostumbrada a las reuniones
> y verbenas que nada conmemoran;
> lugares donde acaban por besarte
> los chicos que jamás recordarías
> si no fuera por eso, y por las copas
> a las que, siempre amables, te invitaban.
> Me arrepentí de todo de repente.
> Corté mi pelo, despinté mis uñas,
> no volví a maquillarme las mejillas
> ni las pestañas, ni besé más labios
> ni bebí más licores. Hice a todos
> creer que estaba loca. Me internaron
> en el mejor lugar y desde entonces
> soy feliz entre tanta pared blanca.
>
> (vv. 1–14)[22]

The speaker recognizes the shallow, sterile social environment in which she moves. Where women and men are assigned limited and limiting roles and where obligatory courtesy is the only reason for coming together, small talk and cocktails do not lead to lasting, satisfying, or meaningful relationships. In fact, the speaker seems bored by this atmosphere, as the phrase *Estaba acostumbrada* and repetition in the sentence "Me arrepentí de todo de repente" suggest. The similarity between *arrepentirse* and *repente,* though deriving from different stems, underscores the conflict. The former is composed of the intensifier *re-* and the verb *poenitere,* connoting thought, reflection, soul-searching, whereas the latter is based on *repons,* denoting rapid, unplanned, unforeseen, or unprepared movement. This antithesis and the phonetic similarity show that the speaker is reacting against the society that encourages superficiality and triviality.

This nodal point calls attention to the speaker's volte-face. Opposed to the dictates of this society, she first cuts her hair and then removes her nail polish and refuses to wear makeup. These gestures signify her rejection of the imposed norms of feminine beauty.[23] Moreover, she forgoes alcohol. Even here a subtle difference is manifest in the change from the word *copas* (v. 5) to *licores* (v. 11). While both refer to alcoholic beverages, *copas* is a metonymic trope based on the container, but *licores* specifies the type of liquid imbibed. The first is more inclusive and general, whereas the second is more precise and specific. The nuances of these distinctions illustrate the speaker's determination to delve ever more deeply into those aspects of herself and her society that restrict her, that tend to intoxicate her so that she cannot see clearly.

Finally, she pretends to be mad. Her performance is so convincing, her actions (cutting her hair, refusing to wear makeup, and ceasing to drink) so alien to the society around her, that they intern her in what she metaphorically and elusively calls "el mejor lugar." On one level, we might gloss this image as an insane asylum or mental institution. But on another level, we might understand that society has simply isolated her, ostracized her, because of her "aberrant" behavior. Since that time, however, the speaker says that she has been happier than ever precisely because of the white walls surrounding her. Again, this image is equivocal. Certainly, the walls of a hospital are traditionally white so as to maintain sanitary conditions; in a mental institution colors can often stimulate violent reactions in patients. The color symbolism might thereby indicate that the speaker's world is now colorless, cheerless, and vapid. Yet, that was the type of world from which she escaped, and she states that she is deeply, spiritually at peace ("Soy feliz" as opposed to "Estoy contenta"). The ungrammaticality of the juxtaposition of the final verse suggests another reading: that white walls are transparent, nonexistent. The speaker no longer finds herself limited by society's norms, especially with regard to feminine beauty. Also, the mental institution implies that a "cure" has been or will be effected. The speaker has started with a clean slate by recognizing the limitations that a patriarchal society has imposed on her and others. Her renunciation of the superficial world has opened new possibilities.

If in the second section of *Cárcel de amor* the speaker looks inward to recognize the ways a patriarchal social structure has limited her, in the third section she looks outward. Through a series of anecdotes and episodes she identifies ways in which men have hypocritically mistreated women. She accuses men of their wrongs against women and the ways in which certain beliefs have instigated misconceptions about women's characters. Although each poem allegorically defines a specific wrong, the opening poem, the title poem of the collection, encompasses all the others by setting the pattern for this section. Here the speaker is a prisoner in the "Cárcel de amor," but she exemplifies the imprisonment of all women in the patriarchal structures of love, especially marriage.

Ironically, even though she appears to be a man's wife, she has less freedom to come and go than other women he has known. Because he loves her more than the others, he has married her, but then their intimacy ceases. She is confined to the house while he comes and goes, leaving each day to return in the evening after work. While it is true that he brings her small presents and talks to her (perhaps about his job or his diversions), these concessions are little more than appeasement: The sweets are supposed to satisfy her body and the commentary her mind. His goodnight kiss suggests the lack of passion with which they go to sleep, only to repeat the same sequence of events the following day ad infinitum. Indeed, the speaker characterizes his kiss on her forehead as "paternal," that is, chaste, dispassionate, condescending, and obligatory.

It is highly understandable, therefore, that the speaker as a woman in a passionless marriage should feel lonely and bored, and that she should seek excitement in another relationship. Because she chooses to do so, patriarchal attitudes accuse her of being unfaithful and insult her with epithets such as "adulteress" or "whore." It is also highly ironic that, as she states in the final verse, he finds her embraced by the jailer, that is, another man! The very system that prohibits and criticizes her seeking an outlet provides the proverbial postman or milkman who takes advantage of the situation. Men hypocritically accuse women of infidelity and sexual appetite when it is men's structure that creates unsatisfied desire and the means of gratification. In both the confinement and the outlet women are trapped in a system that makes them appear guilty. In pointing out this catch-22, the speaker of "Cárcel de amor" establishes the general patriarchal framework in which she will find other instances of men's hypocrisy.

By adopting a number of different stances throughout this section, the speaker calls attention to patriarchal attitudes. In "Desnudo de mujer" (Nude Woman) she is a marble statue sculpted by a man and placed on a pedestal. Such a creation of feminine norms of beauty, however, objectifies, depersonalizes, and dehumanizes woman. In *The Female Nude,* Lynda Nead asserts that "the representation of the female body within the forms and frames of high art is a metaphor for the value and significance of art generally. It symbolizes the transformation of the base matter of nature into the elevated forms of culture and the spirit. The female nude can thus be understood as a means of containing femininity and female sexuality." Later she also argues, "If the female body is defined as lacking containment and issuing filth and pollution from its faltering outlines and broken surface, then the classical forms of art perform a kind of magical regulation of the female body, containing it and momentarily repairing the orifices and tears."[24] We can see these issues raised in Bautista's poem:

> Para ti nunca fui más que un pedazo
> de mármol. Esculpiste en él mi cuerpo,
> un cuerpo de mujer blanco y hermoso,
> en el que nunca viste más que piedra
> y el orgullo, eso sí, de tu trabajo.
> Jamás imaginaste que te amaba
> y que me estremecía cuando, dulce,
> moldeabas mis senos y mis hombros,
> o alisabas mis muslos y mi vientre. . . .
>
> (vv. 1–9)[25]

In these opening verses the speaker complains that the male treats her as nothing but an object, "un pedazo / de mármol." Men define feminine beauty, a white, finely shaped and contoured but lifeless form. Men's hands give shape to breasts and shoulders, thighs and belly, but men expect no response from the figure they caress. They expect a woman to be passive, unresponsive, serving only their gratification. In general, this type of art "sanitizes" the female body by denying her desire. In her discussion of the opposition of contemporary feminist art to the traditional representations of the female nude, Nead states, "Although the female body was on show within high culture, this display denied women's experiences of their bodies and sexual desires."[26] Indeed, men use this object solely for self-gratification. They see themselves and their identities mirrored in the other. Benjamin addresses the issue of mirroring in her discussion of the oedipal model, which—she says—"constructs femininity as a simple mirror image of masculinity." Moreover, she investigates women's desire at length, commenting that, "For Freud, woman's renunciation of sexual agency and her acceptance of object status are the very hallmark of the feminine. And though we may refuse this definition, we are nevertheless obliged to confront the painful fact that even today, femininity continues to be identified with passivity, with being the object of someone else's desire, with having no active desire of one's own."[27] A man is proud of himself when accompanied by a beautiful woman, as if she were a reflection or metonymic indication of his self-worth. Then he places her on a pedestal and exhibits her for all to see.

> Hoy estoy en un parque, donde sufro
> los rigores del frío en el invierno,
> y en verano me abraso de tal modo
> que ni siquiera los gorriones vienen
> a posarse en mis manos porque queman. . . .
>
>   (vv. 10–14)[28]

The statue as woman serves as a public ornament with no concern for her feelings. The contrasting seasons of winter and summer and the temperature extremes of heat and cold attest to the whims of the climate (men's reactions to women or men's emotions—passion or inattention) to which she is exposed. She cannot even enjoy the simple, common pleasures of life, metaphorized in the sparrows, because she is so contingent on the dominant male. What most upsets her, however, is the generic label she has received, which deprives her of her individuality and identity.

> Pero, de todo, lo que más me duele
> es bajar la cabeza y ver la placa:
> "Desnudo de mujer", como otras muchas.
> Ni de ponerme un nombre te acordaste.
>
>   (vv. 15–18)[29]

In fact, in this case the name of the artist overrides the title of the statue, just as the male's surname overrides the woman's when they marry. The act of this woman lowering her head to read the plaque alludes to her humiliation as well as her disappointment. Because this statue is titled merely "Desnudo de mujer," she has lost all sense of individuality, identity, self. She becomes one of a generic category: "woman."[30] Moreover, her nudity exposes her to the gaze of all who pass, further humiliating and debasing her. In addition to being in a public place and set on a pedestal, her nudity makes her exposed and vulnerable to scopic rape. It displays the female body, not only making it an object of the male gaze but also putting women at risk. Thus male art depicting a female nude tends to objectify, dehumanize, and depersonalize women indiscriminately.[31]

In "La croupier" the poet adopts the persona of a woman who works at a roulette table to criticize masculine attitudes toward love, involvement, and commitment. For men, love is like playing roulette: Some lose everything, whereas others win at this game of chance.

> Como todas las noches, yo decía:
> "¡Hagan juego, señores!", y los hombres
> vulgares que llenaban el casino,
> con colonia y gemelos a la moda,
> colocaban sus fichas de colores
> sobre el verde tapete. Yo soltaba
> con desdén la bolita en la ruleta
> que giraba obediente a mis impulsos.
> Así, un día tras otro, y una hora
> tras otra. Me aburrían mortalmente
> el estoicismo del que se arruinaba
> y el goce simple del afortunado. . . .
>
> (vv. 1–12)[32]

The speaker seems aloof, indifferent, and impervious to the risks taken by the bettors around her. This attitude brings to mind the way Spanish women have learned to walk through the streets surrounded by the *piropos* (catcalls) with which Spanish men "try their luck." Several phrases allude to her boredom and indifference as well as to the disdain she feels for these suitors of Lady Luck. Even though they wear cologne and elegant shirts with French cuffs and cufflinks, and even though they seem to have enough money to win or lose stoically, their participation in the game of life does not excite the speaker's interest. In particular, she finds them "mortally" boring. The adverb *mortalmente* suggests not only the depth of her ennui but also the limitations of these men. None of them promises the speaker something extraordinary, "transcendent." The tokens they place on the green felt of the gaming table have the colorful beauty and signify the worth of precious stones, jewelry, and other material pleasures, but they are mere tokens used as a gamble, a substitute for real emotions. The game thus adopts allegorical proportions of an exchange or bartering economy that substitutes for love. One night, however, a different "player" appears at the croupier's table.

> Pero una noche de ruleta y tedio
> llegó un hombre distinto. Sobre el 9
> hizo la apuesta mínima aceptada.
> Jugó sólo esa vez. Perdió su ficha,
> pero permaneció junto a la mesa,

> sin dejar de mirarme ni un momento,
> hasta que se cerró el casino. Entonces
> salimos juntos sin mediar palabra.
>
> (vv. 13–20)[33]

Knowing that the roulette table is based on two contrasting colors, red and black, and that the 9 is red, we can read into this bet. If traditionally red and black are symbolic of passion and death, Eros and Thanatos, we see that this uncommon player has bet on passion. However, he has made the minimum wager. This action would suggest that he has invested very little, and we know that he has lost that. But unlike the others, he has not tried to impress the croupier or to buy her affections. It is obvious that he functions on the margins of society, but it is unclear whether this difference is good or bad. Nonetheless, the speaker is clearly intrigued and even hypnotized by his gaze. Again, we must question whether this attraction is promising or ominous.

When they leave the casino (the public arena of gaming), they do not exchange a word. The phrase *sin mediar palabra* refers to both silence and a lack of representation, a lack of barriers. This metapoetic allusion to the sign and the ambivalent relationship between signifier and signified embodies the relationship between men and women. Communication can be verbal or nonverbal, and either party can send or receive messages. But what is the relationship between language, men, and women? And does the reader always interpret the message as the sender intended it? Do men and women read differently? Does language signify the same thing for men and women?[34]

The allegory of love as roulette, as a game of chance, thus acquires metapoetic proportions that emphasize the arbitrariness of the sign. Recall the speaker's description of her role in the game: "Yo soltaba / con desdén la bolita en la ruleta / que giraba obediente a mis impulsos." She spins the wheel and releases the ball, but the final disposition of the "message" is pure chance. Moreover, that the male has placed his money (again, the minimum amount) on the number 9 (red for passion) are gestures that communicate, but what do they signify? Should we read into the color and number symbolism? How do we interpret his minimum wager and the suspension of his play after losing his token? What does this tell us about him, his life, his past, his attitudes? Ambivalence and ambiguity persist in the final verses of the poem and the speaker's reaction to their encounter.

> Me gustaba aquel rapto silencioso.
> Me condujo a su casa. Al otro día

me fui despacio y le dejé dormido
y en penumbra, con marcas de los pliegues
de la ropa en la cara y en los hombros.
Nunca volvió al casino, porque el juego
no era lo suyo. Nunca he vuelto a verle.

(vv. 21–27)[35]

This one night stand parallels the man's style of betting: a one-time shot, win or lose, with a minimum investment. But how does the speaker feel about this situation? Does she feel the same as he? After all, it is she who leaves him in the morning. In addition, her choice of details in describing the scene leaves the question unresolved. The speaker leaves slowly—to avoid waking him or because she does not want to separate from him? Does the "penumbra" add to the sensuality and mystery of the moment? Or does it allow her to leave unnoticed? And what about the creases in his face and shoulders made by the sheets? They are sensual, but they are also imperfections and impressions that will not last. Would the speaker like to see this man again? Or is it that he and she just do not see eye to eye, do not play the same "game"? Has the female speaker turned the tables on male attitudes toward love and relationships? Or is she still being manipulated by the norms of a masculinist society? When, at the end of the poem, the speaker flatly states that she has not seen this man again, is she matter of fact, or is she disappointed? Was he different from other men, or was he the same?

One last consideration that may shed some light on these issues is the speaker's occupation. The name of this occupation derives from the stick that the croupier uses to remove the bets at the end of the round. On one hand, we might see this "crook" as a satirical allusion to pastoral conventions of love. On another, the croupier uses this implement to "rake in" the colorful tokens that have been placed before her. Who wins and who loses in this situation? What do "winning" and "losing" entail? How do we define them? The croupier controls the table, but what about the casino? Also, *croupier* originally refers to the whip used to urge a horse forward, an image with obvious sexual connotations. The croupier is the one who sits on the horse's croup, its rump, not in the saddle. By calling attention to these issues of power and love, the poet has questioned masculinist attitudes toward love, sex, and relationships, and whether a mere reversal of these positions of power is what women really want.

Another poem that criticizes masculinist attitudes, "En público" (In Public), relies on the anecdotal incident of an encounter between a man and a woman on the platform of a train station and on the train they both board. Traditional connotations allow this anecdotal setting to adopt allegorical proportions of staging in a public place and embarking on an adventure. First, the platform becomes the scopic stage on which the speaker feels herself the object of the male gaze.

> En aquella estación, anocheciendo,
> sentada en mi maleta y esperando,
> te recuerdo mirando mis tobillos
> y ascender, descarado, con los ojos
> siguiendo los dibujos de mis medias.
>
> (vv. 1–5)[36]

With a few quick strokes—the station, the suitcase, dusk—the poet situates us in a typical dramatic situation. But in spite of the drama, this scene is almost comical, too melodramatic, and it seems that we are watching a film directed by Alfred Hitchcock. The gaze of the camera scopes the woman's legs from ankle upward, and the speaker seems taken aback by the boldness and sensuality of this gaze that follows the pattern in her stockings. She describes the man as "descarado": shameless, uninhibited, cheeky. But literally *descarado* means "without a face." Whereas the female figure has specific corporeal presence, the male gaze is anonymous. Hence the speaker feels as if she were on stage, acting a part, doing things as an actor would, the gestures not hers but imposed from outside. Nead notes that the body is always mediated by representation. Contrary to the opinions of many (male) theorists, there is no such thing as "a physical body that is outside of representation. . . . Within social, cultural and psychic formations, the body is rendered dense with meaning and significance. . . ."[37] In other words, this opening makes us acutely aware of the artificiality of the scene.

The encounter between the anonymous male gaze and the female object of the gaze intensifies with the arrival of the train, a phallic symbol. Again the details chosen for emphasis stand out.

> Cuando llegó aquel tren que me llevaba
> no recuerdo a qué sitio, te subiste
> en mi vagón y, al empezar la marcha,
> con tres golpes enérgicos llamaste
> a la puerta de mi compartimento.
>
> (vv. 6–10)[38]

Repetition of the demonstrative adjective *aquel* underscores the sense of estrangement and the feeling that we are watching this scene unfold. Moreover, the speaker has no real destination: She does not recall where she was taking the train. She feels that she is playing a role, going through motions that make little sense to her. This parody defamiliarizes an encounter between a man and a woman in contemporary society and the artificial, mediated position in which a woman finds herself. The detail of his "tres golpes enérgicos" on the door of her compartment again characterizes the male as active, energetic, forceful, dynamic, and determined, as opposed to the passive, overwhelmed female. As a result, the scene adopts the proportions of a fantasy of ideal love, but perhaps also of a nightmare of forced entry and rape. The female is then complicit in this fantasy.

> Te abrí y entraste. Fue todo un asalto,
> pero nunca pensé en gritar pidiendo
> ayuda al revisor. Era más dulce
> rendirse sin hablar, sin preguntarte,
> sin intentar la fuga ni el orgullo. . . .
>
> (vv. 11–15)[39]

If this encounter is truly an assault, why does the speaker refrain from calling for help? In fact, she says that it is sweeter to surrender. However, the contrast in the third-person, impersonal pronoun at the end of the infinitive *rendirse* and the more personal second-person address at the end of *preguntarte* creates an uncomfortable disjunction. This contrast resonates in the two options she then mentions, attempting to flee or adopting a superior, disdainful attitude toward her attacker. Is she complicit in the encounter, or is she powerless to overcome or fight against patriarchal structures? Are we observing a rape, or is she succumbing to societal pressures? The final verses complicate our reaction to this unsettling scene.

> Pensar en los demás me molestaba,
> y más saber que, de un momento a otro,
> nos iba a interrumpir el director
> con sus gritos de "¡corten!" y "¡otra toma!"
>
> (vv. 16–19)[40]

Is this only a film? Or is it a real incident? The figure of the director suggests the presence of a guiding authority figure such as God or patriarchal society. Does the speaker prefer to go through with the lovemaking? Is this fantasy of seduction his or hers? Where do we draw the line between life and art? How is the position of women compromised by their portrayal in film and art? Is a woman always on stage, always the object of a male scopophilia?

The sense of estrangement and distance throughout this poem

defamiliarizes the rape and calls attention to the terror and violence involved in this act. The wider implication is that any public demonstration of affection or approach is culturally determined and responds to a societal script for action. However, because men have power in a patriarchal society, women feel estranged from reality and manipulated by structures over which they have no control. The title "En público" defines the stage on which this drama is played out. Once again, Bautista makes a powerful statement criticizing patriarchal society. Even though her speakers gain in wisdom and insight over the course of these poems, they still present a double-voicing and double-vision. Now, however, the duality is between the external gaze of masculinist mentality and the internal vision of a woman acquiring autonomy.

The fourth and final section of *Cárcel de amor* differs from the previous sections in that each poem portrays a specific, prototypical female figure. As their titles indicate, these historical but not necessarily nonfictional characters can be specific, such as Columbine, Margaret of Provence, or Galatea, or more general types, such as a soldier's wife, a lady playing chess, or a princess. However, the poet situates each of these figures in a contemporary setting, constituting a (dis)junction between past and present that highlights (dis)-continuity. Unfortunately, these poems are disappointing given that they seem to sustain the status quo. In spite of the protests and consciousness-raising carried out in the previous sections, the woman/protagonist/poetic voice remains mired in a patriarchal society that imprisons her in phallocentric relationships with men. In spite of the changes that have occurred in contemporary society, the relations between men and women fundamentally have not changed for centuries, at least since the publication of Diego de San Pedro's *Cárcel de amor* in 1492.

The opening poem, centered on the figure of Columbine, illustrates this dissatisfaction. This figure is taken from the traditional commedia dell'arte, a highly stylized genre that ridicules male and female stereotypes.[41] The daughter of Pantaloon and the sweetheart of Harlequin, Columbine is "dovelike" but clearly dissatisfied with the type of men who surround her, as the opening verses of "Colombina" attest.

> He sido fiel durante muchos años,
> pero no es la virtud, sino la huida
> de un galán aburrido y sensiblero,
> lo que me convirtió en amante esposa
> de un tipo a quien adorna la simpleza.

Aquél es un romántico, suspira,
me escribe cursiladas deleznables,
mira a la luna y llora como un tonto.
Éste es un saltimbanqui confiado,
orgulloso y pagado de sí mismo,
que se escucha al hablar y se cree un genio.
Pero ya me he cansado de los dos. . . .

(vv. 1–12)[42]

The speaker's dissatisfaction could not be clearer. The choices available to her are extremely limited. On the one hand is the romantic, melodramatic, tacky lover who cannot persuade her with tears, sighs, or maudlin declarations to be unfaithful to her husband. The latter, on the other hand, is an egotistical, supercilious tumbler, who derives his self-confidence from his flips, rolls, and somersaults (a reference to his lovemaking?). He is enamored with his own voice, and on hearing himself, believes he is a genius. Clearly self-centered, he does not offer Columbine much of an alternative to her hyperbolic, melancholic suitor. Because she is fed up with these limited choices, the speaker formulates an ideal that will take her out of this comic but not humorous situation.

He decidido que esta misma noche
voy a buscar un hombre que me entienda,
que me acompañe al cine, que me invite
a tomar una horchata o un helado,
que disfrute conmigo y con mi cuerpo
y, ante todo, que no haga payasadas.

(vv. 13–18)[43]

Notwithstanding her determination, the subjunctive mood of the verbs in this passage belies the reality or the possibility of attaining her goal. Does such a man exist? According to this description, he would be concerned with sharing simple pleasures like going to the movies or going out for an ice cream with the speaker. The specific mention of the "cine" and "horchata" not only contemporizes the setting but also points to simple pleasures without the exaggeration or melodramatic emotions of the world in which she currently finds herself. The speaker wishes to extricate herself from the clownlike society where she and others are constrained to play ridiculous parts. Her very formulation of this down-to-earth utopia nonetheless underscores its unreality and the possible futility of realizing it. The double-voicing and double-vision manifest themselves here in the juxtaposition of past and present, theater and reality, reality and utopia, hope and disappointment.

A similar duality is apparent in "Gámbito de dama" (Queen's Gambit), where the game of chess stylizes the competitive relationship between men and women. The woman playing the game of chess and of life identifies with the queen.

> ¿Recuerdas? Me pasaba todo el tiempo
> jugando a amenazarte. Te decía
> "te voy a asesinar" y te contaba
> incluso los detalles de mi crimen:
> el escenario, el arma, los motivos.
> Te había condenado para siempre
> al rol de amante débil y entregado.
> Y yo era inaccesible, altiva, dura
> y algo dulce en contadas ocasiones. . . .
>
> (vv. 1–9)[44]

The opening question engages the speaker in a conversation with the other, herself, and even the reader. This engagement parallels the exchange of moves in the game of chess and posits a tension between two positions. The game thus allegorizes the relationship between men and women, where the phrase *jugando a amenazarte* ironically but ominously alludes to seduction. The speaker even admits that both of them are assigned to certain roles: He is "débil y entregado," whereas she is "inaccesible, altiva, dura / y algo dulce en contadas ocasiones." The speaker's overconfidence in her abilities to play the game, however, has put her in a vulnerable position.

> Pero hace meses que ha cambiado todo
> y de nada me sirve no aceptarlo:
> me enamoré de ti. Sé que estoy loca
> y que vas a matarme cualquier día.
>
> (vv. 10–13)[45]

Instead of maintaining her distance, the speaker has fallen in love with her adversary. The verb *matar* has multiple connotations. Within the game of chess, it refers to checkmate, the winning of the game by taking the king; in traditional poetic terminology à la John Donne, death has a connotation of sexual climax; but even in the literal sense it suggests the danger and vulnerability to which the speaker as woman is exposed both physically and emotionally. She has let down her guard by committing two serious errors: being overconfident and falling in love: "Dos errores rompieron mi proyecto: / el primero, avisarte, y el segundo, / ignorar que jugaba con un hombre" (Two mistakes undid my project: / the first was to warn you and the second / to ignore that I was playing with a man). Because she made her strategy so clear, she left an opening for her opponent. Plus she forgot the nature of her antagonist. In addition to the double-voicing in the image of the game of chess, the speaker's final declaration reveals ambivalence in the words *ignorar* and *hombre*. To ignore is both not to know and to overlook or to lose sight of a fact. This duality combines with the word *hombre* and suggests that there are two different visions or definitions of "a man." As in any game, the opponent may be one who cheats, lies, deceives, and betrays, or one who is noble, honest, fair, and gracious. A foe may be treacherous and dangerous or upright and respectful of the rules of engagement. The speaker's opponent has taken unfair advantage of her, in contrast with the idealized image she had of him.

"Gámbito de dama" lays bare the competitive nature of relationships between men and women and the pitfalls of "playing games." It is apparent, however, that women too are caught in these strategies and deceits because society has imposed them on all equally. Women also internalize these rules of engagement, and they can have disastrous effects for them as well as for men. This consequence is clear in "Judit." The title refers, of course, to the biblical heroine who saved her people by killing the Assyrian general Holofernes. Described as both beautiful in appearance and wise in speech, Judith lays aside her sackcloth of mourning for her deceased husband to save her city from the invaders. In contrast with the men who are fearful of the Assyrians, Judith prays for strength to crush their arrogance with her deceitful words. When Holofernes invites her to eat and drink with him in hopes of an opportunity for seduction and sexual intercourse, he gets drunk, and with two blows of a sword Judith decapitates him.

Though this didactic narrative is well known and has served as the frequent subject of modern art, the Book of Judith is one of the apocrypha, that is, one of the books omitted from the official canon. Judith's courage and wisdom, especially her ability to employ her wiles—her words—has been marginalized by a patriarchal hierarchy. Bautista's poem revisits Judith's story in a contemporary setting in which she questions not only patriarchal power and privilege but also the marginalization of women in relation to the poetic tradition.

> Vino a mi casa a ver el baloncesto
> por la televisión. Y le he matado.

> Estaba ya cansada de sus burlas,
> su superioridad me exasperaba,
> sobre todo cuando era tolerante
> con mis limitaciones. Me ha bastado
> excitar burdamente su lujuria,
> emborracharle un poco y asestarle
> un par de puñaladas en el pecho. . . .
>
> (vv. 1–9)[46]

The contemporary setting has the speaker's boyfriend arriving at her house not to see her but to watch a basketball game on TV. While these anecdotal details may appear trivial, the basketball game bespeaks an atmosphere of competition transmitted over a medium that "mediates" communication. The snub implied in the motivation for the visit unleashes the speaker's anger. Like the Assyrians besetting Bethulia or the patriarchal church hierarchy marginalizing a female heroine, or like the male in the anecdote recounted by Martín Gaite at the beginning of this chapter, the speaker's boyfriend has a superior attitude toward women and hopes to take advantage of the speaker by "invading" her space. Like Holofernes, he is exasperatingly sarcastic and condescending. The phonic repetition of the /a/ in *Estaba ya cansada* and of the /u/ in *burlas* and *su superioridad* subtly underscores the speaker's anger. Like the wise Judith, however, she knows how to capitalize on her opponent's weaknesses. She rechannels (sublimates) her exasperation into seduction. It is enough for her to "excitar burdamente su lujuria" (note the echo of *burla* in *burda*) as she plies him with alcohol. The magnificent rhythm and alliteration of the ninth verse, "un par de puñaladas en el pecho," punctuate the moment when Judith strikes. These "stabbings" are metaphors for his wounded ego, comments that have gone directly to his heart and made him blush severely. After reaching this climactic point, the poet ironically deflates it with absurd understatement.

> Ahora está sorprendido, ensangrentado,
> en el sofá donde hago crucigramas.
> Voy a salir. Me esperan en Retiro,
> en la Feria del Libro. Vendré tarde,
> con el último libro de poemas
> que llevará su nombre. Y en el mismo
> sofá me acostaré, junto a su sangre,
> y lavaré con lágrimas su herida.
>
> (vv. 10–17)[47]

He looks surprised! He is covered with blood! And to think that he lies on the very spot where she does her crossword puzzles! But what are crossword puzzles but word games—like poems—predicated on the simultaneous tension and interdependence of the horizontal and the vertical (metaphor and metonymy, male and female)? Again trivial details adopt symbolic proportions when the speaker announces that she has to go out. The Feria del Libro in the Parque del Retiro has become one of the most popular social events of Madrid. At the beginning of June every bookstore and major publishing house sets up a booth in the park and sells books at a discount. The event draws huge crowds of people, especially because, in addition to the temperate June weather, Spanish writers of all sorts schedule appearances and personally autograph their books.

The metapoetic scope of the poem widens when the speaker nonchalantly states her intention to buy her boyfriend's latest collection of poems at the fair. We could gloss the final image sarcastically as the speaker shedding crocodile tears to soothe her lover's hurt feelings, thus restoring the phallocentric structure of domination to their relationship. We might conversely conclude that the sarcasm overrides any concession and healing, in which case the female speaker has overturned and usurped male power. But this same logic points out that the male writer has success, writes his poems, publishes and sells them because of these relationships with women!

Moreover, the images of blood and tears are grounded in the traditional contrast between Eros and Thanatos. As a conventional symbol of passion, vitality, and the essence of life, blood is positively marked and gendered as masculine. Conversely, tears, bitter outward expressions of grief as a result of death and loss, are negatively marked and gendered as feminine. Although blood is a sign of passion, here the spilling of blood makes it emblematic of death (Thanatos). On the other side of the equation, tears shed sincerely for someone who has died are a sign of deeply felt love (Eros). If earlier in "Enigma" the male character wields the power (his knives) and makes no distinction between Eros and Thanatos, in "Judit" the female speaker uses her power—her beauty, wisdom, and words—to separate Eros and Thanatos and then to reconfigure those terms. While Bautista inscribes these traditional connotations in her appropriation of these images, she resignifies and resemanticizes them. But at the same time that the speaker expresses her anger and metaphorically wounds her boyfriend, thus actively asserting her agency, she is ultimately caught in a tautological trap according to the rules of patriarchal society. As Jessica Benjamin has stated, a reversal of the

Hegelian positions of master and slave, self and other, simply continues the cycle of domination.

The intertextual backdrop for the final poem of *Cárcel de amor* is the myth of the sea goddess Galatea who did not requite the love of the cyclops Polyphemus. In her poem "Galatea" Bautista revises the relationships between the goddess, her lover Acis, and the cyclops by placing them in a contemporary setting—Madrid, specifically the Parque del Oeste (West Park) in winter. In this modern version Galatea and Acis have had an argument, causing her to go for a walk in the park.

> No sabía qué hacer aquella tarde.
> Tú estabas enfadado y no querías
> salir. Me fui al Parque del Oeste
> y estuve paseando mucho rato
> sin encontrar un alma. En el invierno
> casi nadie pasea por los parques.
> No pensé nada. Me senté en un banco
> y encendí un cigarrillo. De repente
> un hombre joven se sentó a mi lado. . . .
>
> (vv. 1–9)[48]

This narrative, told from the female protagonist's point of view, emphasizes the desolation and emptiness of her life. When she and her lover are not getting along and he refuses to go out, she does not know what to do with herself. Because it is winter, the park is empty. Even this season suggests the speaker's state of mind: As an objective correlative (the pathetic fallacy), its coldness, bleakness, and lack of other signs of life reflect the numbness and blankness of the speaker's mind. In an attempt to warm herself, the speaker first walks through the park and then lights a cigarette. Her statement "No pensé nada" indicates a lack of intention in addition to blankness. It implies that she has sat on this bench simply to smoke her cigarette, not with the intention of making herself available. How should she react, then, when a young man suddenly sits next to her?

> Le miré y vi que había un solo ojo
> en mitad de su frente, un ojo oscuro,
> tristísimo y brillante. Me miraba
> como pidiendo ayuda, suplicando.
> Ninguno de los dos dijimos nada.
> Él miraba mis ojos y yo el suyo.

> En silencio empezó a llorar despacio,
> se avergonzó y se fue. Yo no hice nada
> por detenerle. . . .

(vv. 10–18)[49]

This scene presents a perplexing combination of sadness and absurdity, the grotesque and the beautiful. In effect, what the speaker is describing is the sunset onto which she is projecting her fantasies. It is absurd to envision the sun as the single eye of a cyclops, especially in the exchange of gazes: "Él miraba mis ojos y yo el suyo." And yet the speaker clearly receives consolation from imagining that the male cyclops is sad. The silence of their exchange is fraught with emotional intensity, and the speaker clearly undergoes an abreactive experience even though no words are exchanged.

If we read this scene as if it were a daydream or fantasy and analyze it psychoanalytically, it is apparent that the male figure's one eye represents his tunnel vision. The speaker's lover is egocentric and does not take into account her needs and feelings. Nonetheless, he also recognizes this narrow focus—at least in her fantasy—and seeks forgiveness. But he is ashamed of these admissions of weakness (emblematized by his tears). Indeed, if we imagine this scene as an encounter between the patient and his psychoanalyst (a reversal of the usual dynamic of male analyst and female analysand), the silent exchange of gazes betokens the phenomenon of transference and countertransference so central to the psychoanalytic encounter. Ironically, it is the speaker who experiences the cathartic or abreactive alleviation of her emotions by projecting them onto the sunset in her fantasy.

That the speaker does not try to detain the cyclops when he leaves is thus ironic and ambivalent. She is powerless to stop the sun from setting, but because she has come in contact with her emotions, because of the return of her repressed feelings, she no longer needs the presence of the imagined other. If she needed to continue her fantasy, she might have gone to another spot or sought out another (real) man to act out her fantasy. Instead, she returns to her lover and tells him of her "encounter."

> Tú no te creíste
> ni una palabra de esta historia, pero
> yo me lleno de angustia y de tristeza,
> aunque quiera evitarlo, si recuerdo
> al cíclope del Parque del Oeste.

(vv. 18–22)[50]

The speaker's lover is too literal and narrow-sighted to understand what she is saying to him in her recounting of the incident. When he discounts her tale, her reaction once again presents a double-vision. On the one hand, her anguish and sadness could express her disillusionment, resignation, and frustration with her lover. He will never change, and she is fully aware of the evanescence and unreality not only of her vision of the cyclops but also of her hope for an ideal that her lover cannot fulfill. On the other hand, she still maintains that hope and that vision, opening a window of optimism for the future. Maybe she will become so anguished and sad that she will extricate herself from this unfulfilling relationship and seek someone else more in tune with her ideal. Her parenthetical phrase *aunque quiera evitarlo,* with its use of the subjunctive mood, suggests that she does not try to avoid this fantasy and that her remembering the incident in the park is a voluntary act rather than something she wishes to forget.

Because the poem ends with an emphatic repetition of the phrase *[e]l cíclope del Parque del Oeste,* the poem suggests that the narrow-sighted attitudes of the cyclops-type lover will soon disappear from the horizon. It may be that men will finally get the message about what a woman wants. In her discussion of Freud's self-analysis of his dream of Irma (which is regarded as the founding dream of psychoanalysis), Shoshana Felman makes the following observations:

> Is there a difference between female wish fulfillment and male wish-fulfilling fantasies of female wish fulfillment? Is there a difference between what a woman wants and what a man might think a woman wants? Where, exactly, does this difference lie? *What does a woman want?*
>
> The entire dream is up against this question, which its unconscious, searching energy endeavors to articulate, through and beyond its own male plea.[51]

In *Cárcel de amor* Amalia Bautista portrays female speakers involved in various male-female relationships. Several similarities exist between the poet and the protagonist of these poems, but hyperbole and violence vividly mark the differences. The play of similarity and difference between the female speakers and the implied author—a contemporary Spanish woman—illustrates the change in the positioning of female subjectivity in Spanish society and of women poets in the poetic tradition. Ironically, Bautista asserts her individuality via her dependence on the other—her protagonist, the poetic tradition, and her reader. The interaction between self and other is played out on several intra- and extradiegetic levels, making for a dynamic work of art that compels our recognition through the act of reading.

As Jessica Benjamin has cogently argued, domination and submission result from a breakdown in the delicate balance between mutual recognition and self-assertion. She notes, "Recognition is that response from the other which makes meaningful the feelings, intentions, and actions of the self. It allows the self to realize its agency and authorship in a tangible way. But such recognition can only come from another whom we, in turn, recognize as a person in his or her own right."[52] Benjamin's union of the terms *agency* and *authorship* highlights the gendered relationships between the poet and the literary tradition and between poet and reader. We have seen several instances where Bautista has appropriated literary tradition: the title *Cárcel de amor,* traditional adages and wisdom (as that of the messenger), the specific and general female figures, the traditional verse forms and symbolism, and many more. She has nonetheless also asserted her independence and individuality by bringing fresh perspectives to these traditional elements in the use of narrative, the female perspective, absurd hyperbole, and the violent wielding of words. The impact of her words enables the poet to dominate the reader as slave, except that her approach to these issues stresses the absurdity of domination and the necessity of the paradox of mutual recognition. The reader then not only participates in the enjoyment of the ludic, absurd qualities of the poem but can also seek justifications and motivations for this absurdity that address serious issues of life and art. In other words, the reader participates in the double-voicing to appreciate the double-vision of sexual difference. By examining her reflection in the page as mirror, the author invites men and women to alter the status quo, a society governed by behaviors that are both absurd and regrettable.

8

The Two-Way Mirror: Maite Pérez Larumbe's
Mi nombre verdadero

MI NOMBRE VERDADERO (MY TRUE NAME, 1998) BY THE NAVARRESE poet Maite Pérez Larumbe evinces obvious connections with other poets and poems in this book, but significant differences point to an evolution in Spanish women's poetry in the post-Franco era. In this work Larumbe clearly participates in the re-visionist project of mythmaking by contemporary women poets. As Alicia Suskin Ostriker asserts, "The female poet . . . finds something in the myth which nobody noticed before, and which only a woman would be likely to notice. . . . [W]hen meanings already latent in a given story are recovered and foregrounded by a woman's perspective, the entire story appears to change."[1] In each of the twenty-eight poems in Pérez Larumbe's collection, the poet portrays and reinterprets a different woman from the Old or New Testament. These "re-visions" of traditional figures central to the Western imaginary allow the poet to participate not only in the redefinition of women's creative contributions in post-Franco Spain, but also in the wider feminist project of affirming and valorizing women's identity and subjectivity.

As the speaker of Larumbe's poems reflects on women in scripture (in the mirror), she sees images of contemporary women (through the window). Hence the poem functions here as a two-way mirror: a glass that on one side reflects as a mirror but on the other side is a transparent window. Most people call this type of mirror "one-way," but I prefer to call it a two-way mirror in this context. On one side it functions as a mirror, but on the other it is a window. Because Larumbe puts this mirror on a swivel, it would more appropriate to call it a two-way mirror as it functions as both mirror and window for parties on either side. Curiously, there exists a type of "free-standing, full-length mirror on a pivoting frame" that is called a "psyché." According to Sabine Melchior-Bonnet, "Around 1810, the *psyché* came to be known as a piece in which the central pane of mirror could pivot around a horizontal axis to modify the angle of vision. It soon became

298

an indispensable beauty aid during the Empire and the Restoration."[2] The mirror I envision here pivots on a vertical axis, but the name "psyché" is intriguing, especially with regard to the psychological processes of identity inherent in the mirror and the poem as mirror.

Because the poem functions as a mirror reflecting contemporary women in general, these women also serve to define the implied author and her sense of herself as a subject. As Catherine Pastore Blair states, "Women poets write of multiple selves constructed in response to their experiences, selves which 'challenge the validity of the I.'"[3] In her portrayal of Martha and Mary (in comparison with Atencia's use of these figures), Larumbe's poems define a much sharper social edge than earlier poets. This difference is purely one of emphasis, not to gainsay the social importance of Atencia's assertion. In her book *Marta & María*, Atencia affirms the right of a woman to pursue her vocation (in this case, poetic) in the face of a traditional (patriarchal) society's emphasis on woman as mother, wife, and homemaker. After a fifteen-year hiatus in her writing, Atencia rediscovers and reaffirms this aspect of herself in a personal and political context. With the ground already having been prepared for her and others, Larumbe in comparison manifests a clear feminist agenda that goes beyond her individual needs. Though her assertions on behalf of others represent a firm commitment to social change and posit solidarity between herself and other women, her ability to identify with others determines her own sense of identity while "challenging the validity of the I." By giving her "true name" to each of the figures she selects from Scripture, the poet names herself. She explores not only the multiple selves available to her as a contemporary woman but also issues that confront many women. Each of these poets employs the biblical figures of Martha and Mary to define a re-vision of themselves as women in post-Franco Spain; however, the valuation of these figures changes over time and reflects changes in women's consciousness.

Naming and names occupy the foreground of Larumbe's project. As Karla G. Bohmbach notes, "Names can provide insights into a person's character, social location, or future, or *the way in which others perceive the person* [emphasis added]. . . . [T]he act of naming, whether a literary construction or a social reality, may have expressed the name-giver's authority over the named [in biblical times]."[4] Casey Miller and Kate Swift remark that "to be named and defined by someone else is to accept an imposed identity—to agree that the way others see us is the way we really are. . . . What is happening now in language seems simply to reflect the fact that . . . 'women are seeking their own image of themselves nurtured from within rather than imposed from without.'"[5] Gerda Lerner provides similar insights into names and naming in *The Creation of Patriarchy*. As Lerner observes, naming became synonymous with creation itself. Later, in connection with the book of Genesis, Lerner says that "name-giving is a powerful activity, a symbol of sovereignty. In Biblical times, . . . it also had a magical quality, giving meaning and predicting the future. . . . But there is another kind of naming, which we might call 're-naming,' which signifies the assumption of a new and powerful role for the person so re-named."[6] These issues are intrinsic to the characteristics we associate with well known biblical figures.

Through the re-vision of biblical women from a contemporary feminist point of view, Larumbe questions the patriarchal right to name (that is, to characterize, to bring into existence, to identify) these figures. The poet does not change the name (the sign) itself, but rather alters the relationship between signifier and signified, lending new meaning to the figures that the names evoke.[7] Moreover, in addition to the title of her book, Larumbe often employs the image of the name to reflect on her poetic use of language, given that *nombre* can mean "noun" or "word" as well as "name." We can equally apply to Larumbe the same comment that Catherine Pastore Blair states with regard to Ostriker:

> Her conception of women's revisionary mythmaking embroils her in the current question of women's relationship to language. Like myth critics before her, Ostriker sees myths as "sanctuaries of language where our meanings for 'male' and 'female' are stored." Therefore, revisionist mythmaking is the "major strategy" whereby women writers "subvert and overcome" the "'oppressor's language' which denies them access to authoritative expression."[8]

Larumbe recognizes and declares her stance toward language and the act of naming/writing in the opening poem of the collection, "El ángel comadre" (The Angel Godmother). Immediately, the title (name) of this poem attracts attention. It is ironic that the word *ángel* is gendered as masculine if we accept the traditional teaching that angels have no sex. This generic and/or grammatical usage of the masculine gender then contrasts with *comadre*. Because this term designates the relationship of a godparent (a person present at the baptism—naming—of a child and who will stand in for the parents if and when necessary), it establishes a kinship bond with the godchild's family. But the inclusion of the word *mother* implies a relationship between women. The angel in this poem defines the speaker as poet, but a poet with a definitive feminist/feminine interest. The title announces a conflict that will become sharper in the body of the poem. The opening verses specify the act of naming initially as a masculine privilege (Adam was granted the right to name the animals in the Garden of Eden), but one that also encompasses the self-serving naming of his vices.

> En el principio el hombre
> nombró las criaturas.
> Más tarde a sus demonios.
> Cubrió su desnudez para sufrir por ello,
> arrojó el corazón a la intemperie,
> torturó a los cachorros creyendo conjurar
> toda su soledad, su desabrigo.
> Extrañó a sus iguales,
> multiplicó las tribus
> como granos de arena que el viento echa a los ojos.
>
> (vv. 1–10)[9]

Several aspects of the first three verses alert us to the speaker's ironic tone. The echo of the first verse of the book of Genesis, the placement of the noun *el hombre* at the end of the line, and the insistent use of the preterit tense indicate the speaker's distance from the state of affairs created by man. We might also question whether the phrase *el hombre* is a generic usage, a sarcastic reference to linguistic conventions that erase the presence of women. Also, the pithy statement of the third verse contrasts "criaturas" with "demonios." These demons, beings that torment man and have dominion over him, are in all likelihood either his vices or those characteristics that he has chosen to value. The continued use of the preterit verb forms lists these traits. First, man has chosen to cover his nudity, creating a façade that hides and protects his vulnerability, and he has exposed his heart to unpredictable changes in the weather. Ironically, he laments the vicissitudes of life that threaten him physically, but he denies his emotions. His torturing of "los cachorros" may refer to burnt offerings made to God, or these "pups" may be his children, particularly his sons, and their masculinist indoctrination (a similar sacrifice). In either case, man hopes to conjure his solitude and his defenselessness, to dispel these negative feelings by enlisting God's help or by surrounding himself with others like him. Again, he ironically alienates those around him while simultaneously populating the world with his many sons. That the speaker metaphorizes these sons as "granos de arena que el viento echa a los ojos" plays against God's promise to Abraham to make his progeny as numerous as the stars. Because these grains of sand are blown into one's eyes, they are less permanent and more volatile than the stars, and they cause irritation, aversion, and even blindness. At this point the angels descend to men in an attempt to help.

> Hubimos de acudir siquiera a comprenderlos,
> a sorprender su hipo de huérfanos airados.
> Si alguien nos sospechó
> nuestra presencia está justificada.
>
> Los que me acompañaron
> dicen no tener sexo.
> Yo sé que soy mujer.
> No encontraréis mi nombre en la escritura,
> tampoco mis hermanas hablaron demasiado.
>
> (vv. 11–19)[10]

The verb phrase *Hubimos de* suggests that the angels came down from heaven reluctantly and/or because compelled to do so by their compassion. Their task was twofold: first, to understand men; and second, to frighten them out of their hiccups. Inasmuch as the speaker refers to men as "huérfanos airados," she characterizes them as children who are angry because God abandoned them. Their hiccups are the breathlessness caused by intense sobbing. The speaker views men as infantile and pathetic orphans. She doubts, however, that the angels' presence had any effect. It seems that few if any men became aware of their presence and thus of God's concern for his creations. Their descent from heaven symbolizes insight and inspiration that men fail to acknowledge or recognize.

According to the speaker, her companions maintained an asexual identity, perhaps so as to avoid the limitations imposed by naming and categorization or to avoid being subjected to the whims of men. She is quite different from them, as her emphatic, rhythmic declaration "Yo sé que soy mujer" asserts. Unlike the other angels, she is not neutral on this issue; she is taking a stand and assuming a subject position strongly opposed to that of men. In spite of her affirmation, she warns the readers that we will not find mention of her in scripture. Nor will we find that her "sisters" (other angels or perhaps women) are cited. For all but two of the poems in this collection Pérez Larumbe provides specific biblical references pertaining to the figures she has chosen to describe. The only exceptions are this poem and the final poem, the one dedicated to Mary of Nazareth. This lack points to the androcentric bent of the Bible and the intentional silencing of women's voices. Citing recent studies, Meyers states that women probably contributed a great deal to the composition of various parts of the Bible, if only by continuing the oral tradition of storytelling. Yet we have little evidence of their direct act of writing because their contributions were either expunged or not recognized.[11] From the point of view of Pérez Larumbe, women form a minority of the voices participating in literary production until the last quarter of the twentieth century. As a poet, this speaker now makes her voice heard, particularly in the declaration of her sex. The final stanza of this poem compares women with Moses when it comes to the written word.

> La Palabra es país que apenas conocieron,
> murieron en la cima desde donde se avista
> su extensión, su riqueza, murieron codiciosas.
>
> (vv. 20–22)[12]

Just as Moses was denied entry into the Promised Land but was able to see it from the top of Mount Nebo, the women writers who preceded the speaker could only observe their desired goal from afar. Until recently, women found themselves severely limited—for a variety of reasons including lack of education and other societal prejudices—with regard to writing. In response to this exclusion, the speaker here declares that she as a woman will make re-visions in our knowledge of and familiarity with these other voices and perspectives. Her readings of various biblical women will reveal aspects that only a woman poet could perceive, and they will redefine the importance and meaning of these figures in the Judeo-Christian imaginary. For, to recall Ostriker's words, "When meanings . . . in a given story are recovered and foregrounded by a woman's perspective, the entire story appears to change."

This chapter concentrates on pairs of figures that are related in one way or another. Many pairs are sisters, others are contemporaneous or involved in the same sets of circumstances, others are linked thematically. The first pair of sisters, Rachel and Leah, the daughters of Laban, were quite different from one another and offer interesting parallels with the brothers Jacob and Esau. The younger Rachel is described as lovely, well formed, and graceful in comparison with her older sister, Leah, whose main characteristic was that she was "tender-eyed" or "soft-eyed." Whether she was severely myopic or merely "cow-eyed" (which, according to biblical scholars, the etymology of her name supports), she was less attractive than her younger sister. As a result, she was more introspective and spiritually sensitive in contrast with "shallow-minded" Rachel. She was also more fertile, a fact that plays a paramount role in their story, for Jacob fell in love with Rachel as soon as he laid eyes on her, but Laban led him into Leah's tent on the wedding night. According to custom, the younger sister could not marry before the elder one. In this deceit Laban tricked the trickster Jacob, who as the younger son deceived his father, Isaac, into believing that he was Esau and thus inherited Esau's birthright. Even though Jacob then arranged to marry Rachel also, whom he cherished until her death, Leah bore him four sons in succession, establishing a rivalry with her sister. In all, Rachel and Leah and their two maidservants bore twelve sons and are known as the mothers of the twelve tribes of Israel.[13] In "Lía" Pérez Larumbe explores this character's pride in her ability to bear children, but more importantly in her ingenuity, which was the equal of Jacob's. In the poem the speaker addresses Jacob and calls attention to what biblical scholars have called a reversal of sexual knowledge.

> Tanto me consolaste
> que no dije mi nombre
> la noche que mi padre te trajo hasta mi lecho.
>
> A oscuras, la sonrisa
> te crecía en los labios
> mientras me conocías.
>
> Desconocerme al alba
> fue desmentir los cuerpos,
> la certeza que alzamos durante tantas horas,
> desandar de por vida el único camino. . . .
>
> (vv. 1–10)[14]

This passage gives an ironic twist to Levi-Strauss's theory of kinship exchange. While it is true that Laban gave his daughter to Jacob in exchange for seven years' labor, he substituted Leah for Rachel. When Jacob realized that he had been deceived, he must have had mixed emotions. From Leah's statement they both enjoyed themselves on the night in question. The negative prefix of both *desconocer* and *desmentir* attest to the tension. First, *desconocer* plays on the biblical meaning of "knowing" as sexual intercourse. Obviously, Jacob cannot undo what has already been done. However, he now "knows" that he "knew" another woman instead of Rachel, whom he thought he was marrying. The second verb *desmentir* complicates the issue, for Jacob cannot deny what has happened even though it is not what he thought had happened. On one level, the lie is undone, but on another it cannot be undone. When the speaker mentions "los cuerpos,

/ la certeza que alzamos durante tantas horas," the truth of what happened is irrefutable. Undoing the lie does not undo the truth.

Leah has Jacob in a double bind. Through the masculinist practice of kinship exchange she has gained control of the situation. She has used her disadvantage to her advantage. She is Jacob's wife de facto if not de jure. The additional negative prefix of the verb *desandar* could therefore mean "to undo one's steps" or "to retrace one's steps." Because they are married, Jacob will have to retrace his steps (have continued intercourse with Leah) even though he thought he was having intercourse with Rachel. Does the adjective *único* mean "unique" or "sole"? With the help of her father, Leah has tricked the trickster. As she has reversed sexual knowledge, she has also turned the tables on Jacob, who had tricked his father and brother. What was good for Jacob is good for Leah as well. In other words, Leah has shown Jacob that she has as much ingenuity and cleverness as he. If what he did was right, so is what she did. The following verses express Leah's defiance of the patriarchal structures that would condemn her actions.

> ¡Oh, mi Jacob cubierto
> con pieles de cabrito
> ante un padre cansado y moribundo!
> Farsante y temerario.
>
> Veo como acaricias
> la barba que encanece asegurando
> que el Dios de la Promesa te bendijo.
>
> ¿Guardará para mí siquiera una palabra,
> que te amé con mi cuerpo,
> que es más yo que mi nombre,
> que prolongué tu herencia y tu memoria?
>
> (vv. 11–21)[15]

In comparison with Leah, Jacob has been a comic actor: He only had to deceive an aged and blind old man, and he did so by putting on a costume, a disguise, the hairy sheepskins. Her use of the adjectives *Farsante y temerario*, isolated as a sentence fragment and on a single line is blatantly sarcastic, reinforcing the use of exclamations and the interjective *¡Oh!* in the previous sentence. Jacob was "reckless"? What risk was he taking? Yet he is extremely proud of himself, as Leah's overblown portrait of him, stroking his beard (graying with wisdom) and praising God for blessing him, shows. Leah, on the other hand, has not covered her body with a costume, but stripped it of all clothing, of all protection. She has exposed herself much more vulnerably than had Jacob, but will God equate her risk with his? By bearing him sons, she has also prolonged Jacob's heritage and memory, something Rachel has not been capable of doing as we shall soon see. Significantly, Leah considers her body "más yo que mi nombre." Given the importance of names and of the use of language in Larumbe's revision of biblical women, Leah privileges reality and experience over representation. Her body in contact with Jacob's on the night of their marriage supersedes all deceit and all (mis)representation.

This recounting of the past leads us to the present moment, when Leah's firstborn son, Rueben, returns from the fields with mandrake, precipitating another encounter between Leah and Rachel. The root of the mandrake is purported to have aphrodisiac properties and was supposed to cure barrenness. We now know that the root, when eaten, has a relaxing effect on the womb.[16] Because Rachel is still childless and could take advantage of the mandrake, Rachel again manipulates the situation in her favor.

> El quiso hacerme fértil, esa ha sido mi dote.
> Ahora Rubén regresa de los campos,
> me trae unas mandrágoras.
> Mi hermana las desea, se las daré.
> Esta noche la pasarás conmigo, ha sido el trato.
> A oscuras, quiero que reconozcas
> mi nombre verdadero.
>
> (vv. 22–28)[17]

Inasmuch as the declaration of her fertility follows on the heels of the question about God's word for her and as it introduces the issue of the mandrakes, Leah recognizes her control and the power she wields in this situation. Not only does her son bring her the mandrakes so that she can dispose of them (as his mother she owns what he has), her sister is in dire need of their effect. The casual tone of her statement "se las daré" betrays her awareness of her power as the sisters make a deal. Ironically, now it is the women who exchange the man as sexual object, the opposite of Levi-Strauss's theory of kinship exchange! Deen and Frumer-Kensky emphasize that when two co-wives make these types of decisions, the man has little or nothing to say in the matter.[18]

By repeating the phrase *A oscuras* that she used in verse 4 above in the description of the wedding night, the speaker subtly underscores her superiority. Moreover, the prefix in the verb *reconozcas* ludically recalls the play of *conocer* and *desconocer* in the context of the initial deceit, making the verb ambivalent. Leah wants Jacob to recognize her (in the many senses of that term) and "to know" her again. This time there will be no deceit. Jacob will know exactly with whom he lies. Leah is making a declaration (similar to that of the speaker in "El ángel comadre") about who she is and the position of power that she occupies. Once again she has turned the tables on the trickster, who remains silent and powerless. That Larumbe has chosen the last verse of this poem as the title of the entire collection stresses the revisionist project in which she is engaged via her readings of biblical women. "Mi nombre verdadero" refers not just to Leah's emergence from the darkness and the background of the patriarchal system of exchange but to the discovery of latent meaning and understanding that feminist mythmaking reveals.

A reversal similar to that found in "Lía" is also apparent in the counterpart poem "Raquel." At first we might think that Rachel laments her sterility in the expression of grief that opens this poem. In particular, the extent of her wanderings and the infertility that her tears bring about in the regions she travels might indicate the length of her childlessness and her desperation. However, if we look closely, we notice that in this poem Rachel (according to Bible scholars, the first woman to die in childbirth in scripture and an image of tragic womanhood) speaks from beyond the grave, after her death while giving birth to her second child, Benjamin.[19]

> Lloro sobre Sión, me desgañito.
> Nadie crea que duermo bajo la estela de Efratá.
>
> Lloro sobre Betel y Garizím,
> arruino la cosecha en Esdrelón y aún quisiera
> anegar esta cuenca de salitre,
> agostar los retoños, maldecir por los siglos
> esta tierra de lobos.
>
> (vv. 1–7)[20]

The violence connoted in the verb *desgañitarse* might suggest that Rachel is desperate to have a child or even that she is in the moment of giving birth. However, the second line refers to the place where she died in childbirth and where Jacob buried her and placed a stele on her grave to commemorate her. That he buried her in a separate grave rather than with her family and that he erected a stele in commemoration are signs of Jacob's undying love for Rachel.[21] Rachel also disabuses anyone who might think that she lies quietly in her grave. Indeed, her lamentation extends over an even wider area (all of Zion) and causes immense sterility (reminiscent of the myth of Demeter/Ceres). Her tears ruin crops and desiccate vine shoots in an area that could include the Dead Sea ("esta cuenca de salitre") or even the entire Mediterranean because the reference to Ashkelon directs our attention to the west. In keeping with this direction, the phrase *esta tierra de lobos* could refer to Spain. And her curse extends over time: "por los siglos" ("per seculae seculorum"). In spite of the many references to barrenness, Rachel is not lamenting her sterility but rather that she had become pregnant and given birth, as these verses in the middle of the poem demonstrate.

> Olvídese la afrenta de los vientres vacíos,
> dichosa la que tiene muslos de pedernal,
> esparto en las entrañas.
> Alégrese la estéril que no ofrece
> hijos a la catástrofe
> pues no verá maldita su vejez
> ni su reposo humedecido en sangre.
>
> En mi vergüenza volví el rostro a Yavé.
> Y Yavé me escuchó.
> Feliz hallaba entonces la cumplida torpeza,
> felices el pujo y el jadeo,
> felices los cuarenta días de mi impureza
> (los hombres purifican aquello que no entienden).
>
> (vv. 8–20)[22]

The imperatives *Olvídese* and *Alégrese* emphatically speak against the curse of sterility. Rachel thinks that those women who have "muslos de pedernal, / [y] esparto en las entrañas" are fortunate, but her reason for thinking so is unexpected. It is not because of the risk involved for the woman but because sons/children (is *hijo* gender inclusive or solely masculine?) become offerings to "la catástrofe." This word may refer to war, in which the sons would be slain and the daughters taken into captivity, or to the vicissitudes of life and death. In either case, Rachel—as the ideal mother figure—represents for Pérez Larumbe the mother who suffers the loss of a child. These mothers thus find their old age cursed and their repose dripping with blood (probably from war, but possibly from any other cause of death). She now sees that she was foolish for being ashamed of her barrenness. She seems to say that one should be careful what she wishes for because she just may receive it, as Yahweh heard her prayer, gave her children, and thus made her vulnerable to their premature loss. She even seems to say that the veritable curse is not menstruation but pregnancy. When she first became pregnant, she was delighted with the forty days of purification. Her parenthetical expression is doubly ironic as Rachel sees the blessing of pregnancy as a curse and the curse of menstruation (so dubbed by men and internalized by women) as the blessing which men think they must purify, that is, cleanse of defilement.[23] The poet concludes this poem with a poignant protest against death and suffering.

> Hijos de mi dolor,
> corto resultó el tiempo de la leche y la miel,
> breve el arrullo.
> Seréis raza de huérfanos, pasto de la voracidad.
> Grito y me arrastro. Grito.
> De nada servirá la estopa en las rendijas.
> Será inútil la pez. Grito por siempre.
>
> (vv. 21–27)[24]

Aware nonetheless that reproduction will continue, Rachel now addresses herself to her children and those of others and of future generations. The images of milk and honey and of the mother's cradling and cooing define not only infancy but also childhood, and so represent all the pleasures of life. When she says that they will be a "raza de huérfanos, pasto de la voracidad," she emphasizes the loneliness caused by separation and death. All of humanity is fodder for its own voracity for life. How ironic it is that Rachel, symbol of tragic womanhood and image of the happy mother after so long a wait, should so vehemently oppose motherhood! Her lament—not that she is childless, but that life is cruel and that we are all orphans—is so potent that it penetrates all efforts to silence it. It is impossible to ignore her and what she is saying. "La estopa en las rendijas" is oakum or insulation that fills in gaps and cracks in walls, whereas "la pez" is pitch or tar, used for waterproofing and sealing to keep out her cries and her tears. The repetition of the verb *Grito* returns to but intensifies the *Lloro* of the opening verses, reminding us of her continual, bitter complaint and lament that returns even after her death and resounds across the centuries. Rachel's penetrating grief is a rejection of motherhood as a definition of a woman's self-worth.

The next two women paired for this study are not related except by their acts of castrating men: Judith and Jael. Because of her skillful use of language as much as her beauty, Judith is a popular and attractive figure for contemporary women poets.[25] This biblical heroine lays aside her sackcloth of mourning for her deceased husband to save her city. To kill the Assyrian general Holofernes, she prays for strength to crush the Assyrian's arrogance by the deceit of her lips. When Holofernes invites her to eat and drink with him in hopes of an opportunity for seduction, he gets drunk, and with two blows of a sword Judith decapitates him. Though this didactic narrative is well known and has served as the frequent subject of modern art, the Book of Judith is one of the apocrypha, omitted from the official canon. Judith's courage and wisdom, especially her ability to employ her wiles—her words—has been marginalized by the patriarchal church hierarchy. Larumbe's poem revisits Judith's story, drawing a parallel between contemporary women and the biblical heroine.

"Judit ante el espejo" (Judith Before the Mirror) posits a mise en abyme. As the title indicates, the poetic speaker stands in front of a mirror, preparing herself to meet Holofernes. If we consider the poem itself as a mirror, the implied author in turn observes Judith observing herself in the mirror. Likewise, the reader observes the poet observing the protagonist, and in this text you (my reader) observe me observing the poet observing Judith observing herself in the mirror. The cover of Larumbe's book further complicates this pattern given that it reproduces one of Gustav Klimpt's paintings of Judith. This pattern suggests that there are multiple representations of Judith, each varying to a greater or lesser degree from the original. Indeed, Larumbe's protagonist, while representing the biblical Judith, illustrates a contemporary dilemma: a woman's vacillation as to how to make herself attractive and seductive without becoming an object and thus divesting herself of her subjectivity, her agency, and her desires. The opening stanzas of the poem demonstrate the speaker's fear that she may be losing control of her agency.

> Abandona el collar su peso sobre el cuello,
> susurran los zarcillos un canto que me turba.
> Tiemblo como una novia que sospecha,
> en su primera noche,
> capaz su cabellera de enredar un ejército.
>
> Debiera componerme obediente y me agita
> su ansia de soldado que no espera.
>
> (vv. 1–7)[26]

Here she focuses on the jewelry she places on herself, female accoutrements that highlight her attractiveness and her social positioning as object. The necklace she puts on "abandons" its weight on her neck so that it evokes a slave's collar that weighs heavily on the woman who wears it. Moreover, her earrings whisper a song that upsets her. These images are ambivalent in that these adornments are exciting and call attention to feminine beauty, but they also suggest a latent anxiety. In the biblical context Judith is understandably nervous. She must make herself as attractive and seductive as possible while remaining cool and calm. She must keep her wits about her to carry out her task while feigning passion.

In the second stanza her trembling may indicate either apprehension or eagerness, and her suspicion may be from anticipation or fear. Her reference to her hair iterates her lack of agency given that it, rather than she, is capable of ensnaring an entire army of men. Hair is a particularly feminine attribute of beauty that can symbolize a woman's attitude toward a man and her concept of self.[27] With specific regard to mirroring, La Belle notes that "Victorian culture tended to associate a woman's hair with her self-conception. In such a context, to change one's hair—a change usually created before and first registered in a mirror—is to alter the sense of one's identity."[28] In this case the verb *enredar* connotes a plot and a trap as well as seduction. In *Seduction* Jean Baudrillard asserts that "the strategy of seduction is one of deception. It lies in wait for all that tends to confuse itself with its reality."[29] In short, Judith's desire is ambivalent: It causes her both anxiety and desirous anticipation.

The choice of the word *ejército* points to a conflict not only between male and female but also within the speaker herself. She expresses this tension in the third stanza when she says "Debiera componerme obediente," and yet his "ansia de soldado que no espera" makes her apprehensive. Once again we see the speaker feeling that she is becoming anxious and losing control, as the verb phrase *me agita* echoes the earlier *Tiemblo.* These verbs raise the issue of how a woman should act in the presence of a man: To what extent should she be attractive yet cautious? To what extent should she show and delight in her desire? Is she being too aggressive? Or is she making herself vulnerable? Where is the balance between the male soldier's aggressiveness that can readily convert her into an object for his use and her own sense of subjectivity and desire? The two stanzas in the center of the poem form the crux of the speaker's dilemma.

> ¡Bien eligió el Señor aunque yo yerre!
> Para vengar la sed
> alienta el fuego ávido en los pulsos
> y abre bajo mis ojos el océano.
>
> Me asusta esta sabiduría ante el espejo,
> la carne que se muestra como leche y azúcar,

> el cuerpo que se mece como mies de septiembre
> dejándose llevar por un conocimiento
> que yo desconocía.
>
> (vv. 8–16)[30]

On the one hand, she affirms her agency by recognizing that God has chosen her and that she is highly capable. But on the other hand, she is still doubtful of her success in this endeavor. In the biblical context Judith has been designated by God to save her people even though she may have misgivings about her encounter with Holofernes. In a more contemporary setting this Judith could be thanking God for making her a woman and giving her this opportunity to right an injustice: society's double standard that imposes restrictions on women that are not imposed on men (e.g., virginity, desire, subjectivity). The second sentence above is highly equivocal because of its ambiguous grammar. Who is the subject of the verb phrase *Para vengar la sed?* Is it God or Judith? If the thirst belongs to Judith and refers to her desire, is God taking vengeance on her, or is God allowing her to take revenge on Holofernes and his thirst for power? Are the verbs *alienta* and *abre* declarative or imperative? Does Judith acknowledge her empowerment as a direct result of God's intervention and creation? Or does she plead that God grant her these powers? In addition, the image of *el fuego ávido* connotes destruction and regeneration, eagerness and impulsiveness, greed and lack. As a symbol of her blood and the pulse in her veins, this fire is passion and anger, love and hate, desire and aversion. The opening of the vast expanse of the ocean provokes fear as well as ecstasy, whereas the phrase *bajo mis ojos* can indicate Judith's superiority and control over the situation or the dizzying peril that lies before her. It is as if she were on a high cliff and in danger of falling into the vast expanse of the sea, a symbol of losing herself in the rapture of sexual pleasure. Jessica Benjamin discusses Freud's well known description of the oceanic feeling:

> The classic psychoanalytic viewpoint did not see differentiation as a balance, but as a process of disentanglement. Thus it cast experience of union, merger, and self-other harmony as regressive opposites to differentiation and self-other distinction. Merging was a dangerous form of undifferentiation, a sinking back into the sea of oneness—the "oceanic feeling" that Freud told Romain Rolland he frankly couldn't relate to. The original sense of oneness was seen as absolute, as "limitless narcissism," and therefore, regression to it would impede development and prevent separation.[31]

This oceanic feeling is ambivalent, both desired and feared. The next stanza makes specific reference to Judith in front of the mirror and the feelings provoked by her own body as knowledge. If we consider the page as mirror, its whiteness (the blank page) intimidates but also enlightens the poet because of the knowledge she discovers in the act of writing. The speaker is estranged from the other in the mirror, referring to the image of herself as "la carne" and "el cuerpo." The beauty of her own body elicits positive and negative reactions because it is attractive and yet dangerous. The speaker is self-conscious about her own beauty because of the desire it is capable of stimulating —her own as well as the (male) other's. The contrast between *conocimiento* and *sabiduría* and between *conocimiento* and the prefix of *desconocía* points to the speaker's mixed emotions. Her surprise frightens her but also delights her as she recognizes her body as part of herself and yet estranged from her in the otherness of the mirror. The images of milk, sugar, and the golden wheat field lend value to her as indications of purity, sensuality, and fertility, but these images carry her away, literally and figuratively, divesting her of the control she wishes to exert over herself. From a metapoetic point of view, the speaker recognizes her ability to wield language skillfully and gracefully, but she questions the extent of her control over that ability and her inspiration. The final verses of the poem parallel the opening ones, creating the mirror's frame, yet the tone is still ambivalent.

> Quisiera al tiempo darle muerte
> y oír que me desea.
>
> ¿Cuánto deberé odiar
> para no sentir tanto?
>
> Crepitan las ajorcas. Me perfumo.
>
> (vv. 17–21)[32]

The verb form *Quisiera* may express doubt or desire, fear or eagerness. She might like to kill time even though she knows that it is unlikely or impossible, or she may strongly wish to accomplish her end. Does killing time mean that she will prevent time from passing and so defer the moment of contact with Holofernes? Or does she will time to pass so that she does not have to wait any longer? Contradictorily, she wishes to meet Holofernes but also to defer the meeting. She wants to hear that he desires her, but she is also afraid to confront his desire. She is also eager to succumb to her own desire even though it may make her vulnerable and be disastrous for her. It is unclear whether the question in these verses is rhetorical or genuine. To what extent should she feign indifference and lack of passion? Does she need to protect herself from Holofernes or from herself, her own desire? Does the infinitive *sentir* mean "to feel" or "to regret"? Where does she draw the line of her involvement so that she does not make herself vulnerable and thus get hurt, or so that she can enjoy herself giving and receiving pleasure? How much should she *give* and how much should she *take* (in both senses of those verbs)?

The final verse of the poem echoes the sound of the earrings in the first stanza, this time mentioning her bracelets (handcuffs?). The verb *crepitan*, however, suggests not only a ringing sound but also the crackling of fire, evoking again the power of fire to destroy and regenerate and as a symbol of love and hate, attraction and aversion. Likewise, the act of perfuming herself could be a means of heightening her attractiveness or of concealing her deception.[33] At this point we might even question whether Judith is putting on or taking off her jewelry and her clothing. Her portrayal of herself in the mirror of the poem and the act of writing are seductive. The inference that it is time to decapitate (i.e., to castrate) Holofernes represents a renegotiation of power not only in the relationships between men and women but also between poet and reader. We note, however, that the phrase *Me perfumo* that closes the poem is (self-)reflexive in contrast with the earlier verb phrases in which the speaker found herself the object of the action. Here she adopts subjectivity and agency over herself; she controls her own destiny. The figure of Judith as representative of today's women is highly appropriate in light of the biblical figure's prowess as a beautiful woman but also a skillful wielder of words. Whereas it might appear that her words are superficially beautiful and attractive (as many instances of alliteration, rhythm, onomatopoeia, and imagery attest), Judith's beauty is more than skin deep. The mise en abyme pattern shows that the image in the mirror has many layers that lead to profound introspection and recognition of women's subjectivity.

"Yaél la nómada" (Jael the Nomad) speaks to male violence against women. Once again, the female poetic voice directly addresses the male, in this case Sisera, the captain of the army of Jabin, king of Canaan. Sisera was a powerful warrior with "nine hundred chariots of iron" who had oppressed the Israelites for twenty years. Having been approached by them, Deborah, the prophetess who judged Israel at that time, drew out Sisera to the River Kishon, where he was defeated by Barak and a host of Hebrew soldiers. Sisera fled to where Heber the Kenite had pitched his tent, where he hid "for there was peace between Jabin and the house of Heber" (Judges 4). Jael, Heber's wife, greeted him, gave him milk to drink, covered him, and then drove a tent peg through his temple, thus assisting in the subduing of Jabin by the Israelites. In speaking of this passage, Gerda Lerner says, "Although clearly the miracle is the Lord's, who enables even a woman to kill a warrior, the passage is remarkable in its celebration of female strength, both moral (Deborah) and physical (Jael)."[34]

Larumbe's poem is organized around a repeated verse, replicating Jael's hammering of the tent peg into Sisera's temple, to which the alliteration and rhythm contribute: "Clavo la clavija de mi tienda en tu sien" (I pound the peg of my tent into your brain). Elizabeth Lenk maintains that "hammering nails is . . . an archetype of masculinity" and further notes that it is the complement of plying the needle for women.[35] The alternate stanzas emphasize the contrast between Jael as a nomad and Sisera in all his power by inverting binary opposites.

> Mi tienda le hace sombra a tu palacio.
> Lejos, tu favorita,
> se ha bañado y te espera.
>
> (vv. 2–4)[36]

When Jael proclaims that "Mi tienda le hace sombra a tu palacio," she privileges mobility and fluidity (characteristics frequently associated with women) over stability and status (typical male attributes). She exalts the dynamic over the static, the simple over the ornate, necessity over luxury. By casting the shadow of death over Sisera's palace, Jael frees Sisera's favorite (wife or concubine) from her subjection to the male tyrant. This relationship parallels the next stanza's reference to Sisera's mother.

> Las hienas de la noche
> asustan a tus perros.
> En la ciudad tu madre sueña con el botín,
> con un manto bordado.
>
> (vv. 6–9)[37]

First Jael compares herself with hyenas in contrast with Sisera's dogs. These wild scavengers are more ferocious and protective than the domesticated animals, again privileging the supposed inferior over the superior. Then she imagines Sisera's mother waiting for the booty her son will bring her. In Judges 5:30 Sisera's mother tries to justify her son's delay, assuming that he has been dividing the spoils of battle. In addition to the contrast between the beautifully embroidered cloth of the mantle and the coarse cloth of the nomad's tent, the mother's greed displays no concern for the conquered group. Among the spoils she expects her son to have taken "a damsel or two": "Have they not divided the prey; to every man a damsel or two; to Sisera a prey of divers colours, a prey of divers colours of needlework, of divers colours of needlework on both sides, meet for the necks of them that take the spoil?" (Judges 5:30). The repetition in Larumbe's poem imitates and thus subverts that of the biblical passage. In placing herself in opposition to Sisera's mother, Jael denounces the complicity of older generations in privileging masculine rights at the expense of women. Reference to "necks" in the biblical passage maintains a hierarchy of victors and vanquished that Jael overthrows. The spoils of which the mother dreams may even be the grandchildren her son would have engendered, thus continuing the status quo of subjection. In the following passage Jael usurps phallic power in her grasping of the tent peg and the hammer.

> Mi mano no vacila, la tuya se desmaya.
> Tus soldados confían, afanosa me apresto
> a empuñar el martillo.
>
> (vv. 11–13)[38]

According to biblical tradition, the raising of tents was women's work. Thus Jael appropriates the advantages of her domestic responsibilities to usurp power. Her hand is firm and sure, her will and determination resolute, in comparison with the weakness of Sisera. The image of his hand going limp is symbolic of the loss of power (sexual and temporal), like the decapitation of Holofernes. Ironically, Sisera's soldiers stand idly by while Jael becomes the active agent as she grips the hammer. The making of a fist and the verb *empuñar* underscore her taking action with the strength of her own hands. This contrast adopts several manifestations in the next passage, where Jael again privileges the feminine over the masculine.

> Mi velo se mantiene, tu corona se cae,
> mi pie desnudo humilla tus botas de campaña,
> el lino vence al cuero,
> la nómada al caudillo.
>
> (vv. 15–18)[39]

The veil, a traditional Middle Eastern sign of women's subjugation and oppression, stays in place while Sisera's crown (symbol of authority) falls.[40] Delicate cloth is privileged over burdensome metal. Moreover, her bare foot humiliates his combat boots, and her delicate linen dress overpowers his tough leather. In other words, her defenselessness is stronger than his accoutrements of battle, symbols of his aggression, strength, power, and force. It is pointedly significant that the poet juxtaposes "la nómada al caudillo." This contrast reflects prevalent attitudes of the superiority of civilization, centralized power, law, stability, and organization over a shiftless, rootless, barbaric freedom. That which seems insubstantial, flighty, rootless overcomes what is solid, fixed, anchored. The irresistible force prevails over the immovable object. But the choice of the word *caudillo* also evokes the now outdated Franco era and the image of men and women that predominated for so long in Spanish society. This poem has possible political overtones given that Larumbe is from the province of Navarra, between Catalonia and the Basque country. The final repetition of the refrain differs in that it is fully integrated into the last stanza.

> Clavo la clavija de mi tienda en tu sien,
> en tu reino asesino,
> en tu senda de espanto.
>
> (vv. 19–21)[41]

If we recall Barbara Herrnstein Smith's discussion of repetition in poetry, here poetic closure is concomitant with an end to the previously prevailing social practices.[42] As she drives the tent peg into Sisera's temple, Jael also destroys his "reino asesino" and his "senda de espanto." In effect, if his reign is based on murder, threats, and violence, she murders brutality and the exploitation of fear. But the genitive phrase *tu senda de espanto* ambivalently suggests that she simultaneously destroys his fear as well as hers. Jael's act thus becomes a means of liberating all of society from oppression.

In these poems each woman—Judith and Jael—traditionally evokes the idea of betrayal and the emasculation of a powerful male. For Larumbe each biblical setting reflects a contemporary situation. Through her representation of these biblical women the poet illuminates the moral and physical strength of the heroines and thus reconfigures our perception of who they are and what they represent.

The next pair of women is found in the same poem: "La amada" (The Beloved). This figure from the Song of Songs (or Song of Solomon) is said to represent the soul in search of union with God, but in Larumbe's poem "la amada" suggests the relationship between mother and daughter. Larumbe's poem maintains the erotic language so characteristic of the Song of Songs, so that the relationship of mother and daughter adopts overtones of a loving relationship

between two women. The title "La amada" is therefore doubly refer-
ential. The loved one is both mother and daughter as well as the partners of a lesbian relationship. In this poem as in "Lía" and several
other poems of *Mi nombre verdadero* the image of the name figures
prominently, lending a metapoetic aspect to the relationship. The
opening couplet of "La amada" sets the reader up for a surprising
slippage in the next stanza.

> Me abandono en tu nombre
> como lo haría un ciego con una profecía.
>
> Oh, gozosa niñez de la palabra
> que estructura tu cuerpo, lo vertebra y levanta
> ante mí la presencia que le ha dado cobijo,
> la cuerda en que se forma
> hasta que llego yo para reconocerla
> y expiar el silencio.
>
> (vv. 1–8)[43]

The initial verse describes a typical experience of a mystic. The act
of abandoning the self recalls the ecstasies of Santa Teresa de Jesús
and San Juan de la Cruz, translator of the Song of Songs, and the
mention of the name in this context evokes Fray Luis de León's *Los
nombres de Cristo*. Likewise, the simile in verse 2 equates the speaker
with a blind person whose lack of sight augments extrasensory perceptions, allowing her/him to receive the pronouncements of the
gods (cf. Tiresias or the Oracle at Delphi). Whether emphasizing
the act of trust required of the blind person or the trancelike state
in which the blind person loses a sense of self and becomes the
spokesperson of the god, abandonment leads to an experience that
is both erotic and metapoetic. The "nombre" is both the name of the
other and the word, logos. These verses are consistent with the mystic's loss of identity because at this point, in the context of the Song
of Songs, we assume that the other addressed is Christ.

Gradually throughout the second stanza the speaker inserts words
that subtly shift the ground of our perception. The first of these
words is *niñez*. It is only after some reflection that we can accept the
newness of the other's name as the renewal of language itself. The
name of the other brings a new perspective on reality and on the life
of the speaker, giving her a childlike pleasure in discovering and
naming the world around her. Another incongruity occurs because
of the run-on lines of verses 4 and 5. At first we read the verb *levanta*
as the third in a series: The word "estructura tu cuerpo, lo vertebra y

[lo] levanta." The repetition of the object pronoun *lo* would be superfluous, except that *levanta* has another object, "la presencia," which does not appear until the following line. These incongruities gently jar and temporarily disorient the reader, compelling us to adopt a new point of view congruent with the speaker's new perspective on reality thanks to the name of the other.

These abrupt shifts do not negate the effect of the word. Language permits the speaker to know the world around her, especially the beloved whom she addresses. Curiously, we note that the speaker objectifies or reifies the other, referring to that person as "tu cuerpo" and "la presencia." This characterization adopts metaphoric proportions in the words *cobijo* and *cuerda*. Whereas one can readily comprehend the concept of shelter and protection that the other affords the speaker, *cuerda* inserts another ungrammaticality into the discourse of the poem. We might explain this metaphor as the vine on which the fruit grows, indicating the sustenance and attachment the other provides for the speaker. However, we begin to perceive a pattern of incongruities that points to the relationship between mother and child, especially *niñez*, *cobijo* (the womb), and *cuerda* (the umbilical cord). The final two verses of this stanza could describe the literal birth of the speaker or the process of attaining language through separation and individuation from the mother figure (the movement from the imaginary to the symbolic in Lacanian terms). The final act described in this stanza, that of expiating the silence, could represent the child's first cry of life or the uttering of the first word, most likely *mamá*. This word would "expiate the silence," that is, compensate for the mother's loneliness and the tacit and literal expectations before and throughout pregnancy. The birth of a child and the production of the word *mamá* would give voice to the mother's presence, would make the mother another presence, individuating both mother and child/speaker.[44] Nonetheless, there is a bond between them as well as a separation, both represented by the word. Adrienne Rich defines the ambivalent relationship between mother and child: "The child that I carry for nine months can be defined *neither* as me or as not-me. Far from existing in the mode of 'inner space,' women are powerfully and vulnerably attuned both to 'inner' and 'outer' because for us the two are continuous, not polar."[45] We see this duality in the next stanzas of "La amada."

> Esa palabra tuya que te nombra
> es una cordillera, un bálsamo untuoso.
> La protejo en mi boca como a un polluelo de águila
> que ha de surcar el Líbano.

Nombrarte es recrear
la creación al hacerlo,
como si Dios quisiera llevarme a su tarea
y yo pusiera nombre
a lo que sólo espero y reconozco como definitivo,
encontrar en tus sílabas
mi primer balbuceo
y que mi voz madure
al tiempo que te nombro.

(vv. 13–25)[46]

The words that name the (m)other form "una cordillera" and "un bálsamo untuoso," an obstacle or barrier, and a soothing, penetrating unguent, respectively. In this context the psychoanalytic term *(m)other* refers to the ambivalent speaker, who can be either mother or daughter, or either of the two lovers in a lesbian relationship. The speaker as daughter (and as lover) feels both attachment to the (m)other and yet has her own distinct identity and sense of self because of the logos. The word connects through identification and separates by identifying (naming). The beautiful image of the eaglet that the speaker holds in her mouth (the logos that names the [m]other) ambivalently has soft feathers and a sharp beak and talons. By pronouncing that word, the speaker will release the eagle to "plow the air" over Lebanon. The verb *surcar* obtains erotic overtones that refer to the physical and the spiritual (emotional) effects of naming the other. The reference to Lebanon could metonymically refer to the famous cedars of that region, symbols of beauty and majesty in the Song of Songs and of immortality, as are all evergreens.[47] This symbol conveys both erotic and metapoetic overtones.

The near tautology of the second stanza above defines a circular relationship between naming and creating the world anew. Although used in another context, the words of Michel de Certeau are apropos: "Naming is not here the 'painting' of a reality . . . ; it is a performative act organizing what it enunciates."[48] De Certeau relates the act of writing with the body and the coming into being of the subject.[49] The speaker of "La amada" indeed affirms God's purpose in letting her participate in the act of creation through language, by naming "lo que sólo espero y reconozco como definitivo." That which the speaker awaits and recognizes is not an abstraction but concrete, tangible reality, primarily the body of the (m)other. By dint of her first babbling of the mother's name, the poet discovers language. Repetition of that and other words in the act of naming as writing allows the poet's voice to mature over time, leading to her poetic vocation.

"La amada" represents the poet's meditation on language and the acquisition of her "mother tongue." *La amada* as a phrase designates both mother and daughter, the loving relationship that entails union and separation, identification and individuality. But in the context of the Song of Songs this relationship adopts erotic overtones, implying a mature sexual relationship between two women, each of whom is mutually "la amada." This poem thus complicates the mirror image (the image in and of the mirror) via multiple reflections on the use of language. The mother-daughter relationship and the lesbian love relationship comment on the relationship of the poet and language, and vice versa. In every case the speaker grows and matures through contact with the other—mother/daughter, lover, writing. Even though only one poem is involved, there exist three pairs of relationships, adding to the richness of Larumbe's exploration of the act of naming (the other in the mirror).

In the poems examined thus far, several general characteristics of Larumbe's poetics have emerged. In addition to titling each poem with the name of a biblical woman and citing the appropriate passages, the poet tends to divide the poem into short stanzas and to employ short but traditional verses: Heptasyllabic and hendecasyllabic verses predominate. And all the poems are between a page and a page and a half in length. Moreover, she has chosen to structure some of the more memorable poems through repetition of a certain technique or line. For example, in the poem about Jael the nomad the repetition of the refrain "Clavo la clavija de mi tienda en tu sien" neatly organizes the poem and contributes to the theme. In "La amada" cumulative incongruities signal the development of the ambivalent meaning of the central figure. The repetition and variation of the motif *Lloro* in "Raquel" along with other repetitive structures (the commands and the word *feliz*) provide coherence and structure even though the poet significantly alters our perception of this character. In every case the reflections in the page as mirror multiply.

It is appropriate to end this chapter with a consideration of two figures we have seen earlier in this study: Martha and Mary. Thus this study comes full circle. As a member of an older generation, one that grew up during the Franco years, María Victoria Atencia (b. 1931) explored the tensions and complementarity between these two figures within her own life. In contrast, the younger Maite Pérez Larumbe (b. 1962) considers these two sisters separately as distinct possibilities for women.[50] A significant change in attitude is noticeable merely because of a reversal of the order of the two sisters. Normally, with Martha being the older, we always speak of Martha and Mary, and in the biblical text Jesus privileges Mary, saying that she has chosen the better part and that Martha is too agitated and preoccupied with the menial tasks involved in preparing the meal. In Larumbe's collection "María de Betanía" precedes "Marta de Betanía." This reversal does not invert the duality, but rather places Martha and Mary on equal footing. For the younger woman/poet Mary proffers an utopic vision of a future society in which men and women are equals, whereas Martha provides a model of the practical activity necessary to realize this new society. In "María de Betanía" the image of the gaze figures prominently over all the other senses. But even the gaze should not be squandered on the inconstant objects of this world but directed toward a higher goal.

> Para aguardarle,
> sólo los ojos solos,
> las manos no, su torpeza de ciego,
> no el oído que aturde,
> ni el olfato de bestia que agacha la cabeza
> ni el gusto que distrae.
>
> (No dan consolación en tanta espera
> el rayo que ilumina la toronja
> y la hace diferente a cada paso,
> las nubes inconstantes,
> los mil verdes que guarda el limonero.)
>
> (vv. 1–11)[51]

This simple listing of the senses and the parenthetical interruption imitate the passing of time that occurs and for which the speaker warns it is necessary to "aguardar." In comparison with sight, the other senses only confuse and distract one, but even sight can be led astray. Seeing is believing. But even the changing light, the inconstant clouds, and the variety of shades of green on a lemon tree can deceive sight because of their transience. These tangible and visual elements depend on a contrast of dark and light, a binary opposition in which one (light) is privileged over the other (shadow). The arrival that the speaker awaits and expects is beyond the transience of sensorial reality at this moment and even the predominance of sight, as the next stanza asserts.

> Cuando llegue,
> entonces sí el estrépito del pomo,
> derroche de cristales en los tímpanos,
> el frío del perfume,

su olor en mi cabello que le seca,
el sabor de las lágrimas,
antesala de tanta incertidumbre.

(vv. 12–18)[52]

The subjunctive mood of the verb *llegue* further defers the arrival of the expected one, but that arrival will heighten the other senses, which function as a sort of atrium or vestibule prior to actual sight. The images describe the anointing of Jesus's feet with spikenard, and in each case they are synaesthetic, combining various senses. For example, "derroche de cristales en los tímpanos" mixes sound and touch: a liquid being spilled, the tinkling or ringing of glass, the vibration of the tympanum as if it were a drum. Yet here these sensations are only imagined and anticipated. This description of the anointing of Jesus prefigures his washing of the disciples' feet before the Last Supper and symbolizes the act of service that one person extends to another.[53] Once this service is rendered, the focus falls on the mutual gaze exchanged by two people (cf. Atencia's poem).

Y así
presencia pura,
sentido ensimismado,
tiempo que se detiene,
me quedarán los ojos
para seguir mirando
los ojos que los llenan para siempre.

(vv. 19–25)[54]

The brevity of these verses creates a feeling of rapture involved in the experience of a vision. The gaze between the two is reciprocal, but it is still in the future. In her anticipation of Jesus's arrival, this Mary envisions an utopia that she cannot see at this moment. The loved one is "presencia pura," a presence proven by sight and realized by the continual filling of one gaze with the other, but it is only imagined, anticipated, now. This paradox expresses both the longing for what is pending and the joy that she will experience once her vision becomes a reality. "María de Betanía" posits the arrival of a new society, an utopia embodied in the figure of Jesus, the ideal man.

In contrast, "Marta de Betanía" represents a highly capable woman who gets things done, who effects the measures needed to accomplish her sister's goal. That both sisters are identified with their town may suggest that they have the same goal but that they approach it from different perspectives. The prefix *beth-* of Bethany ("Betanía") means "house," which in this case extends to the society in which these women live. It is important to formulate a vision of utopia, but it is just as important to implement it in praxis. Martha distinguishes herself by dint of her industriousness and her tireless effort. The number of activities she accomplishes, the knowledge she possesses, and her ability to delegate tasks and direct others are impressive characteristics that merit recognition. The opening stanza of the poem illustrates her multifaceted talents.

> Madrugué por pintar los higos de aceite,
> así madurarán.
> Oreé las esteras, extendí los sarmientos,
> mandé matar tres pollos y luego recordé
> que quería encargar al alfarero una tinaja alta
> y le envié recado.
> Ayudé a la criada a cepillar las losas,
> me reí con María que aseguró que el aire
> nunca estuvo tan quieto . . .
>
> (vv. 1–9)[55]

The trivial act of brushing oil onto the figs adopts symbolic proportions in the context of the two sisters. Yes, Mary has the vision, but Martha knows how to realize that vision, to make it mature, that is, come to fruition. She has well defined purposes in mind as she looks ahead and makes provisions for what she will need. As the principal person in the house, she is the hub of activity, but she is not averse to getting her hands dirty. She arises before anyone else and accomplishes a great deal before receiving help from others. This eagerness and energy attest to her foresightedness and her drive. Moreover, she has only to send a servant to the potter to order a large jar: The potter must know and trust her because of previous dealings with her. She even demonstrates her sense of humor and of feminine community when her sister complains about the heat. Martha embodies hard work, activity, cooperation with others, and admirable management skills. The next stanza metaphorically continues this process.

> Mientras hacía el pan, de tanto canturrear
> se hizo la masa grande y bulliciosa:
> le dibujé una cara de mujer de rabino.
>
> (vv. 10–12)[56]

Martha is so happy that she sings to herself as she makes the bread. Thus the dough rises even higher and lighter because of her song. Once again this ordinary task is emblematic of the expansion of her spirits and her enthusiasm for fomenting this process. She continues to express her sense of humor as she kneads the bread, making the round, pudgy face of the wife of a rabbi in the dough. This act may be symbolic of her disdain for the traditional roles of women or the reasons behind traditional acts like preparing a large meal. Through her act of kneading the bread she creates something new—a new image of woman—as if she were modeling clay. The ironic humor of this scene again evokes Kathi Weeks's concept of opening an intermediate space for change to occur as a result of ironic laughter.[57] Martha does not even stop to eat because she is so busy.

> No me senté a comer
> porque quise mirar
> si seguiría aquella túnica de una pieza
> en el fondo del arca
> ya de paso,
> bajé un par de jofainas
> para poner el agua a solear.
> Ahora que se oyen ruidos y Lázaro te abraza
> me apresuro en el fuego.
>
> (vv. 13–21)[58]

Bustling here and there, she pays special attention to details: She gets a tunic from the bottom of a chest (where she had undoubtedly stored it) and sets water out to warm so that the ablutions will be more soothing. The washing of feet was a sign of hospitality, but also signifies service to others and a process of purification or renewal (physical and spiritual, personal and societal). That the tunic is all of one piece demonstrates her skill at weaving (bringing something together), and that she "resurrects" it from the chest prefigures Christ's resurrection, the utopia that Mary and Martha anticipate. The chest even suggests an intimate source of Martha's actions and of her love. She is not recovering something from the past (it is not a "baúl," a "trunk") but a chest, as in the Ark of the Covenant or a hope chest. And it is connected with the mention of her brother Lazarus greeting Jesus, who has just arrived. Lazarus represents one of the people—significantly, one of the men—directly affected by this vision of the new society (his resurrection prefigures Christ's). But knowing that Jesus has arrived, that this new society is on the doorstep, only makes Martha work harder! Finally, she sits down to rest.

> Sé que cuando me siente
> con las manos aún rojas
> estaré tan cansada

que apenas si veré las cejas que se arquean
y la sonrisa llena como para los niños
mientras repites Marta, Marta,
agitada y fugaz.
¿Cuándo has de comprender
lo único que importa?

(vv. 22–30)[59]

Martha already knows that she will receive criticism for all of her hustle and bustle. She will even be too tired to see Jesus's eyebrow arch in reproof and his smile that treats her like a child. Ironically, however, I wonder: Who speaks the last question of the poem? Is it Jesus? Or Martha? Having ideals, having vision, having aspirations are important, but one also has to put in the work, apply the elbow grease, get things done. Have the evangelists (incorrectly? unintentionally?) attributed Martha's question to Jesus? Recall Ostriker's words cited at the beginning of this chapter: "[W]hen meanings already latent in a given story are recovered and foregrounded by a woman's perspective, the entire story appears to change." Larumbe's amazing poem "Marta de Betanía" exudes the energy, enthusiasm, and satisfaction in spite of the effort that she (poet and character) invests in the task of the re-vision. In the context of women's architecture, Christiane Erlemann makes a similar point when she says:

> Whoever wants to get on must also have the courage to get out! Our allies are those women who have the same utopias although it would be too narrow to call these "housing utopias". It is more a question of recognising that *under* all the beautiful relationship structures which we so desperately would like to have there lies something else—the so-called "infrastructure". Without this, the basis of our changed relationships can be destroyed overnight. To have a common utopia means sharing the conviction that no one will hand us these mutual goals and understanding on a plate. We must make them for ourselves. Even if it means getting our hands dirty in the process.[60]

Of the twenty-seven poems that comprise Maite Pérez Larumbe's *Mi nombre verdadero,* space and time have allowed analysis of less than half of them, omitting significant figures such as Eve, Sara, Deborah, Delilah, Jezebel, Pilate's wife, and the Virgin Mary, as well as intriguing and well-wrought poems in which they speak, leaving this sample to demonstrate Larumbe's project of revisionist mythmaking in the context of the poem as mirror. The poem functions as a two-way mirror, at once reflecting contemporary society and providing women with revised images. The poet serves as an intermediary reflecting both today's women and traditional figures, and allowing each to peer through from the back of the mirror in a reciprocal relationship.

Nonetheless, or perhaps consequently, one perceives a noteworthy difference in the use of the page as mirror and the act of reflecting (on) the figures portrayed in the poem. The change in the images of Martha and Mary as found in Atencia's early work and later in Pérez Larumbe's appropriation of these same figures epitomizes the changes in thinking that have taken place in Spanish society. If Atencia felt isolated in her struggle to identify herself as a poet as well as a more traditional wife and mother, Larumbe delights in and valorizes the multiple and often conflicting roles of women in the contemporary world, as the pairing of biblical figures often reveals. She can adopt as many different faces as Ana Rossetti, but when she does so, it is not theatre but life itself. In short, she brings together and underscores the multiple roles available to women and the unity/community of women of various types. In the twenty-five years since the death of Francisco Franco, Spanish women poets have wrought major changes in their identity, their subjectivity, and society in general.

Conclusion: Toward Future Studies

THE POETRY EXAMINED IN THIS BOOK REPRESENTS ONLY A SMALL POR-
tion of the works characterizing the "page as mirror" in women's poetry of post-Franco Spain. We could adduce many more examples
from the last quarter of the twentieth century and the beginning of
the twenty-first century to support this reading of women's poetry.
Certainly, it is not the only way in which women poets express themselves during this period. It is, however, a significant phenomenon
and epitomizes some of the issues with which these women and others are dealing. Each new wave of writers contributes to this tendency
in different ways, in accord with the social, historical, and cultural
context around them.

It would be futile merely to list the names of authors and works that
exemplify the page as mirror. It might be helpful, nonetheless, to
trace certain patterns based on the date of birth of the authors to illustrate where further research might occur. One author who, like
María Victoria Atencia, has written a significant amount of her work
in the post-Franco era and is now amassing a significant oeuvre is
Francisca Aguirre (b. 1930). Even in her first work, *Itaca* (Ithaca,
published in 1972), she anticipates the use of the page as mirror.
Adopting the persona of Penelope to relate extremely personal information, she not only rewrites the story of Ulysses' journey from the
woman's point of view, creating a re-vision of the events, but she also
modernizes the context. The parallelism between the classical epic
and the contemporary woman's experiences raises significant issues
through a process of comparison and contrast.

In addition, her autobiographical work, *Espejito, espejito* (1995), a
collection of short prose reflections interspersed with poems, refers
directly to the process of the page as mirror.[1] This title is the Spanish
equivalent of the refrain "Mirror, mirror on the wall" from Snow
White and therefore synonymous with the theme of this book.
Framed as a fairy tale beginning "Había una vez" (Once upon a time),
the introductory passage affirms the relationship between the writer
and the page: "Pasaron los años. Y un día cuando mi corazón creyó

. . . que había empezado 'un nuevo florecer de España,' me acerqué hasta la niña que fui y pregunté con ella: 'Espejito, espejito . . .' Las palabras que siguen son la respuesta que me dio el espejo" (The years passed. And one day when my heart believed . . . that "a new flowering of Spain had begun," I approached the little girl I was and asked with her: "Mirror, mirror on the wall . . ." The pages that follow are the answer the mirror gave me).[2] That Aguirre dedicates this work to her daughter, the poet Guadalupe Grande, and to her sisters, further attests to the significance of these reflections on the theme of identity for Spanish women in democratic Spain. Aguirre continues to explore similar issues in her poetry. In *Pavana del desasosiego* (Pavanne of Helplessness/Despair) we find poems significantly titled "Detrás de los espejos" (Behind the Mirrors) and "Espejos olvidados" (Forgotten Mirrors).[3] In each case the presence of mirrors signals a "reflection" on identity and subjectivity.

The decade of the 1940s introduces another generation of Spanish women poets who have an equivocal relationship with the mirror. The poets of this group—which includes Clara Janés, Dionisia García, and Juana Castro—are much more elusive, self-effacing, and indirect in their self-definition, although they provide subtle glimpses into their identities from time to time. At other times these authors exalt feminine attributes. In books such as Janés's *Creciente fértil* (Fertile Crescent) (1989) and Juana Castro's *Narcisia* (Narcissa) (1986), these poets appropriate images of pre-Judeo-Christian goddesses representing Mother Earth and the origin of life to foreground female sexuality and sensuality.[4] Janés's semi-autobiographical early work, *Libro de alienaciones* (Book of Alienations), also defines the speaker's subjectivity in various poems such as those dealing with her parents and friends, who provide mirror images of otherness, along with what seem to be historical events.[5] Juana Castro also centers works around a well-known female figure, but the act of mirroring in these poems is much less obvious than what we have observed in the previous chapters. In *No temerás* (You Will Not Be Afraid), for example, the central figure is Salomé, and the title of her first work, *Cóncava mujer* (Concave Woman), suggests the mirroring phenomenon.[6] In one of her most recent works, *Del color de los ríos* (Of the Color of the Rivers), several female figures are portrayed and represent various aspects of the speaker as a woman who identifies with other women.[7] As the recent collection of essays edited by Sharon Keefe Ugalde demonstrates, feminine subjectivity constitutes a paramount theme in Castro's poetry.[8]

One more author deserves mention here, particularly because of the tragic circumstances of her life. According to Janés, Paloma Palao was "Como una gacela . . . , alegre y a la vez asustadiza, y capaz de enorme ligereza—en el buen sentido—" (Like a gazelle . . . , happy and at the same time skittish, and capable of tremendous lightness—in the good sense—).[9] This description aptly defines this entire generation of poets. In one of the few books that Palao published in her short lifetime, *Contemplación del destierro* (Contemplation of Exile), she adopts the alter ego of a persona called Annelein, but at the end of this work the poet-speaker writes:

> Eras una mujer desmadejada
> por el amor, Annelein, pero el amor
> era una tortura, que nunca presentías. Estoy
> sintiendo el zureo de la soledad y advierto
> que tu presencia es tan grata, como mi propia imagen.
>
> (vv. 55–59)[10]

The interplay between *you* and *I* in these verses emphasizes the relationship between self and other and the similarities and differences between the writer and the woman portrayed in the page as mirror. Palao's *Contemplación* merits further study as it too illustrates the concept of the page as mirror.

The next decade, the 1950s, offers a plethora of poets who have, in one way or another, conceived of the page as mirror. Whereas the direction these poets' work has subsequently taken generally departs from this type of poetry, poets such as Olvido García Valdés, Angeles Mora, Concha García, Esther Zarraluki, Isla Correyero, Ana María Rodríguez, and Mercedes Castro contribute to this conception of the page as mirror. Many of their poems appear in *Ellas tienen la palabra* (Women Have the Floor), the second major anthology of women's poetry published by Hiperión that, along with Buenaventura's *Las diosas blancas,* frames the period under investigation.[11] In many of the poems of this generation, the poet creates considerable distance between the poetic voice and the woman portrayed. Mercedes Castro's book *El retrato quebrado* (The Broken Portrait), for example, consists of a series of short, proselike poems that by and large deal with an anonymous *ella* (she).[12] Just as the shattered mirror emblematizes psychic distress, the title *El retrato quebrado* can point to the portrayal of a female figure whose world has made her feel psychically dispersed, incomplete, or like a puzzle waiting to take shape. However, it could also be an allusion to cubism, an aesthetic approach that presents many different angles and points of view, indicative of the multiplicity of identities that constitute any individual and represent the varied possibilities for today's women.

Various means of distancing themselves from the images they observe in the mirror are available to the poets of this group. Very often they describe and meditate on women they see in the world around them. Olvido García Valdés, for example, paints a voyeuristic scene in "La mujer entra en el cuartito a oscuras" (The Woman Enters a Small Room in the Dark).[13] Evoking Virginia Woolf's *A Room of One's Own* and Carmen Martín Gaite's *El cuarto de atrás* (The Back Room), this metapoetic statement relates the poet's search for an expression for her emotions. The poets of this era grew up during the paternalistic, patriarchal Franco era, but now as young women they are entering a democracy where men and women should be equals.

These same issues arise in poems of Angeles Mora and Esther Zarraluki. Mora is particularly acerbic in her rejection of traditional roles, as we can see in "La chica más suave" (The Softest Girl), "Yo, feminista, en un concierto" (I, Feminist, at a Concert), and "La chica de la maleta" (The Girl with the Suitcase).[14] Zarraluki's poem "Las pescateras" (The Fishmongers) combines Mora's sharpness with García Valdés's metapoetic slant.[15] Here the speaker observes the women working in a fish market. The fish, then, can be considered as not only words that the poet decapitates and guts for her own purposes but also images of women that she demystifies and deromanticizes.

Another poet who tends to distance herself from the images she portrays in her poems is Ana María Rodríguez. In many of the poems in the first half of *El silencio de la sirena* (The Mermaid's Silence), Rodríguez participates in a revisionist poetics given that she appropriates classical and literary figures to define her identity as a poet.[16] This procedure is clearly evident in poems such as "Victoria alada" (Winged Victory) and "Atenea lemnia" as well as in "Hablando con Emily" (Talking with Emily) (here Emily Brontë rather than Dickinson) and even "Garbo murió soltera" (Garbo Died Unwed).

Although more research needs to be done, it appears that the poets born in the 1950s attempt to separate themselves from traditional renditions of women writers and to define themselves and their poetic voices in apposition with former generations. This revisionist movement becomes more pronounced in the next generation of women, those born in the 1960s. These include Almudena Guzmán and Luisa Castro, studied above. Other poets of this generation who have made and are making an impact are Aurora Luque, Beatriz Hernanz, Mercedes Escolano, Guadalupe Grande, María Angeles Pérez López, and Esther Morillas, among others.

The title of Aurora Luque's *Problemas de doblaje* (Problems with Dubbing) addresses the issue of a woman poet finding her own voice and defining her relationship with symbolic language.[17] Couched in erotic terms, these poems deal with the speaker's search for those ecstatic moments when her true voice will emerge. Like many other women examined here, Beatriz Hernanz draws on a variety of female figures, predominantly mythological, in *La vigilia del tiempo* (The Vigil of Time), although she also includes an "Homenaje a Janis Joplin" (Homage to Janis Joplin) and another to Isidore Ducasse as reflected images.[18] The third section, titled "La urbanidad de los espejos" (The Urbanity of Mirrors), presents a panoply of female figures from Persephone and Penelope to "una mujer . . . a la sombra de una ventana abierta" (a woman . . . in the shade of an open window).[19] This untitled poem also addresses the issue of writing and of finding the words that will appropriately express a woman's emotions.

Although such generalizations must be tentative, we can see that women poets born in the decade of the sixties protest against patriarchal images of women, reject male models of expression as inadequate to their needs, and search for a truer poetic idiom. This trend resurfaces in Esther Morillas's appropriately titled *Mujeres* (Women).[20] This single word could be descriptive of the different types of women found in the situations of these poems, but it could also be an interpolation that directly hails the attention of women readers. Many poems in this collection interrogate the image of woman, as "Himno al sol" (Hymn to the Sun) does when the poet sees a reflection of her mother in herself while polishing her fingernails. Others evince the same ironic tone of protest found in Amalia Bautista's *Cárcel de amor.* The anecdote related in "Miss Nerja 1999," for example, parodies beauty pageants but also calls attention to antiquated provincial customs and attitudes that are still commonplace in Spain and form part of the layers of cultural and social sedimentation that undergird women's lives.

As noted, the tone of protest emerges more strongly in this generation of woman. Their interest in such figures as Lilith reveals a growing sense of independence and rebellion against patriarchal strictures. Whereas Andrea Luca (who does not publish her date of birth) advocates an androgynous/hermaphroditic sexuality that combines male and female characteristics in a flexible, bisexual identity in *El don de Lilith* (Lilith's Gift), Guadalupe Grande is much more acerbic in rejecting accepted roles for and attitudes about women in *El libro de Lilit* (The Book of Lilith).[21]

Poets born in the 1970s are just beginning to come of age, so fewer examples of their work and their stances on these issues are available. Perhaps Miriam Reyes's image of the *Espejo negro* (Black Mirror)—a mirror that reflects no image—is indicative of a change in attitude.[22] Two other poets from the period appear to be leaning in the same direction: Silvia Ugidos in *Las pruebas del delito* (The Proof of a Crime) and Mercedes Castro in *La niña en rebajas* (Girl on Sale).[23] Both poets manifest a sardonic attitude of protest and disillusionment with life. Ugidos employs the page as mirror in a variety of ways, often engaging the reader directly and playing with an image of herself. In this regard her poetry draws not only on Gloria Fuertes, especially in the "autobiographical" poems, but also on Ana Rossetti and Amalia Bautista. Two poems from *Las pruebas del delito* stand out: "Todo lo que nunca quiso saber ni se le ocurriría preguntar sobre Silvia Ugidos" (Everything You Never Wanted to Know or Would Have Occurred to You to Ask about Silvia Ugidos) and "Espejismos, distancias" (Mirages, Distances). In this poem the poetic persona invites us to imagine her seated in front of a mirror, reminiscent of Atencia's visit to Blancanieve's room and Larumbe's Judith before the mirror, among other poems. Again, this poem creates a disjunction or *méconnaissance* (misrecognition) between the gazes of two women who are the same woman at different times in her life.

Mercedes Castro evinces an even more sardonic and disillusioned voice than Ugidos. Castro often employs slang and curse words that may shock some readers, forcing a distance between the reader and the poetic persona, who portrays herself as a rebel. Via this distance the poetic persona asserts her individuality and subjectivity. Ironically, she sets herself apart as other to define herself. In fact, alienation constitutes one of the central themes of *La niña en rebajas*. Her status as a "fish out of water" problematizes her subjectivity by placing her in a double bind: She depends on others to define her, but this definition isolates her and leaves her feeling as though she does not exist, has no identity, no individuality, no subjectivity. We can see this dilemma unfold in "Mar de Madrid" (Sea of Madrid), where the rewriting of the fairy-tale topos of the prince rescuing the princess (re)defines gender stereotypes in a revisionist move because it encourages us to accept the poetic persona "as is," as a real person rather than as an imaginary ideal. Although Castro's tone is harsh and distancing, something of an inner self (or another, less apparent side of the self) comes through the negative image she projects, creating a fascinating tension between sympathy and rejection of the lyric persona. The image reflected in the page as mirror oxymoronically plumbs the interior depths of the self, demonstrating that appearances can be deceiving.

One could adduce many more examples of the page as mirror, of women of various generations (although some of these women prefer not to reveal their age). Just a few of these are María del Valle Rubio Monje's *Derrota de una reflexión* (Defeat of a Reflection); Ana

María Navales's *Los labios de la luna* (The Moon's Lips); Chantal Maillard's *Hainuwele;* Mercedes Escolano's *Estelas* (Steles); María del Carmen Rubio López's *En el bosque del sueño* (In the Forest of Dreams); Magdalena Lasala's *La estación de la sombra* (The Season of Shadows); the sequence on Zabou in Mercedes Yusta's *Las mareas del tiempo* (The Tides of Time); María Luisa Mora's *Meditación de la derrota* (Meditation on Defeat); and the section titled "Hermanas" (Sisters) in Lucía Etxebarría's *Estación del infierno* (Season of Hell).[24] However, the wide range of possibilities of the page as mirror and the extensive occurrence of this phenomenon in the poetry written by women in post-Franco, democratic Spain are patently manifest. The page as mirror can serve a variety of purposes for a woman poet at various moments in her life and her poetic career. The burgeoning of this phenomenon in post-Franco Spain may be a historical occurrence, but that fact does not preclude the recurrence of this device in future generations of women. The poets of the post-Franco era have consolidated a women's tradition in Spain and have laid a solid foundation that will serve as a model for future poets.

Notes

INTRODUCTION

1. See David T. Gies, ed., *The Cambridge Companion to Modern Spanish Culture* (Cambridge: Cambridge University Press, 1999), and John Hooper, *The New Spaniards* (London: Penguin Books, 1995) for an overview.

2. See Carmen Martín Gaite, *Usos amorosos de la posguerra española*, 10a ed. (1987; Barcelona: Anagrama, 1992), and Anny Brooksbank Jones, *Women in Contemporary Spain* (Manchester: Manchester University Press, 1997).

3. Sabine Melchior-Bonnet, *The Mirror: A History*, trans. Katherine H. Jewett (New York: Routledge, 2001), 4, 5.

4. Ibid., 6.

5. Ibid., 99–184.

6. Ibid., xi.

7. See Sandra J. Schumm, *Reflections in Sequence: Novels by Spanish Women, 1944–1988* (Lewisburg, PA: Bucknell University Press, 1999).

8. Jenijoy La Belle, *Herself Beheld: The Literature of the Looking Glass* (Ithaca, NY: Cornell University Press, 1988).

9. J. E. Cirlot, *A Dictionary of Symbols*, trans. Jack Sage, 2nd ed. (New York: Philosophical Library, 1962), s.v. *mirror*, and Michael Ferber, *A Dictionary of Literary Symbols* (Cambridge: Cambridge University Press, 1999), s.v. *mirror*.

10. La Belle, *Herself Beheld*, 9.

11. Ibid., 9.

12. See J. Hillis Miller's study, *Fiction and Repetition: Seven English Novels* (Cambridge, MA: Harvard University Press, 1982), 6.

13. Ibid., 6.

14. Paul Smith, *Discerning the Subject*, Theory and History of Literature, Vol. 55 (Minneapolis: University of Minnesota Press, 1988), xxvii.

15. Ricoeur, *Oneself as Another*, trans. Kathleen Blamey (Chicago: University of Chicago Press, 1992), 16. See Lacan, "The Subject and the Other: Alienation," in *The Four Fundamental Concepts of Psycho-Analysis*, ed. Jacques-Alain Miller, trans. Alan Sheridan (New York: W. W. Norton, 1981), 203–15.

16. Kelly Oliver, *Subjectivity without Subjects: From Abject Fathers to Desiring Mothers* (Lanham, MD: Rowman and Littlefield Publishers, 1998) and *Witnessing: Beyond Recognition* (Minneapolis: University of Minnesota Press, 2001). Also see Kathi Weeks, *Constituting Feminist Subjects* (Ithaca: Cornell University Press, 1998).

17. Oliver, *Subjectivity without Subjects*, 96, 97.

18. Ibid., 151.

19. Ibid., 156. Also see Weeks, *Constituting Feminsit Subjects* and D. W. Winnicott, *Playing and Reality* (London and New York: Routledge, 1971) in chapter 2 on Ana Rossetti.

20. Oliver, *Witnessing*, 4.

21. Ibid., 194.

22. I have appropriated the phrase "chain of reflections" from Melchior-Bonnet, *The Mirror*, 110.

23. See the introduction to Rosalía de Castro, *En las orillas del Sar*, ed. Xesús Alonso Montero (Madrid: Cátedra, 1985), 21–25.

24. Ibid., 109. "Closed rosebud of pale colors, / modest beauty with your graceful brow, / why have you lost the peace of your soul? / to whom have you given the honey of your mouth? // To him who detests you perhaps, and whom your lips / of candid aroma have caused anger, / because he seeks the enflamed rose / that opens its petals to the afternoon sun."

25. Catherine Bellver, *Absence and Presence: Spanish Women Poets of the Twenties and Thirties* (Lewisburg, PA: Bucknell University Press, 2001), 22–42.

26. Susan Bordo, *Unbearable Weight: Feminism, Western Culture, and the Body* (Berkeley: University of California Press, 1993), 241.

27. See John Wilcox, *Women Poets of Spain, 1860–1990: Toward a Gynocentric Vision* (Urbana: University of Illinois Press, 1997). In Sharon Keefe Ugalde, *Conversaciones y poemas: La nueva poesía femenina española en castellano* (Madrid: Siglo Veintiuno, 1991), many of the writers interviewed deny being feminists.

28. See Sylvia Sherno, *Weaving the World: The Poetry of Gloria Fuertes* (University, MS: Romance Monographs, 2001) for a comprehensive discussion of Fuertes's poetic abilities, including the contrast between poetry and antipoetry.

29. Andrew P. Debicki, *Poetry of Discovery: The Spanish Generation of 1956–1971* (Lexington: University Press of Kentucky, 1982), 82.

30. See Margaret Persin, "Humor as Semiosis in the Poetry of Gloria Fuertes," in *Recent Spanish Poetry and the Role of the Reader* (Lewisburg, PA: Bucknell University Press, 1987), 119–36, and Timothy J. Rogers, "The Comic Spirit in the Poetry of Gloria Fuertes," *Perspectives on Contemporary Literature* 8 (1982): 88–97.

31. Wilcox, *Women Poets of Spain*, 226.

32. Ibid., 205.

33. La Belle, *Herself Beheld*, 66.

34. Gloria Fuertes, *Poesía incompleta* (Madrid: Cátedra, 1984), 66. See Sherno's discussion of this poem in *Weaving the World*, 132–34. "Electric hotplates brocades lightbulbs / records of Beethoven siphons for seltzer / I have little lamps at all prices, / used clothing I sell in good condition clothing / bullfighter suits objects of nacre, / miniatures furs books and fans. . . ."

35. "And look at the section of books and novels, / the French magazine with tomes by Verlaine, / with figures postures and human landscapes. / Cervantes Calderón that guy Oscar [Wilde] and Papini / they are very good authors at only a nickel. / Statues of Cupid in all different sizes / and this tapestry in the Velázquez style for your living room, / look at this little mirror, blankets that are almost new, / important stamps, gems . . ."

36. See Margaret Persin, *Getting the Picture: The Ekphrastic Principle in Twentieth-Century Spanish Poetry* (Lewisburg, PA: Bucknell University Press, 1997), 91–98.

37. See Debicki, "La transformación artística del referente en *Marta & María, Los sueños* y *El mundo de M. V.* de María Victoria Atencia," in *La poesía de María Victoria Atencia: Un acercamiento crítico*, ed. Sharon Keefe Ugalde (Madrid: Huerga & Fierro, 1998) and Persin, *Getting the Picture*, 151–53, for other readings of this poem and discussions of dolls.

38. See La Belle, *Herself Beheld*, 76.

39. "The lifeless doll the doll that lives, / the hairless doll the doll that cries, / the doll that laughs, the doll that frightens."

40. For another reading of this poem, see Persin, "La imagen del / en el texto: el ékfrasis, lo postmoderno y la poesía española del siglo 20," in *Novísimos, postnovísimos, clásicos: La poesía de los 80 en España,* ed. Biruté Ciplijauskaité (Madrid: Orígenes, 1990), 43–63.

41. "She is a cross between the Virgin of Fatima and of Lourdes, / a slight impression stamped 'made in USA,' / she has long tresses and open hands / she is washable and if she falls she will not shatter. / There are three colors to choose from, white, blue, pink / —there are three sizes— / —even the largest one is small—."

42. La Belle, *Herself Beheld,* 47.

43. Ibid., 50.

44. See Adrienne Rich, "When We Dead Awaken: Writing as Re-Vision," in *On Lies, Secrets, and Silence: Selected Prose, 1966–1978* (New York: W. W. Norton, 1979), 33–49, where she defines *re-vision.*

45. See David Ray Thompson, "Myth Revision in Spanish Poetry by Women Writers (1972–1998)" (Ph.D. diss., Washington University in St. Louis, 2000).

46. These texts can be found in María Victoria Atencia, *La señal, 1961–1989,* ed. Rafael León, prol. Clara Janés (Málaga: Ayuntamiento de Málaga, 1990). A more recent edition of the *Trances de Nuestra Señora,* prol. María Zambrano (Valladolid: Fundación Jorge Guillén, 1997) has appeared.

47. Atencia, *La intrusa* (Sevilla: Renacimiento, 1992).

48. See Ugalde, *Conversaciones,* 4.

49. See Wilcox, "Blanca Andreu: A "poeta maldita" of the 1980s," *Siglo XX / 20th Century* 7 (1989–90), 29–34, who first applied the term *poeta maldita* to Andreu.

50. Ramón Buenaventura, *Las diosas blancas: Antología de la joven poesía española escrita por mujeres,* 2nd ed. rev. (Madrid: Hiperión, 1986).

51. See his discussion of the etymology of the word *albatara* (clitoris) (13–15) and his introductions to Castro (234–36) and Guzmán (223–24) in particular.

52. See Ugalde, *Conversaciones,* 283–93, as well as Buenaventura, *Las diosas blancas,* 234–36.

53. Lynn Keller, *Forms of Expansion: Recent Long Poems by Women* (Chicago: University of Chicago Press, 1997), remarks on this attitude that Castro (and perhaps Guzmán, Bautista, and others in this study) in her discussion of Marilyn Hacker's poetry. Also see Susan Stanford Friedman, "When a 'Long' Poem is a 'Big' Poem: Self-Authorizing Strategies in Women's Twentieth-Century 'Long Poems,'" in *Dwelling in Possibility: Women Poets and Critics on Poetry,* ed. Yopie Prins and Maeera Shreiber (Ithaca, NY: Cornell University Press, 1997), 13–37.

54. For a discussion of the characteristics of the "poetry of experience," see Enrique Molina Campos, "La poesía de la experiencia y su tradición," *Hora de Poesía* 59–60 (1988): 41–47; Jonathan Mayhew, "The Avant-Garde and Its Discontents: Aesthetic Conservatism in Recent Spanish Poetry," *Hispanic Review* 67 (1999): 347–63; Raquel Medina, "Poesía española 'Fin de siglo': La experiencia y otros fantasmas poéticos," *Revista de Estudios Hispánicos* 32 (1998): 597–612; and María Paz Moreno, "El lugar de la 'poesía de la experiencia' en la literatura del siglo 20: ¿Una posteridad calculada?" *Hispanic Poetry Review* 2 (2000): 72–89.

55. See Carl Dennis, *Poetry as Persuasion* (Athens: University of Georgia Press, 2001).

56. See Hank Lazer, *Opposing Poetries,* Vol. 1, *Issues and Institutions* (Evanston, IL: Northwestern University Press, 1996), 82, where he cites Bernstein's definition of official verse culture.

57. See Kevin Walzer, *The Ghost of Tradition: Expansive Poetry and Postmodernism* (Ashland, OR: Story Line Press, 1998) and R. S. Gwynn, ed., *New Expansive Poetry: Theory, Criticism, History* (Ashland, OR: Story Line Press, 1999).

58. Ostriker, *Feminist Revision and the Bible* (Cambridge, MA: Blackwell, 1993).

CHAPTER 1. THE EKPHRASTIC MIRROR

1. See José Luis García Martín, *Antología poética* (Madrid: Castalia, 1990), 17, for explanations of Atencia's "editorial silence." See also Adrienne Rich, "When We Dead Awaken," in *On Lies, Secrets, and Silence* (New York: W. W. Norton and Company, 1979), 43, apropos this aspect of a woman writer's silence.

2. García Martín, *Antología,* 19.

3. See García Martín, *Antología,* 18–19, for Guillermo Carnero's assessment of the structure of the book.

4. In the introduction to Atencia's *La señal: Antología, 1961–1989* (Málaga: Excmo. Ayuntamiento de Málaga, 1990), xviii, Clara Janés speaks of the construction of an interior self in Atencia's poetry, esp. in *Marta & María.*

5. Murray Krieger, *Ekphrasis: The Illusion of the Natural Sign* (Baltimore: Johns Hopkins University Press, 1992), 6–7. This definition of ekphrasis is consistent with Persin's in her recent work *Getting the Picture: The Ekphrastic Principle in Twentieth-Century Spanish Poetry* (Lewisburg, PA: Bucknell University Press, 1997), 14–20, esp. 17–18, and with W. J. T. Mitchell's approach to the topic in *Picture Theory: Essays on Verbal and Visual Representation* (Chicago: University of Chicago Press, 1994). Ugalde, "Time and Ekphrasis in the Poetry of María Victoria Atencia," *Confluencia* 3 (1987): 7–12), also follows this definition of ekphrasis.

6. Krieger, *Ekphrasis,* 68.

7. The poems cited are from Atencia, *La señal.* All translations of the poems are mine and are provided for those readers who do not know Spanish. "Advent was marching along its course and the gardens / were remaining at the mercy of the west. / Some animals continued in heat. / The fishes dripped their silver on the shores. / The rag dolls spilled their sawdust / and the roof tiles felt their eaves grow green."

8. "The sadness in the ships did not grow greater with the rain / nor did the weeping willows cry more than was convenient. / The newborn calf found the desired udders. / Distant, the lovers continued their dream. / And although an extremely fine chill paralyzed my blood, / the tea was ready, just like it was every day."

9. See W. K. Wimsatt, "The Concrete Universal," in *The Verbal Icon: Studies in the Meaning of Poetry* (Lexington: University of Kentucky Press, 1967), 69–83. See also Krieger, *Ekphrasis,* 47.

10. "You are beneath my bed, shells, algae, sands: / your chill begins where my sheets leave off. / I would graze a fishing smack by letting my arms hang over the side / and I would spread its net over the mizzenmast / of this floating bed between coffin and bathtub. / When I close my eyes, they get covered with scales."

11. "When I close my eyes, the wind from the Straits / leaves the color of Guinea in the damp clothing, / places salt in a basket of flowers and clusters / of green and black grapes on top of my pillow, / make the insomnia swell, and on a bolster then / I sit with my dream to watch the water pass by."

12. *Ekphrasis,* 10–11.

13. "Sometimes at night I return, (a) young woman, to your side / and toward four o'clock I cross your path. / Did my friendship need more time shared / or did

we both have something more serious in common / than my life and your death: a dream of rag / dolls and pinwheels the color of toffee?"

14. "To name you is to possess you, and I say your name / of a repeated candor, and tonight at four o'clock / the name contradicts your definite dark complexion. / Like the last time we were on the beach, / we will sit leaning against the freshly painted boat / to watch the sea together, now that it is dawning."

15. "The window looks out on a silver gray sea, with its fishing smack, / and in the room there is the music of Handel and Corelli. / I reread your sadness, friend Rosalía. / If you could cede me your just correlate / of nostalgia, I might be able to leave this weight behind / and rise little by little along your high tenderness."

16. "How dry this southland and how humid your land! / In Padrón you will tell me the names of the flowers. / We will confront epochs, we will reread your letters, / your writing desk I will open more exhaustively. / Let me see my reflection in your mirror / and may the precise [necessary] word never be lacking in my song."

17. "Move aside the shadowy bird that perched on your eyes / to break forever its flight in your gaze. / Was it a fact of life that I should be first? / I have so much of your love that I am not absent to you / for my blood returns anew to yours / and I await in the dust, florally, your hand."

18. Ugalde, *Conversaciones*, 14.

19. "This house was placed for me beyond decay: / the wind from the land will not be able to do anything against it, that wind that propagates / the lady of the night, nor the wind from the west. / My gardener and father, here it is always spring: / your majesty continues to preside over the red roses; / smile, for you live only for that which is beautiful."

20. See Persin, *Getting the Picture*, 151–53 and 158–60, for another ekphrastic reading of these poems.

21. "You have a renewed duty every night, / dolls that passed one day through my hands. / Like a glass of freshly squeezed orange juice / you arrive at the edge of the sheet of my fever with your / lax corkscrews of dyed tow / and your eyes of watery blue."

22. "Almost human and mine, my plaything of other times, / I am your plaything now, almost yours and human. / This is what life wants: more life possessed, / lived, embodied. / Surrendering to you, you could transport me / forever to the years of the movies of that Shirley."

23. See Simone de Beauvoir, *The Second Sex*, trans. and ed. H. M. Parshley (New York: Alfred A. Knopf, 1952), 273, and her chapter on "The Narcissist," esp. 600–601.

24. "If at some time you could come back to find me / (embroidered suits, white straps, pleated / flutes for the walk, popcorn, / 28 November, 1 Angel Street), / household women, / how I would receive you, now that I understand you."

25. "I used to interrupt your sleep with a sudden fright, / and you would frighten away my fear stroking your hands / along my tight braids, you would wipe my nose / and you would sweeten my nap with Frigilian honey. / Let me go to you, for I want, softly, / to kick as I did then your animal lap."

26. "I will walk through the woods, I will listen to the plaint / of the lark in heat, I will arrive at the rivers / and I will choose the stones that whiten their beds. / At the foot of the araucaria / I will rest a moment and I will find in its trunk / support that is softer than any reasons could be."

27. "From your branches I will hang a crown [a wreath] / and the water will repeat its image a thousand times. / The rhododendron flower will adorn my hair, / I will invent songs different from my own / and I will cover my body with lilies and amaryllis / so that their coolness can temper my madness."

28. "I will not call at your doors, November doorknocker: / the tree of veins beneath my skin rots / and a splinter of a stick pokes at my heart. / Because you are not here, Blanca, your old dressmaker / has forgotten about the tulles, and the Child of the Passion / is filling the glass of La Granja with his tears."

29. "Your mahogany chair has a cold lap, / the marble has your quiet persistent sweetness / and beneath your gaze a dove trembles. / Hopelessly human I could regret one day, / but a world of faded shadows calls me / and to an interminable dream your bed invites me."

30. "One thing, my love, will be indispensable to me / so as to lie at your side on the floor [in the ground]: / that my eyes look at you and that your grace fill me; / that your gaze overflow my breast with tenderness / and, totally estranged, that I may find no other motive / for death than your absence."

31. Ugalde, *Conversaciones,* 14.

32. "But what will become of me when you are gone. / Little or nothing, outside of your reasons, / will the house and its chores, the kitchen and the garden mean. / You are all my leisure: / what does it matter that my sister or the others murmur, / if in my defense you step forward, so that only love counts."

33. Jessica Benjamin, *The Bonds of Love: Psychoanalysis, Feminism, and the Problem of Domination* (New York: Pantheon Books, 1988).

34. Ibid., 33.

CHAPTER 2. PLAYING DRESS-UP

1. *Indicios vehementes (Poesía 1979–1984)* (4th ed. (Madrid: Hiperión, 1990). See the articles by Sharon Keefe Ugalde and Andrew P. Debicki in *P/Herversions: Critical Studies of Ana Rossetti,* ed. Jill Robbins (Lewisburg, PA: Bucknell University Press, 2004). Also see Tina Escaja, "Lenguaje del erotismo: Ana Rossetti," in *Selected Proceedings of the Pennsylvania Foreign Language Conference (1991–1992),* ed. Gregorio C. Martín (Pittsburgh, PA: Duquesne University, Department of Modern Languages, 1995), 63–69. Her discussion of the mirror image is of relevance here.

2. See Mirella Servodidio, "Ana Rossetti's Double-Voiced Discourse of Desire," *Revista Hispánica Moderna* 45 (1992): 318–27.

3. *Femmes Fatales: Feminism, Film Theory, Psychoanalysis* (New York: Routledge, 1991), 25–26.

4. See Margaret A. Rose, *Parody: Ancient, Modern, and Post-Modern* (Cambridge: Cambridge University Press, 1993), 30.

5. Johan Huizinga, *Homo Ludens: A Study of the Play Element in Culture* (Boston: Beacon Press, 1950), 13, 28.

6. Winnicott, *Playing and Reality* (New York: Basic Books, 1971), 54.

7. D. W. Winnicott, *Playing and Reality,* 100. Huizinga speaks to the basis of poetry in play and dedicates an entire chapter to "Play and Poetry," 119–35.

8. Huizinga, *Homo Ludens,* 13.

9. Ibid., 8.

10. Ibid., 9.

11. Ibid., 3

12. See Andrew P. Debicki, *Spanish Poetry of the Twentieth Century: Modernity and Beyond* (Lexington: University of Kentucky Press, 1994), esp. 211–13, and John C. Wilcox, *Women Poets of Spain,* esp. 273–75 and 285–98. In *P/Herversions,* edited by Jill Robbins, several contributors mention Rossetti's connection with the *novísimos.*

13. 2nd ed. (London: Collins, 1971), *devaneo*.

14. Huizinga, *Homo Ludens*, 21.

15. By its nature, parody recuperates other works of the poetic tradition by incorporating and "refunctioning" previous texts; see Rose, *Parody*, 29, for a definition of refunctioning.

16. Ugalde, *Conversaciones*, 156. "When speaking of spring, it is more effective to place Cybele, who as goddess of the earth always implies fertility and renovation. The title also gives me the possibility of using the third person. For Cybele is speaking, not I. . . . It is a way of putting on a mask, or of distancing myself, or of not revealing myself too much. For example, when I have written truly using the third person formally, it has been when I was really implicated in the theme. . . . I seek a formula for not feeling too implicated and for observing myself as if I were another."

17. Pierre Grimal, *The Concise Dictionary of Classical Mythology* (London: Basil Blackwell, 1990), s. v. *Cybele*.

18. Huizinga, *Homo Ludens*, 5.

19. "Detached from its sheath, the bud, / blushing tulip, tight-fitting turban, / infuriated my blood with brusque spring. / Innoculated the sensual delirium, / my saliva lubricates your shaft; / the most turgid stalk that my hand enthrones."

20. See Rose, *Parody*, 33, for a discussion of the comic effect of parody and the incongruous juxtaposition of the low and the high.

21. "That tall flower of yours rising in the dark parks; / oh, beat me, knock me down wounded / with my mouth full of your wet silk. / Like a ring my breasts close around you, / I bring them together, you incrust yourself in me, my lips begin to open / and a drop appears on your mauve bud."

22. Huizinga, *Homo Ludens*, 76.

23. Ibid., 19.

24. "Inimitable age, I question your mirror / in which of my innumerable / cabinets is the mask of the goddess / that covered the marble with shade. / Your fervor, such an obsessive ecstasy, / made her beautiful and distant and proclaimed her unique."

25. Martín Gaite, *Usos amorosos*, 101, addresses the double standard with regard to virginity. Rafael Abella, *La vida cotidiana bajo el régimen de Franco* (Madrid: Temas de Hoy, 1996), 222, also accuses the postwar society of this double standard,

26. La Belle, *Herself Beheld*, 88, addresses the relationship between the mirror, the male gaze, and a woman's concept of self.

27. "Nor could you, through the keyhole, / see how parsimoniously she undressed / making her nakedness grow from the bathtub. / Gray mist of vines. The hand seeking / the sponge. And the fragrant foam, slithering / around her body, introduces itself in her / installing its invisible dominion. / You did not drink from the delicious fountains either / that negated the roiled labyrinths / that a malign virginity sealed closed."

28. "Neither the shadowy armpits, nor the leafy shell / of her pelvis, nor the tangled hair / knew the amiable touch of those fingers / that I know so well. But oh, how you loved her!"

29. "But the memory of her, hurrying, / assaults you and you seek her in me. What a terrible / and inimitable age. Always questioning your mirror. / I try to be reborn, old identity / that fascinated you, that body so unknown, / if such a metamorphosis were possible."

30. See Peter M. Sacks, *The English Elegy: Studies in the Genre from Spenser to Yeats* (Baltimore: Johns Hopkins University Press, 1985), 3–5.

31. "Now I am overly familiar, / invaded country of routine delights. / On pos-

sessing me you lost my inner beauty / and your desires have disappeared. / But if you help me seek / the tunics forgotten in the closets / and rescue the propitious mask, / if I become arrogant, will I be able to convince you?"

32. "So wise is experience / and so indestructible its command / that I left you far behind. / I would even instruct you. And you reproach me for it."

33. "Inimitable age, / where the gods dwelled and admiration / was the only tribute / that you scattered at my feet. // Don't ask me to go back, / for innocence is irrecuperable."

34. *Parody,* 29.

35. Plato, "Symposium," *Selected Dialogues,* trans. Benjamin Jowett (Franklin Center, PA: Franklin Library, 1983), 305–53.

36. For a feminist discussion of the "Symposium" and of the relationship between the physical and the abstract, see the cluster of articles by: Eleanor H. Kuykendall, "Introduction to 'Sorcerer Love,' by Luce Irigaray"; Luce Irigaray, "Sorcerer Love: A Reading of Plato's *Symposium,* Diotima's Speech"; and Andrea Nye, "The Hidden Host: Irigaray and Diotima in Plato's *Symposium,*" in Nancy Fraser and Sandra Lee Bartky, eds., *Revaluing French Feminism: Critical Essays on Difference, Agency, and Culture* (Bloomington: Indiana University Press, 1992), 60–93. For a balanced appraisal see also "Diotima's Discourse on Eros in Plato's *Symposium,*" in Tina Chanter, *Ethics of Eros: Irigaray's Rewriting of the Philosophers* (New York: Routledge, 1995), 159–64.

37. See Huizinga's chapter "Play-Forms in Philosophy."

38. See Huizinga's comparison of play and ritual in *Homo Ludens,* 18–26.

39. "The most enchanting moment of the afternoon / behind the orangish and delicate sheers. / And on the little table the tea / and a bouquet of flowers, roses past their prime, / and on the ottoman of striped silk, / my skirt extended, my foot peeking out / provocatively, I wait for you to come near / to my neck, lowering your look / down the dark funnel of my neckline, / left open on purpose."

40. "I blush / and your fingers begin meditated cautious moves / along my skirt; they linger in the deep tunnels / of the pleating and run along the curly stars / of my lace. . . ."

41. "Hurry, come here, receive these rose / petals, petals like thighs / of unpolluted vestals, veiled. May my mouth / overflow in their silken pieces, terse and dense / as lips brought forward to my teeth / demanding a little nip. Gag yourself, / the panting of your tall dagger, and may your kiss be / the herald of flowers. Hurry, / undo the ribbons, make sure of the heaviest / hanging of the dark breast, look at it, touch it / and in its stiff tips spill your saliva / while I feel, on my legs, your menace."

42. Friedrich Nietzsche, *Beyond Good and Evil: Prelude to a Philosophy of the Future,* trans. Walter Kaufmann (New York: Vintage Books [Random House], 1989), 10 (original emphasis).

43. Ibid., 12.

44. "Illustrious extravagants: 10 portraits of woman," prol. Margarita Rivière (Madrid: Qué Leer [Comunicación y Publicaciones], 1996).

45. Moix, *Extraviadas ilustres,* 22. "a learned woman, brilliant, decadently snobbish and famous among the artistic and intellectual elite of Rome, Paris, and Berlin as a 'collector of celebrities.'"

46. Ibid., 20. "a woman who not only was ahead of her time because of her conviviance with poets and philosophers of renown before, during, and after her marriage, but because she possessed an exceptional talent and intelligence that she refused to sacrifice by conforming to a life corseted and constrained by the burgeois society of her day."

47. Ibid., 23. "feminist before her time and fervent practitioner of free love."

48. Nietzsche, *Beyond Good and Evil,* 185–86 n. 21.

49. See H. F. Peters, *Lou Andreas-Salomé: Mi hermana, mi esposa* (Lou Andreas-Salomé: My Sister, My Spouse), pref. Anaïs Nin (Barcelona: Ediciones Paidós, 1995), 138–39.

50. "Pitiless beauty, you annihilate me. / The light brushes my desert against your skin, / my road of thirst, my incessant passion / for beauty. Behind your back I admire you. / Frightened I contemplate the universe / that excludes me from you. / Lacking in tenderness as you walk, you glow / and you do not look at those who, on seeing you, grow beautiful."

51. John Lechte, *Fifty Key Contemporary Thinkers* (London: Routledge, 1994), 218–19, elaborates the Nietzschean concept of difference.

52. "May my limits / in your disconcerting harmony vanish. / Denuded by your love I remain / in the moor unfamiliar with your seminal rain, / since you engender and fecundate yourself. / Even more, you disdain the obedient mirror. / But what becomes of your power without the submissive slave?"

53. Martín Gaite, *Usos amorosos*, 68, documents the low esteem in which women who studied during the Franco years were held, saying it was deemed necessary to "cortarles las alas" (clip their wings).

54. Cf. Nietzsche, *Beyond Good and Evil*, 50–51. Also see Hélène Cixous, "Sorties," in *New French Feminisms: An Anthology*, ed. Elaine Marks and Isabelle de Courtrivron (New York: Schoken Books, 1980), 90–98.

55. "And I adore you, I adore you blindly, / you who are my distraction, you who are all my dizziness. / In the velvety conjunction / of your legs my eyes get lost with no remedy. / You disturb me. Even when disguised / you repeat voices that I know well, / I elevate you and I surrender myself seduced / when I discover all your ruses."

56. Nietzsche, *Beyond Good and Evil*, 160–61, speaks to the relationship between the surface of the mask and the depth it conceals/reveals.

57. Roger Caillois, *Man, Play, Games*, trans. Meyer Barash (New York: Free Press, 1961), 23, categorizes this type of play as *ilinx*.

58. See Huizinga, *Homo Ludens*, 152.

59. "I throw myself at you, I bejewel myself, I murder myself. / And if my foot rests on your abyss, / nonetheless, I rectify, you must wait faithfully for me. / Nothing can get away from you, nothing can uproot you. / In the end you always win, and in the end they applaud you."

60. Joanna Russ, *How to Suppress Women's Writing* (Austin: University of Texas Press, 1983).

61. "When I was of silk and of camelias, / a panting Duplessis, her mouth full of red / behind the pale lips like pale ribbons, / my fingers would insist on the Nocturnes. // When I would separate my face from the stained handkerchief / my cheekbones copied the whitest vases, / the rarest of porcelain from rare countries, / and tied to my throat there was a brooch for saving a lock of hair."

62. "[Rossetti] has not renounced irony, a joking tone without emphasis, an implicit mockery in [her] heroes, whom—just as happens in life—[she] cannot avoid taking seriously and somewhat jokingly at the same time." I have modified this phrase, taken from the jacket cover of Marías's *El hombre sentimental* (Barcelona: Anagrama, 1986).

63. "Miniscule tomb, golden amulet / deprived of its adored image: / you did not exist. // You did not exist, no, but not for that / were you less beautiful, nor for my predictions / less loved."

64. "My most beloved face suddenly revealed, seductive instant, / inevitable poem, for in my medallion now there is a treasure."

65. See Diana J. Fuss, "'Essentially Speaking': Luce Irigaray's Language of Essence," in Fraser and Gartky, eds., *Revaluing French Feminism*, 94–112.

66. "And when to the garden, with you, we descended, / we avoided as much as possible the apple trees. / Even before the odor of the heliotrope we blushed; / it is well known that this flower explains eternal love. / Your face then was not less inflamed / than your red sash, lying on it, / it competed with the red reflexion."

67. "And ecstatic, mute, we would spy on you; / before wetting our lips in the fountain, / furtive and virginal, you would cross yourself / and clothe yourself in infinite grace. / We would give you holy cards with their edges laced / just like the little plate of raisins / that, with the tea, we offered to visitors, / *vade retros* and relics in which we would sew gold thread / and before you we would sit with childish modesty."

68. Huizinga, *Homo Ludens,* 89–104, addresses the similarity of war to play and competition. See also Martín Gaite, *Usos amorosos,* 167.

69. "My beautiful seminarian so beloved and pure, / how many serpents wrapped around the pots of lilies, / how the roses felt in your hands that thus they lost their petals! / With your gaze lowered we wanted to protect you / from our feminine seduction. / Vain intention."

70. On vamps, see Martín Gaite, *Usos amorosos,* 133–37. On the other hand, see her comments about the triumph of landing a man who was "un hombre difícil" (a difficult man), that is, "un hombre interesante" (an interesting man) (155).

71. "One day, a turgid purple / will stretch, suddenly, your unaware pants / and Adam will spill his provision of milk. / Nothing will be able to stop such a vigorous fountain. / Certainly it will happen, it will happen. / Although you may never bite our apple, / although we may never witness your spasm, / certainly it will happen, it will happen. / And no scapulary is going to save you, / nor will the terrible hell of the white catechism / be able to avert the radiant flow of your sperm."

72. See David T. Gies, ed., *The Cambridge Companion to Modern Spanish Culture* (Cambridge: Cambridge University Press, 1999), xxvii, where he defines the "movida."

73. On 30 July 2005 the Spanish parliament enacted a new law validating same-sex marriages, making Spain one of the most liberal European states in this regard (as well as others).

74. See Luce Irigaray, *This Sex Which Is Not One,* trans. Catherine Porter (Ithaca, NY: Cornell University Press, 1985), 24.

75. "And let us kiss one another, beautiful virgins, let us kiss one another. / Let's hurry to undo ourselves / destroying the booty of our bodies. / I sense the enemy breathing on the other side of the wall, / his covetousness rises between his legs."

76. Both Atencia and Rossetti employ the image of the suitcase as a reference to the past and to those cultural or social elements that they retain (sub)consciously. Also see Gaston Bachelard's chapter on "Drawers, Chests and Wardrobes," in *The Poetics of Space,* trans. Maria Jolas (Boston: Beacon Press, 1964), 74–89.

77. See Alice Schlegel, "Status, Property, and the Value on Virginity," *American Ethnologist* 18 (1991): 719–34.

78. See Irigaray, "When Our Lips Speak Together," in *This Sex Which Is Not One,* 211–12.

79. "And let us kiss one another, beautiful virgins, let us kiss one another. / Don't give prodigally to the sword, / oh virile destiny, the inviolate hymen. / May the crevice, the white battering ram / of our hands, loosen its narrowness."

80. See *Three Contributions to the Theory of Sexuality,* in *The Basic Writings of Sigmund Freud,* trans. and ed. A. A. Brill (New York: Modern Library, 1938), 558.

81. See Hutcheon, *A Theory of Parody,* 44, and Rose, *Parody,* 29, on the relationship between parody and the mock-heroic.

82. "And let us kiss one another, beautiful virgins, let us kiss one another. / Before the conqueror profanes / the citadel, and reveals its circumspection / to sack the

treasures of the temple, / it is preferable always to surrender it to the flames. // And let us kiss one another, beautiful virgins, let us kiss one another. / Singular pillaging: feverish / in our benefit we snatch away / our own dowry. May the haughty conquerer / not obtain his masculine privilege."

83. See Schlegel, "Status, Property, and the Value on Virginity."

84. "And let us kiss one another, beautiful virgins, let us kiss one another. / With the secret font moistened / in the liquor of Venus, / let us anticipate, / drenched in pleasure, Priapus. / And with the thirst of our bodies, let us get drunk."

85. "And let us kiss one another, beautiful virgins, let us kiss one another. / Tearing the orange blossom, let us enjoy for ourselves, let us enjoy ourselves / the prize that our thighs defended. / The phallus, eager to penetrate us / will find, where he thought virtue, a whorehouse."

86. See Abella, *La vida cotidiana*, 74 and 222–23, for comments on prostitution during the Franco era. Martín Gaite, *Usos amorosos*, 102–5, also discusses prostitution and moral double standards in postwar Spain.

CHAPTER 3. THE SHATTERED MIRROR

1. I have used the fifth Hiperión edition of this work (Madrid: Hiperión, 1986). For the most recent version of the text, consult Andreu, *El sueño oscuro: Poesía reunida, 1980–1989* (Madrid: Hiperión, 1994), 13–75.

2. Sherno, "Between Water and Fire: Blanca Andreu's Dream Landscapes," *Revista Hispánica Moderna* 47 (1994): 533–42. See other articles listed in the bibliography.

3. See ibid., 538, on *De una niña* as an "elegy to the decomposition of self." On the mourner's damaged narcissism, see Peter M. Sacks, *The English Elegy: Studies in the Genre from Spenser to Yeats* (Baltimore: John Hopkins University Press, 1985), 10.

4. See Sacks, *The English Elegy,* 171. Also see Jahan Ramazani, *Poetry of Mourning: The Modern Elegy from Hardy to Heaney* (Chicago: University of Chicago Press, 1994), 6.

5. Ramazani, *Poetry of Mourning,* 3.

6. Oliver, *Reading Kristeva: Unraveling the Double-bind* (Bloomington: Indiana University Press, 1993), 107, 109.

7. Zeiger, *Beyond Consolation: Death, Sexuality, and the Changing Shapes of Elegy* (Ithaca, NY: Cornell University Press, 1997), 62–63.

8. See Freud, "Mourning and Melancholia," in *A General Selection from the Works of Sigmund Freud,* ed. John Rickman (New York: Doubleday, 1957) and *Beyond the Pleasure Principle,* Standard Edition, trans. and ed. James Strachey (New York: W. W. Norton and Company, 1961).

9. See Ugalde, *Conversaciones y poemas,* 254–55.

10. Ibid., 250–51.

11. See La Belle, *Herself Beheld,* 85 and 126–27.

12. "Between Water and Fire," 540. Also see Sacks, *The English Elegy,* 199 and 292.

13. Kristeva, *Powers of Horror: An Essay on Abjection,* trans. Leon S. Roudiez (New York: Columbia University Press, 1982). Elizabeth Gross provides an excellent summary of the abject in her article "The Body of Signification" in *Abjection, Melancholia, and Love: The Work of Julia Kristeva,* eds. John Fletcher and Andrew Benjamin (London: Routledge, 1990), esp. 86–93. Kelly Oliver explains the concept of the *sujet-en-procès* in *Reading Kristeva,* 13. Also see John Lechte, "Art, Love, and Melancholy in the Work of Julia Kristeva," in *Abjection, Melancholia and Love,* 27.

14. See Lechte, *Julia Kristeva* (London: Routledge, 1990), 163.

15. Sherno, "Between Water and Fire," 534. Also see Lechte, "Art, Love, and Melancholy," 32.

16. On intertextuality and the thetic, see Oliver, *Reading Kristeva,* 93. For a definition of the paratext, see Gerard Genette, *Paratexts: Thresholds of Interpretation,* trans. Jane E. Lewin (Cambridge: Cambridge University Press, 1997), 1–2.

17. See Sherno, "Between Water and Fire," 537.

18. With regard to elegiac conventions of address, see Sacks, *The English Elegy,* 96.

19. "Say that you wanted to be a sleek horse, the name / of some mythical horse, / or perhaps the name of tristan, and dark. / Say it, Greek horse, that you wanted to be a statue for ten thousand years, say south, and say dove white oleander, / that you had wanted to be in such things, / to die in their substance, to be a column."

20. Sacks, *The English Elegy,* 35–36, addresses the "divided voice" of elegy. See also his discussion of the mirror stage on pp. 9–14 and the implications for women rather than for men on pp. 15–17.

21. Sherno, "Between Fire and Water," 535, echoes these thoughts in her discussion of drugs as related to poetry. Kristeva, *Black Sun: Depression and Melancholia,* trans. Leon S. Roudiez (New York: Columbia University Press, 1989), 36–38, defines the ambivalence of language as a drug.

22. "Say that too many times / astrolabes, stars, the nerves of angels, / came to make music for the poet Rilke, / not for your knees or your soul of walls."

23. See the introduction to *Sonnets to Orpheus,* trans. M. D. Herter Norton (New York: W. W. Norton and Company, 1942), 7–9.

24. "While marijuana distills green seas, / speaks in receptions with green tears, / or robs the light of its greenest light, / you forget who you are, you forget who you are."

25. Andreu considers the colors green, silver, and white extremely ambivalent; see Ugalde, *Conversaciones,* 252.

26. "How strange the air that envelops me will seem, / how strange the cathedral of day, / the cloister that condenses the great age of light / and the character of storms will be thus, / when you are no longer here."

27. See Oliver, *Reading Kristeva,* 56 and 88, on the definition of the abject with regard to boundaries.

28. Kristeva, *Black Sun,* 50–51, examines the dualities of denial in relation to language and poetry.

29. Lechte, *Julia Kristeva,* 72–73, explains Kristeva's concept of negation as a deconstruction of positive and negative.

30. "My love, my love, you without a day for yourself, / swarmed amid mirrors and amid bad things, / the transcendental silver dead / and now the ancient anemones of eclogues, / dead this version that now I obscure, I decline verbs, to read it, younger."

31. "My never love, feverish and pacific, / verses for the small octopus of death, / verses for the rare death that makes the transit of the telephones, / for the mind transformed into verses, for the circuit of the violin, / for the confines of the south, of dreams, / verses that give me no asylum nor are a cause for life, / that give me no sweet umbilical serpent nor the glucose chamber of the womb."

32. Lechte, *Julia Kristeva,* 93–94, discusses the importance of anaphora. Kristeva, *Powers of Horror,* 185, emphasizes the duality of "fear and fascination."

33. See the discussion of "The Maternal 'Thing'" in Oliver, *Reading Kristeva,* 61.

34. In "Stabat Mater" Kristeva urges us to make a distinction between the actual mother and the concept of maternity when it comes to abjection; see Oliver, *Reading*

Kristeva, 162, and Kristeva, "Stabat Mater," in *The Kristeva Reader,* ed. Toril Moi (New York: Columbia University Press, 1986), 160–86.

35. See Sacks, *The English Elegy,* 167–68.

36. See Rainer Maria Rilke, *Letters to a Young Poet,* rev. ed., trans. M. D. Herter Norton (New York: W. W. Norton, 1953), 81–85; 113–15.

37. "look at the trees like the curled nerves of day / crying the water of the scythe. / / This is what I see in the smooth hour of April, / also in the chapel of the mirror I see this."

38. Sacks, *The English Elegy,* 20–21, identifies the pathetic fallacy as a fundamental convention of elegy.

39. "Between Fire and Water," 536 and 539–40.

40. Oliver, *Reading Kristeva,* 55–56, defines the contradictory effect of the abject.

41. See, for example, "In the Morning You Always Come Back" and "Death Will Come and Its Eyes Will Be Yours" in Gian-Paolo Biasin, *The Smile of the Gods: A Thematic Study of Cesare Pavese's Works,* trans. Yvonne Freccero (Ithaca, NY: Cornell University Press, 1968), 21–23.

42. "School: *a girl who drank grapefruit / directly from the lips of night, who swore that she slept with fear in no one's bed, / who swore that fear / had violated her to make two hundred children.* / Love, the Russian girl / who took Communion of roasted reindeer / and who drank lichen. / Love, the Russian girl / who read Tom Wolfe."

43. Andreu mentions having read Wolfe's novels as a result of her friendship with another girl when they both attended the same school; see Ugalde, *Conversaciones,* 247. Wolfe's New Journalism style is based on reality but deploys a new set of conventions for journalistic reporting; see Joe David Bellamy, introduction to *Tom Wolfe: The Purple Decades: A Reader* (New York: Farrar Straus Giroux, 1982), vii–xvi.

44. See Ugalde, *Conversaciones,* 254, where Andreu says that she had bought a reproduction of "El ramo de alhelíes" [The bouquet of wallflowers] by Chagall after seeing an exhibition of his paintings at the Fundación March.

45. See ibid., where Andreu mentions her debt to Perse's poetry.

46. See Kristeva's concept of "reduplication" in Oliver, *Reading Kristeva,* 73.

47. "like the ribbon that was born in the notebook of the Young Bach / and came to die here, / in the girls that nest in records, / while Rainer Maria is no longer as young as on page 38, / is not even a young corpse, / a defunct infant without a pavanne."

48. "and we do not die amid sexes closed like closed books, / but we die, / . . . / Ay, we yawn before the blue cups of methylene, / and we aspire ammonia with a distant air, / we get bored in front of the high sound of vitriol, / we crown ourselves with barbital, / for we can find no sharper blade."

49. See Martín Gaite, *Usos amorosos,* 71, and John Hooper, *The New Spaniards,* rev. ed. (New York: Penguin Books, 1995), ch. 11.

50. "As in my medieval history, / when the school stones burned / for the breaches in the front / and my body granted me opium recently born, / the same hour confuses us, / we make hymns or children of the ancient mythological horse / and of a sad girl with her vein extended, / of a needle raised by the incredible snow / by the yellow of Persian doves."

51. "let's speak of the father horses, / let's allude to the secret hooves that will give us peace / and not to any bridles, / to the future manes delicately anguished, / let's speak of the father horses that will bring us death and of the amphetamine moon, / let's speak of the mother vein that will bring us the final happiness, / let's speak of the extreme virgen drink."

52. "let's not speak of anything but the shore and the slopes of madness / that possess men in the parks and give orders, // nothing but the small dagger that will crown the coronary artery like a supreme diadem / with the infantile metal blade, the rarest and sharpest in the world."

53. Kristeva, *Powers of Horror,* 67, discusses the relationship between the organization of personal identity and the symbolic order of society.

54. "Listen, tell me, it was always this way, / something is missing and we must put a name on it, / to believe in poetry, and in the intolerance of poetry, / or to say *cloud, oleander, / suffering,* / to say *a lone desperate vein,* things thus almost relics, almost far away."

55. Lechte, *Julia Kristeva,* 6 and 111, comments on Kristeva's concept of poetry as a form of subversion.

56. "Thus my hands will die smelling of false lavender / and my plastic neck of moss will die, / thus my cologne of piano or burgundy rose will die. / . . . / thus my hair that before was a barbarous beard of Babilonians / decapitated by Semiramis. / Finally my grammatically elliptical breasts / or the wide hips that made me cry so much. / Finally my lips that became too ferocious."

57. Sherno, "Between Water and Fire," 538–39. See Lynda Nead, *The Female Nude: Art, Obscenity and Sexuality* (London: Routledge, 1992), 70, on the representation of the female body as a "composite" of fragments. Nead also discusses the psychoanalytic grounding of this issue in Melanie Klein's theories about the infant's love/hate relationship with the mother and the move toward separation and subjectivity (78–79).

58. Sherno, 535, refers to Mozart in her passage on drugs and poetry.

59. "The day has the gift of high silk, / petals untread by the foot of night, / coins in corollas, I said that. / But the cloud of magnolia was raised up to arrive at the drowned nucleus, / an electric wire and a triturated pistil of love, / coins deflowered by the terrible Templar check, / or rather the prudent virgin witches / and the leaden millenial nothing. // The day had the gift of high silk, / my love, my love, and for that reason still listen to me, / for that I repeat the boring poem for you."

60. "my love, my love, your voice I loved and that crosses / the purple pupils of the bridges, / and your smell, inhabited, blue, and all / that now I abandon and you abandon / —this fixed perfume—, / I don't know for what reason, / nor do I know in what clandestine manner . . ."

61. "Now, while I break / the idea of your face / and I continue ignoring / what winter, / what baroque artery of that December long ago, / what wakened order is yours / while I live alone, and I sleep, and I detest you."

62. See Sacks, *The English Elegy,* 16–17. Kristeva, *Black Sun,* 18–19, makes a distinction between *nonintegration* and *disintegration.*

63. "Five poems to abdicate, / so that they will be a terrestrial flash in my transit . . . / . . . / Five poems like five ciphered fruits / or like five candles (sails) for the crossing."

64. "while the wavering of my body endows me with the old dream and I have an altar adorned, / while my eyes suspend the aspersion of the briefest liquid, / abandon their lake air and the lightness of the concave tear in which cranes / and other wading birds drink with the foot of a ballerina"

65. For the connection between elegy and ritual, see Sacks, *The English Elegy,* 23–24. On the imagined death of the mourner, see ibid., 16–17.

66. "Five poems for the trek in the countryside of the cotton sheet, / a waste land is old lace, / initials embroidered three thousand days ago / and some stain of love."

67. See Ugalde, *Conversaciones*, 249.

68. Andreu specifically mentions Bernarda Alba when speaking of her school days (ibid., 251–52).

69. "The fourth is for my love. / My love, love, love, love, / I well know that my dream will not spit on you and that your neck will not be slashed / by the last edge of my dream, / that the wounding heart of my dream will not insult you, / because if I sleep I won't love you any longer."

70. "And for that reason I am going to assassinate / with the barbiturate virgin knife / the crowd of heroic madmen who intone for me the nightmare and the yawn, / my love, without coming to the window / old fires, fresh ashes, / wandering families of suns."

71. "I know well that I will gallop in black / because black is the color of dreams, / black the hands of intimacy, / and without spurs, and without bridles, / because the spurs are power, aberration, stars / of scissors and abyss."

72. See "Variations on Death" and "Abdications," in *A Short History of Decay*, trans. Richard Howard (New York: Viking Press, 1975) and "Encounters with Suicide," in *The New Gods*, trans. Richard Howard (New York: Quadrangle/New York Times Book Co., 1974).

73. See Oliver, *Reading Kristeva*, 56–57, on the definition of "the prototypical abject experience, . . . the experience of birth itself."

74. See Lechte, *Julia Kristeva*, 177–78 and Oliver, *Reading Kristeva*, 49–55 for Kristeva's abiding interest in the Virgin Mary.

75. "Death in the gravid time of faded doves, / in the lachrymatory that offers me the foul-smelling ink of May. / Agony of the course in my waist and in the waist of black sloops, / agony in an ogive of water, / May, May, oval poem, brilliance and a leap into the vacuum / a star of nerves that has no pity. // May with crazy masts, May the deer of fever, / May the snout of ocean bit me on the belt of temperature, / May of mauve fevers and the drunken deer of celestial globules / in the tremulous sun of the ventricle, / small lone deer that alone drank devout / all the golden thirst in the arteries."

76. "I wanted death for some eyes without direction, / for some eyes of a sacred compass, / for the young eyes that are raised / to read the wild star at ten o'clock. // Eyes, those eyes of mine, / or rather liturgical eyes widened by torches, / the eyes that carved Gothic initials / in the warrior soul of a child ten years old, / eyes of lilies frozen into needles: / stuck in the sea of taxidermists. // But let's talk of eyes that vanish / the lamps without you . . ."

77. See Patrick Fuery and Nick Mansfield, *Cultural Studies and the New Humanities: Concepts and Controversies* (Melbourne: Oxford University Press, 1997), 80–81.

78. See ibid., 88–89.

79. "let's speak while barefoot I step on this novice line with circles under the eyes, / while I write verses like votive algae, / like wires of tears, while I sense your night and dynasty."

80. "Love, I have broken the nickel of your unfortunate and perfect word. / Love, aching manes of archangel horses comb their hair with cologne of sadness, / because it is May, May the oval poem, May death east . . ."

81. "death in the gravid time of faded doves, / death for their delicate crossings, / and for the crazy storm like a crazy abbess, / death for the underwear that gave Baudelaire the shivers, / death for the nude green wine, / for the stone in heat and the celestial menstruation of May, / death for the drowned calligraphic anguish / in the lachrymatory that offers me the foul-smelling ink of May."

82. See Oliver, *Witnessing: Beyond Recognition*, and Weeks, *Constituting Feminist Subjects*.

83. "And thus, I will speak of your hands that go away and of the hands of the most beautiful burning, / small god with the nose of a deer, my brother, heroes with a confused soul, / girls of hypodermic gold that never think of dying."

84. "how sharp the pupil and the edge of the fingers burning death while an angel flies overhead and passes by / with its beak of silver and of gin, / lips of midday resolved in a bird over your hands that go away and my hands / and the hands of the little deer of savage Greek air, my brother, / and the hands without veins of the heroes, of the amnesiac madonnas."

85. Ovid, *Metamorphoses,* Book 3, 78–80.

86. "My wings of pain robbed by your hands, my love, my heart painted white, / my wings of pain with agonizing bottles and liquids that dissolve life, / and the lips that love you in me and in the convulsed one, / and the music in the thinnest trunks, highly arched trumpets, girl columns, how / sharp the do, / the highest look and the highest complaint, / death bird prince flying, / a bird is an immature angel."

87. These dates can be found in the index of *De una niña.*

88. "In the stables of the seas white terms sleep, / the spume that crackles, the drug made of lichen that moves one to forget: / in the stables of the sea discord, intrigue and the magpie reign, / a new version of water and of the low waves, / a new version of the water spilled from all the lands and the walls of the world."

89. "Between the walls of the sea the birch trees grow quiet, possessing the symbols of the robin, / the last voice of the forest, / the barbarous ivy that poisoned light deer like knives grows quiet, / the boreal oak, / jays asleep like celestial books, fires and owls of the marine gravel."

90. "In the stables of the sea, the sea drowns with its burning meter, / the flora, the ogives and the mouths of the sea, / a council of hickory trees suspended in green wounded, / and someone from very far away abdicating, walking from afar to die amid distant soaked branches: / someone from very far awaiting the flora, the ogives and the mouths of the sea."

91. "Amid November and hooves and corollas / the angel of the oars walks bloodied smelling of wood, / with the pupil of a bird the autumn gravitates, / the angel of the cables and the dark spars, the malign redoubts, lurks, / the angel of clay, womb of bramble bush, / pollen and wake of placenta that in autumn flowers in death."

92. "In the stables of the sea she drowns with her ardent metrics. / Between the walls of the sea the birch trees that possess the symbols of the warning blackbird grow quiet. / In the stables of the sea, as in death, / white terms sleep."

93. Lorenzo Silva, *La flaqueza del bolchevique* (Barcelona: Destino, 1997).

94. "Girl of delicately gilded followers, / girl obsession with the virgin stork / with tufts of damask feathers / that sprinkled death, / of the crazy stork with huge wings / of golden strychnine / that traveled leaving you a corporeal perfume, / a beautiful aroma of lilacs, and of golden, rough dreams."

95. "Girl of a nonexistent concert, / girl of cruel sonatinas and the malevolent books of Tom Wolfe, / or of the lace of witches for binding the wounds of the wounded stags, / of wounded deer appearing in the mysterious knolls, / in places like that. / Pluperfect girl, the girl we never were, / say it now, / say it now, you, now that it is so late, / pronounce the grim adagio scream, / pronounce for me the tear horse, / the purple saliva of the mare, / the shame of the colt that lay down at your feet / awakening the spume."

96. "Declaim with abandon the words of yesteryear, / the shadow of Juan Ramón: *Solitude, I am faithful to you.* / Disdainfully declaim the words of yesteryear, / but not that courtly stanza, / don't speak about queens white as lilies, / snows, and Juana burning, / and the interwoven melancholy / of the beloved Villon, / but the clear

verbs where one can drink the saddest liquid, / pitchers of sea and relief, now that it is so late, / raise your girlish voice and echo executrix and sing: / *Tell life that I remember her,* / *that I remember her.*"

97. "Definitively this small death gets lost in a nascent forest, / the shoot of the comet halted, / this which no one saves, / young volcano of bones and novice gust / made of bird and of eyelid and of a thinking wave / that no book leaves in its wake, / no book stewed with sunny Italian gold, / no book of lava / comes to seal for me."

98. "And thus death so often written / becomes radiant for me, / and I can speak / of desire and of the blind and golden lacquer on the lighthouses, / of the chimerical cadaver of the crew."

99. "And thus death / becomes the history of marine children / enclosed in flower-decorated urns, / or that mute little girl who hanged herself / with the boreal strings of the harp, / because she had a nuptial poison on her tongue."

100. "Definitively I stray while coining litters of rare epitaphs, / girl of the golden followers, / I will tell life that you remember it, / I will tell death that you remember it, / that you remember their lines conjuring your shade, / that you remember their habits and their single character, / their acid laurel, their profound bramble, their shameless error and their aggrieved hords, / . . . / I will tell life to remember you, / to remember me, / now, / when I raise myself with capillary cords and curls / up to the disaster of my head / up to the disaster of my 20 years, / up to the disaster, a light that breaks one's bones."

101. See Ugalde, *Conversaciones,* 254, concerning Andreu's relationship with her generation.

CHAPTER 4. THE FEMALE EUNUCH

1. See Cecile West-Settle, "Luisa Castro and the Poetics of Abandonment" and "Of *War and Peace,* Heroes and Outcasts: The Poetic World of Luisa Castro's *Odisea definitiva* and *De mi haré una estatua ecuestre.*" I am grateful to Prof. West-Settle for sharing these unpublished documents with me.

2. My translation of the following passage from Ugalde, *Conversaciones y poemas,* 292–93.

"SKU: . . . ¿[T]e parece que dentro del mundo literario existen todavía prejuicios sutiles en contra de la mujer?

"LC: Pienso que los hay y que no son sutiles. Los prejuicios son descarados y el más grande . . . viene del lado de los escritores y las escritoras aposentados ya en su lugar de escritor, tanto de hombres como de mujeres. Como todas las que estamos escribiendo somos demasiado jóvenes a sus ojos, siento que para ellos eso tenga algún tinte de amenaza. . . . O sea, veo que no son vistos con buenos ojos los escritos de la gente joven. Y si eres mujer, peor aún, porque tiene la coartada de echarte en cara que has tenido éxito porque eres tía, y si no esgrimen la excusa de que te han publicado porque eres mujer, dicen que has conseguido publicar gracias a tal y cual. Me parece sórdido y eso existe. Es una presión con la que he vivido el año pasado, con la que ha vivido alguna colega mía más, una presión que seguramente muchas han tenido antes de ponerse a publicar algo. Es una situación que no es normal en absoluto y baraja tanto el hecho de que eres mujer como el hecho de que eres joven. Son dos cosas que de alguna forma imponen a la gente que ya está en su trono."

3. Diana Fuss, "'Essentially Speaking': Luce Irigaray's Language of Essence," in *Revaluing French Feminisms: Critical Essays on Difference, Agency, and Culture,* ed.

Nancy Fraser and Sandra Lee Bartky (Bloomington: Indiana University Press, 1992), 94–112.

4. Ibid., 103.

5. Hélène Cixous, "Sorties: Out and Out: Attacks/Ways Out/Forays," in Hélène Cixous and Catherine Clément, *The Newly Born Woman*, trans. Betsy Wing, intro. Sandra M. Gilbert, (Minneapolis: University of Minnesota Press, 1986), 63–132.

6. Diana Fuss, *Essentially Speaking: Feminism, Nature and Difference* (New York: Routledge, 1989), 66.

7. Miriam Brody, *Manly Writing: Gender, Rhetoric, and the Rise of Composition* (Carbondale: Southern Illinois University, 1993), 20.

8. Lacan emphasizes the distinction between penis and phallus, but he is inconsistent in maintaining the separation between them. See Nancy Fraser, "Uses and Abuses of French Discourse Theories for Feminist Politics," in *Revaluing French Feminisms*, 192, n. 14.

9. Suzanne Guerlac, *The Impersonal Sublime: Hugo, Baudelaire, Lautréamont* (Stanford: Stanford University Press, 1990), 97–122.

10. Luisa Castro, *Los versos del eunuco*, 2nd ed. (Madrid: Hiperión, 1989). "I want to tell you the story of the Eunuch. // My father was dying as if willingly and we were sleeping with the bald light of sunset making esses, little drawings to be good. We slept hugging the wave as if with fear and little cloth and my father who knew nothing was dying as if with the pain of a transoceanic workman. // I want to tell you the story of the eunuch, which is sad. The eunuch who is sad normally inhabits the woods of withering leaves; the other, the one who is not sad and gets along well, is abundant and fibrous and makes his nest in the winter treetop."

11. "I had the august aspect of something bitter, I had some fervent shoes and I had a hole in my earlobe and I had an umbrella the color of iron that the neighbors liked a lot. // I had very big hands and from afar we smelled of potatoes."

12. See Kristeva, *Powers of Horror*, 102.

13. Arnold Rubin, "The Tattoo Renaissance," in *Marks of Civilization: Artistic Transformation of the Human Body*, ed. Arnold Rubin (Los Angeles: University of California, 1988), 255. Also see Elizabeth Grosz, *Volatile Bodies: Toward a Corporeal Feminism* (Bloomington: Indiana University Press, 1994), 139 and 141, concerning the difference between "civilized" and "primitive" body art.

14. "The story of the Eunuch is so that you will see: There were all sizes to choose from to try on; it was a time pregnant with eunuchs and alarm clocks. It was an incessant shuffling of empty bottles and daily divine immolations, stains on my name devoid of lanterns, stains on the foreheads of chauffeurs who brought impeccable visitors, stains on the pawned calendar of memory; it was a respectable time of eunuchs without flourishes, white shirts, and power, duty and deceits. // I, who deciphered the hands of the clock with my sweat, I knew the legs of the eunuch from afar, striped pants with a cadaver inside and a plastic phallus in his hand for love of honor and of devotion to the sky that looks at us."

15. See Susan Gubar, "'The Blank Page' and the Issues of Female Creativity," in *The New Feminist Criticism: Essays on Women, Literature and Theory*, ed. Elaine Showalter (New York: Pantheon Books, 1985), 292–313, esp. 294 and 301, where she comments on blots and equates the female body and bleeding with telling or singing.

16. "There were also the Great eunuchs with the best plastic phallus, colorful and a little more erect, but my voice did not reach their eardrums yet and I already knew their houses of theatre curtains and weasels with dogs at the door and behind strange occupations. // In their hands the billfold with magic and spare knives and a Sunday phallus just in case of an emergency so as not to improvise. // But there my soli-

tude like a whipped sail. But there my skin that would have to be sold for the tooth of an elephant. There the fear, the terror of the ignorant rabbits that walk hours and hours with their eyes open without expecting anyone to arrive with an engraving."

17. "The Great Eunuch bombards the world but does not know my hands in the mud. // The Great Eunuch sleeps peacefully and doesn't think about my heart that beneath the earth knows all the names of hate. // The Great Eunuch drinks in the summer parties with his wooden offspring around him / smiling / and doesn't see me among the people who frequent the swimming pools, on the long pathways that the city treads, in the high theatres that fill with families in the evenings. // But there my solitude making a place for some messenger without a face. / But there my solitude. / It vomits the meals, unmakes the beds / for a long time it hasn't dreamed of anything pleasant / and it foresees the end."

18. See Rafael Abella, *La vida cotidiana bajo el régimen de Franco* (Madrid: Temas de Hoy, 1996), 26, for remarks on Franco.

19. See Kristeva, *Revolution in Poetic Language,* trans. Margaret Waller (New York: Columbia University Press, 1984), 23–24 and 152–53, where she summarizes the difference between the semiotic and the symbolic.

20. Gubar, "'The Blank Page,'" 305, comments on the blank page as a subversive space.

21. Castro mentions having been influenced by Plath in Ugalde, *Conversaciones,* 290.

22. Buenaventura, *Las diosas blancas,* 235.

23. Hélène Cixous, "The Laugh of the Medusa," in *New French Feminisms: An Anthology,* ed. Elaine Marks and Isabelle de Courtrivron (New York: Schoken Books, 1980), 245–64, 254.

24. "While a herd of rosy butts spied on us from behind the red world of the afternoon, let's see what it has inside, he said, open (me) up, let's see, let's see, take a broken cup, let's see what it has inside. // So that I disposed myself to enter with glass and we saw white blood fall on the white floor of the bathroom and we knew the pained eyes of those who do not love. // That closed in a few days; the eunuch didn't come to see me for two weeks."

25. Cixous, "The Laugh of the Medusa," 251.

26. "At night when the eunuch / sleeps / dreaming about my third death and my heart / divides the gold of the blood / a little tremor inhabits my mouth."

27. "To pluck useful harps / then, / to temper the hot iron, to close / one's hands around some sex still shouting / I can only die, I can only die, / perhaps means / being close / to my solitude with a knot. / Perhaps it means to pour photographs on a zone / often foreign / beating a cemented sand."

28. "But when he sleeps or insists on the sale of / my goods, / on my face on a stick, / there only remains / to die, there only / remains to die, the painful part / is the morning with hymns and housemaids, / the painful part / is my body with scaffolding in waves like a edifice / of / air."

29. "At five o'clock it fills with women like / a park. // At six a wind that darkens runs through it like a / sword."

30. *Diccionario de los símbolos,* s. v. *espada, sable.*

31. "My body that the world touched with a start, / that grew with its bones straight / to the branches slash, that went along conquering / to reach slash the white roof of the houses slash in which it lived / dispossessed."

32. "My body / that burned and belonged / to the poor thin badly dressed boys of / letters slash and tuberculosis / who loved it with / pustules slash and fever so many slash times. / Here it is slash."

33. Compare this passage with a similar one in Andreu's *Una niña de provincias* in

the previous chapter. Lynda Nead, *The Female Nude: Art, Obscenity and Sexuality* (London: Routledge, 1992), 7, 72, and 82, addresses these issues.

34. "It is obvious that it hates with its name and / a number next in the line of pain / that asks slash one slash, two hours slash / how much time, how much time."

35. "At nine the moss inhabits / my heart and the game warden comes / and / a shopkeeper / comes with a box of matches to set fire to / the sunset in my ear and to burn the blood / of nine o'clock / of my body / like / plastic."

36. See John Briggs, *Fractals: The Patterns of Chaos* (New York: Simon and Schuster, 1992), for a discussion of fractals in chaos theory.

37. See Juliet Mitchell, "Introduction—I," in Jacques Lacan, *Feminine Sexuality: Jacques Lacan and the école freudienne,* ed. Juliet Mitchell and Jacqueline Rose, trans. Jacqueline Rose (New York: W. W. Norton and Company, 1982), 5. Also see Paul Verhaeghe, "Causation and Destitution of a Pre-ontological Non-entity: On the Lacanian Subject," in *Key Concepts of Lacanian Psychoanalysis,* ed. Dany Nobus (New York: Other Press, 1998), 164–89.

38. "At ten mistaken suitcases arrive / and we dress it with hate in lace / and disjunctions arise on its skin through the lining / but there is no salt, or future, or / audience. // The recently arrived observe how I disrobe senselessly. / It is a punishment. I operate on my body."

39. "A eunuch writes me verses, verses / of death, verses of stick, / verses of almond tree for judges and arenas. // A eunuch writes me verses turned green / . . . // A eunuch writes me verses and I / love him . . . // A eunuch fatigues me since forever with his verses. // I love him like a proviso of stone / that has bloomed, like a tax of blood, like a scar / that I don't possess."

40. "Verses like burning up in beds, sinking / the spur and give me / the dark trinity of your soul, / the strange drawer of your body, and high / parabola of yourself."

41. "And / I / who live on the other side of the fire / absent and silenced / and singing sad things, I / so far from the blacksmith and without a soul / and a bitter body to keep quiet / I will have to say well, that's it, my love, / that's it."

42. "And to burn myself in beds, to sink / the spur and give him / the dark trinity of my soul, / the strange drawer of my body, / my highest parabola, / these things that I know / and that I keep quiet."

43. Tina Chanter, *Ethics of Eros: Irigaray's Rewriting of the Philosophers* (New York: Routledge, 1995), 215.

44. Ibid., 183.

45. Ibid., 192.

46. "He suckles me with simplicity. He pulls back his tongue, / he smells my supplies and he goes away. / Dizziness and childbirth."

47. "The children of the snow do not understand it, / they do not understand this place that we leave forever / each day, never to return, each day. / We cede to the place all its site, we reduce / each time even time, we think that it is / better thus, that it never belongs to us, we leave it / to grow, to grow old, to fart in freedom / and we go along knowing that one cannot return."

48. See Mikhail Bakhtin, *Rabelais and His World,* trans. Hélène Iswolsky (Bloomington: Indiana University Press, 1984), 317, for a definition of the "grotesque body" (an apt description of the eunuch and of the castrated or mutilated body) and "the mighty thrust downward into the bowels of the earth, into the depths of the human body," 368–436.

49. *What Does a Woman Want? Reading and Sexual Difference* (Baltimore: Johns Hopkins University Press, 1993), 65.

50. Gloria Fuertes also uses this comparison in "Carta explicatoria de Gloria," in

Obras incompletas, 293. Along with the images of the penis and breast as pens, Bakhtin, *Rabelais and His World,* 319, implies a connection between secretions of the body, and speaking and writing. Also see Dominique Laporte, *History of Shit,* trans. Nadia Benabid and Rodolphe el-Khoury (Cambridge, MA: MIT Press, 2000) for the connection between excrement and the emergence of subjectivity. For a discussion of the Freudian concept, see Julia Kristeva's chapter "Freud's Notion of Expulsion: Rejection" in *Revolution in Poetic Language,* trans. and intro. Leon S. Roudiez (New York: Columbia University Press, 1984), 147–64. Also see Sherno's discussion of the carnivalesque in Fuertes's poetry in *Weaving the World,* 197–222.

51. Recall Lacan's definition of desire as Elizabeth Grosz explains in *Jacques Lacan: A Feminist Introduction* (New York: Routledge, 1990), 64.

52. See Ronald Bogue, *Deleuze and Guattari* (London: Routledge, 1989), 107.

53. "Since we founded the city / in the schools / phalloi / of desk and sermon / ill-loved / amid the all-too-well-known fauna and flora of the funerary working / hands."

54. "I am the finacee of high heels / and ships in her voice. / Neither the muscle recognizes me / nor am I its only child, / I am going to eat with the old man / and I leave my statue in the bathroom and / in the schools / a book about generals and autumns with my testicles / within / miserable identical twins."

55. "I am the sickly consul of the first time. / I recount with intrigue. I dishevel my hair slowly. // Let's see, come very quietly. I brush off the uniform of misfortune / and we get along terribly, / I foresee her breviary of trips, I imagine her literary / botchings / and I disappear profoundly // I go away without charging a cent."

56. "Drop by drop we go along making this bad love / disordered and / lethal. / His eyes don't look at me / in a way / lamentable."

57. "IF YOU COME NEAR MY MOUTH YOU CAN SEE PSALMS / GROW ON ME / IF YOU COME NEAR MY ASS / YOU CAN SEE TAILORS IMPALED / RAFFLES GREETINGS EXPECTATION / AND YOU SAY TO PAIN / WHAT BAD CHOREOGRAPHY."

58. Jean-Luc Herring, *Rear View: A Brief But Elegant History of the Bottom,* qtd. in Erin J. Aubry, "The Butt: Its Politics, Its Profanity, Its Power," in *Adiós Barbie: Young Women Write About Body Image and Identity,* ed. Ophira Edut (Seattle: Seal Press, 1998), 22.

59. "I AM A PEOPLE IN T-SHIRTS WORKING / BUT THERE ARE NO WIVES (HANDCUFFS) WITHIN // I AM A NEIGHBOR OF SIXTY YEARS WHO CRIES. / THIS IS MY HOUSE."

60. "And thus it was that each day he would arrive more yellow, with yellow cow's breath and his eyes hanging out on a yellow background. And thus it was that each time he would arrive more dead, without words to speak, unconnected verses beating against my heart. // But no one wanted to believe me."

61. "They had arrived from all the countries to see him and to interrogate me and curse me and bury me at his side with tears and effort. Thus they punish the woman who slices off a phallus in this glorious neck of the woods."

62. "Forgetfulness is a natural decency. // And I wait seated for the end. I know the death that awaits me. It is appropriate to wash one's hands."

63. Tibullus, *Erotic Elegies,* 2–3.

64. See Deborah Cameron, *Feminism and Linguistic Theory,* 2nd ed. (New York: St. Martin's Press, 1992), 128–86, on women's relationship with symbolic language.

65. "I want to know how one falls into the flames, / how one falls to the high and double / bonfire of the / best pain of all pain. I am / an angel lacking in recourses, don't look at me, I am / made slowly / with the poor heart of an angel's poverty, / with the indigence in the center / attentive / like a noble messenger of the error / to the pain / of mammals."

66. "And the women whom I count in my head, that I recount, / that I forget, / their blue dresses that I will have to hang up, their / aching hands, true virgens. / The women whom my mother opened to me so that I would not begin / all the verses with a noun. So that I not begin / all the verses with their glass of noun. / All the women that I remember / seeking a hard bowl where one can shelter the womb. / All the women that my mother opened to me."

67. "My hate awaits hate with the smell of a tablecloth / and spilled vinegar, that hate that one pisses on the heel of the librarians / until they grow lilies / and the earth muddies the taxis watching / a school."

68. "My body is sweeter; / here it is with medals and / hips, with the verb of tabacco and fallen leaves. / It is sweeter / thus / with tiny traces of a live bird's teeth / in my sex like old clothes that devour / the salt, on the dwarf breasts like proofs, held back / and on my waist that burned / with dead people, barricades, bottles, / armor / and a useless almanac dated the eighth / and the children of the valley, the dogs and the reeds."

CHAPTER 5. THE MIRROR AS MALE GAZE

1. See the interview with Sharon Keefe Ugalde, "Entrevista con Almudena Guzmán," in *Literatura Femenina Contemporánea de España: 7 Simposio Internacional*, ed. Juana Arancibia, Adrienne Mandel, Yolanda Rosas (Northridge: California State University, 1991), 219–30; and personal communication.

2. Prior to *Usted* (Madrid: Hiperión, 1986), Guzmán had published two books of poetry: *Poemas de Lida Sal* (Madrid: Libros Dante, 1981) and *La playa del olvido* (Gijón: Altair, 1984). Following the publication of *Usted* in 1986, she also published *El libro de Tamar* (Melilla: Rusadir, 1989). She was silent until the publication of *Calendario* (Madrid: Hiperión, 1998), a hiatus of nearly ten years.

3. Luis M. Marigómez, "La seducción lúcida: lectura de poemas de Almudena Guzmán," *La Ciudad* (5 April 1988): 15.

4. Buenaventura, *Las diosas blancas*, 223–24.

5. See Genette, *Paratexts*, 117–36, for a discussion of the dedication.

6. Adam Phillips, *The Beast in the Nursery: On Curiosity and Other Appetites* (New York: Pantheon Books, 1998), 126.

7. Almudena Guzmán, *Usted*, 2nd ed. (Madrid: Hiperión, 1986). "You, sir, slip in under my scarf / from a very white aura that makes my lips reverberate. // I don't move, / I don't smoke—maybe that wrinkle in the snow will bother your silence—; / and only when you go away do I realize / that I have been holding my urge to piss the whole time."

8. Martín Gaite associates the cigarette with the image of the vamp in Hollywood films (*Usos amorosos*, 134–35). Abella notes that when rationing of tobacco began in 1940, ration cards were issued only to males, not to females (*La vida cotidiana bajo el régimen de Franco*, 61).

9. See Kristeva, *Powers of Horror*, 8, where she defines the "stray."

10. "You, sir, escape from me in the hallways like a discus thrower slathered with oil. // But everything you say is like a gloved hand on my stockings. / (Naked, I rub your voice against the hips of the sheet / so as not to fall asleep so sad.)"

11. "Today you are wearing a tie with sparrowhawks in my favorite shade of blue. / We have lunch together thanks to poetry / and, over coffee, / I cannot avoid look-

ing at you over the edge of the cup, / and later smiling from my bangs on down like the bad girl / that / I was: / We are exactly alike. And neither of us knows the existence of mirrors."

12. See Brownmiller, *Femininity,* 97, and Doane, *Femmes Fatales,* 48–49 and 54–55, for a discussion of the veil, which is similar in effect to fans, hat brims, and other ways of "blocking off" parts of the face.

13. "We lunch together again. / This man each day more good-looking and the circles under your eyes get deeper. / Who cares. / Who cares about the little time you have to enamour him, / who cares about the cold soup / —you can't allow the luxury of losing him from sight a single moment, Almudena—, / just when you are about to cite *I am always sad* / he speaks first and caressing your eyes says that your joy is enchanting."

14. Cf. Atencia's poem, "Con la mesa dispuesta" from *Marta & María,* where the speaker has to leave her family at table to respond to the urge to write.

15. This quote derives from a poem titled "Farewell" in Pablo Neruda's *Crepusculario* (Barcelona: Seix Barral, 1977), 29–31.

16. La Belle, *Herself Beheld,* 27, 40, 88, and 143, remarks about how the male gaze serves as a mirror and extends to society.

17. "You have gone. But it won't do to dramatize things. // When I go out, / I still have many happy hors d'oeuvres in my heels, / and my fishnet stockings manage to reduce the waist of sadness / if your absence makes me silent in a hangover of frost."

18. "Or rather, I'm not so badly off. / Because I will be able to be from time to time an eclipse. But / never / an eclipse without the blood of light."

19. Kristeva, *Black Sun: Depression and Melancholia,* trans. Leon S. Roudiez (New York: Columbia University Press, 1989). Her definition of the term *black sun* encompasses the concept of the eclipse (151) and associates the black sun with the maternal Thing (13). Moreover, she addresses the feeling of emptiness on p. 243.

20. Ibid., 82.

21. Ibid., 81–82. Rather than menstruation, Kristeva views this type of image as a manifestation of castration.

22. "A woman of rum and black fingernail polish, / bangs and a cosmopolitan vagina, / spreads her legs for me behind the window of the bordello. // It is fog."

23. Brownmiller, *Femininity,* 185, makes a comparison between spiked high heels and fingernails.

24. Abella, *La vida cotidiana bajo el regimen de Franco,* 75, uses this term in his discussion of brothels during the Franco era.

25. La Belle, *Herself Beheld,* 5, mentions the possibility of using a window as mirror in her listing of possible reflectors.

26. "Secretly, / opening dead bolts, / it has arrived in my room, / a translucid panther with its diamond fur / that will bite the nape of my neck when I least expect it. // It is desire."

27. "Censer of thorns / and vomit. // Last night's rum, / Alka Seltzer / —Isn't anybody going to make me an herbal tea?—, / seaport roaches unaffected by bug spray. // Acid mist of a dune uprooted in a mirror."

28. La Belle, *Herself Beheld,* ch. 5, esp. 112, comments on this type of situation.

29. "I only preserve / —thanks to the rearview mirror— / a vague lyrical refraction / of two hands, / that, squeezed before a challenge of unequal touches, / became lovers."

30. ". . . and I wonder if it wouldn't be better / —there's still time— / to flee from his eyes like someone who flees from a traffic jam, / because you, sir, drive me crazy."

31. "Exquisite quarrel that of my mouth and his / because of that finger, a bee that sipped amid murmurs and sweet-toothed distentions, / the successive flowerings of my nocturnal anemone."

32. Clara Janés, *Creciente fértil* [Fertile crescent] (Madrid: Hiperión, 1989), 24, uses the same image, but she reverses the roles of male and female. Both authors thus subvert typical masculine and feminine roles and the privileging of the phallus.

33. "With each contraction of the mirror / my skin kept becoming more beautiful / while I fulfilled / —all veiled eyes— / that indecent promise of ours at twelve o'clock."

34. This is precisely the image Weeks, *Constituting Feminist Subjects,* 140, uses when talking about opening a space for the modification of female subjectivity through ironic self-laughter. Weeks stresses that ironic self-laughter is not the only means of accomplishing this change.

35. "Sir, / the Sunday rain / is an immense bathtub / that submerges me in slow motion / in the frothy curtain of your Saturday curls."

36. "I am a bunch of grapes / and I resist as much as I can / the growing tide of your mouth / spurring me toward the sun. // Until I explode."

37. "Sir, / if you know / that I now am jealous / because of what you have said to me, / at least have the courtesy of not calling it to my attention during supper. // (Never in my life have I twirled spaghetti with such hate.)"

38. My thinking throughout this chapter has been shaped by Joanna Russ's delineation of the different ways masculinist readers suppress women's writing. Note especially her categories of "Pollution of Agency" ("She wrote it, but she shouldn't have"), the "Double Standard of Content" ("She wrote it, but look what she wrote about"), and "False Categorizing" ("She wrote it, but 'she' isn't really an artist and 'it' isn't really serious, of the right genre—i.e., really art"). See *How to Suppress Women's Writing* (Austin: University of Texas Press, 1983).

39. Again, see Buenaventura, *Las diosas blancas,* 223–24, for comments on Guzmán's poetry.

40. "—Do you have an extra pen? / —Here, and let's see if you can stop asking me for things, / because with you at one's side nobody can take a single note, Mari Carmen."

41. "Ah, / I forgot to tell you / that the cold was the dominant note of the day / and that night, in spite of everything, we slept together. // Back to back."

42. "Before, // there was never the necessary silence between one embrace and another / to notice the blink of this guillotine / that today, / grazing by surprise the nape of my neck with its hands of bleach / has made my eyes bitter. // I myself can't hear myself when I scream. / I would like to flee. But it's already too late: / the sheets have become muddy water mixed with glue. // And in a little while, / as something horrible follows behind me / and you continue sleeping, / I die of laughter before the portrait of Leonardo that I have before my cadaver."

43. Kristeva, *Black Sun,* 254, posits the ambiguity of Mona Lisa's smile.

44. "Who is this shadow / that lands cleanly on my body / like a falcon. // Its talons hold me by the wrists and prevent my fleeing. // Its misty breath goes slowly slicing through / the terse and now bright red sheer curtains of my belly."

45. "And writing time and again that life is the most painful / foreshortening / that even Mantegna could have painted in his nightmares."

46. "Because I am terribly bored / while my fingernails dry, / I look askance at the calendar: / today is the twenty-second / and this Sunday from its puddle of red ducks / piques my memory: / I think that you have a birthday, / but I don't know that for sure, / nor will I call you, in truth, / more than anything because of my nails."

47. Phillips, "Just Rage," 123.

48. "What torment, / before I used to have them all bitten and full of hangnails, / in spite of the strategies of "tata" Carmen / so that I would abandon that, my first vice: / candy, slaps on the hands, sweet talk, scowls, / making me feel ashamed in front of my aunts . . . // Although my nails may dry soon, / I still won't be able to call / because I'm supposed to meet someone at nine, / and it's already eight thirty / and I still haven't even shaped this tangle of hair that I have. . . ."

49. "It's curious, / at times I wonder on what tree of the park I hung my childhood. / The only thing I have left of it is this sweet hair of mine, / and the memory of those water pistols that I would steal from the boys / with a face of absolute innocence."

50. "At that time I was going out with David / —and how jealous that Fatima with her big tits was / each time she saw us abandon some dark corner, / with our hands sticky with so much timid pipe!— / a nice little friend who always spent his pay inviting me to the movies on Sundays . . . / (The other day, as a matter of fact, I ran into him / and we both went crazy.)"

51. "Piedad is now calling on the intercom at the front door, / but if I open it for her now I will ruin my nails; / let her wait, / after all, / that way we can avoid her anger / at seeing me still in my pajamas / and without knowing which miniskirt to wear to the party."

52. Phillips, "Just Rage," 125, 132.

CHAPTER 6. THE ABANDONED WOMAN

1. Lawrence Lipking, *Abandoned Women and Poetic Tradition* (Chicago: University of Chicago Press, 1968).

2. Ibid., "Series Editor's Foreword," viii.

3. Ibid., viii–ix.

4. Ibid., xvii.

5. Ibid., xxvi.

6. For an overview of intertextuality, see Graham Allen, *Intertextuality* (London: Routledge, 2000).

7. Margarita Merino, *Baladas del abismo* (Madrid: Endymión, 1989). "I see you, Emma, with your wild eyes, / you are so beautiful with your complexion transfigured / by all the revelation of your sadness. // Ay, Emma, so beautiful, subtle and refined, / fighting to flee from the tenacious monotony / your ambition did not know how to conform to the vulgar / and you dreamed of flying, anxiously abandoning / a hick city that has always scrutinized / enviously, rapaciously, the beauty that renews you / each day, the brilliant pallor that dawn / gives you when you approach the window / melancholic for the absence of full passion / and tenderness that will snatch from you / the renewed and miserly day that dawns."

8. "Emma, you who wanted to leave behind the intranscendence / of this yokel, narrow town that oppresses you / to delight in a frivolous life, as desired women / know how to do, who bring together a graceful skeleton / and an inquisitive head and learn per force / the exercise of thinking freely while alone, / to use—after deceits and betrayals— / their sharp intelligence delayed for so long a time / thanks to the turgid aspect of a body perceived / beneath the folds of taffeta and cotton. // Emma, you who as a child enjoyed the cultivated / disciplines that produce an indelible pleasure / in aesthetics: rotund music that satiates / the disposed mind, the

sublime mysticism / that raises one to the devouring of other more earthy / passions, the tenuous message of books / that continue to be irrepeatible with the passing of years, / Emma, dear, who had your sensitivity / awakened to the clear perception of things."

9. "They said of you, Emma, that you possessed that feminine / something that can inspire all the poems / that they write, that you are 'she' in all / the novels: a perturbing presence eternally / inspiring feelings of possession / that later enchain you."

10. "You stopped to contemplate that demolishing / image in the mirror, teaching your bones / motives for seduction and you didn't know how / to attend to the mute call of authenticity. / You believed that you would be a perennial youth, / an unthroned goddess, the mortal incarnation / of tremulous beauty. You thought capriciously / that the moon existed to illuminate / your bedroom, that you could make yourself a brooch / with the stars."

11. La Belle, *Herself Beheld,* 175.

12. "Choosing your clothing with care, sprucely, / surrounding yourself with objects that are now useless, / you softened the tearing lack of your intuited absence / that material things can never banish. Amassing household goods, / knickknacks that would take so much room away from you."

13. See poem 97 from *Campos de Castilla* in Antonio Machado, *Poesías completas* (11th ed., Madrid: Espasa-Calpe, 1966), 77.

14. "the clumsy lovers / who successively possessed you made you skillful / at the cost of taking away your tender desire for enjoyment / that used to move you at will."

15. "No one told you that the suitor who attains / the prey that motivates him then becomes disdainful / and no longer spoils that which was the delirious object / of his fantasies, that all the gifts / with which your love regaled him (for your zeal / for him would have a drop of the maternal mixed in it) / he will receive suddenly as if he were the owner, / a tyrant by right. Other vain little women / will necessarily seem to him the height of wisdom, / models of good taste and manners, suddenly / singular mistresses. Don't be surprised, Emma, / for overcoming timidity and becoming an expert / takes away agency from the one who in these battles / aspires for the first fragrance of the rose."

16. "The men that you chose don't enjoy the ember, / just like you they are ecstatic in the flames / and no powerful fire is about to start / there where the sparks are waning, / there where the sonorous crackling / of the ashy remains of what was wood is less frequent / and that the voracious combustion has insanely consumed / without largesse, leaving only a scant ash / of its recent glow in the hearth, a funereal dust / that a sigh raises at its convenience."

17. "Love is as huge and luminous as a cosmos, / it discovers the astral vertigo suddenly, / the halucinatory magma that generated the beginning."

18. "The enchantment of a perfect oval, / the eyes half-closed in sidereal blinks / of a woman wounded by the trembling of love, / the splendor of a body that offers itself / make a man who is not extraordinary / —unaware of other rhythms—look away / from the rip in your heart pierced by anguish, / from the self-centered presentiment that assaults you / on the ungraspable magic of happiness / and the ephemeral nature of the world unaware of its spinning / to the feelings that are bound to know the loneliness / of the cold, the silence, that dwell in tombs: / the humid looms of worms, kingdoms of shadow / where the placid, comforting sun / will never place his warm, generous fingers."

19. *Metamorphoses,* trans. and intro. Mary M. Innes (London: Penguin Books, 1955), 100.

20. "Ay Emma, nothing has respected your disdained / search for luxury, for harmony, and for pleasure / and you have lost everything. Rapaciously they stole from you / your esteem, the capacity to tolerate haughtily / the sooty life that afflicts you, / and in the end you never managed to find your soulmate / who would know how to attune the delicate instrument / that your estranged soul would have made resonate / vibrating and moved returning to purity."

21. "I cry impotently when I see you, feverish, eat / rat poison, and a horrible death / seduces you bursting your viscera for such a long time, / the obscene talons of vengeful guilt / dig into your stiff throat, death rattles / provoke a blackish vomit sealing / the mouth that moaned in the moments of climax / and that learned to tell lies in infidelity. / The pain of abandonment is now filling you / the arsenic runs throughout your corrupt organism, / the poison penetrates denied crevices: / the secret pathways that unbridled love / knew not how to concede to happiness."

22. Lipking, *Abandoned Women,* 69.

23. "The lady sighed looking at the helpless rose / that, snatched by insomnia from the dew, / was spilling itself on the heat of her thighs / in desolate petals, in shadowy leaves / like the dried blood and the nectar of mature / blackberries, on her statue-like knees / of changed flesh that grows quiet."

24. "She tried, the taciturn lady, / to distract her melancholy with the thread of remembrance / of distant springtimes, when in her youth / she had not recognized, bitter, / the acrid taste of events on her tongue: / 'Where now does happiness hover / as noisy as a waterfall . . .' / 'Where will the clamorous fountains spill forth / with which the fresh joy of life splashes.'"

25. "It is time to concede freedom / to the falcons that equally enjoyed / rides while perched on the fist of my lord."

26. "When the centuries offer us / the brutal spectacle of demolitions, / inferring the decadence of the stones, / the sanguinary impulse of the barbarians / and the night-roving hordes; / when the denuded skeleton of a castle / conquered in the assault testifies / to the helplessness of the artistry / in the flames, / the rigor of the befallen fire, / the sadness that inherits the footsteps / that measured the agile escarpments / masters of the subdued space; when the past bears testimony / to the madness, to the illiterate hunger, / to intolerance, misery, / to the sinister spirit, the foolishness / that wars awaken; / we will know that the parlors / will never remain unharmed / by the touch of the sentence with which the tolling / of the four horsemen of hopelessness / condemn the slave and the pariahs."

27. *Powers of Horror,* 13.

28. Lipking, *Abandoned Women,* 12.

29. "Nearly eleven years have elapsed / since you offered me your gaunt face, / eleven years since your lips were sealed / by the invincible rigor of the last silence. / So much time has passed without you in my life, / so much time that your house has been / without your care, / that the blond coins in the corner, / the diminished elephants that called / to luck with their trunks raised, / the little banners of tin, / the stone tortoise, / the little spare parts for everything, / the pens and markers, / the little boxes of cardboard that housed ink bottles, / have disappeared from your dresser."

30. "Now you never again fall asleep / in the wingback chair that sheltered your nap, / nor will your study be filled to bursting / with beautiful editions of beloved books, / no one will again save bearded paper / in the drawer, and I will not find / anything inspiring when I shuffle through the spaces / that your surprising things occupied, / your things that offered the exact image / of a kindly and delicate man / while you were alive."

31. "I have not seen repeated that placid parade / of pajamas and berets and leather slippers / in which you gave refuge to your nostalgia, / oh prince dressed like a pauper / who wore a toga and morning coat / from time to time / to appease the spirits of the closed circle."

32. "Now no one gets excited about legendary dreams / of justice and songs, culture and community, / for the others—just like you—have gone to sleep, / the old comrades of mythologies and ethics, / the same ones who with you shared the spectacle / of so many birds of youth mixed up in the mire."

33. "And I, I am no longer the one you knew, / that legitimate heiress, / that rebellious princess of a miraculous kingdom, / for I have been changed into discouragement / by the umpteenth disaster: I too / —my scaffolding thrown down into the pits / of slime and phosphorus in which are sunken / the clear towers and the eagles—I have been buried."

34. "I groan from this sticky, repugnant bed / before the embalmed crowd of mummies, / but to my pathetic sighs respond / only a homogeneous beat of guffaws / since you went away in the black tunic / and you left me in the paths of the unsupportive, / oh my father."

35. See Sacks, *The English Elegy*, ch. 3.

36. "The days of my infancy have crossed The Threshold. / They are now on the other side of the mirror. On the other side. / I cannot find the spring that will make the hinges / of that livid door squeak anew / where the luminous gifts that belonged to me / are snatched from me forever. / Nor can I make them come back / to the bitter shore where death lies in wait / drying my pores at each nightfall."

37. See Lacan, "The Mirror-Stage," in *Ecrits*, 1–7.

38. "Ay the stiffness crackling my mouth, / the bitterness of the saliva shipwrecked on my tongue, / my violet lips gone thin . . . / Ay my skin turning into a wasteland, / into leather insensitive to that warm touch, / now all of me the booty of the dusk: "Rosebud . . ." / (Rosebud burning insignificant amid useless objects.)"

39. "Look at the pale image the icy moons / in which I am reflected return to me / lethargic because of abandonment pondering my memories, / licking the wounds with which love crowns / those who do not consent to the liturgy of the meek: / the preamble, chalice of whipping and branding. / Now I am the Queen of the Cold Ones. Little by little, / my sparkling combustion has turned to frost. / The days of the past have dissolved into smoke / erasing familiar faces."

40. See Gaston Bachelard, *The Poetics of Space*, trans. Maria Jolas (Boston: Beacon Press, 1969), esp. ch. 2, "House and Universe."

41. "I seek the complicity of statues / in their orbits blind because of contemplating / The Miniscule Nothingness that presides / over the hope of one who listens forewarned / to the formula that will inspire the torrential spark / of life, the blow that surprises / the vertiginous light."

42. See Carl Dennis, *Poetry as Persuasion* (Athens: University of Georgia Press, 2001), 46.

43. "Before my mother's mirror, / I would dress up with delicate veils of light / that the comets offered me from their tails. / Melancholic asteroids exchanged with me / their radiant necklace with an indefinable aura / for marbles of glass and beads of colors. / A constant risk, a new surprise, / fed my daily impatient awaiting, / and thus the furniture, the enormous armchairs, / the spaces between the drapes and the wall, / the dark angles of the long hallway, / took the place of the yard I didn't have, / became virgin jungle in my distillery."

44. See Weeks, *Constituting Feminist Subjects*, 139–40.

45. See Sandra M. Gilbert and Susan Gubar, *The Madwoman in the Attic: The Woman Writer and the Nineteenth-Century Literary Imagination* (New Haven, CT: Yale University Press, 1979), 339–43.

46. "don't be surprised either that they should feel pity / for so many outrages that history has perpetrated / without shame on the singular lineage of little girls: / of little girls who—like I was then—aspire only / to enjoy their own autonomy in peace, / to dream softening the atrocious burrs / of life, to read, to think, to sing, to dance, / to surrender themselves to drawing an eccentric and celestial / world where everything tender has a place, / to deal with the wise animal species / that teach so much about necessary things."

47. Martín Gaite criticizes the Francoist policy of segregated education in *Usos amorosos*, 91–92. Abella also mentions this situation briefly in *La vida cotidiana*, 106.

48. "They accused me of all the vices united: / I was disorganized, curious, I didn't leave / a puppet with its head, I beseiged everything, / —and they adorned me with pretty sayings about Atilla, / his horse, his huns, the barbarians, the hordes, / the devil, hell, a hurricane, / that served to illustrate the rosary / of the harangue with examples—."

49. "When I would swear to them that I did nothing of all that, / when I rebelled a second against the punishments / and I tattled loudly the true name / of their authors, denouncing them, / revealing impiously their rites and their household gods, / they—the others, the upright ones, the adults— / called me the worst of insults, / I was a liar, so much imbibing / of crazy fantasies was robbing me / of my precarious sanity with no remedy."

50. Gilbert and Gubar, *Madwoman in the Attic*, 338–39.

51. "But I learned to squelch the name / of my comrades and my beasts, / silencing their deeds forever."

52. See La Belle, *Herself Beheld*, 7.

53. "Barely noticing it, I reached precociously / the time of growth. / How rare I felt, what long legs / I had, in heels. Hearing the praises, / stimulus now of sudden silences / at my passage, I daubed my lips / with red, and like all the other girls / I would smile stupidly as I walked along. / Like all the other girls, I would cry remorsefully / and I would walk away from the shop windows on seeing myself / reflected in the glass, twisting / my ankles while running down Ordoño Street."

54. See Brownmiller, *Femininity*, 83–84.

55. "Suddenly, the Reign of the Evil One settled / around there. They took over the sidewalks, a troop / of Spiritual Exercises, Mortal / Sin. The Forbidden. Then the pointed / breasts and the selfless vigilance of Mom / planted themselves in a fence and a belt, / and I saw the hours of dusk consume themselves / from the verandah, numbing me, / divining the prodigious labyrinths / through which—material of the thighs—we spring / from the elemental egg / to this dissimulated hemisphere of the chaste."

56. See Gilbert and Gubar, *Madwoman in the Attic*, 402–3.

57. "I can't decide if it has been worth the pain / the trick of learning at the cost / of going along looking at the real without seeing / and I distractedly dust off the baggage I had. / There is a circling of moths in the weaving, / my companions fall ashily like lead / in the attic of my out-of-tune conscience / for those textures that will never return."

58. "Diana pursues a ray of tenuous light / of The Dark Side of the Moon, / and from her tunic there escapes a snowy breast / with a nipple of silver spilling a drop / of milk that falls into her quiver. / No longer will I ride frenetically through the

night / beside the Amazons, my madness barks, / my pulse accelerates, a captive of nostalgia, / I listen to the clean hooves of the horses / profaning the silence of the cemeteries / and the domes go deaf from the echo."

59. *The Concise Dictionary of Classical Mythology* (London: Basil Blackwell, 1990), s.v. Artemis.

60. See Weeks, *Constituting Feminist Subjects,* 145–50, on the concept of self-valorization as affirmation to construct a feminist standpoint.

61. *Women in Scripture,* Carol Meyers, gen. ed., et al. (Boston: Houghton Mifflin Company, 2000), 179.

62. "I smell of wet earth, the beasts sweat / urged on by the spur, I shoot a precise / dart at a Chimera, and it shouts, / it shouts with an atrocious lament, / when it falls dead on the grass."

63. "I will seal the revived pact with my blood: / Perhaps the gods without power that encouraged me / will be able to return if I invoke them, ignoring the rules / that the conquering legion of The Gray Ones imposed. / Fearless, I will scratch on the paper the purple liquid / inundating each letter with all the helplessness / that afflicts me aging the dreams that I feigned / were immortal."

64. "My sweet comrades will accompany me / impassioned, warriors will attack / to yoke this terrible calm that has tried / to become the lady of the narrow hallway of my house."

CHAPTER 7. DOUBLE-VOICING, DOUBLE-VISION

1. Carmen Martín Gaite, *Usos amorosos,* 45, my translation.

2. See "Women and Madness: The Critical Phallacy (Balzac, 'Adieu')," in Shoshana Felman, *What Does a Woman Want?: Reading and Sexual Difference* (Baltimore: Johns Hopkins University Press, 1993), 20–40, esp. 21–22.

3. This phrase derives from Jessica Benjamin, *The Bonds of Love: Psychoanalysis, Feminism, and the Problem of Domination* (New York: Pantheon Books, 1988).

4. Amalia Bautista, *Cárcel de amor* (Sevilla: Renacimiento, 1988). "I am not that type of woman / incapable of love and tenderness. / I know what courage is and what blood is, / although I may hate sacrifices and may be disgusted by / the vanity that is born of violence. / I want to be the wife of a mercenary, / of a poet or of a martyr, whatever. / I know how to look into the eyes of men. / I know who deserves my tenderness."

5. Sigrid Weigel, "Double Focus: On the History of Women's Writing," in *Feminist Aesthetics,* ed. Gisela Ecker, trans. Harriet Anderson (Boston: Beacon Press, 1985), 61.

6. "He tells me that I'm not in love, / and at times I feel like swearing to him / that I would forget the sun in his arms, / or that I would like to kiss his lips / forever, or that time doesn't matter to me / when he looks at me darkly, fixedly and crazily. / But what good would all that do? / I know that he would never believe a word of it."

7. See Rosalía de Castro's poem discussed in the Introduction.

8. "The first day that I went out with you / you said your job was strange. / Nothing more. However, I felt / that my skin was tearing, being shredded / each time your hands caressed me / and that your eyes were like steel / that made my eyes ache. / From then on, it was always the same: / you were proud of your art, / more subtle and direct every day, / and I never understood anything."

9. See Benjamin, *The Bonds of Love*, esp. 80–81.

10. See Sigmund Freud, *Freud on Women*, ed. Elisabeth Young-Bruehl (New York: W. W. Norton and Company), 212 and 272.

11. "That uprising, absolutely unpardonable, / merited death, one by one, / for all those who participated in it. / My brain and my unmoved eyes / contemplated dozens of heads, / terrible, separated from their trunks."

12. "But you arrived. With your gaze, / shameless and valiant, you rendered useless / all the authority of my crown. / You, stronger or weaker than the others, / deserved pardon and you deserved / to be the caprice of your queen, and always, / as long as I do not order otherwise, / you will be my lover."

13. "At times I think / that this is a worse punishment than death, / and I do not know if you conspire in silence / or if your abnegation is cowardice."

14. Felman, *What Does a Woman Want?* 71.

15. Ibid., 40; original emphasis.

16. "I couldn't confess to you where I had / been for such a long time, nor explain to you / my unexpected return. I could only / make you suspect that in that year / I had been unfaithful to you with impunity. / And it was better thus. Once again I surrendered / before your eyes and your forgiveness. / I forgot that I was in that center / for the mentally ill. Everything returned / to what it always was before I went away. / The heart-wrenching, sweet love returned, / and the poisonous passion, and in my chest / that pain and the former flames / returned, burning without clemency."

17. See Benjamin, *The Bonds of Love*, esp. 31–36.

18. "I would do anything that he wanted / because now I see only through his eyes. / My will is annulled by his caprice. / I continue to get thrilled if he calls me / on the phone and says let's go out. / His kisses melt me or excite me, / but I never find them indifferent."

19. Benjamin, *The Bonds of Love*, 23.

20. See Lechte, "Art, Love, and Melancholy in the Work of Julia Kristeva," 30, where he discusses perfume.

21. Felman, *What Does a Woman Want?* 65; original emphasis.

22. "I was accustomed to the gatherings / and festivities that commemorated nothing; / places where they ended up kissing you / those boys you would never remember / if it weren't for that, and for the drinks / to which, always amiable, they invited you. / I regretted everything suddenly. / I cut my hair, I removed the polish from my nails, / I never again put make-up on my cheeks / or my eyelashes, I never kissed other lips / or drank more liquor. I made everyone / believe that I was mad. They committed me / in the best place and since then / I am happy amid so many white walls."

23. See Naomi Wolf, *The Beauty Myth: How Images of Beauty Are Used Against Women* (New York: Doubleday, 1991) and Lourdes Ventura, *La tiranía de la belleza: Las mujeres ante los modelos estéticos* [The Tyrrany of Beauty: Women Facing Aesthetic Ideals] (Barcelona: Plaza & Janés, 2000). Although heavily indebted to Wolf's study, Ventura includes recent statistics on Spanish (and other European countries') incidence of such topics as anorexia and plastic surgery. Also see Brownmiller, *Femininity*.

24. Nead, *The Female Nude*, 2 and 7.

25. "For you I was never more than a piece / of marble. You sculpted my body of it, / a woman's white beautiful body, / in which you never saw more than stone / and the pride, of course, in your work. / You never imagined that I loved you / and that you made me shiver when, sweetly, / you would mold my breasts and my shoulders, / or you smoothed my thighs and my belly."

26. Nead, *The Female Nude*, 63.

27. Benjamin, *The Bonds of Love*, 170 and 87, respectively.

28. "Today I am in a park, where I suffer / the rigors of cold in winter, / and in summer I burn in such a way / that not even the sparrows come / to perch on my hands because they burn."

29. "But, of everything, that which hurts the most / is to lower my head and see the plaque: / "Nude woman," like so many others. / You didn't even remember to give me a name."

30. See Marina Warner, *Monuments and Maidens: The Allegory of the Female Form* (London: Weidenfield and Nicholson, 1985) for a discussion of the difference between the specificity of the statues of specific men and the anonymity of women in sculpture. Also see Susan Gubar, "'The Blank Page' and Issues of Female Creativity," in *The New Feminist Criticism: Essays on Women, Literature and Theory*, ed. Elaine Showalter (New York: Pantheon Books, 1985), 292–93.

31. Nead addresses the link between art and obscenity in part 3 of *The Female Nude*.

32. "Like every night, I would say: / 'Place your bets, sirs!', and the vulgar / men who filled the casino, / with fashionable cologne and cufflinks, / would place their colored chips / on the green felt. I would release / the little ball disdainfully on the roulette / that would spin obediently to my impulses. / Thus, one day after another, and one hour / after another. I was bored to death / by the stoicism of him who was ruined / and the simple delight of the lucky one."

33. "But one night of roulette and tedium / a different man arrived. On the 9 / he placed the minimum bet accepted. / He played only once. He lost his chip, / but he remained beside the table, / without taking his eyes off me for a moment, / until the casino closed. Then / we left together without exchanging a word."

34. See Deborah Cameron, *Feminism and Linguistic Theory*, 2nd ed. (New York: St Martin's Press, 1992), ch. 9.

35. "I liked that silent rapture. / He drove me to his house. The next day / I left slowly while he still slept / in shadows, with the marks of wrinkles / of the sheets on his face and his shoulders. / He never returned to the casino, because gaming / was not for him. I never saw him again."

36. "In that station, at nightfall, / sitting on my suitcase and waiting, / I remember you looking at my ankles / and raising your eyes, shamelessly, / following the design in my stockings."

37. Nead, *The Female Nude*, 16.

38. "When that train arrived that would take me / I can't remember where, you got on / my car and, as the train started rolling, / with three energetic taps you knocked / at the door of my compartment."

39. "I opened the door and you entered. It was a full assault, / but I never thought about shouting / to the conductor for help. It was sweeter / to surrender, without questioning you, / without attempting either flight or pride."

40. "Thinking about others bothered me, / and even more so knowing that, from one moment to the next, / the director was going to interrupt us / with his shouts of 'Cut!' and 'Another take!'"

41. Bakhtin, *Rabelais and His World*, 374, mentions the comic effect of this technique as it appears in the commedia dell'arte.

42. "I have been faithful for many years, / but it is not a virtue, but an escape / from a boring and touchy man, / who changed me into the loving wife / of a guy whom simplicity adorns. / That one is a romantic, he sighs, / he writes me ephemeral tripe, / he looks at the moon and cries like a fool. / This one is a confident tumbler, / proud and full of himself, / who listens to himself speak and thinks he's a genius. / But I am tired of both of them."

43. "I've decided that this very night / I'm going to seek a man who will understand me, / who will go to the movies with me, who will invite me / to an horchata or an ice cream, / who will enjoy himself with me and with my body / and, above all, who will not clown around." (Horchata is a drink made of rice, similar to a milkshake but thinner and a little gritty, and served well chilled. It is a popular drink during the hot summer months in Spain.)

44. "Do you remember? I spent all my time / pretending to threaten you. I would say / 'I'm going to kill you' and I would even tell you / the details of my crime: / the scene, the weapon, the motives. / I had condemned you forever / to the role of the weak and surrendered lover. / And I was aloof, haughty, hard / and somewhat sweet on certain occasions."

45. "But months ago everything changed / and it means nothing for me to accept it: / I fell in love with you. I know that I am crazy / and that you will kill me any day now."

46. "He came to my house to watch a basketball game / on TV. And I killed him. / I was just tired of his deceits, / his superior attitude exasperated me, / above all when he was tolerant / of my limitations. It was enough for me / to excite his lust grossly, / to get him a little drunk and plunge / a dagger in his chest a couple of times."

47. "Now he lies surprised, bloodied, / on the sofa where I do my crossword puzzles. / I am going out. They're waiting for me in the Retiro, / at the Book Fair. I will return later, / with the latest book of poems / that bears his name. And on the same / sofa I will lie back, next to his blood, / and I will wash his wound with tears."

48. "I didn't know what to do that afternoon. / You were cranky and didn't want / to go out. I went to West Park / and I walked around for quite a while / without meeting anyone. In winter / almost nobody goes for walks in the parks. / I didn't think about anything. I sat on a bench / and lit a cigarette. Suddenly / a young man sat down beside me."

49. "I looked at him and saw that there was only one eye / in the middle of his forehead, a dark eye, / very sad and shiny. He was looking at me, / as if asking for help, begging. / Neither of us said anything. / He was looking at my eyes and I at his. / In the silence he began to cry slowly, / he became ashamed and he left. I did nothing / to stop him."

50. "You didn't believe / even one word of this story, but / I am filled with anguish and sadness, / even though I would like to avoid it, if I remember / the cyclops of West Park."

51. Felman, *What Does a Woman Want?* 107 (original emphasis).

52. Benjamin, *The Bonds of Love,* 12.

CHAPTER 8. THE TWO-WAY MIRROR

1. Alicia Suskin Ostriker, *Feminist Revision and the Bible* (Cambridge, MA: Blackwell, 1993), 29.

2. Sabine Melchior-Bonnet, *The Mirror: A History,* trans. Katharine H. Jewett (New York and London: Routledge, 2001), 85.

3. See the introduction to Ostriker, *Feminist Revision,* 5–6.

4. Karla G. Bohmbach, "Names and Naming in the Biblical World," in *Women in Scripture,* ed. Carol Meyers et al. (Boston: Houghton Mifflin Company, 2000), 33, 37.

5. Casey Miller and Kate Swift, *Words and Women: New Language in New Times,* updated ed. (New York: HarperCollins Publishers, 1991), 17–18.

6. Gerda Lerner, *The Creation of Patriarchy* (New York: Oxford University Press, 1986), 182.

7. Cf. Jacques Derrida, *On the Name,* ed. Thomas Dutoit, trans. David Wood, John P. Leavey, Jr., and Ian McLeod (Stanford: Stanford University Press, 1995), 98, on the distinction between appellation and names.

8. See Ostriker, *Feminist Revision,* 4.

9. Maite Pérez Larumbe, *Mi nombre verdadero* (Pamplona: Pamiela, 1998), 11. "In the beginning man / named the creatures. / Later [he named] his demons. / He covered his nakedness to suffer for that, / he threw his heart to the winds, / he tortured his pups thinking that he was conjuring / all his loneliness, his lack of shelter. / He alienated his peers, / he multiplied the tribes / like grains of sand that the wind throws in one's eyes."

10. "We had to appear just to understand them, / to surprise their sobs of angry orphans. / If someone suspected us / our presence is justified. // Those who accompanied me / say they have no sex. / I know that I am a woman. / You will not find my name in the scriptures, / nor did my sisters speak too much."

11. See "An Introduction to the Bible," in Meyers et al., *Women in Scripture,* 9–10.

12. "The Word is a country that they barely knew, / they died on the mountain top from where one can view / its extension, its richness, they died desirous."

13. See Edith Deen, *All of the Women of the Bible* (New York: Harper and Row, 1955) and Meyers et al., eds., *Women in Scripture,* s.v. *Leah and Rachel.*

14. "You consoled me so much / that I did not say my name / the night my father brought you to my bed. // In the darkness, your smile / kept growing on your lips / while you were knowing me. // To unknow me at dawn / was to deny our bodies, / the certainty that we raised during so many hours, / to unwalk for a lifetime the only road."

15. "Oh, my Jacob, covered / with goatskins / before a tired and moribund father! / Farcical and reckless. // I see how you caress the beard that grows gray assuring / that the God of the Promise blessed you. // Will you keep even one word for me, / that I loved you with my body, / that it is more I than my name, / that I prolonged your inheritance and your memory?"

16. Meyers et al., *Women in Scripture,* s.v. *Rachel.* Deen, *All of the Women of the Bible,* 32.

17. "He made me fertile, that has been my dowry. / Now Rueben returns from the fields, / he brings me some mandrake roots. / My sister wants them, and I will give them to her. / You will spend this night with me, that has been the agreement. / In the darkness, I want you to recognize / my true name."

18. See Deen, *All of the Women of the Bible,* and Meyers et al., *Women in Scripture.*

19. Ibid., s.v. *Rachel.*

20. "I cry over Zion, I dishevel myself. / Let no one believe that I sleep beneath the stele of Ephratha. // I cry over Bethel and Garizim, / I ruin the crop in Ashkelon and I would still like / to smash this bowl of saltpeter, / to burn up the stalks, to curse throughout the centuries / this land of wolves."

21. See Deen, *All of the Women,* and Meyers et al., *Women in Scripture.*

22. "Forget the affront of empty wombs, / happy the woman who has thighs of flint, / dry grass in her entrails. / The sterile woman should rejoice that she does not offer / sons to the catastrophe / for she will not see her old age cursed / nor her repose soaked in blood. // In my shame I turned my face to Yahweh. / And Yahweh heard me. / The fulfilled clumsiness I then found happy, / happy the thrusting and the panting, / happy the forty days of my impurity / (men purify that which they do not understand)."

23. For Kristeva's view of menstruation as the abject, see the chapter on Blanca Andreu.

24. "Sons of my grief, / short was the time of milk and honey, short the cuddling. / You will be a race of orphans, the fodder of voracity. / I shout and drag myself along. I shout. / Caulking in the cracks will serve no purpose. / The pitch will be useless. I shout forever."

25. See the chapter on Bautista above for another poem on Judith.

26. "The necklace abandons its weight on my neck, / the earrings whisper a chant that disturbs me. // I tremble like a bride who suspects, / on her first night, / that her hair is capable of ensnaring an army. // I ought to compose myself obediently and I am agitated by / his eagerness of a soldier who does not wait."

27. See Nadia Julien, *The Mammoth Dictionary of Symbols: Understanding the Hidden Language of Symbols* (New York: Carroll and Graf Publishers, 1996), s.v. *hair.* Also see Brownmiller, *Femininity,* 57 and 76.

28. La Belle, *Herself Beheld,* 145.

29. Jean Baudrillard, *Seduction,* trans. Brian Singer (New York: St. Martin's Press, 1990), 69–70.

30. "How well the Lord chose even if I err! / To revenge the thirst / he stirs the avid fire in the pulse / and he opens the ocean beneath my eyes. // This wisdom before the mirror frightens me, / the flesh that is revealed as milk and sugar, / the body that rocks back and forth like the wheatfields in September / letting itself be carried along by a knowledge / of which I was unaware."

31. Benjamin, *The Bonds of Love,* 46–47.

32. "I would like to give death to time / and to hear that he desires me. // How much ought I to hate / so as not to feel so much? // The bracelets crackle. I put on perfume."

33. See the chapter on Amalia Bautista, where the same image appears in her poem on Judith.

34. Lerner, *The Creation of Patriarchy,* 165.

35. See Elizabeth Lenk, "The Self-reflecting Woman," in *Feminist Aesthetics,* ed. Gisela Ecker, trans. Harriet Anderson (Boston: Beacon Press, 1986), 53.

36. "My tent puts your palace in a shadow. / Far away, your favorite / has bathed and awaits you."

37. "The hyenas of the night / frighten your dogs. / In the city your mother dreams about the booty, / about an embroidered mantle."

38. "My hand does not waver, yours grows limp. / Your soldiers are trusting, I lend myself gladly / to grasping the hammer."

39. "My veil stays on, your crown falls, / my naked foot humbles your campaign boots, / linen conquers leather, / the nomad conquers the captain."

40. See Brownmiller, *Femininity,* 97, and Mary Ann Doane, *Femmes Fatales,* 46, 48–49, 54–55.

41. "I nail the peg of my tent in your temple, / in your murderous kingdom, / in your path of terror."

42. Barbara Herrnstein Smith, *Poetic Closure: A Study of How Poems End* (Chicago: University of Chicago Press, 1968).

43. "I lose myself in your name / as a blind man would do with a prophecy. // Oh, delightful childhood of the word / that structures your body, gives it backbone and raises / before me the presence that has given it shelter, / the rope in which it is formed / until I arrive to recognize it / and to expiate the silence."

44. See Hanna Segal, *Introduction to the Work of Melanie Klein,* 2nd ed. (New York: Basic Books, 1974), 68, and Nancy J. Chodorow, *Feminism and Psychoanalytic Theory*

(New Haven: Yale University Press, 1989), 184–87, on the mother as an individual with her own feelings and subjectivity, especially her pre-oedipal role. See Klein, "The Psychogenesis of Manic-Depressive States," in *The Selected Melanie Klein,* ed. Juliet Mitchell (New York: Free Press, 1986), esp. 141–42, on the mother as a "whole person."

45. Rich, *Of Woman Born,* 64. Also see Chodorow, *Feminism and Psychoanalytic Theory,* 23–65, on the differences between girls' separation from mother as opposed to boys'.

46. "That word of yours that names you / is a mountain range, a smooth balm. / I protect it in my mouth like a little eaglet / that will someday fly over Lebanon. // To name you is to recreate / the creation by making it, / as if God would like to take me to his task / and I could put a name / on that which I only hope for and recognize as definitive, / to find in your syllables / my first babbling / and that my voice mature / while I name you."

47. See J. A. Pérez-Rioja, *Diccionario de símbolos y mitos,* s.v. *cedro.*

48. Michel de Certeau, *The Practice of Everyday Life,* trans. Steven Rendall (Berkeley: University of California Press, 1984), 155. We can also compare this phrase in Larumbe's poem with Atencia's poem "Ahora que amanece," where she says "Nombrarte es poseerte" (see ch. 1 above).

49. Ibid., 138.

50. See W. Michael Mudrovic, "Revisiting Mary and Martha: Passing the Torch from One Generation to the Next," *Journal of Hispanic Higher Education* 1 (2002): 195–210, which includes a poem by Margarita Merino from *Baladas del abismo* that deals with the same issues.

51. "To wait for him, / only my eyes alone, / not my hands, their clumsy blindness, / not my ear that confuses, / nor my bestial sense of smell that lowers its head, / nor my distracting taste. // (They give no consolation during such a wait: / neither the ray that illuminates the grapefruit / and makes it different at each turn, / nor the inconstant clouds, / the thousand shades of green that protect the lime grove.)"

52. "When he arrives, / then yes, the din of the scent bottle, / excess of crystals on the eardrums, / the coldness of perfume, / its aroma in my hair that dries him, / the taste of tears, / vestibule of such uncertainty."

53. See Meyers et al., *Women in Scripture,* s.v. *Mary 2.*

54. "And thus, / pure presence, / introspective sense, / time that stops, / my eyes will remain / to keep on looking / at the eyes that fill mine for ever."

55. "I got up early to brush the figs with oil, / thus will they ripen. / I aired out the mats, I spread out the vines, / I ordered three chickens killed and then remembered / that I wanted to order a tall jar from the potter / and I sent him a message. / I helped the maid polish the floor tiles, / I laughed with Mary who swore that the air / had never been so still."

56. "While I was making the bread, from so much singing / the dough grew large and airy: / I drew the face of the rabbi's wife in it."

57. Weeks, *Constituting Feminist Subjects,* 140.

58. "I didn't sit down to eat / because I wanted to see / if that one-piece tunic was still / in the bottom of the chest / just in passing, / I brought down a couple of washbasins / to put water in the sun to warm. // Now that we hear noises and Lazarus embraces you / I dive into the fire."

59. "I know that when I sit down / with my hands still red / I will be so tired / that I will barely see your eyebrows arch / and your full smile as when you look at children / while you repeat Martha, Martha, / anxious and hurried. / When will you understand / the only thing that matters?"

60. See Erlemann, "What is Feminist Architecture?" in Ecker, ed., *Feminist Aesthetics,* 134.

CONCLUSION: TOWARD FUTURE STUDIES

1. Aguirre, *Espejito, espejito* (Madrid: Ayuntamiento de San Sebastián de los Reyes, 1995). *Itaca* can be found in Aguirre, *Ensayo general (Poesía completa, 1966–2000)*, (Madrid: Calambur, 2000), 25–87.

2. Aguirre, *Espejito*, 13.

3. Aguirre, *Pavana del desasosiego* (Madrid: Torremozas, 1999).

4. Clara Janés, *Creciente fértil* (Madrid: Hiperión, 1989) and Juana Castro, *Narcisia* (Barcelona: Taifa, 1986).

5. Clara Janés, *Libro de alienaciones* (Madrid: Endymión, 1980).

6. Juana Castro, *No temerás* (Madrid: Torremozas, 1994) and *Cóncava mujer* (Córdoba, 1978).

7. Juana Castro, *Del color de los ríos* (Esquío-Ferrol: Fundación CaixaGalicia, 2000).

8. See Sharon Keefe Ugalde, *Sujeto femenino y palabra poética: Estudios críticos de la poesía de Juana Castro* (Córdoba: Diputación de Córdoba, n.d.).

9. See the inside cover of Palao's *Música o nieve* (Zaragoza: Cuadernos de Aretusa, 1987).

10. Paloma Palao, *Contemplación del destierro* (Madrid: Endymión, 1982), 78. "You were a woman disheveled / by love, Annelein, but love / was a torture, that you never imagined. I am / feeling the cooing of solitude and I perceive / that your presence is as pleasing as my own image."

11. See Noni Benegas and Jesús Munárriz, eds., *Ellas tienen la palabra: Dos décadas de poesía española* (Madrid: Hiperión, 1997) and the introduction of this book for discussion of Buenaventura's anthology.

12. It seems that Mercedes Castro is the name of two women poets. One is from León and was born in 1953; she has published *El retrato quebrado* (Madrid: Rialp, 1996). The other is from Ferrol (A Coruña) and was born in 1972. She has published *La niña en rebajas* (Esquío-Ferrol: Fundación CaixaGalicia, 2001), cited below.

13. Benegas and Munárriz, *Ellas tienen la palabra*, 129–30.

14. Ibid., 159.

15. Ibid., 252.

16. Ana María Rodríguez, *El silencio de la sirena* (Madrid: Torremozas, 1996).

17. Aurora Luque, *Problemas de doblaje* (Madrid: Rialp, 1990). See Silvia Bermúdez, *Las dinámicas del deseo: Subjetividad y lenguage en la poesía española contemporánea* (Madrid: Editiones Libertarias Prodhufi, 1997), 159–85, for another approach to this poetry.

18. Beatriz Hernanz, *La vigilia del tiempo* (Madrid: Rialp, 1996).

19. Ibid., 46.

20. Esther Morillas, *Mujeres* (Valencia: Pre-Textos, 2001).

21. Andrea Luca, *El don de Lilith* (Madrid: Endymión, 1990) and Guadalupe Grande, *El libro de Lilith* (Sevilla: Renacimiento, 1996).

22. Miriam Reyes, *Espejo negro* (Barcelona: DVD, 2001).

23. Silvia Ugidos, *Las pruebas del delito* (Barcelona: DVD, 1997) and Mercedes Castro, *La niña en rebajas* (Esquío-Ferrol: Fundación CaixaGalicia, 2001). As mentioned above, this Mercedes Castro is from Ferrol (A Coruña) and was born in 1972.

24. See the bibliography for information concerning these texts.

Bibliography

Abella, Rafael. *La vida cotidiana bajo el régimen de Franco*. Madrid: Temas de Hoy, 1996.

Aguirre, Francisca. *Ensayo general (Poesía completa, 1966–2000)*. Madrid: Calambur, 2000.

———. *Espejito, espejito*. San Sebastián de los Reyes: Universidad Popular, 1995.

———. *Pavana del desasosiego*. Madrid: Torremozas, 1999.

Allen, Graham. *Intertextuality*. London: Routledge, 2000.

Andreu, Blanca. *De una niña de provincias que se vino a vivir en un Chagall*. 5th ed. Madrid: Hiperión, 1986.

———. *El sueño oscuro: Poesía reunida, 1980–1989*. Madrid: Hiperión, 1994.

Atencia, María Victoria. *Antología poética*. Edited by José Luis García Martín. Madrid: Castalia, 1990.

———. *Ex Libris*. Prologue by Guillermo Carnero. Madrid: Visor, 1984.

———. *La señal: Antología, 1961–1989*. Málaga: Excmo. Ayuntamiento de Málaga, 1990.

———. *Trances de Nuestra Señora*. Prologue by María Zambrano. Valladolid: Fundación Jorge Guillén, 1997.

Bachelard, Gaston. *The Poetics of Space*. Edited by Maria Jolas. Foreword by Etienne Gilson. Boston: Beacon Press, 1969.

Bakhtin, Mikhail. *Rabelais and His World*. Translated by Hélène Iswolsky. Bloomington: Indiana University Press, 1984.

Baudrillard, Jean. *Seduction*. Translated by Brian Singer. New York: St. Martin's Press, 1990.

Bautista, Amalia. *Cárcel de amor*. Sevilla: Renacimiento, 1988.

Bellamy, Joe David. Introduction to *Tom Wolfe: The Purple Decades: A Reader*. New York: Farrar Straus Giroux, 1982.

Bellver, Catherine. *Absence and Presence: Spanish Women Poets of the Twenties and Thirties*. Lewisburg, PA: Bucknell University Press, 2001.

Benegas, Noni, and Jesús Munárriz, eds. *Ellas tienen la palabra: Dos décadas de poesía española*. Madrid: Hiperión, 1997.

Benjamin, Jessica. *The Bonds of Love: Psychoanalysis, Feminism, and the Problem of Domination*. New York: Pantheon Books, 1988.

Bermúdez, Silvia. *Las dinámicas del deseo: Subjetividad y lenguaje en la poesía española contemporánea*. Madrid: Ediciones Libertarias Prodhufi, 1997.

Biasin, Gian-Paolo. *The Smile of the Gods: A Thematic Study of Cesare Pavese's Works*. Translated by Yvonne Freccero. Ithaca, NY: Cornell University Press, 1968.

Biedermann, Hans. *Dictionary of Symbolism: Cultural Icons and the Meanings Behind Them*. Translated by James Hulbert. New York: Meridian, Penguin Books USA, 1994.

Bogue, Ronald. *Deleuze and Guattari*. London: Routledge, 1989.

Bordo, Susan. *Unbearable Weight: Feminism, Western Culture, and the Body*. Berkeley: University of California Press, 1993.

Briggs, John. *Fractals: The Patterns of Chaos*. New York: Simon and Schuster, 1992.

Brody, Miriam. *Manly Writing: Gender, Rhetoric, and the Rise of Composition*. Carbondale: Southern Illinois University Press, 1993.

Brownmiller, Susan. *Femininity*. New York: Fawcett Columbine, 1984.

Buenaventura, Ramón. *Las diosas blancas: Antología de la joven poesía española escrita por mujeres*. 2nd ed. rev. Madrid: Hiperión, 1986.

Bundy, Nancy L. "Entrevista con Ana Rossetti." *Letras Femeninas* 16 (1990): 135–38.

Caillois, Roger. *Man, Play, and Games*. Translated by Meyer Barash. New York: Free Press, 1961.

Cameron, Deborah. *Feminism and Linguistic Theory*. 2nd ed. New York: St. Martin's Press, 1992.

Cano, José Luis. "La poesía de María Victoria Atencia." *Insula* 398 (1980): 8–9.

Carnero, Guillermo. Prologue to *Ex libris*, by María Victoria Atencia. Madrid: Visor, 1984). 9–13.

Casado, Miguel. "Sobre la poesía de María Victoria Atencia . . . *El libro de las aguas*." *Vuelta* 217 (1994): 54–56.

Castro, Juana. *Del color de los ríos*. Esquío-Ferrol: Fundación CaixaGalicia, 2000.

———. *Narcisia*. Barcelona: Taifa, 1986.

———. *No temerás*. Madrid: Torremozas, 1994.

Castro, Luisa. *Los versos del eunuco*. 2nd ed. Madrid: Hiperión, 1989.

Castro, Mercedes. *La niña en rebajas*. Esquío-Ferrol: Fundación CaixaGalicia, 2001.

———. *El retrado quebrado*. Madrid: Rialp, 1996.

Cavarero, Adriana. *In Spite of Plato: A Feminist Rewriting of Ancient Philosophy*. Introduction by Rosi Braidotti. Translated by Serena Anderlini-D'Onofrio and Áine O'Healy. New York: Routledge, 1995.

Chanter, Tina. *Ethics of Eros: Irigaray's Rewriting of the Philosophers*. New York: Routledge, 1995.

Chesler, Phyllis. *Women and Madness*. New York: Four Walls Eight Windows, 1997.

Chevalier, Jean, and Alain Gheerbrandt. *Diccionario de los símbolos*. Barcelona: Herder, 1991.

Chodorow, Nancy J. *Feminism and Psychoanalytic Theory*. New Haven, CT: Yale University Press, 1989.

Cioran, E. M. *The New Gods*. Translated by Richard Howard. New York: Quadrangle/ The New York Times Book Co., 1974.

———. *A Short History of Decay*. Translated by Richard Howard. New York: Viking Press, 1975.

Ciplijauskaité, Biruté. "Los diferentes lenguajes de amor." *Monographic Review / Revista Monográfica* 6 (1990): 113–27.

———. "Purificación y esencialidad en la más joven poesía española." In *After the War: Essays on Recent Spanish Poetry*. Edited by John Wilcox and Salvador Jiménez-

Fajardo. Boulder, CO: Society of Spanish and Spanish-American Studies, 1988. 109–28.

Ciplijauskaité, Biruté, ed. *Novísimos, Postnovísimos, Clásicos: La poesía de los 80 en España.* Madrid: Orígenes, 1990.

Cirlot, Juan Eduardo. *Diccionario de símbolos.* Barcelona: Labor, 1991.

———. *A Dictionary of Symbols.* 2nd ed. Translated by Jack Sage. New York: Philosophical Library, 1962.

Cixous, Hélène, and Catherine Clément. *The Newly Born Woman.* Translated by Betsy Wing. Introduction by Sandra M. Gilbert. Vol. 24, Theory and History of Literature. Minneapolis: University of Minnesota Press, 1986.

Cooper, J. C. *An Illustrated Encyclopaedia of Traditional Symbols.* London: Thames and Hudson, 1978.

Correyero, Isla. *Diario de una enfermera.* Madrid: Huerga & Fierro, 1996.

Courteau, Joanna. "New Horizons in Iberian Poetry." *Poet and Critic* 8 (1987): 25–26, 32–34.

de Beauvoir, Simone. *The Second Sex.* Edited and translated by H. M. Parshley. New York: Alfred A. Knopf, 1952.

de Castro, Rosalía. *En las orillas del Sar.* Edited by Xesús Alonso Montero. Madrid: Cátedra, 1985.

de Certeau, Michel. *The Practice of Everyday Life.* Translated by Steven Rendall. Berkeley: University of California Press, 1984.

Debicki, Andrew P. "New Poetics, New Works, New Approaches: Recent Spanish Poetry." *Siglo XX / 20th Century* 8 (1990–91): 41–53.

———. *Poetry of Discovery: The Spanish Generation of 1956–1971.* Lexington: University of Kentucky Press, 1982.

———. *Spanish Poetry of the Twentieth Century: Modernity and Beyond.* Lexington: University of Kentucky Press, 1994.

Deen, Edith. *All of the Women of the Bible.* New York: Harper & Row, 1955.

Dennis, Carl. *Poetry as Persuasion.* Athens: University of Georgia Press, 2001.

Derrida, Jacques. *On the Name.* Edited by Thomas Dutoit. Translated by David Wood, John P. Leavey, Jr., and Ian McLeod. Stanford: Stanford University Press, 1995.

Diccionario de la Lengua Española. 19th ed. Madrid: Real Academia Española, 1970.

Doane, Mary Ann. *Femmes Fatales: Feminism, Film Theory, Psychoanalysis.* New York: Routledge, 1991.

Ecker, Gisela, ed. *Feminist Aesthetics.* Translated by Harriet Anderson. Boston: Beacon Press, 1985.

Edut, Ophira, ed. *Adiós, Barbie: Young Women Write About Body Image and Identity.* Seattle: Seal Press, 1988.

Ehrmann, Jacques, ed. *Game, Play, Literature.* Boston: Beacon Press, 1968.

Escaja, Tina. "Lenguaje del erotismo: Ana Rossetti." *Selected Proceedings of the Pennsylvania Foreign Language Conference (1991–1992).* Edited by Gregorio C. Martín. Pittsburgh, PA: Duquesne University, Department of Modern Languages, 1995). 63–69.

Escolano, Mercedes. *Estelas.* Madrid: Torremozas, 1991.

Etxebarría, Lucía. *Estación de infierno.* Barcelona: Lumen, 2001.

Felman, Shoshana. *What Does a Woman Want?: Reading and Sexual Difference.* Baltimore: Johns Hopkins University Press, 1993.

Ferber, Michael. *A Dictionary of Literary Symbols*. Cambridge: Cambridge University Press, 1999.

Ferradans, Carmela. "La (re)velación del significante: Erótica textual y retórica barroca en 'Calvin Klein, underdrawers' de Ana Rossetti." *Monographic Review / Revista Monográfica* 6 (1990): 183–91.

Fletcher, John, and Andrew Benjamin, eds. *Abjection, Melancholia, and Love: The Work of Julia Kristeva*. New York: Routledge, 1990.

Fraser, Nancy, and Sandra Lee Bartky, eds. *Revaluing French Feminism: Critical Essays on Difference, Agency, and Culture*. Bloomington: Indiana University Press, 1992.

Freud, Sigmund. *The Basic Writings of Sigmund Freud*. Translated and edited by A. A. Brill. New York: Modern Library, 1995.

———. *Beyond the Pleasure Principle*. Standard Edition. Translated and edited by James Strachey. New York: W. W. Norton and Company, 1961.

———. *Freud on Women: A Reader*. Edited by Elisabeth Young-Bruehl. New York: W. W. Norton and Company, 1990.

———. *A General Selection from the Works of Sigmund Freud*. Edited by John Rickman. New York: Doubleday, 1957.

Fuertes, Gloria. *Obras incompletas*. 9th ed. Madrid: Cátedra, 1984.

Fuery, Patrick, and Nick Mansfield. *Cultural Studies and the New Humanities: Concepts and Controversies*. Melbourne: Oxford University Press, 1997.

Fuss, Diana. *Essentially Speaking: Feminism, Nature and Difference*. New York: Routledge, 1989.

Genette, Gerard. *Paratexts: Thresholds of Interpretation*. Translated by Jane E. Lewin. Foreword by Richard Macksey. Cambridge: Cambridge University Press, 1997.

Gies, David T., ed. *The Cambridge Companion to Modern Spanish Culture*. Cambridge: Cambridge University Press, 1999.

Gilbert, Sandra M., and Susan Gubar. *The Madwoman in the Attic: The Woman Writer and the Nineteenth-Century Literary Imagination*. New Haven: Yale University Press, 1984.

Gómez Segade, M. A., et al. "Rumbos de la poesía española de los ochenta." *Anales de la Literatura Española Contemporánea* 9 (1984): 175–299.

Grande, Guadalupe. *El libro de Lilit*. Sevilla: Renacimiento, 1996.

Grimal, Pierre. *The Concise Dictionary of Classical Mythology*. London: Basil Blackwell, 1990.

Grosz, Elizabeth. *Jacques Lacan: A Feminist Introduction*. New York: Routledge, 1990.

———. *Volatile Bodies: Toward a Corporeal Feminism*. Bloomington: Indiana University Press, 1994.

Guerlac, Suzanne. *The Impersonal Sublime: Hugo, Baudelaire, Lautréamont*. Stanford: Stanford University Press, 1990.

Guzmán, Almudena. *Calendario*. Madrid: Hiperión, 1998.

———. *El libro de Tamar*. Melilla: Rusadir, 1989.

———. *La playa del olvido*. Gijón: Altair, 1984.

———. *Poemas de Lida Sal*. Madrid: Libros Dante, 1981.

———. *Usted*. 2nd ed. Madrid: Hiperión, 1986.

Gwynn, R. S., ed. *New Expansive Poetry: Theory, Criticism, History*. Ashland, OR: Story Line Press, 1999.

Halperin, David M. "Why is Diotima a Woman? Platonic *Eros* and the Figuration of Gender." In David M. Halperin, John J. Winkler, and Froma I. Zeitlin, eds. *Before Sexuality: The Construction of Erotic Experience in the Ancient Greek World.* Princeton: Princeton University Press, 1990. 257–308.

Hart, Anita M. "The Relational Self in Almudena Guzmán's Dialogic Poetry." *Rocky Mountain Review* 48 (1994): 143–60.

Hernanz, Beatriz. *La vigilia del tiempo.* Madrid: Rialp, 1996.

Hooper, John. *The New Spaniards.* Rev. ed. New York: Penguin Books, 1995.

Huizinga, Johan. *Homo Ludens: A Study of the Play Element in Culture.* Boston: Beacon Press, 1950.

Hutcheon, Linda. *A Theory of Parody: The Teachings of Twentieth-Century Art Forms.* New York: Routledge, 1985.

Irigaray, Luce. *This Sex Which Is Not One.* Translated by Catherine Porter. Ithaca, NY: Cornell University Press, 1985.

Jaffe, Catherine. "Gender, Intersubjectivity, and the Author/Reader Exchange in the Poetry of María Victoria Atencia." *Letras Peninsulares* 5 (1992): 291–302.

Janés, Clara. *Creciente fértil.* Madrid: Hiperión, 1989.

———. *Libro de alienaciones.* Madrid: Endymión, 1980.

Jones, Anny Brooksbank. *Women in Contemporary Spain.* Manchester: Manchester University Press, 1997.

Julien, Nadia. *The Mammoth Dictionary of Symbols: Understanding the Hidden Language of Symbols.* New York: Carroll and Graf Publishers, 1996.

Keller, Lynn. *Forms of Expression: Recent Long Poems by Women.* Chicago: University of Chicago Press, 1997.

Klein, Melanie. *The Selected Melanie Klein.* Edited by Juliet Mitchell. New York: Free Press, 1986.

Krieger, Murray. *Ekphrasis: The Illusion of the Natural Sign.* Baltimore: Johns Hopkins University Press, 1992.

Kristeva, Julia. *Black Sun: Depression and Melancholia.* Translated by Leon S. Roudiez. New York: Columbia University Press, 1989.

———. *The Kristeva Reader.* Edited by Toril Moi. New York: Columbia University Press, 1986.

———. *Powers of Horror: An Essay on Abjection.* Translated by Leon S. Roudiez. New York: Columbia University Press, 1982.

———. *Revolution in Poetic Language.* Translated by Margaret Waller. Introduction by Leon S. Roudiez. New York: Columbia University Press, 1984.

La Belle, Jenijoy. *Herself Beheld: The Literature of the Looking Glass.* Ithaca, NY: Cornell University Press, 1988.

Lacan, Jacques. *Feminine Sexuality: Jacques Lacan and the école freudienne.* Edited by Juliet Mitchell and Jacqueline Rose. Translated by Jacqueline Rose. New York: W. W. Norton and Company, 1982.

———. *The Four Fundamental Concepts of Psycho-Analysis.* Edited by Jacques-Alain Miller. Translated by Alan Sheridan. New York: W. W. Norton, 1981.

———. "The Mirror Stage." *Ecrits: A Selection.* Translated by Alan Sheridan. New York: W. W. Norton and Company, 1977. 1–7.

LaFollette, Martha. "Writing the Book of Life: The Word and the Flesh in Ana Rossetti's *Punto umbrío.*" Unpublished paper presented at the Blue Ridge Conference, Appalachian State University, April 2001.

Laporte, Dominique. *History of Shit.* Translated by Nadia Benabid and Rodolphe el-Khoury. Cambridge, MA: MIT Press, 2000.

Lasala, Magdalena. *La estación de la sombra.* Madrid: Huerga & Fierro, 1996.

Lazer, Hank. *Opposing Poetries.* Vol. 1, *Issues and Institutions.* Evanston, IL: Northwestern University Press, 1996.

Lechte, John. *Fifty Key Contemporary Thinkers: From Structuralism to Postmodernity.* London: Routledge, 1994.

———. *Julia Kristeva.* London: Routledge, 1990.

Lerner, Gerda. *The Creation of Patriarchy.* New York: Oxford University Press, 1986.

Levine, Linda Gould, Ellen Engelson Marson, and Gloria Feiman Waldman, eds. *Spanish Women Writers: A Bio-Bibliographical Source Book.* Westport, CT: Greenwood Press, 1993.

Lipking, Lawrence. *Abandoned Women and Poetic Tradition.* Chicago: University of Chicago Press, 1988.

Lliteras, Margarita. "Funcionamiento de la Intertextualidad en la Poesía de Margarita Merino." *Romance Languages Annual* 4 (1993): 491–96.

———. "'Viaje americano' de Margarita Merino: un homenaje a América." *Letras Peninsulares* 5 (1992): 123–36.

Luca, Andrea. *El don de Lilith.* Madrid: Endymión, 1990.

Luque, Aurora. *Problemas de doblaje.* Madrid: Rialp, 1990.

Machado, Antonio. *Poesías completas.* 11th ed. Madrid: Espasa-Calpe, 1966.

Maillard, Chantal. *Hainuwele.* 1990. Lucena: Excmo. Ayuntamiento de Lucena, 2001.

Makris, Mary. "Mass Media and the 'New' Ekphrasis: Ana Rossetti's 'Chicho Wrangler' and 'Calvin Klein, underdrawers.'" *JILS* 5 (1993): 237–49.

Mandlove, Nancy. "Oral Texts: The Play of Orality and Literacy in the Poetry of Gloria Fuertes." *Siglo XX* 5 (1987–88): 11–16.

———. "Used Poetry: The Trans-Parent Language of Gloria Fuertes and Angel González." *Revista Canadiense de Estudios Hispánicos* 7 (1983): 297–309.

Marigómez, Luis M. "La seducción lúcida: lectura de poemas de Almudena Guzmán." *La Ciudad* 5 (April 1988): 15.

Marks, Elaine, and Isabelle de Courtrivron, eds. *New French Feminism: An Anthology.* New York: Schoken Books, 1980.

Martín Gaite, Carmen. *Usos amorosos de la postguerra española.* 1987. 10th ed. Barcelona: Anagrama, 1992.

Martínez Ruiz, Florencio. "*Indicios vehementes (Poesía 1979–1984).* Ana Rossetti." *Insula* 418 (1981): 9.

Mayhew, Jonathan. "The Avant-Garde and Its Discontents: Aesthetic Conservatism in Recent Spanish Poetry." *Hispanic Review* 67 (1999): 347–63.

Medina, Raquel. "Poesía española 'Fin de siglo': La experiencia y otros fantasmas poéticos." *Revista de Estudios Hispánicos* 32 (1998): 597–612.

Melchior-Bonnet, Sabine. *The Mirror: A History.* Translated by Katherine H. Jewett. New York: Routledge, 2001.

Merino, Margarita. *Baladas del abismo.* Madrid: Endymión, 1989.

Mesa Toré, José Antonio, ed. "El vuelo: María Victoria Atencia." *Litoral* 26 (1997).

Metzler, Linda D. "Images of the Body in the Poetry of María Victoria Atencia." *ALEC* 18 (1993): 173–81.

Meyers, Carol, et al., eds. *Women in Scripture: A Dictionary of Named and Unnamed Women in the Hebrew Bible, the Aprocryphal / Deuterocanonical Books, and the New Testament.* Boston: Houghton Mifflin, 2000.

Miller, Casey, and Kate Swift. *Words and Women: New Language in New Times.* Updated ed. New York: HarperCollins Publishers, 1991.

Miller, J. Hillis. *Fiction and Repetition: Seven English Novels.* Cambridge, MA: Harvard University Press, 1982.

Miller, Martha LaFollette. "Continuidad y ruptura: *Punto umbrío* de Ana Rossetti." *Alaluz* 32 (2000): 31–41.

Miró, Emilio. "*De la llama en que arde,* de María Victoria Atencia." *Insula* 517 (1990): 10–11.

———. "Dos premios para dos nuevas voces: Blanca Andreu y Ana Rossetti." *Insula* 418 (1981): 6.

———. "El mundo lírico de María Victoria Atencia." *Insula* 462 (1985): 6.

Mitchell, W. J. T. *Picture Theory: Essays on Verbal and Visual Representation.* Chicago: University of Chicago Press, 1994.

Moix, Ana María. *Extraviadas ilustres: Diez retratos de mujer.* Prologue by Margarita Rivière. Madrid: Qué Leer [Comunicación y Publicaciones], 1996.

Molina Campos, Enrique. "La poesía de la experiencia y su tradición." *Hora de Poesía* 59–60 (1988): 41–47.

Mora, María Luisa. *Meditación de la derrota.* Madrid: Torremozas, 2001.

Moreno, María Paz. "El lugar de la 'poesía de la experiencia' en la literatura del siglo 20: ¿Una posteridad calculada?" *Hispanic Poetry Review* 2 (2000): 72–89.

Morillas, Esther. *Mujeres.* Valencia: Pre-Textos, 2001.

Mudrovic, W. Michael. "Revisiting Mary and Martha: Passing the Torch from One Generation to the Next." *Journal of Hispanic Higher Education* 1 (2002): 195–210.

———, ed. "Contemporary Spanish Women's Poetry." *Revista de Estudios Hispánicos* 29 (May 1995).

Nantell, Judith. "Writing Her Self: Ana Rossetti's 'Anatomía del beso'." *Anales de la Literatura Española Contemporánea* 27 (1997): 253–63.

Navales, Ana María. *Los labios de la luna.* Madrid: Torremozas, 1989.

Nead, Lynda. *The Female Nude: Art, Obscenity and Sexuality.* London: Routledge, 1992.

Neruda, Pablo. *Crepusculario.* Barcelona: Seix Barral, 1977.

The New Jerome Biblical Commentary. Edited by Raymond E. Brown, SS, et al. Englewood Cliffs, NJ: Prentice Hall, 1990.

Newton, Candelas. "La reflexión sobre el signo en la poesía de Blanca Andreu." *Letras Peninsulares* 2 (1989): 193–209.

———. "Retales y retórica: Jugando a las prendas con Ana Rossetti." *Romance Languages Annual* 8 (1997): 615–20.

Nietzsche, Friedrich. *Beyond Good and Evil: Prelude to a Philosophy of the Future.* Translated by Walter Kaufmann. New York: Vintage Books, 1989.

Nobus, Dany, ed. *Key Concepts of Lacanian Psychoanalysis.* New York: Other Press, 1998.

Núñez, Antonio. "Encuentro con Ana Rossetti." *Insula* 474 (1986): 1, 12.

O'Donnell, Cathryn Collopy. "A New Poetics of the Self: María Victoria Atencia, Clara Janés, and Ana Rossetti." Ph.D. diss., University of California, Irvine, 1996.

Oliver, Kelly. *Reading Kristeva: Unraveling the Double-Bind*. Bloomington: Indiana University Press, 1993.

———. *Subjectivity without Subjects: From Abject Fathers to Desiring Mothers*. Lanham, MD: Rowman and Littlefield Publishers, 1998.

———. *Witnessing: Beyond Recognition*. Minneapolis: University of Minnesota Press, 2001.

Ortiz, Fernando. "María Victoria Atencia." In *La estirpe de Bécquer*. Jerez de la Frontera: Fin de Siglo, 1982. 187–92.

Ostriker, Alicia Suskin. *Feminist Revision and the Bible*. Cambridge, MA: Blackwell, 1993.

Ovid. *Metamorphoses*. Translated and Introduction by Mary M. Innes. London: Penguin Books, 1955.

The Oxford Classical Dictionary. 3rd ed. Edited by Simon Hornblower and Antony Spawforth. Oxford: Oxford University Press, 1996.

Palao, Paloma. *Contemplación del destierro*. Madrid: Endymión, 1982.

———. *Música o nieve*. Zaragoza: Cuadernos de Aretusa, 1987.

Pasero, Anne M. "Contemporary Spanish Women's Poetry: Ode to the Goddess." *Letras Femeninas* 16 (1990): 73–84.

Pérez-Rioja, J. A. *Diccionario de símbolos y mitos*. 4th ed. Madrid: Tecnos, 1992.

Pérez Larumbe, Maite. *Mi nombre verdadero*. Pamplona: Pamiela, 1997.

Pérez López, María Angeles. *Carnalidad del frío*. Sevilla: Algaida, 2000.

Persin, Margaret H. *Getting the Picture: The Ekphrastic Principle in Twentieth-Century Spanish Poetry*. Lewisburg, PA: Bucknell University Press, 1997.

———. "La imagen del / en el texto: el ékfrasis, lo postmoderno y la poesía española del siglo 20." In *Novísimos, postnovísimos, clásicos: La poesía de los 80 en España*. Edited by Biruté Ciplijauskaité. Madrid: Orígenes, 1990.

———. *Recent Spanish Poetry and the Role of the Reader*. Lewisburg, PA: Bucknell University Press, 1987.

Pertusa, Inmaculada. "El culturalismo particular de María Victoria Atencia." *Ariel* 8 (1992): 17–32.

Peters, H. F. *Lou Andreas-Salomé: Mi hermana, mi esposa*. Preface by Anaïs Nin. 3rd ed. Barcelona: Ediciones Paidós, 1995.

Phillips, Adam. *The Beast in the Nursery: On Curiosity and Other Appetites*. New York: Pantheon Books, 1998.

Plato. "Symposium." *Selected Dialogues*. Translated by Benjamin Jowett. Franklin Center, PA: Franklin Library, 1983. 305–53.

Prins, Yopie, and Maeera Shreiber, eds. *Dwelling in Possibility: Women Poets and Critics on Poetry*. Ithaca, NY: Cornell University Press, 1997.

Ramazani, Jahan. *Poetry of Mourning: The Modern Elegy from Hardy to Heaney*. Chicago: University of Chicago Press, 1994.

Reyes, Miriam. *Espejo negro*. Barcelona: DVD, 2001.

Rich, Adrienne. *Of Woman Born: Motherhood as Experience and Institution*. Tenth Anniversary Edition. New York: W. W. Norton and Company, 1986.

———. *On Lies, Secrets, and Silence: Selected Prose, 1966–1978*. New York: W. W. Norton, 1979.

Ricoeur, Paul. *Oneself as Another*. Translated by Kathleen Blamey. Chicago: University of Chicago Press, 1992.

Rilke, Rainer Maria. *Duino Elegies*. Translated by David Young. New York: W. W. Norton and Company, 1978.

———. *Letters to a Young Poet*. Translated by M. D. Herter Norton. Rev. ed. New York: W. W. Norton, 1953.

———. *Sonnets to Orpheus*. Translated by M. D. Herter Norton. New York: W. W. Norton and Company, 1942.

Robbins, Jill. *P/Herversions: Critical Studies of Ana Rossetti*. Lewisburg, PA: Bucknell University Press, 2004.

Rodríguez, Ana María. *El silencio de la sirena*. Madrid: Torremozas, 1996.

Rodríguez Padrón, Jorge. "María Victoria Atencia: Indagando en la soledad." *Insula* 458–59 (1985): 30 (suplemento verde).

Rogers, Timothy J. "The Comic Spirit in the Poetry of Gloria Fuertes. " *Perspectives on Contemporary Literature* 8 (1982): 88–97.

Rosas, Yolanda and Hilde F. Cramsie. "Ana Rossetti: Novísima poesía." In *Literatura Femenina Contemporánea de España*. Edited by Juana Arancibia, Adrienne Mandel, and Yolanda Rosas. Northridge: California State University at Northridge; Instituto Literario y Cultural Hispánico, 1991. 189–97.

———. "La apropiación del lenguaje y la desmitificación de los códigos sexuales de la cultura en la poesía de Ana Rossetti." *Explicación de Textos Literarios* 20 (1991–92): 1–12.

Rose, Margaret A. *Parody: Ancient, Modern, and Post-Modern*. Cambridge: Cambridge University Press, 1993.

Rossetti, Ana. *Indicios vehementes (Poesía, 1979–1984)*. 4th ed. Madrid: Hiperión, 1990.

Rubin, Arnold. "The Tattoo Renaissance." In *Marks of Civilization: Artistic Transformations of the Human Body*. Arnold Rubin, ed. Los Angeles: University of California, 1988, 233–62.

Rubio López, María del Carmen. *En el bosque del sueño*. Talavera de la Reina: Colección Melibea, 1992.

Rubio Monge, María del Valle. *Derrota de una reflexión*. Madrid: Rialp, 1987.

Russ, Joanna. *How to Suppress Women's Writing*. Austin: University of Texas Press, 1983.

Sacks, Peter M. *The English Elegy: Studies in the Genre from Spenser to Yeats*. Baltimore: John Hopkins University Press, 1985.

Schechtman, Marya. *The Constitution of Selves*. Ithaca, NY: Cornell University Press, 1996.

Schlegel, Alice. "Status, Property, and the Value on Virginity." *American Ethnologist* 18 (1991): 719–34.

Schumm, Sandra J. *Reflections in Sequence: Novels by Spanish Women, 1944–1988*. Lewisburg, PA: Bucknell University Press, 1999.

Segal, Hanna. *Introduction to the Work of Melanie Klein*. 2nd ed. New York: Basic Books, 1974.

Servodidio, Mirella. "Ana Rossetti's Double-Voiced Discourse of Desire." *Revista Hispánica Moderna* 45 (1992): 318–27.

Sherno, Sylvia R. "Between Water and Fire: Blanca Andreu's Dream Landscapes." *Revista Hispánica Moderna* 47 (1994): 533–42.

———. "Blanca Andreu." *Dictionary of Literary Biography* 134, 3–10.

———. "Blanca Andreu: Recovering the Lost Language." *Hispania* 77 (1994): 384–93.

———. *Weaving the World: The Poetry of Gloria Fuertes*. Romance Monographs, No. 57. University, MS: Romance Monographs, 2001.

Showalter, Elaine, ed. *The New Feminist Criticism: Essays on Women, Literature and Theory*. New York: Pantheon Books, 1985.

Silva, Lorenzo. *La flaqueza del bolchevique*. 1997. Madrid: Ediciones Destino, 2000.

Smith, Barbara Herrnstein. *Poetic Closure: A Study of How Poems End*. Chicago: University of Chicago Press, 1968.

Smith, Paul. *Discerning the Subject*. Foreword by John Mowitt. Vol. 55, Theory and History of Literature. Minneapolis: University of Minnesota Press, 1988.

Terence. *The Lady of Andros, The Self-Tormentor, The Eunuch*. Translated by John Sargeaunt. Vol. 1. Cambridge, MA: Harvard University Press, 1979.

Thompson, David Ray. "Myth Revision as Discursive Practice in Clara Janés's *Creciente fértil*." Unpublished manuscript.

———. "Myth Revision in Spanish Poetry by Women Writers (1972–1998)." Ph.D. diss., Washington University, St. Louis, 2000.

Tibullus, Albius. *The Erotic Elegies of Albius Tibullus with the poems of Sulpicia arranged as a sequence called No Harm to Lovers*. Translated by Hubert Creekmore. New York: Washington Square Press, 1966.

Ugalde, Sharon Keefe. *Conversaciones y poemas: La nueva poesía femenina española en castellano*. Madrid: Siglo Veintiuno, 1991.

———. "Entrevista con Almudena Guzmán." *Literatura Femenina Contemporánea de España. 7 Simposio Internacional*. Edited by Juana Arancibia, Adrienne Mandel, Yolanda Rosas. Northridge: California State University, 1991. 219–30.

———. "Erotismo y revisionismo en la poesía de Ana Rossetti." *Siglo XX / 20th Century* 7 (1989): 24–29.

———. "The Feminization of Female Figures in Spanish Women's Poetry of the 1980s." *Studies in Twentieth-Century Literature* 16 (1992): 165–84.

———. "Masks of Canvas and Stone in the Poetry of María Victoria Atencia." *Anales de la Literatura Española Contemporánea* 24 (1999): 227–42.

———. "La subjetividad desde «lo otro» en la poesía de María Sanz, María Victoria Atencia y Clara Janés." *Revista Canadiense de Estudios Hispánicos* 14 (1990): 3511–23.

———. "Time and Ekphrasis in the Poetry of María Victoria Atencia." *Confluencia* 3 (1987): 5–12.

———, ed. *La poesía de María Victoria Atencia: Un acercamiento crítico*. Madrid: Huerga & Fierro, 1998.

———, ed. *Sujeto femenino y palabra poética: Estudios críticos de la poesía de Juana Castro*. Córdoba: Diputación de Córdoba, n.d.

Ugidos, Silvia. *Las pruebas del delito*. Barcelona: DVD, 1997.

Ventura, Lourdes. *La tiranía de la belleza: Las mujeres ante los modelos estéticos*. Prologue by José Antonio Marina. Barcelona: Plaza & Janés, 2000.

Walzer, Kevin. *The Ghost of Tradition: Expansive Poetry and Postmodernism*. Ashland, OR: Story Line Press, 1998.

Warner, Marina. *Monuments and Maidens: The Allegory of Female Form*. London: Weidenfield and Nicholson, 1985.

Weeks, Kathi. *Constituting Feminist Subjects*. Ithaca, NY: Cornell University Press, 1998.

West-Settle, Cecile. "Luisa Castro and the Poetics of Abandonment." Unpublished manuscript.

———. "Of *War and Peace,* Heroes and Outcasts: The Poetic World of Luisa Castro's *Odisea definitiva* and *De mí haré una estatua ecuestre.*" Unpublished manuscript.

Wilcox, John. "Ana Rossetti y sus cuatro musas poéticas." *Revista Canadiense de Estudios Hispánicos* 14 (1990): 525–40.

———. "Blanca Andreu: A 'poeta maldita' of the 1980s." *Siglo XX / 20th Century* 7 (1989–90): 29–34.

———. "Visión y revisión en algunas poetas contemporáneas: Amparo Amorós, Blanca Andreu, Luisa Castro y Almudena Guzmán." In *Novísimos, postnovísimos, clásicos: La poesía de los 80 en España.* Edited by Biruté Ciplijauskaité. Madrid: Orígenes, 1990. 95–113.

———. *Women Poets of Spain, 1860–1990: Toward a Gynocentric Vision.* Urbana: University of Chicago Press, 1997.

Wimsatt, W. K. *The Verbal Icon: Studies in the Meaning of Poetry.* Lexington: University of Kentucky Press, 1968.

Winnicott, D. W. *Playing and Reality.* London: Routledge, 1971.

Wolf, Naomi. *The Beauty Myth: How Images of Beauty Are Used Against Women.* New York: Doubleday, 1991.

Yusta, Mercedes. *Las mareas del tiempo.* Zaragoza: Prensas Universitarias de Zaragoza, 1997.

Zardoya, Concha. *Diotima y sus edades.* Barcelona: Victor Pozanco, 1981.

Zeiger, Melissa F. *Beyond Consolation: Death, Sexuality, and the Changing Shapes of Elegy.* Ithaca, NY: Cornell University Press, 1997.

Index